COMMENCEMENT-LEVEL

UNITED STATES HISTORY & GOVERNMENT

STAREVIEW

USH&G

Authors
Paul Stich
Susan F. Pingel
John Farrell

Editor
Wayne Garnsey

Artwork & Graphics
Eugene B. Fairbanks & Wayne Garnsey

N&N Publishing Company, Inc.

18 Montgomery Street   Middletown, New York 10940-5116

For Ordering & Information
1-800-NN 4 TEXT
www.nn4text.com   email: nn4text@nandnpublishing.com

Dedicated to our patient families

and
the perseverance of
the staff of N&N Publishing Company

Especially
Ed Stich
Fran Harrison
Jim Bennett
and Joanne Stich

and
the enduring support of **Gary** and **Michelle Gluckow**
and their staff at BookMart Press

© Copyright 2001, **Revised 2008**

N&N Publishing Company, Inc.

phone: 1-800-NN 4 TEXT
internet: www.nn4text.com   email: nn4text@nandnpublishing.com
SAN # - 216-4221   ISBN # - 0935487-69-7

7 8 9 10 11 12 13 14 15   BookMart   2013 2012 2011 2010 2009 2008

TABLE OF CONTENTS

THE ☆ CAPSULES COMBINE TEXT AND GRAPHICS TO GIVE THE STUDENT A SYNTHESIS OF KEY TOPICS ON WHICH TEST WRITERS OFTEN BASE QUESTIONS.

☆ LESSON

INTRO

PAGE 5

APPROACHES FOR THE U.S. HISTORY EXAM

STRATEGIES FOR THE U.S. HISTORY AND GOVERNMENT EXAMINATION

PREFACE

You are reading this because there is a serious challenge before you – a difficult final examination in United States History and Government. You need help in sorting through the concepts, the ideas, the relationships, and the facts presented as you studied the history of this country. Lessons 1 through 9 of this book concentrate on major course themes and historical details that relate to them.

Before plunging into all that history, this lesson requires you to take some time to analyze the task itself. If you know the task, you can effectively organize your review time and focus your energy.

Educational research shows that there is a consistent pattern of student achievement on examinations of this nature. Students achieve a higher percentage of points on the <u>multi</u>-choice (used here in place of <u>multiple</u> choice) or objective segment (Part I) than on the written, subjective segments (Parts II and III). To that end, this book places greater emphasis on material and skills that aid in answering essay questions.

Exam Blueprint

Part I   Objective Response: 50 multi-choice questions

Part II   Subjective Response: 1 Thematic essay

Part II   Subjective Response: 1 Document-Based Question composed of:

Part A   scaffolded short answer questions on 4 to 8 documents

Part B   essay based on Part A documents and outside knowledge

Exam Hints

- On multi-choice questions, you can eliminate answers that are too extreme – watch for answers that contain "all," "none," or "only" and/or have no logical connection to the question.
- Never leave any questions blank. There is no penalty for guessing.
- When you take practice exams, time yourself, even if you do it in segments. You will get an idea about how long it takes to do certain parts.

PART I: MULTI-CHOICE QUESTIONS

On U.S. History & Government examinations, there are many kinds of multi-choice questions. There are very few straight, factual recall questions (e.g., "The current Secretary of State is ..."). Most questions are "compound questions." This means they require (*a*) some basic knowledge, and (*b*) an application of that knowledge.

SAMPLE 1 - COMPOUND QUESTION STRUCTURE

In the South, Jim Crow laws passed during the late 19th century were designed to
1   make sure the Fourteenth Amendment would be enforced
2   provide employment opportunities for the newly freed African Americans
3   create separate societies for whites and African Americans
4   guarantee civil rights for African Americans

In the Sample 1 question, the basic knowledge (*a*) is knowing that Jim Crow laws were segregation laws enacted after Reconstruction ended. It was a clearly negative event aimed at keeping the races apart in Southern society after the Thirteenth Amendment abolished slavery. You must apply (*b*) that basic knowledge to events in the South in the late 19th century. Answers 1, 2, and 4 all denote positive policies for the newly freed African Americans and had effects opposite the Jim Crow laws.

> ## Note:
> The Part I multi-choice questions are arranged chronologically. Sometimes this can help you eliminate some wrong answers because they either happened long before or after the time period that is the focus of the question.

There are a number of other types of multi-choice questions used on U.S. History & Government examinations. Commonly, multi-choice questions ask you to complete a statement. Often these questions will ask you to identify a cause (see Sample 2), or identify an effect (see Sample 3).

SAMPLE 2 - COMPLETE A STATEMENT (CAUSATION)

One reason for the United States imperialistic overseas expansion in the late 19th century was to
1   gain new sources of raw materials and markets
2   break up monopolies
3   help unions organize workers
4   set up an electoral college system overseas

Sample 3 – Analyze an Event (Results)

Which was an immediate effect of the use of new production techniques during the period from 1900 to 1929 in the United States?

1 loss of commitment to the work ethic
2 a flood of consumer products on the market
3 an increase in the rate of unemployment
4 a sharp decline in business profits

Some multi-choice questions test your knowledge of concepts. In this
type, you are presented with a series of situations and asked to identify
the one that clearly illustrates one of the "big ideas" of U.S. History &
Government such as federalism, judicial review, laissez-faire, or nationalism. You will have to know some definitions and be able to recognize
them at work. You will find a general list of concepts later in this lesson.
You will also find them **boldfaced** in the narrative of Lessons 1 through
9 as well as in the **glossary-index** at the back of the book.

Sample 4 – Identify a Concept at Work

Which conditions are most characteristic of a depression?

1 high production and high demand
2 few jobs and little demand
3 much money in circulation and high stock prices
4 supply meeting demand and high employment

Another popular type of multi-choice question gives multiple clues in
the stem and asks you to find similarities or make comparisons. In this
type you are presented with a series of situations or individuals and you
must look for a common thread. The simplest approach is to look for
something you know is true or false about one of the situations or persons. If it is false, you can eliminate that answer. If it is true, see if it can
be universal enough to be applied to the others. It could be the common
thread you need. Try this with Sample 5. Besides identifying the correct
answer, be aware of *why* you rejected the other answers.

Sample 5 – Compare Several Similar Situations
that Occurred at Different Times

Which statement applies to the foreign policies of James Madison,
Woodrow Wilson, and Franklin Roosevelt?

1 They managed to expand the size of the country through conquest.
2 Economic depressions forced them to restrict exports by U.S.
manufacturing.
3 Neutrality positions failed to prevent involvement in wars.
4 They founded major international peacekeeping organizations.

GROWING POPULARITY
OF DATA-BASED QUESTIONS
– CHARTS, GRAPHS, MAPS, AND CARTOONS –

Up to 20% of the multi-choice questions will measure your ability to comprehend visual data. "Visual stimulus" questions (such as a chart, a graph, a map, or a cartoon) are very popular on tests because they help to assess a broad range of skills beyond historical knowledge. On Part I, often more than one multi-choice question will be asked on a visual's data. The first is often a very basic, straightforward question to test your skill at extracting information from the data. A second question may ask you for an explanation, analysis, comparison, or the relation of the data to some historic circumstances.

Cover the question(s) – A simple technique on visual questions is to cover the question(s) with your hand or scrap paper and just look and think about the visual. Ask yourself some questions:

- What does the data represent?

- What point is being made?

- What do you know about the time period involved?

When you uncover the questions, you may be surprised at how this simple "brainstorming" has helped. Try it as you look at the different samples of data-based questions below.

Another strategy to practice as you look at the question samples is to take note of a particular type of visual that gives you trouble. During the review, you will want to practice with this type more than others.

Focus on the rough spots – When you actually take the test, remember to do Part I in pencil so that you can make changes easily. Also, when you are not sure of the answer, it is best to put down a *tentative* answer, circle the question number, and check back on it later. Let time work for you. Wait until you have "warmed up" and had some time to look over the examination to finalize your answers. When you have "settled in," you will be less tense than when you first started. By then, you will be thinking differently, and you will be able to address questions more logically. Try to see data-based questions as "gifts." Remember, the answer is in the visual and it is something *obvious* – rarely is it tricky or obscure.

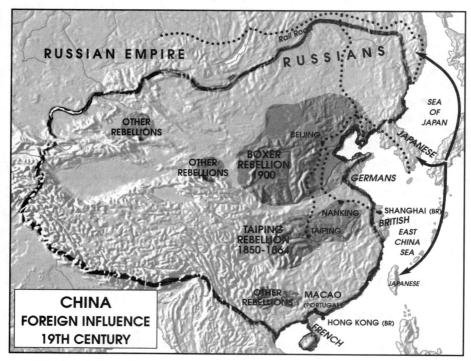

CHINA
FOREIGN INFLUENCE
19TH CENTURY

Which of the following resulted from foreign influences (commercial spheres) shown on this map?

1   U.S. Congress declared war on foreign powers occupying China
2   use of the atomic bomb against Germany
3   presidential proclamations of neutrality
4   nationalist uprisings and the Open Door Policy

SAMPLE 7 – GRAPHS (PIE)

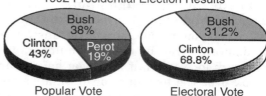

1992 Presidential Election Results

Bush 38%
Clinton 43%
Perot 19%
Popular Vote

Bush 31.2%
Clinton 68.8%
Electoral Vote

Which generalization is supported by the information provided by the graphs?

1   The electoral vote often fails to reflect the popular vote.
2   The House of Representatives must settle elections in which third parties participate.
3   The electoral college system weakens the two-party system.
4   Electoral college members often vote against their party's candidates.

Sample 8 – Graphs (Bar)

U.S. Foreign Aid, 1946–1954
(Billions of Dollars)

Which United States program is most likely reflected in the amounts of nonmilitary foreign aid given from 1947 to 1950?

1 Open Door
2 Lend Lease
3 Marshall Plan
4 Peace Corps

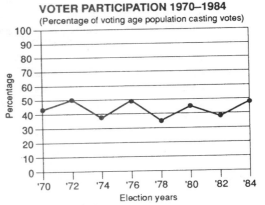

NONMILITARY	YEAR	MILITARY
$ 4.0	1946	$ 0.7
$ 5.8	1947	
$ 5.0	1948	$ 0.1
$ 5.7	1949	$ 0.4
$ 4.3	1950	$ 0.2
$ 3.3	1951	$ 1.1
$ 2.8	1952	$ 1.8
$ 2.0	1953	$ 4.4
$ 1.7	1954	$ 3.5

Sample 9 – Graphs (Line)

Why did voter turnout change throughout the period from 1970 to 1984?

1 The number of citizens eligible to vote decreased dramatically.
2 Presidential elections attracted more voters than "off-year" elections did.
3 Increases in minority voter registration resulted in greater total voter turnout.
4 Many Americans still could not vote because of poll taxes.

VOTER PARTICIPATION 1970–1984
(Percentage of voting age population casting votes)

Percentage (y-axis: 0 to 100)

Election years ('70 '72 '74 '76 '78 '80 '82 '84)

Source: U.S. Bureau of the Census

Sample 10.1 – Chart

Which factor was a major cause of the farm problem indicated by the data in the chart?

1 major droughts in the Midwest
2 low farm prices set by government regulations
3 widespread crop failures during the late 1800s
4 overproduction of these farm crops

UNITED STATES CROP PRICES, 1878–1897

Years	Wheat (per bushel)	Corn (per bushel)	Cotton (per pound)
1878–1881	$1.00	$.43	$.09
1882–1885	$.80	$.39	$.09
1886–1889	$.74	$.35	$.08
1890–1893	$.70	$.41	$.07
1894–1897	$.63	$.29	$.05

Source: *History of the United States*, Houghton Mifflin, 1991

Sample 10.2 – Chart: (use chart on page 11)

To help solve the problem indicated by the data in the chart, American farmers wanted the federal government to
1 reduce the regulation of railroads
2 increase the money supply
3 provide funds to increase crop yields
4 raise tariffs on foreign manufactured goods

Sample 11 – Cartoon

The cartoon indicates the foreign policy position of the United States in response to the
1 start of the League of Nations
2 collapse of the global economy
3 beginning of World War II
4 spread of communism in Eastern Europe

Sample 12 – Timeline

1781	Congress adopts Articles of Confederation
1782	
1783	Treaty of Paris
1784	
1785	Shays' Rebellion
1786	Economic depression
1787	Constitutional Convention at Philadelphia
1788	Ninth state ratifies the Constitution
1789	Washington inaugurated in New York

Which period of American history is represented by this timeline?
1 Colonization
2 Great Awakening
3 Critical Period
4 Manifest Destiny

"Those of us who shout the loudest about Americanism in making character assassinations are all too frequently those who, by our own words and acts, ignore some of the basic principles of Americanism."

– Senator Margaret Chase Smith (Maine), 1950

Which of the following statements would support Senator Smith's criticism of Senator Joseph McCarthy and his supporters?

1   Senator McCarthy did not do enough to protect the nation from a communist conspiracy.
2   The tactics of Senator McCarthy were necessary to protect the basic principles of democracy.
3   Free speech must be limited in times of national crisis.
4   Senator McCarthy was a greater threat to freedom than communist sympathizers were.

Exam Hints: Speaker Questions

Cover the questions then read the four statements, ask yourself:

• What is the general topic under discussion? [restriction of immigration]
• Who are these people? [A = for ethnically restricted immigration; B = elitist; C = fears economic competition; D = for unrestricted immigration].)

SAMPLE 14.1 – SPEAKER QUESTION

SPEAKER A: To preserve our American culture, people whose national origins do not match the origins of our nation's founders must be refused admission.

SPEAKER B: ...let us admit only the best educated from every racial and ethnic group ....

SPEAKER C: ...there is an appalling danger to the American wage earner from the flood of low, unskilled, ignorant, foreign workers who have poured into the country ...

SPEAKER D: Give me your tired, your poor, your huddled masses yearning to breathe free...

In the early 20th century, most labor unions supported the view of Speaker

1   A   3   C
2   B   4   D

SAMPLE 14.2 – SPEAKER QUESTION (use question on page 13)

People who support unrestricted immigration would agree most with Speaker

1   A
2   B

3   C
4   D

SAMPLE 14.3 – SPEAKER QUESTION (use question on page 13)

United States immigration legislation of the 1920s most closely reflected the views of Speaker

1   A and C
2   A and D

3   B and C
4   C and D

SAMPLE 15 – HEADLINES OR EVENTS

"SENATE FAILS TO RATIFY TREATY OF VERSAILLES"

"PRESIDENT TRUMAN VETOES TAFT-HARTLEY ACT"

"SENATE REJECTS NOMINATION OF ROBERT BORK TO SUPREME COURT"

These headlines illustrate the constitutional principle of

1   federalism
2   executive privilege

3   due process of law
4   checks and balances

USE YOUR "SENSE OF HISTORY"

A final thought on multi-choice questions: use the general awareness of history you have built up over the years. There are certain patterns in the American experience and they have a logical flow. Whether you are aware of it or not, from elementary, middle, and high school experience, most U.S. History & Government students have a sense of how institutions such as the government and the economy have evolved. Put your awareness of these patterns and your broad chronological consciousness to work. No matter what the form of the question or type of visual presented, there are going to be answers suggested that are just plain wrong. Your "sense of history" will tell you that these answers do not square with your grasp of what has happened. If you keep the "big picture" of the American experience in mind, it will help you see whether a multi-choice answer is appropriate.

PART II: APPROACHES FOR WRITING QUESTIONS (ESSAYS)

Both the thematic essay and the document-based question require thought and preparation before writing. This "prewriting" is a vital part of the writing process and helps you focus on the task. You need to summon the writing skills you have acquired not just in social studies, but in your English classes, too. You should block out your answers in a simple outline:

- Introduction Paragraph – The introduction is critical. It must state your purpose, and your **thesis** (proposed answer that you will argue in the essay).

- Body Paragraphs – The body is a series of paragraphs in which you must present evidence in support of your thesis.

- Conclusion Paragraph – Lastly, there should be an effective conclusion in which you must restate your thesis, summarize your ideas, and re-emphasize evidence that proves them.

Exam Hints
- Watch spelling, grammar, and punctuation. The easier and clearer your work is to read, the easier it is to grade.

In the model essays that follow, there are suggestions for prewriting as well as ideas about effective writing.

Keep things in perspective. Remember that the point values matter, too. On all examinations, the designation of points on a question indicates how much time and effort to spend on a particular section. On the U.S. History & Government examination, there are 50 multi-choice questions on Part I, but you are only half way through the exam when you complete them. There is still considerable writing to do on Part II. The DBQs Part *A* is a series of short answers about each of the individual documents. It is really a prewriting exercise designed to give you ideas to incorporate into the Part *B* essay.

Check the point values. At the end of each question, there are point values. They tell you that the thematic essay and the DBQ Part *B* essay are worth about the same. In the past, students have lost credit when they put enormous effort into the thematic essay, linger on the

DBQs Part *A* short responses, and then find that they do not have enough time to write an effective response on the DBQ essay. Strive for a balance. Do not overdo one essay and not write enough on the other.

SAMPLE THEMATIC ESSAY

Directions: Write a well-organized essay that includes an introduction, several paragraphs explaining your position, and a conclusion.

Theme:

> Government flexibility
> Throughout United States history, many changes have been made in the federal government

Task:

> Using your knowledge of United States history and government, write an essay in which you select three specific changes in the federal government. For *each* change,
>
> • describe the historical circumstances that led to the adoption of the change
>
> • discuss the effect of the change on the functioning of the government

Suggestions:

You may use any governmental change from your study of U.S. history and government. Some suggestions you might wish to consider include the ratification of the *Constitution of the United States*, the expansion of voting rights, direct election of United States Senators, two-term limit on the presidency, limitation of Presidential war powers. **You are *not* limited to these suggestions**.

WRITING STRATEGY FOR THEMATIC ESSAY

- Set up five (5) paragraphs. After you have written your introduction and stated your thesis in the first paragraph, divide the body into three (3) evidence paragraphs (one for each change and its effects), and construct a final fifth paragraph for your conclusion.

- For each of the central three evidence paragraphs focusing on government change:

  use transition – phrases that link each paragraph to the thesis

  identify the change – say what it was and when it happened; explain why it was needed; say how it helped America

★ REVIEW – SAMPLE THEMATIC ANSWER

INTRO & THESIS PARAGRAPH

Democratic government is designed to serve the needs of people. Therefore, it is a living thing that must change as people's needs change. Throughout United States history, many formal and informal changes have been made in the federal government that have broadened American democracy. (THESIS =) These changes continually renew the process of democracy.

EVIDENCE PARAGRAPH A

(TRANSITION =) The adoption of Constitution of the United States revitalized American democracy. By 1787, it was clear to many leaders that the government under the Articles of Confederation was failing the people. States were feuding. Congress could not collect taxes, and there was no body to enforce the few national laws that were made. The Constitutional Convention in Philadelphia produced a stronger form of government. It had limited power, but it gave the people an effective system for producing, enforcing, and interpreting national laws. With a stable, powerful government, the economy grew and the nation prospered.

EVIDENCE PARAGRAPH B

(TRANSITION =) The gradual expansion of voting rights broadened democracy and changed American government. In the early 1800s, states changed laws to drop property-owning requirements for male voters; the 15th Amendment declared that former slaves could vote; the 19th Amendment (1920) gave women the right to vote in national elections; the 26th Amendment (1971) gave 18 year-olds the right to vote. With more and more people involved in choosing leaders, more points of view have to be considered and the society is more open to the ideas of a broad variety of people.

EVIDENCE PARAGRAPH C

(TRANSITION =) The adoption of the two term limit on Presidential terms (22nd Amendment, 1951) strengthened democracy. It formalized an unwritten rule broken only by Franklin D. Roosevelt during World War II. This change insured democracy by avoiding long term accumulation of power that might undermine the democratic process. It insured change and therefore promoted the vitality of the elective system.

CONCLUSION PARAGRAPH

(TRANSITION =) The ability to change as new situations, viewpoints, and technology alter the times is critical in a democracy. (CONCLUSION =) Stability is important, but the capacity to live, grow, and develop depends on taking into account many views. The constitutional changes experienced in American history demonstrate that careful change is critical to the process of democracy.

SAMPLE DOCUMENT-BASED QUESTION (DBQ)

Document-based questions test your ability to analyze information, organize it, and use it to present a point of view. Follow the same structural rules as above for writing thematic essays. The exception is that you have to incorporate reference to and analysis of the Part *A* documents.

- **Introduction paragraph** must contain your **thesis** (the position you are trying to prove), some details which set the scene, and transition to the first paragraph.

- **Body paragraphs** must organize, compare, add other information, and show how the document(s) prove your thesis.

- **Final paragraph** (**conclusion**) must summarize your ideas and use quotations to re-emphasize how the evidence proves your thesis.

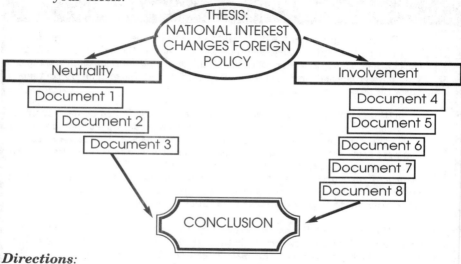

Directions:

The following question is based on the accompanying documents. Some of the documents have been edited for the purposes of this exercise. The task is designed to test your ability to work with historical documents. As you analyze the documents, take into account both the source of the document and the author's point of view. Read the documents in Part *A* and answer the question after each document. Then read the directions for Part *B* and write your essay.

- Write a well-organized essay that includes an introduction with a thesis statement, several paragraphs explaining the thesis, and a conclusion.
- Analyze the documents.
- Use the documents and refer to them by title, author, or number.
- Use evidence from the documents to support your thesis position.
- Do not simply repeat the contents of the documents.
- Include specific related outside information.

Historical Context:

United States' foreign policy decisions are often difficult to make. Policy makers must take into account its national interests at the time. Over the course of its more than two hundred year existence, the United States of America has made certain key decisions which have become cornerstones to United States foreign policy.

Task:

Using the information from the documents and your knowledge of United States history and government, write an essay in which you

- identify *two* (2) key foreign policies of the United States

- describe the policies chosen, including reasons for their development

- discuss how these policies complement or contradict each other

Part A – Short Answer

Analyze the documents and answer the questions that follow each document in the space provided.

Document 1

> "The great rule of conduct for us in regard to foreign nations is, in extending our commercial relations to have with them as little political connection as possible...It is our true policy to steer clear of permanent alliances with any portion of the foreign world, so far, I mean, as we are now at liberty to do it...Taking care always to keep ourselves by suitable establishments on a respectable defensive posture, we may safely trust to temporary alliances for extraordinary emergencies..."
>
> – President George Washington, *Farewell Address*, 1796

Questions for Document 1

1 What foreign policy precedent did President Washington establish?
(sample answer) <u>Washington urged his countrymen to avoid permanent alliances, but entertain temporary ones to meet their prevailing interests.</u>

2 What did President Washington state about trade with other countries?
(sample answer) <u>Expand international trade as much as possible.</u>

Document 2

Questions for Document 2

1   What foreign policy approach is depicted in the cartoon?
    (sample answer) <u>The U.S. (Uncle Sam) is warning European powers to stay</u>
    <u>out of the affairs of the Western Hemisphere.</u>

2   How was this foreign policy an extension of the precedent set by
    President Washington?
    (sample answer) <u>The second part of the Monroe Doctrine was a pledge by</u>
    <u>the U.S. to remain neutral in regard to European political conflicts.</u>

Document 3

> "Either we should enter the League [of Nations]
> fearlessly, accepting the responsibility and not fear-
> ing the role of leadership which we now enjoy, con-
> tributing our efforts towards establishing a just and
> permanent peace, or we should retire as gracefully as
> possible from the great concert of powers by which
> the world was saved."
>
> – President Woodrow Wilson, commenting of the *Treaty of Versailles*,
> 1920

Questions for Document 3

1   What did President Wilson see as the foreign policy role for the
    United States after World War I?
    (sample answer) <u>According to Wilson, the U.S. had a responsibility to</u>
    <u>become actively involved in keeping world peace.</u>

2   What alternative did the United States have if it rejected this role?
    (sample answer) <u>Wilson (despairingly) saw the alternative as a retreat from</u>
    <u>world involvement.</u>

Document 4

> "Our policy is directed not against any country or doctrine but against hunger, poverty, desperation and chaos. Its purpose should be the revival of a working economy in the world so as to permit the emergence of political and social conditions in which free institutions can exist. Any assistance that this government may render in the future should provide a cure rather than a mere palliative to reduce the suffering..."
>
> – George Marshall (President Truman's Secretary of State), speech at Harvard University, June 1947

Questions for Document 4

1 What was Marshall Plan aid to Europe intended to do?
(sample answer) Marshall wanted the U.S. to send aid to revive the global economic structure as a foundation to restore a free political and social order.

2 What would be the goal for United States foreign policy?
(sample answer) The goal should be preservation and nurturing of free political and social institutions.

Document 5

> "This is the message of...the 'Nixon Doctrine' ...Its central thesis is that the United States will participate in the defense and development of allies and friends, but that America cannot – and will not – conceive all the plans, design all the programs, execute all the decisions, and undertake all the defense of the free nations of the world. We will help where it makes a real difference and is considered in our interest..."
>
> – President Richard Nixon, *Department of State Bulletin*, 1970

Question for Document 5

1 How does President Nixon modify United States growing internationalism?
(sample answer) Nixon wanted the U.S. to help friends, but back away from broad-based involvement.

Document 6

> "The post-Cold War world remained an unsettled and uncertain place. While the United States was committed to nourishing democracy and protecting its economic interests, Americans remained wary of foreign intervention, even to prevent genocide or massive violations of human rights. They continued to be haunted by the specter of Vietnam, 20 years after the war's end..."
>
> – Nash, et al, *The American People*, 1998

Question for Document 6

1 How did the Vietnam Conflict continue to impact on United States foreign relations in the 1990s?

(sample answer) In the wake of Vietnam, the U.S. became more wary sending its troops to solve foreign problems.

Document 7

Defense Employment Levels, 1980-2001
(numbers in millions)

Military Personnel	Department of Defense Civilians	Defense Industry
1980 . . . . . .2.0	1980 . . . . . . .3.2	1980 . . . . . .4.8
1985 . . . . . .2.2	1985 . . . . . . .3.4	1985 . . . . . .6.2
1990 . . . . . .2.0	1990 . . . . . . .3.2	1990 . . . . . .6.0
1995 . . . . . .1.5	1995 . . . . . . .2.5	1995 . . . . . .4.5
2001 . . . . . .1.2	2001 . . . . . . .2.0	2001 . . . . . .3.5

Source: *Statistical Forecasts of the United States,*
James E. Person, Jr., Editor, 1993, 583.

Question for Document 7

1 What has happened to employment opportunities in the government and private defense and the military from 1980 to 2001?

(sample answer) Employment decreased by roughly 33% in each category for the period shown.

Document 8

> "So the U.S. is likely to remain 'No. 1,' but being No. 1 won't be what it used to be. New issues in international politics-ecology, debt, drugs, AIDS, terrorism-involve a diffusion of power away from larger states to weaker states and private actors. Unilateral action and hard power resources such as military force cannot solve these problems. Instead, they require cooperative responses. The U.S. and other countries will have to pay much more attention to the problems of organizing cooperation through a wide variety of multilateral arrangements."
>
> – Source: Joseph S. Nye, Jr., "Soviet Decline and America's Soft Power," *The Christian Science Monitor*, No. 181, August 14, 1990, p. 19.

Question for Document 8

1   What foreign policy problems will the United States be facing after the fall of communism?

(sample answer) <u>According to Nye, national interests that will guide U.S. policy makers include drug trafficking, terrorism, AIDS, and environmental issues.</u>

Part B – Essay

Task:

Using the information from the documents and your knowledge of United States history and government, write an essay in which you

- identify *two* (2) key foreign policies of the United States
- describe the policies chosen, including reasons for their development
- discuss how these policies complement or contradict each other

Be sure to include specific historical details. You must also include additional information from your knowledge of United States history and government.

DBQ KEY TO ORGANIZATIONAL NOTES IN SAMPLE ANSWER

(A)   Be sure to restate the task as you begin.

(B)   Thesis: Take a clear position on what you want to prove.

(C)   Transition: Be clear about where your argument is going next.

(D)   Name the document and incorporate its information.

(E)   Add information from your own knowledge of U.S. history and government.

(F)   Use a brief quote from the documents to strengthen your conclusion.

(G)   Restate your thesis in your conclusion paragraph.

A country's national interests determine its foreign policy [A]. As the United States' national interests have changed, so has its foreign policy [B]. In the 20th century, the U.S. shifted its foreign policy from neutrality and general isolation, to widespread global involvement, and then began modifying the extent of that involvement.

[C] The young United States was weak economically and militarily [E]. Survival demanded that it shrewdly follow George Washington's recommendation in his Farewell Address [D]. The U.S. generally "steered clear" of entangling alliances with European countries, but could not avoid Europe's problems completely. In 1812 it was drawn into a war with Great Britain that was a near disaster [E]. During President Monroe's tenure, the United States established the Monroe Doctrine [D], which sought to limit European control in the Western Hemisphere and formally pledged the U.S. would stay out of European affairs.

[C] In the second half of the 19th century, industrialization broadened America's interests and it became an imperial power [E]. In the early 20th century, the isolationist tradition was still strong enough to keep the U.S. out of Europe's "Great War" until 1917 [E]. In the aftermath of World War I, that strong isolationist sentiment blocked American entry into the League of Nations despite the vigorous involvement diplomacy of Woodrow Wilson [D].

[C] Actually, it wasn't until after World War II that the United States adopted a broad policy of global involvement. The U.S provided Marshall Plan [D] aid to help rebuild Europe and prevent the spread of communism and the conditions that had led to the rise of fascism during the 1920s and 1930s [E]. This more expansive role of fighting communism also led the U.S. to an active presence in Asia.[E].

During the 1960s and 1970s, the U.S. actively fought communism in Vietnam [C]. Due to the lack of a clear victory in this prolonged conflict, American public opinion turned against active American military involvement [E]. This is reflected in the Nixon Doctrine's ideas [D] – that America cannot "…undertake all the defense of the free nations of the world." In the aftermath of Vietnam, the United States is more reluctant to assume the role of world's policeman.

[C] In the 1990s, the collapse of the U.S.S.R. led to more rethinking and reevaluating of national interests, as the comments by Nash in Document 6 [D] show. The fading of the Soviet military threat led to policy modification. The Document 7 table [D] shows that, in the past two decades, policy makers followed through with this new approach by cutting back defense expenditures by nearly one-third.

[C] The fall of the United States' historic enemy of the post-WWII period (the U.S.S.R.), changed America's view of the world. It caused new shifts and a more modified approach to involvement. Joseph Nye's [D] comments in "Soviet Decline and American Soft Power" show that the national interests are still changing. As he says, "The U.S. and other countries will have to pay much more attention to the problems of organizing cooperation …" [F]. He indicates that nuclear weapons, terrorism, epidemic diseases are new national interests. When national interests change, they cause a reshaping of the United States foreign policy [G].

USING THIS BOOK FOR REVIEW

Now you have an idea of the parts of the examination and the types of questions on it. You should see the task before you in a clearer light. The next step is to understand how this book will help you to prepare for the examination.

Geographic Influences – You need to concentrate on the essential concepts, ideas, and patterns of events. While the bulk of the examination is devoted to historical concepts and patterns, geography plays a powerful, universal role in the shaping of human affairs. It is important that you see how geography touches every era of U.S. history and government, including the present. So that you can carry this geographic knowledge through the chronological eras, this is where the review begins. The next part of this introductory lesson is on geographic influences. Lessons 1 through 9 deal with content studied in the major chronological eras of U.S. history and government. Finally, there is a full practice examination.

Standard Lesson Structure – Content Lessons 1 through 9 are structured in similar fashion, although they are of different lengths. For consistency, each lesson begins with a time line of the main political, economic, and social occurrences of the era. From there, the lessons go into detail on the interplay of the forces that shaped the era. Along the way, there are illustrated charts and profiles to help visualize and deepen the broad patterns shown in the lesson. **Graphics are extremely important** and they are often used to provide "mental triggers" to help you visualize key ideas and events.

Lesson Assessment – At the end of each lesson there is an assessment. It will help train you for the examination as well as deepen ideas about what you have read. The assessment features multi-choice questions similar to the actual test questions. You should do the questions and look back in the book for those of which you are unsure.

Emphasis on Writing Questions – It is a fact that students lose a higher percent of credit on the Part II written responses than on the Part I multi-choice questions. Each lesson's assessment has a thematic essay. To succeed on the examination, you must practice prewriting, planning, and outlining the written responses. At the end of each lesson there is a short, two document "Practice for DBQ" exercise. It will strengthen your ability to deal with the longer, full version of the DBQ on the examination. For guidance, it is worth referring back to the model thematic essay and model DBQ you have just seen in this introductory lesson. Be sure to work the answers out on scrap paper first. Getting your ideas on paper –no matter what the order of ideas – is one of the most vital parts of the writing process.

ESSENTIAL CONCEPTS

Concepts are "core ideas" that are essential to mastering U.S. history and government. They are guaranteed to appear on every examination. The list that follows merely presents the terms to jog your memory. It is artificial to define them here. They are only valuable if they are presented in context – associated with historic people, places and things. However, you should be on the lookout for them throughout this book. As you progress through the review lessons, you will find them introduced and defined as their associated content is presented.

Political: Anarchy, Appeasement, Civil Disobedience, Common Law, Communism, Compromise, Confederation, Constitution, Containment, Demagogue, Democracy, Dictatorship, Divine Right, Due Process, Fascism, Federalism, Genocide, Imperialism, Implied Power, Intervention, Isolationism, Judicial Activism, Judicial Review, Limited Government, Lobbying, Loose Constructionist, Nationalism, Neutrality, Parliamentary, Polarization, Precedent, Reactionary, Reform, Representative Government, Republic, Reserved Power, Revolution, Sectionalism, Self-determination, Separation of Power, Social Contract, Socialism, Sovereignty, Strict Constructionist, Suffrage, Terrorism, Totalitarian, Unwritten Constitution

Geographic (Physical): Altitude, Climate, Continent, Current, Hemisphere, Island, Isthmus, Latitude, Longitude, Maps, Mountain Range, Peninsula, Plain, Plateau, Region, River Valley, Spatial Relationships, Strait, Topography, Savanna

Economic: Agrarian, Boycott, Capitalism, Cartel, Collective Bargaining, Command Economy, Commercial Revolution, Consumerism, Consumption, Contraction, Deficit, Depression, Diversification, Embargo, Government Stimulation, Gross Domestic Product and Gross National Product, Income, Industrialization, Interdependence, Investment Capital, Laissez-faire, Less Developed Country, Market Economy, Marxism, Mercantilism, Monopoly, Per Capita, Rationing, Recession, Reciprocation, Revenue, Sanction, Scarcity, Service Industry, Socialism, Subsistence Farming, Supply and Demand, Surplus, Tariff, Traditional Economy, Unionism

Environmental: Acid Rain, Conservation, Global Warming, Green Revolution, Greenhouse Effect, Ozone Depletion, Strip Mining

Social: Acculturation, Affirmative Action, Assimilation, Birth Rate, Culture, Cultural Diffusion, Diversity, Infant Mortality Rate, Integration, Literacy Rate, Modernization, Nativism, Racism, Segregation, Social Darwinism, Social Mobility, Traditionalism, Urbanization, Xenophobia

Religious: Christianity, Ethic, Fundamentalism, Heresy, Puritanism, Separation of Church and State

"THE MAIN THING IS ... DON'T GET EXCITED."

Some people get very frantic as examinations loom. They put pressure on themselves that drives them into an emotional state that is counter productive. Here are some important ideas to keep you calm and help you make the most of a big task:

- **Allow sufficient time** – Any review of a course as broad as U.S. History & Government is going to take time. It cannot be done quickly, and it cannot be done alone. So, give yourself time. On your own, work in a quiet environment, get rid of distractions, and always have pen and paper handy. The act of writing helps cement ideas in your consciousness.

- **Get Verbal Feedback** – During part of your review, you might try working one-on-one with a friend or parent. Verbal feedback and dialog about the content helps build your confidence. Above all, take it slowly – in small doses, a few pages at a time. A long, drawn-out session is counterproductive.

- **Work With Teacher** – This book was designed to be used following a teacher's advice in the classroom and at home. Each lesson can be read in one or two nights and followed up in class the next day. Perhaps your teacher will have you pre-write a thematic essay or DBQ at home and then work on writing the actual essay the next day in class. Perhaps you will start prewriting by brainstorming in a cooperative group in class and finish an essay for homework. There are many ways to approach the review, but use your teacher's system – and don't look for short cuts. At this point, there aren't any.

- **Lean on a Textbook** – When you are working on your own, remember to have your textbook handy. It has much more material and background than this brief review book. When you feel you need more depth to understand something, use your textbook as a reference book. Go to the index and look up key words, then skim the text material connected with them. Look carefully at the textbook page. Just the appearance of the page or some illustration should remind you of when you originally studied the material. Take some time to jot down a few notes about the event, person, or movement from the text. Write them in the margin of this book so they are there when you are going over the material later.

There is no single, right method for review. There are many possible ways to review. Your teacher is the best guide for designing the review procedure. The key is working at the material calmly, systematically, and gradually over several weeks.

GEOGRAPHIC BACKGROUND

Geography is the study of the Earth and its features. It also studies the distribution of life on Earth, including human life and the effects of human activity. Geographic features have a significant impact on where and how people live. Relationships to climate, water, land forms, and mineral deposits shape how people live and act toward others. For example, once railroads began crossing the undeveloped western U.S., settlement increased in a very short time. Indications are that more attention is being paid to geographic factors on the new U.S. history and government exams than in the past. Review of some key factors should be beneficial.

As a geographic factor, **climate** often plays a key role in human development. It shapes culture (e.g., Amerindian plains dwellers were usually nomadic). In each region of the country, the general climatic conditions govern human progress. An area's livelihood may spring from geographic factors (e.g., fishing has been a chief industry for New England, water power from the rapids of short rivers of the east aided industrial development, and the Great Plains lent themselves to large-scale grain farming).

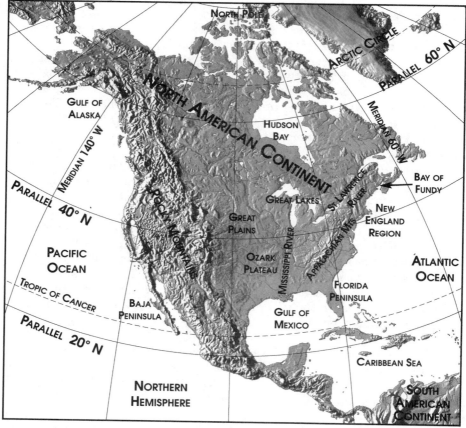

GEOGRAPHIC TERMS

Term - Explanation

Meridian (U.S.: approx. 67°W (Maine) – 160°W (Hawaii/ 170°W Aleutians) – an imaginary great circle passing through the North and South geographic poles; **lines of longitude** measured East or West to 180 degrees of the Prime Meridian (0° – running through Greenwich, England and 180° at the International Date Line)

Parallel (U.S.: approx. 18°N (Puerto Rico / Hawaii) – 72°N (Alaska) – any of the imaginary lines representing **degrees of latitude** that encircle the Earth parallel to the plane of the Equator zero degrees (0°) measured North and South to 90 degrees (90° North or South – geographic poles)

Hemisphere (Western) – either the northern or southern half of the Earth as divided by the Equator, or the eastern or western half as divided by a meridian

Continent (North America) – one of the principal landmasses of the Earth (other continents include: Africa, Antarctica, Asia, Australia, Europe, North America, and South America)

Region (New England, Middle Atlantic, Midwest, South, Southwest, Northwest) – a large portion of the country unified by physical or human characteristics such as language, culture, economic activity, or a political system

Ocean (Atlantic, Pacific) – any of the principal divisions of the Earth's salt water surface (71%), including the Atlantic, Pacific, and Indian Oceans, their southern extensions in Antarctica, and the Arctic Ocean

Sea (Caribbean) – a relatively large body of salt water completely or partially enclosed by land

Bay (New York, Chesapeake, San Francisco) – a body of water partially enclosed by land with a mouth accessible to the sea

Gulf (Gulf of Mexico) – a large area of a sea or ocean partially enclosed by land

Lakes (Great Lakes) – a large inland body of fresh water or salt water

River (St. Lawrence, Hudson, Ohio-Missouri-Mississippi, Colorado, Columbia) – a large natural stream of water emptying into an ocean, a lake, or another body of water

Mountains (Appalachian, Rockies) – a significant natural elevation of the Earth's surface having considerable mass, generally steep sides

Plateau (Allegheny, Ozark, Intermountain) – an elevated, level expanse of land; a tableland

Plain (Eastern Coastal, Great Plains) – an extensive, level, usually treeless, area of land

Peninsula (Florida, Baja Calif.) – a piece of land that projects into a body of water

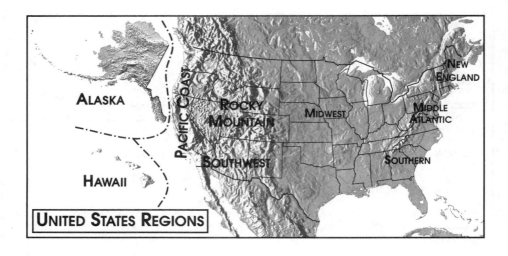

UNITED STATES REGIONS

SIZE OF THE UNITED STATES

Area: 3,700,000 square miles (4th largest country after
            Russia, Canada, and China)
Borders: 4,000 mile northern border with Canada, 1,900 mile southern
            border with Mexico
Center of
Population: 1790 - east of Baltimore, Maryland, 1990 - southwest of St. Louis,
            Missouri

GEOGRAPHIC FACTORS THAT SHAPED
THE IDENTITY OF THE UNITED STATES

The **topography** (physical features of the Earth's surface) of the
United States has greatly influenced the settlement and development of
the nation. Modern technological developments in the 20th century have
helped to reduce the impact that many of these features presented in
prior years.

MAJOR MOUNTAIN RANGES

The Appalachian Mountains extend 1,500 miles from New England,
southwestward to Georgia and Alabama. They form a nearly continuous
chain and were at one time a formidable barrier.

The Rocky Mountains extend in an irregular pattern from northern
New Mexico to northern Canada. The Continental Divide (the line that
divides those rivers that flow east from those that flow west) runs
through the Rockies.

MAJOR RIVER SYSTEMS

The Mississippi River has served as a vital north-south water highway in the United States. The main tributaries of the Mississippi, the Ohio in the east and the Missouri to the west, extend the reach of the Mississippi from the Appalachians to the Rockies. The delta at the mouth of the Mississippi results in a fertile agricultural region.

Rivers east of the Appalachian Mountains (Delaware, Hudson, Potomac, Connecticut) are generally much shorter than the great rivers of the Middle West. Also in the east is the St. Lawrence River that, with the construction of the St. Lawrence Seaway and other locks and canals, provides a route from the Atlantic through the Great Lakes to the cities of the Middle West such as Chicago, Cleveland, and Detroit.

Rivers west of the Rockies include the Columbia and the Colorado. They flow through large areas of desert and semi-arid lands on their way to the Pacific. The flow of water on many western rivers has been impeded by the construction of dams for irrigation and drinking water.

GREAT PLAINS

Much of the large area between the Rocky Mountains and the Appalachian Mountains is called the Interior Plains. The eastern part of these plains are the Central Lowlands, today the Middle West. This is a fertile area with adequate rainfall. Farther west, from an area west of

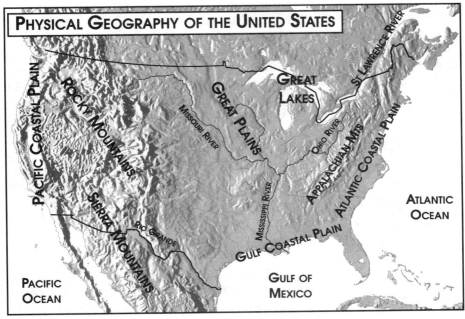

PHYSICAL GEOGRAPHY OF THE UNITED STATES

the Mississippi to the foothills of the Rockies is the Great Plains. This grassland, with a slightly upward slope, is much drier than the area to the east. Americans who saw it 150 years ago called it the Great American Desert. Prairie grasses dominated the landscape, though today little of the native grass remains. It has been transformed to pastureland and farming.

COASTAL AREAS

The Atlantic and Gulf Coastal Plains extend in a broad sweep from New York to Texas. These lowlands result in fertile soil and adequate transportation routes. The gentle slope to the sea, together with the eastern rivers, give the region excellent ports for shipping.

ATLANTIC AND PACIFIC OCEANS

These two oceans provided a boundary thousands of miles wide from Europe and Asia. Until the 20th century, it usually took weeks or even months to cross these oceans. The nation was able to use the oceans as barriers from the political problems and upheavals of much of the world.

VEGETATION ZONES

Most of the area from the Atlantic Coast to the edge of the Great Plains was at one time covered by forests. Evergreen forests dominated in the northern and mountain regions, while deciduous forests (broad leaf) were prevalent in much of the rest. The grasslands of the Great Plains contained prairie grasses. The area from the Rockies westward was, like the climate, more varied. Forests were predominant in the mountains, grasses and small plants in the basins and semi-arid regions, and a mixture in the coastal areas of central and southern California. Human settlement has swept away much of the naturally growing vegetation of the United States, especially in the areas east of the Rockies.

AGRICULTURAL AREAS

Fewer than 3% of the workers in the United States today are involved directly in agriculture, yet the nation produces enormous surpluses of food. Nearly 40% of the world's corn is grown in the United States, and between 10% - 20% of the world's cotton and wheat. The Midwest is the most productive agricultural region, while California produces the greatest value of agricultural products.

From New England to the Upper Midwest, dairy farming is common, with smaller farms growing a variety of corn, grain, and vegetables in the relatively short growing season. The Midwest and the Plains are the centers of America's farming region. Corn, soybeans, wheat, and oats are grown in large quantities, and pastures are filled with cattle. The longer growing season in the South permits farmers to cultivate cotton, tobacco, and in Florida and Texas, citrus fruits. Irrigation and a mild climate give California farmers the ability to grow fresh vegetables and produce a large citrus crop.

NATURAL RESOURCES

The richness of the United States in natural resources helped it to become the leading industrial nation in the world. Historically, the discovery of gold and silver in places such as California, Nevada, and Alaska set off rushes in which thousands would race to a location to claim their fortune. Most came away disappointed. More important in the long run have been other resources, such as petroleum, natural gas, iron ore, and coal.

Petroleum and natural gas are found mostly in Texas, Louisiana, California, and Alaska. The Mesabi region around Lake Superior provided the United States during the years of industrial expansion with iron ore for steel. Throughout the Appalachian Mountains, coal has been mined for over 100 years. Arkansas provides most of the domestic production of bauxite, used to make aluminum. Copper comes from Arizona and Utah. Lead, phosphorus, zinc, and uranium are a few of the many other minerals that are mined in the United States.

SUMMARY

A knowledge of national history gives an individual a better perspective on the society in which they live. Understanding of how historians analyze facts and ideas is the beginning point. Achieving proficiency in U.S. history requires meeting standards in a broad range of the social sciences – a basic knowledge of analytical tools of historians, political scientists, economists, and geographers. These basic standards are commonly used to assess students' knowledge on history examinations. This book should help you review these standards as well as the general content of United States history.

SAMPLE GEOGRAPHY QUESTIONS

1   Which action would most likely have occurred as a result of climate variations in the United States?
1   discovery of gold in California
2   nomadic lifestyle of Native American plains dwellers
3   growth of Puritan religious influences in colonial America
4   the southerly flow of the Mississippi River

2   Which features of United States topography acted most as a barrier to the movement of people and goods?
1   Mississippi and Missouri Rivers
2   St. Lawrence River and the Great Lakes
3   Rocky and Appalachian Mountains
4   Atlantic and Gulf Coastal Plains

3   Until the 20th century, which of the following provided the United States with effective barriers from the upheavals and problems of much of the rest of the world?
1   Atlantic and Pacific Oceans
2   Appalachian and Rocky Mountains
3   Mississippi and Missouri Rivers
4   Great Plains and Interior Plains

4   In the mid 18th century, the British Parliament issued the *Proclamation of 1763* in an attempt to reduce defense costs by containing colonial settlement to
1   east of the Appalachian Mountains
2   south of the St. Lawrence River
3   west of the Mississippi and Missouri Rivers
4   the New England colonies

5   The Louisiana Purchase (1803), the *Oregon Treaty* (1846), and the victory of the U.S. in the Mexican War (1848) resulted in
1   an expansion of the Monroe Doctrine
2   a settlement of the slavery issue
3   completion of the southern route of the transcontinental railroad
4   more than doubling the size of the country since the American Revolution ended in 1781

6   Which of the following was an independent nation before becoming part of the United States?
1   New England   3   Texas
2   West Virginia   4   Florida

7   Which was the most formidable barrier to early to mid-19th century settlers' travel to the Pacific coast?
1   extensive swamp areas
2   slow flowing rivers
3   dangerous grade-level railroad crossings
4   treacherous mountain passes

8   One of the most effective strategies of the Union in the Civil War was
1   blockading the South's transatlantic trade
2   fortifying the Great Lakes Region
3   retreating and forcing Southern armies to fight in the colder climates
4   refusing to fight in open plains

Base your answer to question 9 on the map at the right and on your knowledge of U.S. history and government.

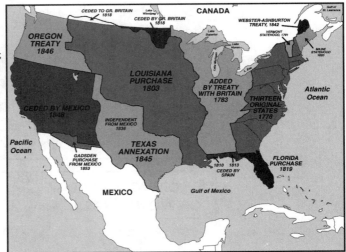

9   Which statement about U.S. expansion is most accurate?
1   U.S. expansion was primarily achieved by military victories over Great Britain.
2   Territories added to the U.S. were gained by a variety of methods.
3   Most of the territory west of the Mississippi was purchased from Mexico.
4   The first areas added to the thirteen original states were on the west coast.

10 These maps indicate that the participants in the Paris Peace Conference attempted to
1 expand Russian influence in Eastern Europe
2 provide self-determination for subject peoples
3 establish a German-Russian common border
4 increase the size of the Austrian Empire

PRE-COLUMBIAN CIVILIZATIONS PRE-1492

COLUMBUS' VOYAGES (1492)

1500

1600

JAMESTOWN (1607)

1625

EXPLORATION AND

PURITAN
REVOLUTION
(1648)

1650

COLONIZATION

OF THE AMERICAS

1675

ENGLISH BILL OF RIGHTS (1689)

1700

1725

GREAT AWAKENING (1720s-1740s)

1750

FRENCH & INDIAN WAR (1754-1763)

STAMP ACT (1765)

1775

DECLARATION OF INDEPENDENCE (1776)

BATTLE OF SARATOGA (1777)

TREATY OF PARIS (1783)

1800

©1993 PhotoDisc Inc.

EXPLORATION AND COLONIZATION OF THE AMERICAS

INTRODUCTION

Long before the voyages of Christopher Columbus to the Western Hemisphere, Native American peoples developed communities in the Americas. Early inhabitants in the American continents came from the steppes of Asia across the Bering Sea / land bridge approximately 12,000 years ago. However, new findings suggest the migrants came by land and sea from several regions of Asia and possibly Europe more than 17,000 years ago. Regardless of origin, hundreds of Native American societies developed with different customs, languages, dialects, and appearances.

PRE-COLUMBIAN AMERICA

Despite their diversity, pre-Columbian Native American societies lacked technologies widely used in Europe, including the wheel, the plow, and the use of draft animals such as horses and oxen. Ideas regarding land ownership differed drastically as well. Native Americans believed in communal ownership (land belonged to the whole society), whereas, the Europeans believed in private ownership of land.

AFRICA AND THE ATLANTIC SLAVE TRADE

Several empires rose and fell in western Africa from 300 AD to 1600 AD. These empires had large armies, traded extensively, and engaged in agriculture. Some areas were heavily influenced by Islam, but often retained many aspects of traditional religions, including a single all-powerful God, lesser gods, and ancestor worship. Extended families held lands in common with individual nuclear families being assigned plots where men and women worked to cultivate the fields.

Although slavery existed in Africa before the Europeans entered the trade, African slavery differed considerably from European and Middle Eastern forms. In Africa, slavery was more social than economic. Slavery was a way to cut off people from their families. Prisoners of war and others banished by their kin became slaves. Slaves generally lived under the protection of law in West Africa. They could be sold, but their children could not. The Portuguese developed the plantation system and a com-

☆ CAPSULE – CHARACTERISTICS OF NATIVE AMERICAN SOCIETIES BEFORE 1492

NORTH AMERICAN CULTURES (c 1500)

MESOAMERICA
(Mexico, Central America, South America)

- included the Olmec, Mayan, Aztec and Incan Empires
- highly organized societies with codified laws, roads and communications systems, great cities, astronomical calendars, accounting systems, bureaucracies, religious systems
- agricultural, especially important was the development of maize (Indian corn)

NORTH AMERICA

- fewer people than in Mexico, Central America, South America
- lived in clans and related tribal groups
- generally hunter-gatherers, but also cultivated crops
- diversity based on geography – Plains Indians nomadic (Sioux and Crow), Pacific Northwest fishing cultures (Kwakiutl), eastern woodlands cultures established villages surrounded by cultivated fields (Delaware, Mohawk), southwestern cultures adapted to a more arid climate (Anasazi)
- most tribes consisted of independent members loosely joined together under the leadership of a chief; some groups did organize stronger governments, including the Powhatan Confederacy in Virginia and the Iroquois League or Confederacy in upstate New York
- Eastern Woodland Indians divided labor; women raised crops, gathered nuts and fruits, cared for the children and prepared meals; men cleared land, hunted, fished and provided protection

mercial system to purchase large numbers of slaves from African traders. The Portuguese needed labor to cultivate sugar cane in the islands off the coast of Africa. This same plantation slave system – the fazenda – was transferred by them to their American colonies, spread to the encomiendas of the Spanish colonies and on to the New World colonies of the British.

EUROPEAN COLONIZATION

Despite early exploration by the Norse (Vikings) of the land rimming the North Atlantic, permanent European settlement of the American continents did not occur until hundreds of years later.

Because the Spanish recognized Portugal's claim to Africa and an eastern route to Asia, Spanish explorers looked for another way to Asia. In Spain's pay, Italian Christopher Columbus looked westward across the Atlantic Ocean. Most educated people at the time believed the world to be round, but seriously underestimated its circumference. In 1492, Columbus and his crew discovered a "new world" for the Europeans, despite initially believing they landed in the East Indies.

Columbus' voyages also led to friction between Portugal and Spain. Portugal claimed Columbus' findings were part of Portugal's sphere of

---

☆CAPSULE – CHANGES THAT ENCOURAGED EXPLORATION

As Europe emerged from the Medieval Era, changes in thinking and technology led to a period of exploration and discovery. Changes included:

- demand for spices for food preservation increased after the Crusades (11th -13th C)
- greater world view and broader learning as a result of the Renaissance (15th -16th C)
- creation of nation-states under strong monarchs, such as Ferdinand and Isabella of Spain and Elizabeth I of England (15th - 17th C)
- technological innovations, including the astrolabe to determine latitude, ship design, and guns allowing mariners to travel further from known waters
- expansion of trade and capital allowed for supply of capital to fund expeditions

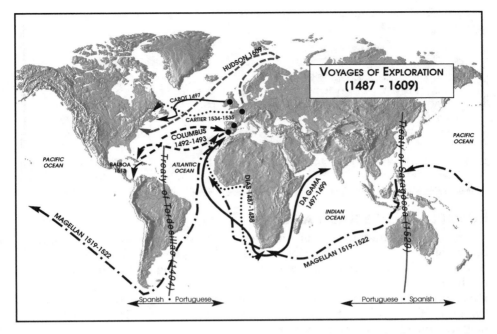

Voyages of Exploration (1487 - 1609)

influence. Spain rejected Portugal's claim. These Catholic countries allowed the Pope to resolve matters. In 1494, the ***Treaty of Tordesillas*** granted Portugal the rights to the Atlantic slave trade and the sea route around Africa to India. Spain received the right to explore and conquer lands to the west of the treaty line that was about 1000 miles west of the Azore Islands.

Although Columbus' voyages did not extend beyond the Bahamas and Caribbean islands, these voyages inspired further European exploration to the Americas. France and England sent their own explorers, ignoring Spain and Portugal's monopolies.

Major changes occurred for four continents when Native Americans, Europeans, and Africans came into contact at the end of the 1400s. In addition to the transfer of plants and animals between Europe and the Americas, the colonial labor shortage led to an increase in the African slave trade.

This so-called "Columbian Exchange" included the acquisition of seeds and plants, including potatoes, and corn, from the Americas which enriched the diets of Europe and Africa. The Europeans introduced new diseases, livestock, European wheat, the wheel, and firearms to the Americas. A significant number of Native Americans (estimates range as high as 90%) died largely as a result of lack of immunity to virulent European diseases and germs, especially smallpox.

☆ Capsule – The Columbian Exchange

To the Americas	To Europe
diseases – smallpox, measles, plague, influenza, scarlet fever. (A significant number of Native Americans, estimates range as high as 90%, died largely as a result of lack of immunity.)	diseases – hepatitis, syphilis
foods – wheat, rice, sugar cane, coffee, bananas	foods – corn, potatoes, yams, peanuts, pumpkins, beans, squash, tomatoes
animals - horses, pigs, sheep, goats	animals – turkeys, llamas
other – the wheel, firearms	other – tobacco

European Imperial Patterns

Spain's conquistadores helped develop a vast empire in the Americas before other European countries successfully explored and colonized the Americas. The northern European countries of France, England, and the Netherlands were focused on the religious and political struggles of the **Protestant Reformation** and their own national development. England's defeat of the Spanish Armada in 1588, its growing commercial power, and strengthened monarchy fueled nationalism and overseas interest. By the 17th century, northern European Protestant countries sought to challenge Spain's supremacy in the Americas.

☆ Capsule – European Colonization Patterns

Spanish – 16th century	Dutch – 17th century
Location: Gulf of Mexico area, Caribbean, Central America, and much of South America	**Location**: Hudson River area
Motivations: gain territory and wealth; religious conversion of natives	**Motivations**: expand commerce and trade; seek profit for investors in joint stock companies
Pattern of Settlement: national enterprises financed and coordinated by the Crown; Spanish elite appointed by the Crown dominated and submitted the large Indian population to a forced labor system (encomienda); few Spanish immigrants settled in the Americas; society was hierarchical and closely tied to Spain.	**Pattern of Settlement**: manorial (patroon) system and prosperity of the Netherlands in the 17th century discouraged settlement
Success: much success in extracting mineral wealth (gold and silver); less initial emphasis on trade and agriculture; sugar plantations in the West Indies	**Success**: trading conflicts and leadership problems limited success. English took control of New Netherlands in 1664

EUROPEAN
COLONIAL EMPIRES
(17TH - 18TH CENTURIES)

French – 17th century

Location: St. Lawrence River and Great Lakes area, lower Mississippi River area, French West Indies in the Caribbean

Motivations: develop fur trade; religious conversion of natives

Pattern of Settlement: few immigrants led to sparse settlement; focus on fur trade led to more cooperative relations between the French trappers (coureurs de bois) and the native populations

Success: fur trade and sugar cultivation highly profitable

English – 17th century

Location: Atlantic seaboard of North America, Caribbean islands

Motivations: strengthen national prestige and wealth; seek profit for investors in joint stock companies; achieve religious freedom for certain groups (Puritans, Catholics); create outlet for surplus population; Explore new route to Asia

Pattern of Settlement: established own communities; separated native populations from English settlements; immigration of large numbers of English (approx. 160,000 from 1600-1680 to the Atlantic coast colonies); religious persecution of Protestants or Catholics (depending on monarchy) led these groups to seek religious freedom; eventual focus of colonies on farming and permanent settlement

Success: initial attempts at colonization failed, e.g., Roanoke colony; success increased when colonists met the area on its own terms instead of trying to follow the Spanish model

☆ Capsule – Early English Settlements in Virginia and Massachusetts Bay

Similarities

- colonial charter (development license) initially granted to a joint stock company (the Virginia Company had two divisions)
- both eventually became royal colonies (controlled by the Crown)
- English settlers brought a heritage governed by English principles
- both met with Indian resistance after initial assistance

Differences
Virginia

- Jamestown Colony established in 1607
- introduction of tobacco as a cash crop insured the colony's success
- indentured servitude supplied labor – indenture contracts ran from 4-7 years of labor in exchange for passage to the colonies
- great proportion of early settlers were male
- slavery introduced to supply labor
- life expectancy initially was very short
- tobacco cultivation and many navigable rivers led to scattered population.

Differences
Massachusetts and New England

- Plymouth Colony established in 1620 by Pilgrims (Separatist Puritans - no ties to the "corrupt" Church of England) seeking religious freedom
- Massachusetts Bay Colony established as a charter colony in 1630 by Puritans (Protestants seeking to reform the Church of England or Anglican Church) seeking religious freedom. They wished to become "a city upon a hill" – a model Christian society.
- immigrants generally settled in family groups
- towns developed following the English model of houses clustered around a village green
- tight knit communities did not tolerate religious dissenters
- other New England colonies developed out of religious conflicts within the Puritan communities, eg. Rhode Island, Connecticut

Despite the common economic goal of increasing national wealth which would lead to greater national political power, the patterns of European colonization differed significantly. Only along the Atlantic coastline did European influence dominate. In the interior of North America numerous Native American societies existed between scattered European settlements and beyond them.

MERCANTILISM

The economic policy of mercantilism guided European colonization of this period. Under mercantilism, colonies existed for the benefit of the mother country.

> ### BASIC MERCANTILIST PRINCIPLES
> * national wealth measured in precious metals (gold and silver)
> * achieve a favorable balance of trade
> * acquire colonies to provide raw materials and markets
> * forbid colonial manufacturing
> * prohibit colonies from trading with any other country

EARLY ENGLISH SETTLEMENT

By the early 1600s conditions were suitable for English colonization of the land explored 100 years earlier. These conditions included: growing national political power, increased naval and maritime power, and the formation of joint stock companies which brought together middle class money to fund potentially profitable colonization efforts.

SETTLEMENT OF OTHER ENGLISH ATLANTIC COLONIES

As the English colonies grew and prospered, the English Crown became more reluctant to grant charters to joint stock companies. Instead, individuals or groups directly responsible to the Crown, known as **proprietors**, received the charters for these proprietary colonies. Despite the similarities of the English colonies being in the same imperial network, there were tremendous differences in their settlement. By the later colonial period, the Crown kept ownership of some colonies and took over control and ownership of most proprietary and charter colonies (see map and charts on pages 46 and 47).

POLITICAL DEVELOPMENT OF THE ENGLISH COLONIES

The English colonists brought with them a political heritage that drew heavily from English civil experience.

* In the *Magna Carta* of 1215, noblemen began to limit absolutism.

* English common law, drawing from the precedents established in earlier and similar court cases, became the basis for the colonial legal system.

* The *English Bill of Rights* of 1689 limited the power of the British monarchy and established the supremacy of Parliament.

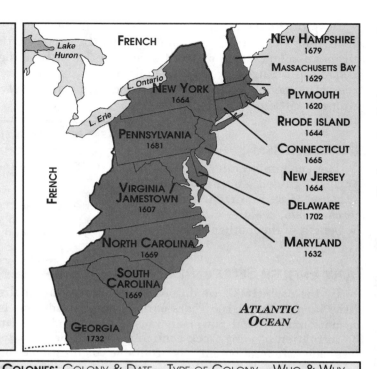

BRITISH ATLANTIC COAST COLONIES:

SETTLEMENT PATTERNS

(1607 – 1732)

FRENCH

Lake Huron

L. Ontario

L. Erie

FRENCH

NEW YORK
1664

PENNSYLVANIA
1681

VIRGINIA / JAMESTOWN
1607

NORTH CAROLINA
1669

SOUTH CAROLINA
1669

GEORGIA
1732

NEW HAMPSHIRE
1679

MASSACHUSETTS BAY
1629

PLYMOUTH
1620

RHODE ISLAND
1644

CONNECTICUT
1665

NEW JERSEY
1664

DELAWARE
1702

MARYLAND
1632

ATLANTIC OCEAN

NEW ENGLAND COLONIES: COLONY & DATE – TYPE OF COLONY – WHO & WHY

Colony & Date	Type of Colony	Who & Why
Plymouth 1620	Virginia Company Contract; later royal charter	Pilgrims (Separatists from Anglican Church)
Massachusetts Bay 1629	charter	Massachusetts Bay Company; Puritan religious freedom
Rhode Island 1644	charter	Roger Williams; religious toleration; Puritan dissenters from Massachusetts
Connecticut 1665	charter	Puritan dissenters from Massachusetts (*Fundamental Orders of Connecticut*)
New Hampshire 1679	royal	originally part of Massachusetts Bay Colony

MIDDLE COLONIES: COLONY & DATE – TYPE OF COLONY – WHO & WHY

Colony & Date	Type of Colony	Who & Why
New York, 1664	royal	taken from the Dutch
New Jersey, 1664	proprietary (royal, 1702)	part of land taken from Dutch
Pennsylvania, 1681	proprietary	William Penn; Religious refuge for Quakers; Liberal government ideas
Delaware, 1702	proprietary (royal, 1729)	separate assembly, but governor same as Pennsylvania

SOUTHERN COLONIES: COLONY & DATE – TYPE OF COLONY – WHO & WHY		
Virginia/ Jamestown, 1607	charter (royal, 1624)	sharp class differences; tobacco trade important
Maryland, 1632	proprietary	Lord Baltimore; Catholic safe-haven; economic similarities to Virginia
Carolinas, 1669	proprietary (royal, 1729)	split into South Carolina and North Carolina; primarily supplied food to West Indies; dependent upon slave labor; small, self-sufficient mixed farming of tobacco, livestock, foodstuffs; naval stores and lumber
Georgia, 1732	proprietary (royal, 1702)	James Ogelthorpe; Last colony created; defensive buffer against Spanish Florida; established as penal colony

This background, combined with the English government being 3,000 miles away and often lax in enforcing colonial regulations, led to the colonists having some measure of control over their own affairs.

The **European Enlightenment** influenced colonial political thought as well. The writings of **John Locke** and **French philosophes** such as Jean Jacques Rousseau focused on the social contract, the relationship between the government and those being governed. These philosophers believed that the government received its authority to govern from the people and not through divine right. At the same time, British kings sought to strengthen their economic and political control over the Anglo-Atlantic colonies by revoking certain charters. Many former charter and proprietary colonies became royal colonies (eight out of thirteen) before the Revolutionary War.

GENERAL PATTERNS OF COLONIAL POWER

CHARTER COLONIES	PROPRIETARY COLONIES	ROYAL COLONIES
• land granted by monarch to company	• land granted by monarch to individual or group	• crown owned land
• peoples' power specified in charter	• governor, with veto power, appointed by proprietor(s)	• governor, with veto power, appointed by monarch
• governor, with veto power, elected by colonists	• usually bicameral legislature with upper house appointed and lower house elected by the colonists	• bicameral legislature with upper house appointed by monarch and lower house elected by the colonists
• bicameral legislature with both houses elected by the colonists		

Within these three general patterns of English colonial government, great variations existed. The governments had both democratic and undemocratic aspects. Despite the limitations of colonial democracy, the availability of land allowed a greater proportion of freeholders (land owners) to participate in political affairs than in England of the same time. Regional variations did exist.

- **House of Burgesses** (1619) – lower house of Virginia's legislature; first representative body in England's North Atlantic colonies; governed local matters; made laws for the colony (subject to governor's and later the Crown's approval)

- *Mayflower Compact* (1620) – signed by the Pilgrim men aboard the Mayflower; agreement to make "…just and equal laws for the general good…" of the colony; recognized the people as the source of power (in theory)

- *Fundamental Orders of Connecticut* (1639) – written constitution; granted all Connecticut men the right to vote, not just church members; judges and governor elected annually

- **New England town meetings** – example of direct democracy; free discussion of public matters; only property owners and those belonging to the established church could vote for officials or on local matters in most New England colonies

- **County or parish governments** – more important in the southern colonies; county officials appointed by the governors; lower house legislators chosen by colonists in most southern colonies

DEMOCRATIC AND UNDEMOCRATIC ASPECTS OF COLONIAL RULE	
Democratic Aspects	**Undemocratic Aspects**
• written constitutions • popularly elected assemblies • separation of powers • guaranteed rights of the people • "power of the purse" – locally elected legislatures could levy and collect taxes	• governors appointed, except in Rhode Island and Connecticut • monarchs claimed right to review and veto colonial laws • voting rights based on religious qualifications for some colonies • voting rights based on land ownership in all colonies • freedom of speech and press not guaranteed rights (the Zenger case in 1735 in New York helped to establish the principle that truth is a valid defense against libel)

Colonial governments generally focused on the local affairs of their own colonies and their place within the imperial framework. Before the American Revolution, there was little interest or success in bringing the colonies together. French colonial policy posed a common threat to the English colonies, but Benjamin Franklin could not find firm support for his **Albany Plan of Union** in 1754. Economic rivalry and geographic isolation kept the colonies from forming an effective union until the late 1770s.

ECONOMIC DEVELOPMENT
OF THE BRITISH COLONIES

Initially, England hoped its explorers would uncover a new supply of gold and silver or at least new, safer, and shorter trade routes to the Orient. They did not. As the colonies developed, they supplied England with raw materials and staple goods while buying goods produced in England. Both sides benefited, but the goal of economic independence for the mother country (England) kept the colonies economically dependent on England. This economic relationship was known as mercantilism.

The **Navigation Acts** provided the basic economic framework for England's Atlantic colonies. Starting in 1650, Parliament passed acts that:

- banned foreign shipping from the colonies
- forbade the colonies from exporting certain "enumerated goods" to anywhere but England
- routed all European and Asiatic trade with the colonies through England
- prohibited colonial manufacturing

The English did not strongly enforce these mercantilistic laws nor provide clear direction for British economic policy before the end of the French and Indian War in 1763. This left the colonies with a great deal of economic independence, known as a period of "salutary" or "benign neglect."

Partly as a result of mercantilist policies, England fought a series of wars between 1689 and 1763 to determine which European nations would control North America. Combatants included Spain, France, and France's Indian allies. The English victory over the Dutch in 1664 led to New Netherland becoming the colonies of New York and New Jersey. The British victory in the **French and Indian War** (1754-1763) eliminated France as a major power in North America.

DIFFERENT ECONOMIC REGIONS DEVELOP

Although over 90% of the colonists were engaged in agriculture, England's Atlantic colonies developed along different economic lines. Differences in geography, including climate, terrain, and population patterns, had a major impact.

Less than 5% of the colonial population lived in towns and cities, but coastal towns were the center of the colonies' commercial and intellectual life. Merchants linked producers and consumers by extending credit, building ships, and trading goods. Major colonial cities included Philadelphia, New York City, Boston, Charleston, and Baltimore.

QUESTION OF LABOR

Despite considerable European immigration and a high native birth rate by 1700, a labor shortage existed in the English Atlantic colonies,

REGIONAL COMPARISONS IN ENGLAND'S ATLANTIC COLONIES

NEW ENGLAND COLONIES

Geography	Dominant Economic Activities
• rugged terrain • rocky soil • cold climate • irregular coastline containing numerous harbors • abundant fishing grounds • abundant forest land	• subsistence farming on small plots of land • land ownership more widespread than in the southern colonies • smaller gap between rich and poor than in the southern colonies or Europe • shipbuilding and fishing major industries • commerce and trade significant, including triangular trades between the Atlantic colonies (fish, grain, lumber, rum), and Africa (slaves), the West Indies (sugar, molasses), England (manufactured goods)

MIDDLE COLONIES

Geography	Dominant Economic Activities
• fertile farmland • temperate climate • harbors • long, navigable rivers	• production of abundant foodstuffs, including grains, led to label of "bread colonies" • family sized farms • interior trade with Native Americans for furs • commerce with other colonies and Europe

SOUTHERN COLONIES

Geography	Dominant Economic Activities
• fertile soil • wide coastal plain • numerous wide, navigable rivers • warm, semi-tropical climate • forests	• export of staple crops, such as tobacco (Chesapeake), rice and indigo (South Carolina and Georgia) • single crop export plantation system • production of naval stores (pitch and tar) necessary for colonial shipping

COMPARISON OF INDENTURED SERVITUDE AND SLAVERY	
Indentured Servitude	**Slavery**
• 4-7 year work contracts in return for passage to colonies • over one-half of European immigrants to the colonies • worked as farm laborers, artisans, household servants • free at end of indenture sometimes receiving tools or land • existed in every colony	• life slavery based on mother's condition became legal norm in mid 1600s • forced migration from Africa under horrendous conditions known as "middle passage" • approximately 20% of population by 1775 with 90% living in the southern colonies • worked as farm laborers, artisans, household servants • existed in every colony

especially in the southern colonies. Settlers were unwilling to work for others when they could acquire their own land. Consequently, the use of indentured servants and African slaves developed. As the colonial era unfolded, the use of African slaves far surpassed the dwindling supply of indentured servants.

SOCIAL DEVELOPMENT OF THE AMERICAN COLONIES

Although heavily influenced by England over the course of the colonial period, the Atlantic colonies developed many aspects of a distinctly American culture.

- **Diversity of Population**
  The English outnumbered other ethnic groups, but there were a half million slaves (most from the West Indies and Africa) and settlers from other European countries, including Scotch-Irish, Germans, French, Swiss, Swedes, Dutch, Irish, and Welsh.

- **Class Structure**
  Generally, most colonies had a three-tiered class structure, although it was less distinct than in Europe. The upper class was an aristocracy of wealthy merchants and planters and a small professional group of lawyers and clergymen. The majority of population was of the "middling sort" (yeomen or small farmers, skilled workers, shopkeepers, and laborers). Shopkeepers and laborers were found in larger numbers in the northern than in the southern colonies). The lower class included indentured servants, African slaves, and Native Americans.

- **Education**
  The amount and type of education children received varied from colony to colony and class to class. In New England, literacy rates were high because Bible reading was central to the religious life. The wealthy often employed private tutors. Most children were taught at

home. The general education level in the colonies was higher than in Europe. The need for trained clergy led to the establishment of many colonial colleges, including Harvard, Yale, Princeton, and William and Mary.

- **Religion**
  Separation of church and state was not the common rule in the 17th and 18th centuries. Most colonists were Protestants and most colonies had an established church. The Anglican Church dominated in the southern and middle colonies. The Congregational Churches (Puritan) dominated the New England colonies. Despite the initial religious intolerance of Puritans toward other denominations, there was a wide number of religious groups in the colonies by the 1700s. This led to greater toleration, especially for other Protestant groups. The **Great Awakening** – a Protestant revival that swept across the colonies in the early 1700s – caused **schisms** (arguments and divisions) within churches and challenges to religious authority. The fragmentation of congregations eventually led to greater toleration of diversity. However, Christianity was central to the religious beliefs of overwhelming majority of American colonists.

By the eve of the American Revolution, the American colonists began to forge an identity that drew heavily upon their European, especially English background. Their colonial experiences created a society more dynamic, fluid, and healthier than in Europe.

COLONIAL DISCONTENT AND REVOLUTION (1763-1781)

CHANGES IN COLONIAL RELATIONS

In the mid-18th century, warfare among the major European powers spilled over into North America. In **King George's War** (1744-1748), colonists battled the French at Louisbourg in Nova Scotia. The **French and Indian War** (1754-1763) was known in Europe as the **Seven Years War**. It had the greatest impact upon colonial America. Victory over the French gave the British a greatly enlarged empire in North America. The end of the War also saw a shift in the relationship between Britain and its American colonies. This changed attitude resulted in a series of events leading up to revolution and independence a decade later.

France lost the French and Indian War and nearly all its colonies in North America. Large parts of Canada and the Mississippi region came under the control of Great Britain.

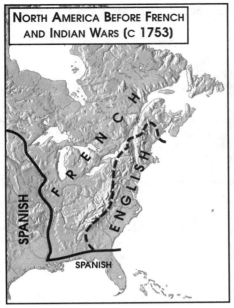

NORTH AMERICA BEFORE FRENCH AND INDIAN WARS (C 1753)

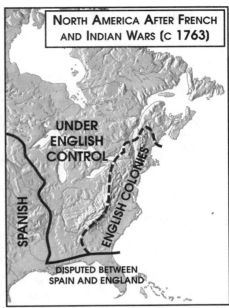

NORTH AMERICA AFTER FRENCH AND INDIAN WARS (C 1763)

During the War, at the **Albany Congress** in 1754, some British and colonial officials attempted to unify the colonies by strengthening defenses. With seven colonies represented, some delegates discussed the need for a continental legislature and an executive. The separate colonial assemblies had little enthusiasm for the plan, however, and nothing came of it.

The cost of the War, combined with administering the new colonial areas was a large financial burden for Britain. In London, some members of Parliament demanded that the colonists pay a greater share of the costs. Parliamentary leaders decided that revenue could be raised through new taxes and stricter enforcement of existing mercantilist trade laws.

Most British Ministers and Members of Parliament held the view that colonists should be subordinate to Parliament. They believed that the colonists should conform to the will of the British government. This included laws of navigation, trade, and taxation. Tradition and practice worked against their designs, however. For many years, elected colonial legislatures controlled most of the internal affairs of the colonies. They rarely looked to London to solve problems. Now, after many years of "salutary neglect," colonists resented taking orders from Parliament and the King. This was especially true concerning taxation.

PARLIAMENTARY ACT	PURPOSE	COLONIAL REACTION
Navigation Acts 18th century	Act forced colonists to trade with Britain and its possessions. Parliament imposed **customs duties** (tariffs) to enforce the regulations.	Colonists engaged in smuggling, importing foreign items, and bribing colonial officials.
Writs of Assistance 1760	Parliament provided British officials with *Writs of Assistance* – general search warrants – to find smuggled goods. Officials searched colonial homes and businesses, even if no probable cause for suspect activity was present.	Massachusetts colonists failed at convincing the British to halt the random searches. For the 1st time, British took enforcement of trade regulations seriously.
Proclamation of 1763	Native American uprisings, led by Chief Pontiac made life on the frontier dangerous and deadly. To diminish the cost of frontier defense, British Finance Minister George Grenville banned white settlement west of the Appalachian Mountains.	Colonists (land speculators and farmers) defied the order, and continued westward.
Sugar Act 1764	Grenville cut the duty on sugar in half to take the incentive out of bribing customs officers. British naval vessels strictly enforced the new regulations in and around American waters. Violators were to be tried in vice-admiralty courts, instead of civil courts with local juries.	Colonists continued smuggling sugar and molasses to make rum.
Stamp Act 1765	For the first time, Parliament imposed an "internal tax" – a tax on goods bought and sold within the colonies. The tax required colonists to purchase specially stamped paper for documents, licenses, papers, pamphlets, almanacs, and playing cards. Once again, vice-admiralty courts were to try any violators.	Houses of those who were to sell and supervise distribution of stamps were destroyed. Riots and mob violence spread. Reacting to the *Stamp Act*, Congress issued a declaration of grievances.
Quartering Act – 1765	At the end of the French and Indian War, the British kept a standing army in America to minimize conflicts between colonists and Native Americans. To defray the military cost, Parliament forced colonists to provide certain supplies, rations, and shelter for the troops.	Samuel Adams and others wrote protests against the tyranny of a standing army in peacetime.
Townshend Acts – 1767	Parliament imposed new import taxes on glass, lead, paint, paper, and tea, and a Board of Customs Commissioners in Boston for enforcement and levying fines.	Colonists pressured merchants to halt importation of British goods.

COLONIAL RESISTANCE TO NEW REGULATIONS

As in any protest, the main obstacle facing the American colonists was their lack of unity. Rarely had they ever cooperated on anything. Though in many instances cultures and ways were similar among the thirteen colonies, numerous differences existed. Opposition to the new British taxes and regulations brought about unprecedented unity among the colonies. The chart (on page 54) summarizes the actions taken by Britain, and the colonial response.

LEADERS ARISE

A small but influential number of colonists became more vocal in their criticism of the British.

- **Patrick Henry** (VA) – denounced Parliament's power to impose the Stamp Tax

- **John Dickinson** (PA) – wrote *Letters from a Farmer in Pennsylvania* which said that Parliament had no right to tax commerce if the sole intent was to raise revenue

- **John Hancock** (MA) – criticized Parliamentary actions that suppressed trade, and provided financial support for the Sons of Liberty, a group that led protests against British policies

- **Samuel Adams** (MA) – helped form the committees of correspondence to inform other colonies of unfair British actions

By 1770, the British Parliament had repealed most of the previously imposed taxes. Only a small tax on tea remained, and animosity between the colonies and Britain temporarily declined.

MOVING TOWARD WAR (1770-1775)

In 1768, Britain sent troops to Boston to protect British officials. Bostonians protested, as they associated standing armies with tyranny. A chain of events began that led to revolution in 1775.

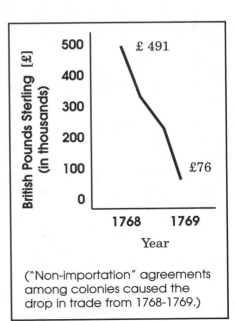

("Non-importation" agreements among colonies caused the drop in trade from 1768-1769.)

EVENTS LEADING TO THE AMERICAN REVOLUTION

1770	Boston Massacre (1770)
1771	
1772	
1773	Boston Tea Party (1773)
1774	Intolerable Acts (1774)
	First Continental Congress (1774)
1775	Patriots Attack British at Lexington and Concord (1775)
	Patriots take Ft. Ticonderoga (1775)
	Second Continental Congress (1775)
1776	*Declaration of Independence* (1776)

The Boston Massacre started as a disturbance outside the Boston customs house, and escalated into a violent confrontation between colonists and British soldiers. After attempts to restrain the crowd failed, the troops fired back, killing five colonists. Sam Adams wrote extensively to the other colonies, propagandizing the incident as a "massacre."

The Boston Tea Party was the colonial response to the *Tea Act* passed by Parliament. Britain placed restrictions on the sale of tea in the colonies, which infuriated colonial merchants. One night in December, 1773, a group of colonists disguised as Native Americans boarded British ships in Boston harbor and dumped the cargo of tea overboard in protest. This illegal Boston "Tea Party" infuriated British authorities.

Britain imposed a series of measures called by the colonists the "Intolerable Acts" in response to the Tea Party. The British Prime Minister, Lord North, urged Parliament to pass the Boston Port Bill. This closed Boston harbor until colonists paid for the tea. A new *Quartering Act* extended the right of troops to demand housing on private property. Another act gave new powers to the governor and limited the number of town meetings.

The **First Continental Congress** included representatives from twelve of the thirteen colonies who met at Philadelphia in the Fall of 1774. Most still hoped for reconciliation with Great Britain. Though unhappy with Parliament, a certain loyalty to England still existed. Despite these feelings, a majority decided to support Boston, and urge repeal of the "Intolerable Acts."

In passing the ***Declaration of Rights and Grievances***, the Congress demanded that colonists have the right of assembly and petition, to be tried by one's peers, and to be free of a standing army. They also stated that Parliament could not tax the colonies except to regulate external commerce. A letter sent to King George said that Parliament, not he, was the problem.

THE UNANIMOUS DECLARATION OF THE THIRTEEN UNITED STATES OF AMERICA

© Wildside Press

"When in the course of human events, it becomes necessary for one people to dissolve the political bonds which have connected them with another, and to assume, among the powers of the earth, the separate and equal station to which the laws of nature and nature's God entitle them, a decent respect to the opinions of mankind requires that they should declare the causes which impel them to the separation. ... We hold these truths to be self-evident, that all men are created equal; that they are endowed by their Creator with certain unalienable rights; that among these are life, liberty, and the pursuit of happiness. ... That, to secure these rights, governments are instituted among men, deriving their just powers from the consent of the governed;... That, whenever any form of government becomes destructive to these ends, it is the right of the people to alter or to abolish it, and to institute a new government, laying its foundation on such principles, and organizing its powers in such form, as to them shall seem most likely to effect their safety and happiness..."

– Thomas Jefferson, *Declaration of Independence*, 1776

Congress organized a boycott of British goods. Members urged colonists to form committees to enforce the non-importation, non-consumption, and non-exportation agreements of British goods. It hoped that British merchants, ruined by a boycott, would pressure Parliament to give in.

OUTBREAK OF FIGHTING (1775)

In April of 1775, General Thomas Gage, the British commander in Massachusetts, was ordered to arrest the leading troublemakers of the colony. With little hope of catching them, he attempted to seize military weapons the colonists had hidden at **Concord**. After some brief encounters with the colonists at **Lexington**, the British moved onto Concord, but found few weapons. Enraged colonists mistakingly thought the British were burning the town. Angry colonial minutemen arrived on the scene and harassed the British on their 16 mile march back

General Washington Takes Command
© Wildside Press

to Boston. The British lost hundreds of men to enemy fire. In June, the British defeated the colonists at the **Battle of Bunker Hill** (actually Breed's Hill) in Boston. However, the British suffered over 1000 casualties compared to less than 100 for the American Patriots.

THE SECOND CONTINENTAL CONGRESS (MAY 1775)

Between Concord and Bunker Hill, the **Second Continental Congress** convened in Philadelphia on May 10, 1775. This time, all of the colonies were represented. Though they composed a petition to the King seeking peace, most realized the need to prepare for war. Congress took control of the army surrounding Boston. The unanimous selection as commander in chief was George Washington of Virginia. Attempts were made to keep the Native Americans neutral during the conflict. The Congress also urged the individual colonies to designate Committees of Safety to supervise security and defense.

THE DECLARATION OF INDEPENDENCE

Even after fighting began, there was a reluctance to blame the King for colonial troubles. However, the publication of the pamphlet *Common Sense* by Thomas Paine in January of 1776 altered the view held by many colonists. In simple language, Paine condemned monarchies, saying they had no right to rule others. He urged that an independent America be established.

In June, John Adams and Richard Lee of Virginia arose at the Second Continental Congress to call for a complete break with Britain. Although some still hoped for compromise with Britain, support for independence grew. Congress urged the individual colonies to form their own governments. Members of Congress wanted a written statement to rally the people. Adams joined Benjamin Franklin, Virginia's Thomas Jefferson, New York's Robert Livingston, and Connecticut's Roger Sherman in composing one. Jefferson did most of the writing.

The greatest influence on Jefferson was English Enlightenment thinker John Locke. In *Two Treatises on Government* (1690), Locke wrote that people have the right to life, liberty, and property, and people had a right to remove a government from power if it failed to protect these rights. Locke's thinking was part of a long heritage of democratic thinking that included the *Magna Carta* (1215), English Common Law, and the *English Bill of Rights* (1689). Congress made several changes in Jefferson's original document. On 2 July 1776, Congress formally voted for independence. On 4 July 1776, Congress approved the **Declaration of Independence**.

The *Declaration* did not set up a framework for a new government. Its basic philosophy on government, however, reflected later designs for the American government, including the *Constitution of the United States*. Three parts of the *Declaration of Independence* are

- a proclamation of democratic ideals, embodying the ideas of John Locke

- a statement of grievances against King George III of England

- a concluding statement declaring the break with Britain

THE AMERICAN REVOLUTION (1775-1781)

As commander in chief of the Patriots' Continental Army, George Washington relied on the assistance of many military figures from Europe. Examples include the Marquis de Lafayette from France and Baron von Steuben from Germany who led and trained American troops.

AMERICAN REVOLUTION: ADVANTAGES AND DISADVANTAGES	
ADVANTAGES	
American	**British**
fighting on familiar territory largely rural population hard for British to control	superior weapons experienced armies control of the seas long established, unified government larger population greater wealth
DISADVANTAGES	
American	**British**
constantly short of money and supplies worthless paper money troops not always well trained and disciplined	vast distance between the battlefields and Britain indecisive commanders in battle unpopular war in Britain

Not all colonists supported the Revolution. Some were apathetic. Others, known as Loyalists or Tories, pledged loyalty to King George. Some of the middle colonies, especially New York, were centers of Loyalist activity. Often, Loyalists faced the hostility of the Patriot community. Patriots confiscated vast amounts of Loyalist property during the Revolution, and nearly 100,000 Loyalists left the country.

KEY BATTLES

- Brooklyn / Long Island (1776) – British victory which led to Washington's retreat from New York

- Trenton / Princeton (1776) – American victory when Washington surprised German Hessian troops on Christmas night

- Saratoga (1777) – American victory which led to French military help and a treaty of alliance with France

- Yorktown (1781) – final battle of the war which resulted in the British surrender by General Cornwallis

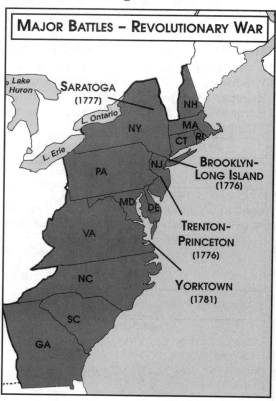

MAJOR BATTLES – REVOLUTIONARY WAR

Mistakes by British commanders, an influx of French foreign aid to the Americans, and the cost and unpopularity of the war in England led up to the eventual defeat at Yorktown. Britain agreed to American independence, and peace negotiations started. Benjamin Franklin, John Adams, and John Jay went to Paris to conclude the *Treaty of Paris* with the British.

TREATY OF PARIS
(1783)

- recognition by Britain of American independence

- western boundary of the United States set at the Mississippi River

- American fishing rights secured off the Canadian coast

- British agreed to remove all troops from American soil

- Americans promised to restore Loyalist properties

- Americans agreed to let Britons attempt to collect debts in America

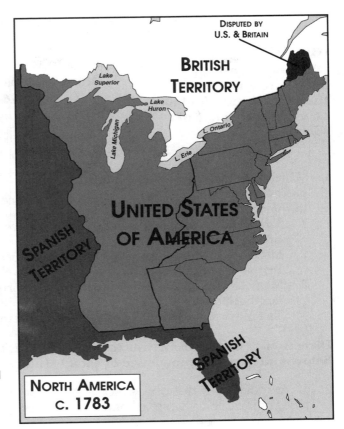

DISPUTED BY
U.S. & BRITAIN

BRITISH TERRITORY

Lake Superior

Lake Huron

Lake Michigan

L. Ontario

L. Erie

UNITED STATES OF AMERICA

SPANISH TERRITORY

SPANISH TERRITORY

NORTH AMERICA
c. 1783

SUMMARY: THE COLONIAL EXPERIENCE

Nearly two hundred years under British colonial rule greatly influenced America. The new nation's written laws, elected legislatures, and separation of government power among the branches reflected common Anglo-Saxon traditions. While royal governors and the British Crown exerted powerful vetoes on colonial legislatures, the new nation's government checked that kind of power. Property and religious qualifications restricted those who could vote, slavery still existed, and there was no expansion of rights for women. However, diversity of colonial religion voided out the power of any one church. The new American nation, born of revolution, turned to making independence work. It could apply to that problem an experience built on almost two hundred years of sociopolitical evolution and experimentation.

LESSON ASSESSMENT

MULTI-CHOICE

Directions: Base your answer to question 1 on the chart at the right and on your knowledge of social studies.

DESTINATION OF AFRICAN SLAVES 1526-1810
Source: Curtin, *The Atlantic Slave Trade*
British North America 427,000
Mexico & Central America . .224,000
West Indies 4,040,000
Spanish America 746,000
Portuguese America 3,647,000

1 Which statement is supported by the information in the chart?

  1 The English took control of the African slave trade from the Spanish.

  2 More African slaves ended up in the Caribbean islands than in British North America.

  3 More African slaves ended up in British North America than in South America.

  4 The Mexicans controlled the African slave trade until 1750.

Directions: Base your answer to question 2 on the quotation below and on your knowledge of social studies.

2 "...To molest any person, Jew or Gentile, for either professing doctrine, or practicing worship merely religion or spiritual, it is to persecute him..." – Roger Williams (1644)

According to this quotation, Roger Williams would most clearly support

1	trial by jury	3	consent of the governed
2	freedom of the press	4	religious toleration

3 In writing about North America, Englishman Richard Haklyut (c. 1597) called for England "...to plant religion among those infidels... enlarge the dominions of the Queen... [send] the woolen cloth of England... and [receive] commodities that we receive... from Europe..." Haklyut supported a policy of

1	mercantilism	3	leaving the colonies alone
2	religious toleration	4	isolation

4 Which statement is accurate regarding the American colonies by 1750?

  1 The majority of American colonists were small landowners.

  2 Women had an active and equal political role in colonial affairs.

  3 Slavery had been outlawed in the majority of the colonies.

  4 The majority of American colonists lived west of the Appalachian Mountains.

5   The Columbian Exchange had negative consequences for the Native Americans because
    1   their important technology like the wheel was taken by Europeans
    2   their lack of immunity to European diseases resulted in widespread death
    3   the Europeans brought pesticides to kill insects in their corn crops
    4   Europeans copied their methods of raising horses, pigs, and other livestock

6   Which statement regarding African slavery during the colonial period is accurate?
    1   American slavery followed the African model.
    2   Slavery existed in every American colony.
    3   Life servitude (slavery) was determined by the father's condition.
    4   More African slaves worked in the southern colonies than in lands under Spanish or Portuguese control.

7   The middle colonies of New York and New Jersey differed significantly from either the New England or the southern colonies because
    1   the population of the middle colonies was more diverse
    2   slavery provided more of the labor force
    3   they contained a greater number of broad, navigable rivers
    4   they relied more heavily on shipbuilding and trading

8   Colonial governments possessed some democratic characteristics including
    1   appointment of governors
    2   property or religious qualifications for voting
    3   granting women the right to vote
    4   popularly elected lower houses of the legislatures

9   The indenture system was important in the development of some early colonies because it provided
    1   a favorable balance of trade
    2   workers to solve a labor shortage
    3   freedom of religion to all settlers
    4   for the development of democratic government

10 The ideas of John Locke and Jean Jacques Rousseau in colonial thinking showed the influence of what European movement?
    1   Renaissance
    2   Reformation
    3   Enlightenment
    4   Industrialization

11 The term "salutary neglect" refers to British policies that
1 resulted in lax enforcement of mercantile policies
2 permitted the colonies to be directly represented in Parliament
3 caused the colonial economy to collapse
4 ended all trade between the American colonies and England

12 Which factor helped account for a relatively high literacy rate in many American colonies?
1 the establishment of free public schools in every colony
2 the Protestant belief that required reading of the Bible
3 the requirement that all children be educated in England
4 the existence of universal suffrage laws

13 American colonists did not like many of the Navigation Acts because the Acts
1 placed trade restrictions on the colonists
2 forbid colonists from travelling to England
3 imposed the Anglican religion on the colonists
4 restricted travel in the colonies

14 Colonists used boycotts and non-importation agreements in order to
1 build support for direct democracy in the colonies
2 raise revenue in colonial governments
3 raise an army to fight British troops
4 pressure Parliament to change colonial policies

Directions: Base your answer to question 15 on the illustration at the right and on your knowledge of social studies.

15 What is the main idea of the drawing?
1 Colonists should join European alliances.
2 The colonies unite as one.
3 All colonies should have equal populations.
4 Every colonial land owner should be allowed to vote.

16 Thomas Paine influenced American colonial thought by encouraging colonists to
1 seize lands west of the Mississippi
2 break away from British rule
3 ban the importation of African slaves
4 vote in Parliamentary elections

17 "...it is their right, it is their duty, to throw off such Government and to provide new Guards for their future security."

– Thomas Jefferson, 1776

Thomas Jefferson wrote these words in order to encourage the American colonists to
1   seek colonial representation in Parliament
2   allow colonists to fight in the British army
3   revolt against British rule
4   compromise with the British monarchy

18 Which principle of government comes from the *Declaration of Independence*?
1   Political power originates with a strong central government.
2   The primary function of government is to protect natural rights.
3   A system of checks and balances is necessary in any government.
4   Individual liberties must be guaranteed by a Bill of Rights.

19 An advantage of the Americans over the British in the American Revolution was the
1   professional military training of the Americans
2   superior American navy
3   Americans' familiarity with the land
4   American access to an unlimited supply of European mercenaries

20 The *Treaty of Paris* in 1783 established the western border of the United States at the
1   Appalachian Mountains   3   Rocky Mountains
2   Mississippi River   4   Pacific Ocean

THEMATIC ESSAY

Directions: Write a well-organized essay that includes an introduction, several paragraphs explaining your position, and a conclusion.

Theme:

Colonial Experience; Development of Democracy

The American colonial experience supported and challenged the growth democracy in the United States.

Task:

Explain how *three* aspects of the American colonial experience supported or challenged the growth of democracy.

Support your explanation by citing specific examples from the American colonial experience that helped or hindered the development of democracy. Your choices do not have to both help and hinder at the same time.

Suggestions:

You may use any examples from your study of United States history and government. Some suggestions you might wish to consider are slavery, colonial legislatures, voting requirements, religious reforms, types of colonies or the Enlightenment. **You are *not* limited to these suggestions**.

PRACTICE SKILLS FOR DOCUMENT BASED QUESTIONS

Directions:

The following task is based on the accompanying documents. The documents may have been edited for the purposes of this exercise. The task is designed to test your ability to work with historical documents. As you analyze the documents, take into account both the source of the documents and the author's point of view.

Historical Context:

Although the British monarchy controlled the American colonies on the Atlantic coast of North America during the colonial period, the thirteen colonies made up a land of contrasts.

Part A – Short Answer

Analyze the documents and answer the scaffold questions that follow each document.

Document 1

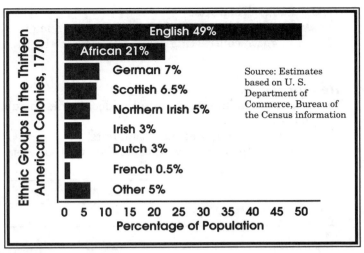

Question for Document 1

Approximately what percentage of the settlers in the thirteen colonies came from ethnic groups associated with the British Isles? What is an impact of that figure?

Document 2

"There are several churches in the town [New York City], which deserve some attention. 1. The English church... 2. The new Dutch church... 3. The old Dutch church... 4. The Presbyterian church... 5. The German Lutheran church... 6. The German Reformed church... 7. The French church, for Protestant refugees... 8. The Quakers' meeting-house... 9. To these may be added the Jewish synagogue..."

– Diary of Peter Kalm, Swedish naturalist,
Travels into North America, 1772

Question for Document 2

What type of diversity is Kalm writing about?

Part B – Essay Response

Task: Using only the two documents, write one or two paragraphs describing two contrasting social patterns in the thirteen colonies.

State your thesis:

- use only the information in the documents to support your thesis position
- add your analysis of the documents
- incorporate your answers from the two Part A scaffold questions

_____

_____

_____

_____

Additional Suggested Task:

From your knowledge of United States history and government, make a list of additional examples of diversity in colonial American society.

_____

_____

_____

_____

_____

_____

_____

_____

_____

_____

_____

_____

_____

_____

_____

1650

ENLIGHTENMENT (1640-1740)
    LOCKE
    MONTESQUIEU
    ROUSSEAU

1675

ENGLISH BILL OF RIGHTS (1689)

CONSTITUTIONAL FOUNDATIONS

1700

1725

Independence Hall, Philadelphia, PA
– ©1993 PhotoDisc Inc.

1750

ALBANY PLAN OF UNION (1754)

1775 **AMERICAN REVOLUTION**
(1775-1783)

ARTICLES OF CONFEDERATION
(1781-1789)

CONSTITUTION OF THE U.S. (1789)

WASHINGTON AS PRESIDENT (1789-1797)

1800 **BILL OF RIGHTS** (1791)

CONSTITUTIONAL FOUNDATIONS

INTRODUCTION

While England's American colonies fought to gain their independence, they created new state and national governments. These new governments created the first nation in modern times to have a government designed and run according to democratic principles. The United States government is drawn from many different sources. Europe's Enlightenment thinkers influenced the United States' Founding Fathers. Colonial experience included democratic features which influenced the new government. The experiences of the new nation also shaped its government.

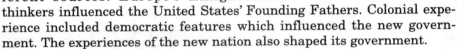

THE ARTICLES OF CONFEDERATION (1781-1789)

America's rebelling colonists knew they needed to rewrite their colonial charters after independence was declared. Starting in 1776, colonial assemblies began replacing their English colonial charters with new state constitutions. These state constitutions did differ from each other, but they had several key similarities.

ORIGINAL CONSTITUTIONS FOR ALL STATES	
Recognized:	**Created:**
• the need to protect citizens' natural rights to life, liberty, and property • the people as the proper source of authority (popular sovereignty) • that people created the government to protect their rights (social contract)	• governments, where most of the power went to an elected legislature (legislative supremacy); only Massachusetts created a state government with separation of powers; Its constitution provided a model for the later *Constitution of the United States* • a system of checks and balances within the legislative branch (most states) • a declaration of rights (providing models for the later *Bill of Rights*)

PROBLEMS AT THE END
OF THE AMERICAN REVOLUTION

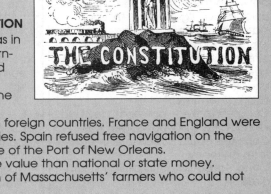

- The American economy was in disarray. The national government could not get needed money from the states.
- Violence broke out along the frontier.
- Trade became difficult with foreign countries. France and England were unwilling to sign trade treaties. Spain refused free navigation on the Mississippi River and free use of the Port of New Orleans.
- Foreign currency held more value than national or state money.
- Daniel Shays led a rebellion of Massachusetts' farmers who could not pay their debts.
- Border and trade disputes broke out between the states.

In addition to creating the new state governments, the states needed to create a central or national government to conduct the affairs of the new nation. For example, the Revolutionary War needed to be fought and won. Pennsylvania congressional delegate John Dickinson proposed the first national government for the new United States. Dickinson's proposal became the basis for the *Articles of Confederation*. It took the states almost four years to ratify the *Articles of Confederation*. They did not want to give up their authority or land claims.

The *Articles of Confederation* was very weak as a national government. The new national government was a confederation or loose union with power shared between the states and the national (central government). Consequently, Congress had to depend on the good will of the states to raise money and make its laws work. Some comparison can be made with the Iroquois Confederacy (Haudenosaunee Union) of the pre-colonial and colonial period. Members of the Seneca, Cayuga, Onondaga, Oneida, and Mohawk tribes met periodically to deal with common problems.

The *Articles of Confederation* governed the United States during its "Critical Period" from 1783-1789. Despite its faults, there were notable achievements of the government under the *Articles*.

- successfully negotiating the end to the American Revolution with the *Treaty of Paris*, 1783

ARTICLES OF CONFEDERATION V. CONSTITUTION OF THE UNITED STATES

Weaknesses of Government under the *Articles of Confederation*	Changes under the new *Constitution of the United States*
• no chief executive • no courts to handle disputes between the states • unicameral legislature with each state having an equal vote regardless of population • nine of thirteen states' approval needed to pass a law • unanimous approval needed to ratify an amendment • Congress lacked "power of the purse" - it could levy, but not collect taxes • Congress could not create one uniform currency • Congress could not recruit an army directly • Congress did not control interstate or foreign commerce	• executive department headed by single President to enforce the laws • national judiciary headed by the Supreme Court • bicameral legislature - proportional representation in House; equal representation in Senate • simple majority needed to pass laws • Congress can levy and collect taxes • Congress can create one currency • Congress can raise a military directly • Congress can control interstate and foreign commerce

- passage of the *Land Ordinance* of 1785 which allowed for the sale and survey of western lands

- passage of the *Northwest Ordinance* of 1787 which created a model for the admission of new states into the Union.

The problems of the Critical Period led some leaders to believe the national government under the *Articles* was too weak. Several regional meetings in the mid-1780s sent out a call for a general meeting of all the states in Philadelphia in 1787 to consider revising the *Articles of Confederation*.

THE CONSTITUTIONAL CONVENTION

Twelve states sent delegations to the Philadelphia meeting in 1787. Only Rhode Island refused to send a delegation. Attendees were all white males – mostly lawyers, large landholders, and a few merchants. The common people – yeoman farmers and frontiersmen – were not well represented. Major revolutionary figures (Thomas Jefferson and John Adams) were off representing the United States in Europe and others were suspicious of the proposed meeting. Key figures in attendance included George Washington (the presiding officer); Benjamin Franklin, Alexander Hamilton, and James Madison (whose notes earned him the title of the "Father of the Constitution").

Although the convention was to revise the *Articles of Confederation*, the delegates immediately accepted the proposal of the Virginia delegation to create an entirely new form of government that became the *Constitution of the United States*. This caused some of the delegates to leave the convention and others to refuse to sign the final document.

Independence Hall,
Philadelphia, Pennsylvania
© Wildside Press

POLITICAL BACKGROUND TO THE CONSTITUTIONAL CONVENTION

The delegates' ideas on government flowed from many different sources. Classical thought of the Ancient Greeks and Romans influenced them. Greek influence included juries and salaries for public officials. Roman contributions included representative government, veto power and codified law.

The European Enlightenment thinkers of the 17th and 18th centuries strongly influenced the Philadelphia delegates. **John Locke** of England was especially influential. His *Two Treatises on Government* (1690) laid out his beliefs of natural rights, the social contract, and the right of revolution. A trio of French 18th century *philosophes* were strong influences, too. **Voltaire** had advocated religious tolerance, natural rights, and the abolition of torture. Baron de **Montesquieu** had supported limiting the power of government through separation of power into separate branches. Jean-Jacques **Rousseau** had expanded Locke's ideas. **Rousseau** popularized the concept of the social contract and consent of the governed and spoke against the divine right of kings.

Also influential was the colonial experience. It reflected the commitment to certain democratic principles such as written law, elected legislatures, separation of powers, and limitations on the power of government.

Despite the vast differences of opinion among the convention delegates on the type and extent of changes to be made to the existing government, certain key points received strong support.

- The Congress should have greater power to levy and collect taxes and regulate foreign and domestic commerce.
- National executive and legislative branches were needed.
- Guarantees of property rights should be strengthened.

☆ Capsule –
Compromises at the Constitutional Convention

The Constitution has been called a "bundle of compromises." True to the democratic spirit that brought them to Philadelphia, the delegates worked to find middle ground on the issues that divided them the most.

- **The Great Compromise** – Fair representation in the Congress became a critical issue. The large states, led by Virginia, wanted a *bicameral* (two chambers) national legislature with representation in the lower house based on the population of the state. The lower house would choose the upper house from a list of nominees submitted by the state legislatures. The small states, led by New Jersey, called for a *unicameral* (one chamber) legislature with all states represented equally. The compromise worked out a bicameral legislature with equal representation (2 per state) in the upper house (Senate) and representation determined by population in the lower house (House of Representatives.)

- **The Three-Fifths Compromise** – How slaves would figure in the representation caused great disagreements. Heavily slave-populated southern states wanted to count the slaves for purposes of representation, but not taxation. The northern states considered slaves property and therefore should be taxed, but not counted for representation. It was finally agreed that five slaves would be counted as three persons for both purposes.

- **The Slave Trade Compromise** – contentions arose over the institution of slavery itself. Opponents did not succeed in having it abolished, but importation of slaves was forbidden after twenty years (1808). Slavery itself was allowed to continue.

- **The Tariff Compromise – Taxing imports and exports gave rise to problems**. Southern agricultural exporters wanted no federal tariffs to hurt their trade. Northern business interests wanted tariffs to protect against foreign competition. The Constitution gave Congress the authority to tax imports but forbade taxing exports.

- **The Presidency Compromises** – Fears of excessive executive power led to two debates. One dealt with the length of the President's term of office. Proposals ranged from three years to life. The other dealt with the selection of the President. Proposals ranged from appointment to direct popular election. Compromises worked out four year terms and an indirect election through the "electoral college" system.

THE DOCUMENT

The *Constitution of the United States* is the world's oldest functioning written plan of government. This document created a general framework of government with several key features:

- **The Preamble** lists the purposes of the U.S. government including "...to form a more perfect union, establish justice, insure domestic tranquility, provide for the common defense, promote the general welfare, [and] secure the blessings of liberty..."

- **Limited government** insures control by writing down and specifying what the national government can and cannot do and what the states may not do.

- **Representative government** (a republic) allows for the people to choose officials (some directly and most indirectly) who would deal with issues and administer policies.

- **Federalism** provides a dual system of dividing power between the state and national governments. The states accept the overall power (sovereignty) of the national government, but they retain power over local matters.

- **Separation of power** creates three distinct branches (legislative, executive, and judicial) within the national government with certain powers and functions to help avoid concentrations of power in one group or individual.

- **Checks and balances** gives each national government branch special controls to block the other branches from illegally expanding their powers.

RATIFICATION

To put the new government into effect, nine out of the thirteen states needed to ratify the Constitution. The ratification battle was not an easy one. Federalists supported the ratification of the Constitution and Anti-Federalists opposed it.

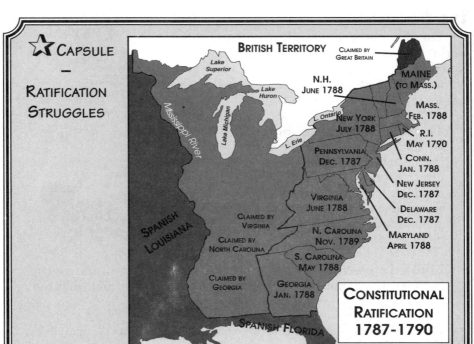

CONSTITUTIONAL RATIFICATION 1787-1790

Federalist Arguments	Anti-Federalist Arguments
• strong, stable government necessary to peace and economic growth • personal liberties protected by the state constitutions • states retained powers under the new constitution • checks and balances prevented any branch from becoming too powerful (Supporters were mainly business and propertied interests.)	• document ignored the rights of the people • state governments lost too much power to the national government • the power of the President resembled that of a monarch • personal liberties not guaranteed (Supporters were generally less well-to-do and less educated)

Some states ratified the Constitution quickly, but bitter ratification battles broke out in the "linchpin" states of Virginia and New York. In Virginia, Washington, Madison, and John Marshall turned the governor's opinion to support ratification. A bill of rights was proposed to encourage ratification, which finally took place on 25 June 1788.

In New York, staunch Federalists Alexander Hamilton and John Jay were joined by Madison in writing a series of essays that appeared in newspapers. The series was widely circulated in the rest of the country.

These essays, written under the pen name "Publius," are now collectively known as the *Federalist Papers*. They are still considered the most able defense of the Constitution. Hamilton delayed voting at the New York ratifying convention until news of Virginia's ratification arrived. With that momentum, New York voted on 26 July 1788 to become the 11th state. By 1790, all the states had joined the Union under the Constitution.

ESTABLISHMENT OF THE NEW GOVERNMENT

Once the Constitution was ratified, the new government went into effect. Representatives were chosen and the electors unanimously selected George Washington as the nation's first President. In the spring of 1789, Congress began passing laws. Throughout these early years, Congress and the Presidents set precedents for the new nation that scholars refer to as the "unwritten constitution."

THE *BILL OF RIGHTS*

As promised during the ratification struggle, Congressman James Madison (VA) proposed a series of amendments to the Constitution to insure individual civil liberties. His ideas became the basis for the first ten amendments proposed by Congress and sent to the states for ratification in 1789. They were ratified in 1791 and became known as the ***Bill of Rights***.

☆ CAPSULE – MAJOR PROVISIONS OF THE *BILL OF RIGHTS*

- freedom of speech, press, religion, assembly and petition
- right to bear arms
- no quartering of soldiers without consent of the owner in peacetime
- no unreasonable searches and seizures; no vague warrants
- grand jury indictment; no double jeopardy; no self-incrimination; due process guarantees; no taking of property without just compensation
- speedy and public trial by peers; informed of charges; confront accusers; call favorable witnesses; right to a lawyer
- jury trial in civil cases
- no excessive bail nor cruel or unusual punishment
- no laws denying rights not listed
- reserved powers to the states

Many of the civil liberties protected by these amendments directly relate to the colonial experience (e.g., British "writs of assistance" prompted search and seizure protections). These protections limit the power of the national government. Most of the original state constitutions already included bills of rights. For more than two hundred years, the federal courts have interpreted the meaning of these amendments in different ways.

THE AMENDMENT PROCESS

One way the Constitution may be altered to fit changing times is through formal amendment. This is a procedure specified in the Constitution. Two steps must be followed to amend the Constitution:

THE AMENDMENT PROCESS

- **Step One: Proposal**
  Amendments may be proposed by either a 2/3 vote of Congress or by a special national convention called by Congress at the request of 2/3 of the state legislatures (latter never used).

- **Step Two: Ratification**
  Ratification occurs either by A) approval of 3/4 of the state legislatures, or B) approval of 3/4 of special state conventions called to vote on ratification.

BASIC PRINCIPLES OF AMERICAN GOVERNMENT

The Constitution established a democratic republic (indirect democracy) which divided and limited the powers of government.

- **Democratic Republic** – When people vote, they delegate their power to govern themselves to representatives. Despite the Enlightenment ideals of "consent of the governed" and the social contract, the framers of the Constitution were reluctant to let the people, whom they thought might be easily swayed, directly chose their national government officials. Originally, the only national office directly elected from the very beginning is that of United States Representative. Senators, federal judges, the heads of the executive departments, the president, and the vice president were all chosen indirectly. (Later, the 17th Amendment [1913] allowed for direct popular election of senators.)

- **Division of Powers** (federalism) – The concept of federalism is complex and dynamic. The Constitution grants the national government delegated and implied powers and grants the states reserved powers under the 10th Amendment.

- **Separation of Powers** (for the legislative, executive, judicial branches) – The desire for limited government led to the creation of the three branches. Each branch has a primary purpose and ways to prevent abuse of powers in the other two branches (checks and balances).

Constitution Article I – The Congress
Powers & Functions

The bicameral Congress is considered the "people's branch" and makes the laws for the nation.

Congress	
House of Representatives	**Senate**

House of Representatives

- apportionment determined by population; total 435 (set by law); number of seats per state is redetermined every 10 years as a result of the census.

- member must be U.S. citizen for seven years, at least 25 years old, and reside in state represented

- elected directly for two year terms

- presiding officer is the Speaker of the House

- may bring impeachment charges; chooses the President if there is no electoral majority; starts all revenue bills

- size and short terms of office make this house more responsive to the people and representative of local concerns.

Senate

- 2 per state (currently 100 from 50 states)
- Senator must be U.S. citizen for nine years, at least 30 years old, reside in state represented

- since the Seventeenth Amendment, directly elected by state voters; (originally chosen by state legislatures)
  - Vice President is presiding officer, but a President Pro Tempore also chosen by Senators

- acts as jury in impeachment trials (2/3 vote necessary), chooses Vice President if no electoral majority; ratifies treaties (2/3 vote necessary), approves presidential appointments (majority needed)

- size and length of terms make this a more stable and deliberative body reflecting statewide interests.

THE CAPITOL

WASHINGTON

FEDERALISM

CONCURRENT POWERS
(both governments)

pass laws
borrowing
penal systems
general welfare of citizens

taxation
court systems
law enforcement agencies
charter banks and
corporations

DELEGATED POWERS
Contained in Art. I, Sec. 8
(national government only)

interstate & foreign commerce
declare war
foreign relations
coin and regulate money
Immigration rules
postal service
maintain army and navy
grant patents and copyright

&

IMPLIED POWERS
contained in the
"elastic clause" of Art. I, Sec. 8:
Allows Congress to stretch the delegated
powers when "necessary and proper"

RESERVED POWERS
**Granted by the Tenth
Amendment**
(state governments only)

regulate Intrastate commerce
establish local governments
Provide for public health
qualify voters
supervise elections
license occupations

AMERICANS ARE CITIZENS UNDER
TWO GOVERNMENTS:
NATIONAL (U.S. FEDERAL)
GOVERNMENT AND THE STATE IN
WHICH THEY RESIDE.

The powers used by Congress to rule the United States fall into three categories: delegated power, implied power, and concurrent power.

The national government's implied powers and the state governments' reserved powers have been the sources of conflicts over the years. Supporters of the use of the implied powers are called **loose constructionists**. They believe Congress may liberally stretch the seventeen delegated powers in Article I, Section 8 – the so-called **"elastic clause"** – to meet any problems confronting American society. Their opponents are called **strict constructionists**. They believe Congress should conservatively stretch the powers only when absolutely necessary to meet only the most serious problems confronting society.

POWERS DENIED BY THE CONSTITUTION	
Powers Denied to the National Government	**Powers Denied to the State Governments**
• suspension of habeas corpus, except in rebellion or invasion • bills of attainder (declaring guilt without a trial) or ex post facto laws (make an act a crime after it has been committed) • export taxes • titles of nobility	• treaty making • coin money • bills of attainder or ex post facto laws • levy duties without consent of Congress • entering into agreements with other states without consent of Congress

Often, Congress' use of the elastic clause's implied powers bring it into conflict with the states' reserved powers. As technology and industrialization changed the country, many activities crossed state borders (railroads). Congress used the elastic clause to stretch into many areas traditionally under the exclusive control of the states. This conflict of state versus federal power led to some of the great constitutional debates of American history. Often, the Supreme Court has been asked to judge whether state or congressional laws have exceeded their constitutional authority. In some cases, the Court has declared acts of states and Congress unconstitutional.

In addition to granting power, the Constitution specifically denies certain powers to the national and state governments. The above chart gives a summary of the powers denied government by the *Constitution of the United States*.

CONGRESS IN ACTION

Congress operates by taking **bills** (proposed laws) submitted by its members and processing them through subcommittees, committees, and public floor debates. The process is lengthy and involved for a reason. Making laws for the entire nation is complex, and Congress must avoid passing unworkable or unjust laws.

For a bill to become a law, it must be approved by both houses of Congress and be signed by the President. Over the years, Congress developed the **committee system** (part of the unwritten constitution) to study and report on proposed legislation. Rank and position on key committees gives members of Congress prestige and power over legislation. The President checks Congress' legislative power through the **veto**. However, there is a balance in the process. If the President vetoes a law, Congress may override the veto by a $2/3$ vote of both houses.

CONSTITUTION ARTICLE II – THE PRESIDENT

POWERS & FUNCTIONS

THE WHITE HOUSE
WASHINGTON

The executive branch is outlined in Article II and the Twelfth, Twentieth, Twenty-second, Twenty-third, and Twenty-fifth Amendments. According to the Constitution, to be President or Vice President, a person must be at least 35 years of age, a native born citizen, and a resident of the U.S. for at least 14 years. Presidential terms are four years (two term limit set by Twenty-second Amendment). Presidents are chosen indirectly by special electors (the Electoral College). Removal is possible through the impeachment process.

The Constitution outlines a number of official roles and duties for the President. However, much about the office has evolved over time. Presidents have acquired "extra-constitutional" roles as times have changed along with the power and prestige of the United States.

PRESIDENTIAL ROLES	
Constitutional Roles	**Extra-Constitutional Roles**
• chief executive – implements and administers Congressional laws and programs • chief of state – represents the country on ceremonial occasions • chief diplomat – conducts foreign affairs • commander-in-chief – supervises military forces • chief legislator – proposes legislation, calls special sessions of Congress • delivers State of the Union Address • grantor of pardons and reprieves • appointer of federal judges and other officials	• world leader – exerts a powerful role in influencing international events • voice of the people – spokesman for interests of general public • director of emergency actions – mobilizes federal action in the event of a disaster • manager of economic prosperity – attempts to maintain growth • head of political party – ranks highest elected official in the country

ELECTING THE PRESIDENT

In modern times, political campaigns have become difficult and expensive tasks. Presidential candidates begin campaigning for office years before the election. A complex system of local caucuses and primary elections choose delegates to national party nominating conventions. The delegates then officially nominate party candidates at these conventions. The candidates of each party then face each other in a general election in November.

Unwilling to place too much power in the hands of the people, the framers of the Constitution provided for an indirect election for the President and Vice President. Nicknamed the "electoral college," special officers are chosen in each state called **Electors of the President**. It is they who actually vote for the President and Vice President after the general public indicates its preferences in November of an election year. Each state sets its own rules for choosing electors.

Each state is allotted a number of electors equal to its total congressional delegation (# of Representatives + 2 Senators). U.S. territories do not have electors, but by the Twenty-third Amendment in 1961, the District of Columbia was granted a minimum of three.

There are a total of 538 electoral votes (435 Representatives + 100 Senators + 3 for DC). To win the presidency, a candidate must receive a majority (270). In most states, the "unit rule" operates. This means that if a party's candidate wins the simplest majority of the popular vote, all of that state's electors will be chosen from that party.

This "winner take all" principle makes it possible for a candidate to win a majority of the national popular vote but still lose the electoral vote. A candidate can win by large popular margins in some small electoral vote states, and just barely lose in enough big electoral vote states, thus failing to achieve the needed 270 votes. In 1888, incumbent President Grover Cleveland won in total popular votes, but lost the electoral vote to Benjamin Harrison.

More recently, in the 2000 presidential election, the Democratic candidate, Albert Gore (President Clinton's 2-term Vice President), won the national popular vote by a slim 500,000 votes, but the struggle came down to who won Florida's 25 electoral votes. Recounts of Florida ballots led to six weeks of legal wrangling in the state and federal court systems and even in the U.S. Supreme Court. In the end, Florida awarded its electoral votes to the Republican candidate – Texas Governor George W. Bush – who won with 271 electoral votes to Gore's 267.

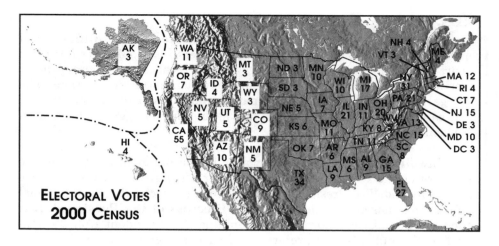

ELECTORAL VOTES
2000 CENSUS

The electoral vote system forces candidates to spend more time and money campaigning in states with high electoral vote counts. Just barely winning the popular vote in five states – CA (55), NY (31), TX (34), FL (27), and PA (21) gives a candidate 31% of the total electoral votes and 61% of the 270 majority needed to win. Consequently, candidates may often seem to ignore voters in states with a small number of electoral votes. In 1960, Vice President Nixon pledged to campaign in all 50 states. In the closing days of a close campaign, he spent hours on planes to Alaska and Hawaii, while Senator Kennedy focused his energies on New York, Michigan, and Illinois which had large numbers of electoral votes.

According to Article II, if a vacancy occurs through the President's death, disability, retirement, or resignation, the Vice President takes over. If there is no Vice President, Congress decides the order of succession. In 1947, Congress passed the *Presidential Succession Act*. It set the order after the Vice President as: Speaker of the House, President Pro Tempore of the Senate; then secretaries of the Cabinet starting with the Secretary of State.

However, the adoption of the Twenty-fifth Amendment in 1967 (Presidential Disability and Succession Amendment) makes it unlikely there will ever be a vacancy in the Vice Presidency. The President appoints a new Vice President with the approval of both houses of Congress if there is a vacancy. This amendment also allows the Vice-President to become acting President in the event of presidential disability.

The Twentieth Amendment of 1933 moved the inauguration of the President from the March 4th to the January 20th after an election. At the inauguration, the President takes an oath to "preserve, protect, and defend the *Constitution of the United States.*"

CONSTITUTION ARTICLE III – THE JUDICIARY

The judicial branch interprets the nation's laws. Article III of the Constitution deals with the national courts, but only mentions one by name – the Supreme Court of the United States. Congress may create other lower national courts by passing laws. The first Congress did this under the *Judiciary Act* of 1789. All federal judges are appointed by the President with the approval of the Senate. Federal judges are appointed for life, as long as they serve in "good behavior," and they may be impeached for violations of law.

THE POWER OF JUDICIAL REVIEW

The Supreme Court's main power involves **judicial review** (deciding if cases involving local, state, and federal laws or government actions violate the *Constitution of the United States*). If the Supreme Court finds them in violation, it will declare these laws or actions "null and void" or unconstitutional. This power is not specified in Article III, but was assumed by the Court in the *Marbury v. Madison* decision (1803) during the tenure of Chief Justice John Marshall (1801-1835). This power has placed the Court at the center of controversy throughout American history. It enables the Court to overrule and block actions of Congress, the president, other courts, and the states.

FEDERAL BUREAUCRACY

Today, several million people work for a federal government that has grown enormously in size and scope since

U.S. SUPREME COURT

1 Chief Justice & 8 Associate Justices (has original & appellate jurisdiction hearings on Constitutional issues)

U.S. CIRCUIT COURTS OF APPEAL (11)

have only appellate jurisdiction, operate as hearing panels, decisions are final in most cases

U.S. DISTRICT COURTS (94)

have original jurisdiction, operate using normal jury trial procedure the early years of the republic. **Bureaucrats** are the civil servants and appointees who oversee hundreds of government activities from delivering the mail to processing income tax returns to guarding national parks.

SUMMARY

Over the course of a turbulent fifteen year period from 1776 until 1791, the American people fought a revolution and created a series of new governments based on principles untried in the modern world. America's leaders created new state and national constitutions based on republicanism, limited government, and the consent of the governed. Early attempts at a national confederation of states failed, but the federal union created under the Constitution proved to be a lasting achievement.

LESSON ASSESSMENT

MULTI-CHOICE

1   Which provision of the *Constitution of the United States* has contributed most to its ability to adapt to changing times?
    1   "[Congress shall have the power...] to make all laws necessary and proper for carrying into execution the foregoing powers..."
    2   "The Senate of the United States shall be composed of two Senators from each state..."
    3   "All bills for raising revenue shall originate in the House of Representatives..."
    4   "The judicial power of the United States shall be vested in one Supreme Court..."

2   In the United States, the electoral college system influences Presidential candidates to
    1   make personal appearances in every state
    2   campaign extensively in states with large populations
    3   state their platforms in very specific terms
    4   seek endorsements from state governors

3   How does the *Constitution of the United States* currently require that the office of the Vice President be filled if it becomes vacant before the completion of a four year term?
    1   The office remains vacant until the next regularly scheduled election.
    2   The Secretary of State succeeds to the Vice Presidency.
    3   A special election takes place within three months of the vacancy.
    4   The President nominates a new Vice President who must be confirmed by Congress.

4   Which action best exemplifies the principle of checks and balances in the *Constitution of the United States*?
    1   The President negotiates a treaty.
    2   The House of Representatives initiates a revenue bill.
    3   The Vice President presides over a Senate meeting.
    4   The Senate ratifies a Presidential appointment.

5   Which is the main reason why the *Constitution of the United States* specifies no time limit on how long Supreme Court Justices serve?
    1   Qualified people will not seek the job unless there is life tenure.
    2   The selection process for qualified candidates is too time consuming for short term appointments.
    3   Justices should be free of political or economic pressures in making their decisions.
    4   It requires at least twenty years experience to train a successful justice.

6   Which is an example of an implied power of the federal government rather than a power specifically delegated by the *Constitution of the United States*?
    1   distribution of federal tax revenue to the states
    2   establishment of military forces
    3   conduct of foreign affairs
    4   control over interstate commerce

Directions: Base your answer to question 7 on the quotation below and on your knowledge of social studies.

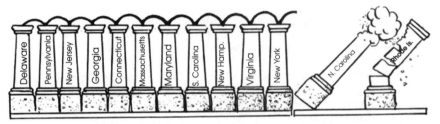

"On Erection of the eleventh pillar of our National Dome...The foundation is good – it may yet be saved"

7   The "National Dome" mentioned in the cartoon's text refers to the
    1   dome of the Capitol building in Washington, DC
    2   new structure of government under the *Articles of Confederation*
    3   new federal union formed under the *Constitution of the United States*
    4   influence of newspapers and public opinion on government

Directions: Base your answer to question 8 on the quotation below and on your knowledge of social studies.

"In framing a government which is to be administered by men over men, the great difficulty lies in this: you must first enable the government to control the governed; and next, oblige it to control itself."
                                            – James Madison, *Federalist No. 10*, 1788

8   Which concept of government is used to achieve Madison's observation?
    1   unicameral legislature
    2   a system of checks and balances
    3   a decentralized executive branch
    4   a cabinet system

9   The purpose of most of the amendments to the *Constitution of the United States* is to
    1   guarantee individual civil and political rights
    2   insure the proper functioning of the checks and balances system
    3   strengthen the authority of the state governments
    4   expand the powers of the Presidency

10 The major reason for a nation to have a written constitution is to
    1   fulfill the requirements of international law
    2   prevent change in the structure of government
    3   define the nature of the government's powers and processes
    4   encourage official recognition of a government by other nations

11 Flexibility is provided in the *Constitution of the United States* mainly by the
    1   Preamble and the *Bill of Rights*
    2   amending process and the elastic clause
    3   provisions for separation of powers
    4   system of checks and balances

12 Which power of the President of the United States is judicial in nature?
    1   presiding at an impeachment trial of a Vice President
    2   determining the legality of Cabinet decisions
    3   reviewing decisions made by the Supreme Court
    4   granting pardons and reprieves

13 Which newspaper headline best illustrates the principle of checks and balances in the United States government?
    1   *STATES MUST ENFORCE 21-YEAR-OLD DRINKING AGE OR LOSE FUNDS*
    2   *U.S. WARSHIPS SENT TO THE PERSIAN GULF*
    3   *CONGRESS OVERRIDES PRESIDENTIAL VETO ON TAX BILL*
    4   *FEDERAL AID TO CITIES CUT 10%*

14 The *Constitution of the United States* attempted to solve a major problem that existed under the *Articles of Confederation* by providing for
1 federal control of interstate commerce
2 stronger state governments
3 the direct election of the President by the people
4 a balanced federal budget

15 Which is an example of the unwritten constitution in the United States?
1 a system of political parties
2 operation of checks and balances
3 guarantee of freedom of religion
4 sharing of power between state and national governments

16 Those who supported the ratification of the *Constitution of the United States* promised to add a bill of rights in order to
1 encourage economic development
2 prevent the return of English control over the new nation
3 increase the power of the national government over the states
4 persuade the Anti-Federalists to accept the Constitution

Directions: Base your answer to question 17 on the passage below and on your knowledge of social studies.

"Its size and short terms of office make this house more responsive to the people and representative of local concerns."

17 The passage above best describes the
1 Electoral College
2 United States Senate
3 United States House of Representatives
4 Supreme Court of the United States

18 Which best illustrates the concept of federalism as it relates to the structure of the United States government?
1 The constitutional system of checks and balances concentrates power in the hands of Congress.
2 The Constitution assigns some responsibilities to the federal government and some to the states, while other powers are shared by both.
3 According to the Constitution, economic power is shared by the President, union leaders, and the heads of major corporations.
4 Authority to make, enforce, and interpret laws is provided for in the Constitution.

19 A major objection to the *Constitution of the United States* when it was presented for ratification in 1787 was that the Constitution
    1   reserved too much power for the states
    2   contained too many compromises
    3   required approval of all the states for ratification
    4   provided insufficient guarantees of civil liberties

20 A government based on a federal union differs most from one based on a confederation in that
    1   a federal union creates a stronger national government
    2   a federal union has greater protection of individual liberties
    3   a confederation creates a stronger national government
    4   a confederation divides power among three branches

THEMATIC ESSAY

Directions: Write a well-organized essay that includes an introduction, several paragraphs explaining your position, and a conclusion.

Theme:

> **Power in Government**
>
> The *Constitution of the United States* both divides and limits the powers of government.

Task:

> Discuss the reasoning behind creation of a government that divides and limits power.
> Describe with details how the Constitution both divides and limits the powers of the government.

Suggestions:

You may use any examples and details from your study of the *Constitution of the United States* and United States history and government. Some suggestions include federalism, separation of powers, checks and balances, limits on the power of the people, limits on branches. **You are *not* limited to these suggestions**.

PRACTICE SKILLS FOR DBQ
Directions:

The following task is based on the accompanying documents. The documents may have been edited for the purposes of this exercise. The task is designed to test your ability to work with historical documents. As you analyze the documents, take into account both the source of the documents and the author's point of view.

Historical Context:

Growing dissatisfaction with the *Articles of Confederation* in the 1780s led leaders of the new nation to create a controversial plan for a new government under the *Constitution of the United States* based on certain key principles.

Part A – Short Answer

The documents that follow present views of the *Constitution of the United States*. Examine each document carefully, then answer the scaffold question that follows it.

Document 1

> "We the People of the United States, in Order to form a more perfect Union, establish Justice, insure domestic Tranquillity, provide for the common defense, promote the general Welfare, and secure the Blessings of Liberty to ourselves and our Posterity, do ordain and establish this *Constitution for the United States* of America."
>
> – Preamble to the *Constitution of the United States*.

Question for Document 1

What is the purpose of the national government created by the Constitution?

Document 2

> "Certainly no single interest or view was wholly satisfied, and many specific provisions did represent a middle term between opposing requirements. The most creative of the compromises was the formation of a federal union, combining state authority over local affairs with a national government authorized in specific ways... Underlying the compromises of the Constitution were certain fundamental agreements... The general government, no less than the state(s), ...as to be republican in basis, end, and form. The founders had in view a government resting on the consent of the governed which would be strong enough to serve the needs of a growing nation and yet could not destroy the rights of men."
>
> – Meyers, Cawelti, Kern, *A More Perfect Union, Sources of the American Republic*, Vol. I, 1967, p. 149

Question for Document 2

What are two governmental principles the founders included in the new Constitution?

Part B – Essay Response

Task: Using only the two documents, write one or two paragraphs describing the Constitution's underlying principles of government.

State your thesis:
- use only the information in the documents to support your thesis position
- add your analysis of the documents
- incorporate your answers from the two Part *A* scaffold questions

_____

_____

_____

_____

Additional Suggested Task:

From your knowledge of United States history and government, make a list of ways that the Constitution combines European tradition and American colonial experiences.

_____

_____

_____

_____

_____

_____

_____

_____

_____

_____

_____

_____

_____

_____

_____

_____

1800	LOUISIANA PURCHASE (1803)
	MARBURY V. MADISON (1803)
1810	WAR OF 1812 (1812-1814)
1820	MISSOURI COMPROMISE (1820)
1830	TARIFF CONFLICT (1828-1833)
	ABOLITIONIST CRUSADE (1830-1860)
1840	
	MEXICAN WAR (1846-1848)
1850	COMPROMISE OF 1850 (1850)
	DRED SCOTT DECISION (1857)
1860	CIVIL WAR (1861-1865)

CONSTITUTIONAL CONFLICTS

President Abraham Lincoln
Civil War CD, Digital Stock ©1995

CONSTITUTIONAL CONFLICTS

THE NEW REPUBLIC (1789-1865)

In 1789, a new government based on a federal union began operation. The actions of the early Presidents and other governmental figures set precedents (initial actions that become patterns of future procedures) still in effect today. Taken together, these precedents make up a body of procedures called the "unwritten constitution."

DOMESTIC PRECEDENTS DURING THE EARLY PRESIDENTIAL ADMINISTRATIONS

THE CABINET

In 1789, Congress created three executive departments to assist President Washington – State, Treasury, and War. President Washington consulted with the secretaries (heads of the departments) together as a **Cabinet** (an advisory group) when making difficult executive decisions. All subsequent presidents have followed the precedent of having a cabinet, but the degree to which they have used it as their chief advisory group has varied.

CURRENT DEPARTMENTS OF THE EXECUTIVE BRANCH

1 State - 1789
2 Treasury - 1789
3 Justice (Attorney Gen.) - 1789
4 Interior (federal lands) - 1849
5 Agriculture - 1889
6 Commerce - 1903
7 Labor - 1913
8 Defense - 1947
9 Housing/Urban Develop. - 1965
10 Transportation - 1966
11 Energy - 1977
12 Health & Human Services - 1977
13 Education - 1979
14 Veterans Affairs - 1989
15 Homeland Security - 2002

POLITICAL PARTIES

The writers of the Constitution had a distaste for party politics, yet political groups formed during Washington's Administration. The first two parties were the **Federalists**, led by Alexander Hamilton and John Adams, and the **Democratic Republicans**, led by Thomas Jefferson and James Madison. Once the precedent was set, parties evolved to influence Congress, and eventually they determined who candidates would be for political offices at every level of government.

THE FEDERALISTS

Leaders:

Alexander Hamilton   John Adams

Supported:
- loose construction of the *Constitution of the United States*
- stronger central government
- central control of economic affairs, pro-national bank and protective tariffs

Supporters: Wealthy and propertied groups – merchants and manufacturers

Foreign Affairs: pro-British

THE DEMOCRATIC–REPUBLICANS*

Leaders:

Thomas Jefferson   James Madison

Supported:
- strict construction of the *Constitution of the United States*
- stronger state government
- less central control of economic affairs; against a national bank and high tariffs

Supporters: "Common People" - small farmers, city labor, frontier people

Foreign Affairs: pro-French

*For a while after 1800, the group was called "Republicans," but it is no relation to the modern Republican Party which formed in the 1850s. By the 1830s, the group took the permanent name of "Democrats."

LAW ENFORCEMENT

In 1794, western Pennsylvania distillers and farmers seized the federal marshals who were charging them with evading the new excise tax. Washington ordered federal authorities to use a large armed force to suppress resistance to the federal laws. This **Whiskey Rebellion** episode set a precedent for law enforcement not clearly defined in the Constitution's list of executive branch powers.

JUDICIAL REVIEW

Judicial review, the power of the Supreme Court to determine if local, state, or federal statues and governmental actions violate the Constitution, grew out of the decision in *Marbury v. Madison* (1803). In the decision, Chief Justice **John Marshall** overturned part of a Congressional law – the *Judiciary Act of 1789*. By assuming the power of judicial review, the Court strengthened its power considerably. To this day, judicial review remains the Supreme Court's most important and most controversial power.

EXECUTIVE AND CONGRESSIONAL SEPARATION

In the early days, many observers assumed that presidents would merely act at the disposal of Congress as the British Prime Minister acts at the disposal of Parliament. Washington altered that assumption. He set his own rules for dealing with Congress. He limited how often his cabinet officers appeared to testify before Congress. This **executive privilege** precedent underlined the independence and separation of the executive branch.

SIGNIFICANT DECISIONS OF THE SUPREME COURT UNDER CHIEF JUSTICE MARSHALL		
YEARS	DECISIONS	SIGNIFICANCE
1810	*Fletcher v. Peck*	Supreme Court established its power to review state laws.
1819	*Dartmouth College v. Woodward*	Set precedent that states may not pass laws impairing private contracts.
1819	*McCulloch v. Maryland*	Upheld the constitutionality of the Bank of the United States by denying the state of Maryland's attempt to tax a federal institution.
1824	*Gibbons v. Ogden*	Established broad interpretation of the federal government's authority over interstate commerce.

LOBBYING

In any government, groups and individuals pressure officials to see their side of an issue. From the early days, it became customary for these individuals and groups to approach Congressional representatives in the entrances of the Capitol. Hence, the name "lobbyists" emerged.

Lobbyists currently represent every major business, economic group, foreign nation, and other special interest. Many members of Congress believe that lobbyists present vital information they would not be able to obtain otherwise. Opponents of the influence of lobbyists say the information is always biased, and that lobbyists even lean toward unethical behavior (bribes) to get their way. Today, laws force lobbyists to register with the federal government and publicly report their financial activities.

HAMILTON'S FINANCIAL PLAN – KEY PRECEDENT IN DOMESTIC STABILITY

Washington appointed Alexander Hamilton as Secretary of the Treasury. Hamilton wanted to establish the credit of the United States among other nations and provide a sound currency, strengthen the central government, and secure the support of the propertied classes. To do this, Hamilton proposed five key actions, most of which were approved by Congress.

- repay the foreign debt
- assume debts still unpaid by states from the Revolutionary War
- raise revenue through excise taxes on luxury items (liquor and jewelry) and tariffs
- impose a protective tariff to encourage domestic industries
- create a Bank of the United States to coordinate public and private financial activities

Thomas Jefferson and others opposed the Bank, claiming that the Constitution did not delegate such powers to Congress. However, Hamilton successfully argued that the "elastic clause" allowed the Bank because it was "necessary and proper." The establishment of the Bank of the United States became one of the first uses of the elastic clause and legitimized the doctrine of the implied powers by Congress.

EARLY PRECEDENTS IN FOREIGN POLICY

Early presidential administrations also set precedents in foreign affairs. In regard to foreign wars, trade, and territorial expansion, many of these policies guided America's behavior in the world into the 20th century.

NEUTRALITY

Realizing that the new nation was militarily and economically weak, President Washington adopted policies which kept the United States out of unstable European politics. While the Atlantic Ocean provided realistic protection in a time of slow-moving transportation, the United States was still surrounded by British and Spanish possessions. President Washington wanted to keep the United States neutral, and avoid being drawn into the conflicts between Britain and France. To this end, he issued the *Proclamation of Neutrality* in 1793. Later, he counseled his fellow citizens to "steer clear of permanent alliances" in his *Farewell Address* in 1796. This advice became a cornerstone of a long-standing American isolationist tradition.

ECONOMIC PRESSURES OF NEUTRALITY

In this early period, the country's economic needs often determined the path Presidents took in foreign affairs. **Jay's Treaty** (1795) with Britain led to the removal of the remaining British troops from the western regions of the U.S., and improved trade between the two countries. **Pinckney's Treaty** (1795) with Spain gave western farmers the right of deposit to transship goods through the Spanish port of New Orleans safely. Thomas Jefferson in 1807 asked Congress to pass the *Embargo Act* in response to the impressment (the act or policy of seizing people or property for public service or use) of American sailors by Britain and France. The *Embargo Act* forbade all U.S. foreign trade. This was extremely unpopular with trading interests, and was repealed in favor of a law which restricted trade only with warring Britain and France.

THE WAR OF 1812

President James Madison (term: 1809-1817) inherited the foreign problems from Jefferson. He failed at diplomatic efforts to keep the United States from being drawn into the European conflicts of the Napoleonic Era. British naval blockades and continuing impressment threatened America's economy. A group in Congress, called the "War Hawks," pressured Madison into asking Congress for a declaration of war against Britain. Congress declared war in June, 1812.

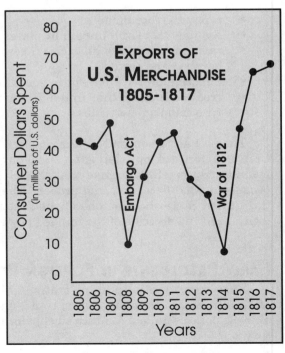

EXPORTS OF U.S. MERCHANDISE 1805-1817

Several attempts by the United States to invade British controlled Canada failed. Although American ships had some success in naval battles with the British, the British blockade of the American coasts ruined American trade. In 1814, British troops marched into Washington D.C. and burned most of the public buildings. In January 1815, General Andrew Jackson won a final victory at New Orleans, but by then Napoleon had been defeated and a peace agreement had already been signed with Britain. The *Treaty of Ghent* (1814) acknowledged the War as a draw. Although none of the causes of the War were addressed, relations with Britain improved throughout the next decade.

TERRITORIAL EXPANSION

In 1800, the vast Louisiana Territory west of the Mississippi was ceded by the Spanish government to France. President Jefferson grew alarmed at the prospects of dealing with the much more powerful French, and the possibility of a new French Empire in the Americas. Westerners worried that the previously negotiated right of deposit would end. Jefferson wanted to buy New Orleans from Napoleon, but was offered all of Louisiana for $15 million. Not expecting to be offered the

☆ CAPSULE – TERRITORIAL EXPANSION

The Louisiana Purchase doubled the size of the United States, and extended the western boundary of the nation to the Rocky Mountains. Shortly after the Purchase, **Meriwether Lewis** and **William Clark** led an expedition into the new territory. Along the way they were given valuable assistance by **Sacajawea**, a Shoshone Native American. Stories of the trip helped spark added interest in western lands, although large scale settlement was still decades away. The interest in western lands did spur road and canal building however.

The Cumberland (National) Road was financed by Congress, and New York State built the **Erie Canal**, which made Buffalo a major western port by connecting it to Albany and New York City.

entire territory, Jefferson had doubts about the constitutionality of the purchase. The Constitution is vague on the acquisition of new territory, and Jefferson was for strict interpretation of the Constitution. But delaying might lead Napoleon to change his mind, and Jefferson saw the need this one time for a loose interpretation of the Constitution. The Louisiana Purchase was set in a treaty which the Senate soon ratified.

DEMOCRATIC IDEALISM IN FOREIGN POLICY: THE MONROE DOCTRINE

President James Monroe set another major foreign policy precedent in 1823. Monroe warned Europe that no further colonization would be allowed in the Western Hemisphere. The United States pledged it would not interfere with existing colonies, and repeated its determination to remain neutral in European affairs. The Monroe Doctrine became a cornerstone of United States foreign policy throughout the 19th and 20th centuries.

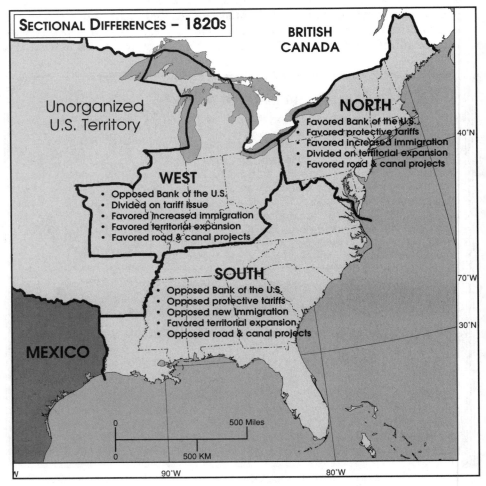

SECTIONAL DIFFERENCES – 1820s

BRITISH CANADA

Unorganized U.S. Territory

NORTH
- Favored Bank of the U.S.
- Favored protective tariffs
- Favored increased immigration
- Divided on territorial expansion
- Favored road & canal projects

40°N

WEST
- Opposed Bank of the U.S.
- Divided on tariff issue
- Favored increased immigration
- Favored territorial expansion
- Favored road & canal projects

SOUTH
- Opposed Bank of the U.S.
- Opposed protective tariffs
- Opposed new immigration
- Favored territorial expansion
- Opposed road & canal projects

70°W

30°N

MEXICO

0   500 Miles

0   500 KM

90°W   80°W

THE CONSTITUTION TESTED

SECTIONAL DIFFERENCES DEVELOP

An **"Era of Good Feeling"** followed the War of 1812. It was a short-lived period of national harmony and political cooperation. By the late 1820s, the Era of Good Feeling fell victim to sectionalism (giving primary loyalty to a state or region rather than to the nation as a whole). The map on page 100 summarizes the sectional differences.

THE TARIFF CONTROVERSY

In 1828, Congress passed a very high protective tariff (Southerners called it the "Tariff of Abominations"). While its aim was to protect infant Northern industries from foreign competition, Southerners felt that the tariff could ruin their economy. High rates would increase the cost of foreign manufactured goods in the South and lead to **reciprocation** (retaliation by foreign nations raising their tariffs against Southern cotton exports). This tariff controversy featured the ideas and actions of these four individuals:

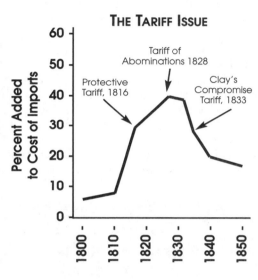

THE TARIFF ISSUE

- Vice President **John C. Calhoun** (South Carolina) wrote the *South Carolina Exposition and Protest* (1828), in which he said a state could declare the federal tariff "null and void."

- Senator **Daniel Webster** (Massachusetts) argued that the federal government is supreme and opposed Calhoun's doctrine of nullification.

- President **Andrew Jackson** stated that states must obey all federal laws, and that the Federal government could use force to make sure the laws are obeyed.

- Senator **Henry Clay** (Kentucky) introduced a compromise tariff bill in Congress that gradually reduced tariff rates and averted a showdown between South Carolina and the federal government.

Despite Clay's tariff compromise, the larger issues of states' rights and nullification were not resolved. It plagued the nation for another generation, and it was the main cause of the Civil War in the 1860s.

THE BANK OF THE UNITED STATES CONTROVERSY	
Supporters	**Opponents**
• provided economic stability • maintained a sound currency	• controlled by rich businessmen • made it difficult to borrow money

THE BANK CONTROVERSY

The first Bank of the United States ceased operation in 1811, but a second Bank of the United States was created by Congress in 1816. As with the first one, this second Bank was also controversial.

The constitutionality of the Bank was decided by the Supreme Court in *McCulloch v. Maryland* (1819). In the decision, Chief Justice Marshall said that Congress is given implied power in the Constitution's Article I, Section 8 (the "elastic clause") to do what is "necessary and proper" to carry out its delegated powers. According to Marshall, the Bank of the United States was a constitutionally proper use of the elastic clause. In the same landmark case, Marshall also ruled on the supremacy of the federal law, saying that a state (in this case Maryland) had no right to interfere with the functioning of a federal agency like the Bank.

☆ CAPSULE –
SUFFRAGE EXPANDS IN THE EARLY 19TH CENTURY

YEAR	POPULAR VOTE	TOTAL POPULATION VOTING (%)
1824	356,000	3.3 %
1828	1,155,000	9.5 %
1840	2,404,000	14.1 %

Reasons for the Increase in Voting in the Early 19th Century	Groups Still Prohibited from Voting
• elimination of property requirements to vote • national nominating conventions met to name Presidential candidates (replacing the old caucus system, where small groups of party members made the choices) • states begin to let voters select the electors for the electoral college (instead of electors being selected by state legislatures)	• women • African Americans • Native Americans

---

☆ Capsule – American Culture Emerges (1830-1860)

New ideas flowed freely in religion, education, and literature during this period. Some of the most important individuals and their actions are summarized below.

Religious Reforms

Charles Grandison Finney helped lead the "Second Great Awakening", which challenged the beliefs of traditional faiths such as Congregational, Episcopalian, and Presbyterian.

Brigham Young helped build the Mormon community into a prosperous and growing religion near the Great Salt Lake in Utah. Controversial for its new scriptural revelations and the practice of polygamy.

Mother Ann Lee led the Shakers, whose members practiced celibacy and believed the end of the world was near.

Educational Changes

Horace Mann pushed for reforms in Massachusetts schools, including state funding, longer school year, and teacher training.

Emma Willard and **Mary Lyon** opened some of the first schools and colleges for women, including Lyon's Mt. Holyoke College in Massachusetts.

Literary Achievements

Ralph Waldo Emerson promoted transcendentalist thought through lectures and essays (*Nature, Representative Man*).

Henry David Thoreau supported an individuals right to disobey unjust laws (*On Civil Disobedience*).

James Fenimore Cooper successfully depicted the American scene in his novels of frontier life and the sea (*The Last of the Mohicans, The Deerslayer, The Pilot*).

Washington Irving created the mythical lives of Rip Van Winkle and Ichabod Crane (*Sketch Book*).

Edgar Allen Poe wrote macabre themes in poetry and short stories (*The Raven, The Fall of the House of Usher*).

Walt Whitman was a news editor, and poet who celebrated American diversity (*Leaves of Grass*).

Nathaniel Hawthone penned transcendental themes (*The Scarlet Letter, The House of the Seven Gables*).

Herman Melville wrote allegorical sailing and adventure novels (*Moby Dick*).

Social Reforms

Lyman Beecher called for the total prohibition of alcohol.

Elizabeth Cady Stanton helped lead the Seneca Falls meeting in 1848 to demand equality for women.

Dorothea Dix fought for better treatment of the mentally ill and those in prison.

Robert Owen founded New Harmony, a utopian community hoping to achieve perfection.

President Andrew Jackson despised the Bank. He said it was a misuse of government power and created privileges for the rich. Jackson vetoed the bill to recharter the Bank of the United States in 1832. Four years later, the Bank went out of existence. Afterwards, unregulated "wildcat" state banks proceeded to issue paper securities of little value. These state banks made unwise loans and speculated in Western lands with depositors' money. A long and dismal depression began as Jackson left office in 1837. While changes in foreign investment and other economic factors helped to cause the depression, unregulated banking made matters worse.

TERRITORIAL EXPANSION AND MANIFEST DESTINY

Americans used the term "Manifest Destiny" to describe what they saw as the "divine mission" of the United States to spread American rule all the way to the Pacific Ocean. Three events in the 1830s and 1840s saw the United States make this a reality – the annexation of Texas, settlement of the Oregon border, and the Mexican War.

TEXAS

Led by Stephen Austin, Americans began moving into Texas during the 1820s. Texas proclaimed independence from Mexico in 1836, and, led by Sam Houston, established the Republic of Texas. Texas requested annexation by the United States, but this met opposition by some in the United States. Northerners feared that Texas would become a slave state and add to Southern influence in Congress. However, support for annexation slowly grew, and in 1845, Congress admitted Texas as the 28th state.

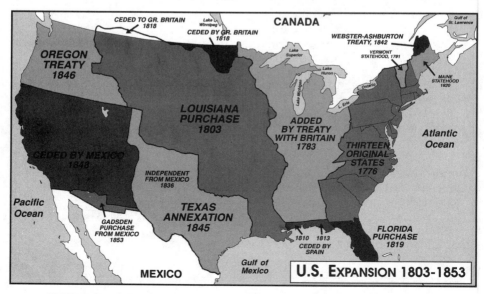

U.S. EXPANSION 1803-1853

OREGON

This territory was jointly occupied by the United States and Great Britain. As the American population of Oregon grew, some wanted the United States to claim all of Oregon – to Latitude 54° 40' North. War was avoided when Britain and America agreed to a compromise at the 49th parallel, which extended the already existing boundary between the United States and Canada.

MEXICAN WAR (1846-1848)

Disputes with Mexico, including the annexation of Texas and border questions led President James Polk to ask Congress to declare war in 1846. Generals Zachary Taylor and Winfield Scott invaded Mexico and led American forces to important victories. A defeated Mexico had no choice but to agree to the *Treaty of Guadalupe Hidalgo* in 1848. The Treaty established the Rio Grande as the southern border of Texas and gave California and New Mexico Territory (known as the Mexican Cession) to the United States. In return, the United States paid Mexico $15 million and agreed to settle any disputed debts. The new territories added many new Spanish-speaking people to the United States.

THE DEBATE ON SLAVERY

When the Constitution was written in 1787, many people believed that the institution of slavery would become unprofitable and gradually die out in the United States. While this is what occurred in the North, the South saw the demand for slaves increase through the first half of the 19th century. The invention of the cotton gin, the expansion of territory, and the increased demand from the North and from overseas for raw cotton, all contributed to this rejuvenation of slavery.

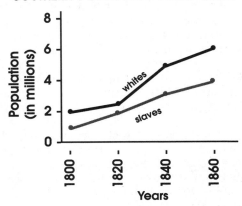

SOUTHERN POPULATION 1800-1860

From the period 1820-1860, Southerners were concerned about the balance between free and slave states, and about allowing slavery in new federal territories. Several compromises were worked out to satisfy all sides.

- **Missouri Compromise (1820)**, devised by Henry Clay, admitted Missouri as a slave state, Maine as a free state, and banned slavery in territories north of 36° 30' North Latitude.

ABOLITIONIST LEADERS

- **William Lloyd Garrison**: A Boston resident who through his newspaper, *The Liberator*, demanded an immediate end to slavery.

- **Frederick Douglass**: A former slave who made frequent speaking appearances in which he described his life as a slave, and called for immediate abolition.

- **Harriet Tubman** and **Sojourner Truth**: Two former slaves who were involved in the Underground Railroad, through which escaped slaves could reach freedom in the North and Canada.

> ### Read and Ponder
> # THE FUGITIVE SLAVE LAW!
> Which disregards all the ordinary securities of PERSONAL LIBERTY, which tramples on the Constitution, by its denial of the sacred rights of Trial by Jury, Habeas Corpus, and Appeal, and which enacts, that the Cardinal Virtues of Christianity shall be considered, in the eye of the law, as CRIMES, punishable with the severest penalties.
> *Fines and Imprisonment.*
> Freemen of Massachusetts, REMEMBER, That Samuel A. Elliott of Boston, voted for this law, that Millard Filmore, our whig President approved it and the Whig Journals of Massachusetts sustain them in this iniquity.

- **Wendell Phillips**: founder and president of the American Antislavery Society; became abolitionists' most eloquent platform speaker.

- **Compromise of 1850** – California was admitted as a free state, a Fugitive Slave Law designed to capture escaped slaves was enacted, and declared that new territories from the Mexican Cession were to have slavery decided by "popular sovereignty," by the vote of the inhabitants of the territory. (Again, devised by Henry Clay.)

Opposition to slavery was growing, however, with the help of leaders in the abolitionist movement. Some southerners continued to defend slavery. They said that African American slaves had been civilized by their white masters, who Christianized them, educated them, and gave them better living conditions. Of course, economic prosperity in the South depended on labor-intensive cotton exports. Though less than 25 percent of white Southerners owned slaves, most supported the continuation of slavery.

The lines in the slavery argument became more rigidly drawn in the 1850s. A newspaper barrage of extreme abolitionists and "hard-line" states' rights positions made compromise less and less feasible. In the North, the abolitionist crusade gained even more momentum in 1852 after Harriet Beecher Stowe published her novel of harsh treatment on the plantations, *Uncle Tom's Cabin*. At the same time, the two national political parties of the era, the Democrats and the Whigs, tried to avoid alienating voters by refusing to take a stand on the slavery issue. By the mid 1850s, many abolitionists joined the newly formed **Republican Party**. Generally, the Republicans were moderates who opposed the extension of slavery into the new territories but did not seek full emancipation.

On 4 March 1861, Abraham Lincoln was inaugurated as the 16th President of the United States. Addressing the nation that day, Lincoln said he wished to preserve the Union. He promised not to interfere with slavery in the states where it already existed. The South rejected Lincoln's offers and formed the **Confederate States of America**. The attack on the federal Fort Sumter in Charleston (SC) harbor took place just six weeks later. Fort Sumter's surrender the next day was a turning point in the secession crisis. By June 1861, a total of 11 states had left the Union, and the tragedy of the American Civil War began.

☆ CAPSULE – DISCORD OVER SLAVERY – 1854-1860

- **Kansas-Nebraska Act** (1854) allowed the settlers of these territories to decide the slave issue through popular sovereignty, but the result was five years of fighting when opposing pro and anti slave groups rushed into the territory.

- **Dred Scott v. Sanford** (1857) decision of the Supreme Court ruled that slaves were property, and the 5th Amendment forbids Congress from depriving people of their property without due process of law. As a result, all attempts to ban slavery in federal territories were unconstitutional.

- **John Brown's Raid** (1859), a failed attempt to lead a slave revolt, further infuriated Southern supporters of slavery.

- **Election of Abraham Lincoln** (1860), an Illinois Republican who opposed the extension of slavery in the territories was despised by Southern supporters of slavery.

- **Secession of South Carolina** (1860) after the election of Lincoln, but while "lame duck" President James Buchanan was still in power, followed by the secession of other states, made confrontation inevitable.

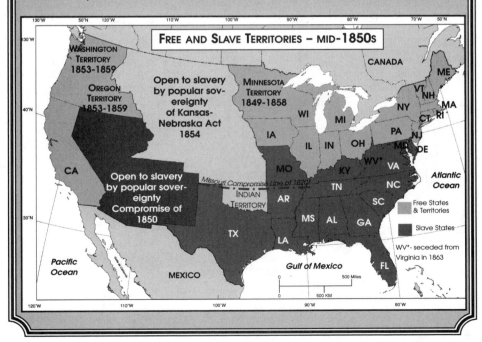

FREE AND SLAVE TERRITORIES – MID-1850s

THE CONSTITUTION IN JEOPARDY:
THE AMERICAN CIVIL WAR

While slavery was a leading cause of the Civil War, it was by no means the only cause. The issue of states' rights, differing economic and cultural patterns, the territorial expansion issue, and the rising power of the industrial North all contributed to the breakdown of unity. While initially fighting to preserve the Union, the North was later led by Lincoln into making abolition of slavery a major aim. Slavery was abolished by the end of the War, but bitterness between the North and the South remained long after the last shot was fired.

THE NATION DIVIDES

As hostilities began, volunteers from both the North and the South rushed to join their respective armies. The most difficult decisions were made by those in the **border states** – where slavery existed, but which remained loyal to the Union (Delaware, Maryland, Kentucky, Missouri, and West Virginia after it seceded from Virginia later in 1861). Although much of the population in these states leaned toward the Confederate side, Lincoln was able to convince them, sometimes by force, to remain in the Union.

People were mainly loyal to their section and fought to defend their homes, but support was by no means unanimous. It is doubtful that a majority of Southerners really favored secession, and a number joined

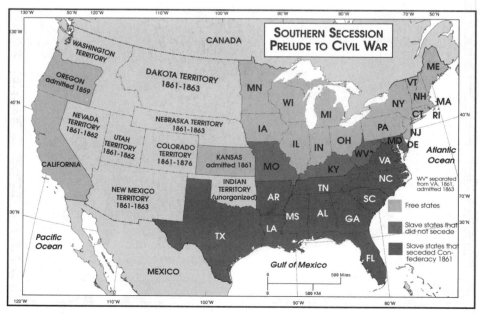

the Union forces. While most Northerners were willing to fight to preserve the Union, the goal of abolishing slavery was not universally supported at the outset of the War. Others in the North, called "Copperheads" demanded an immediate, negotiated settlement and were constant critics of President Lincoln and Congress.

LINCOLN STRETCHES POWER

For the most part, President Lincoln acted within constitutional guidelines as commander in chief, but he did exceed his authority on a number of occasions:

PRESIDENT LINCOLN AND THE *CONSTITUTION OF THE UNITED STATES*	
THE CONSTITUTION STATES:	LINCOLN'S ACTIONS WERE:
Congress is given the power to raise and support armies	increased the size of the army without Congressional authorization
no money can be taken from the treasury unless approved by law	withdrew $2,000,000 for military purposes without authorization
the *Writ of Habeas Corpus* shall not be suspended, except in cases of rebellion or invasion	arrested and jailed anti-Unionists giving no reason (no permission was obtained from Congress)
no law shall be made abridging freedom of speech or the press	censored some anti-Union newspapers and had editors and publishers arrested
accused persons have the right to a speedy trial and impartial jury in the state or district where the alleged act was committed	even though U.S. civil courts were operating, he set up military courts to try Confederate sympathizers

(Setting up military courts in the border states was declared unconstitutional by the Supreme Court in *Ex parte Milligan*, 1866)

OTHER CONTROVERSIAL ACTIONS

Besides Lincoln's stretching of his powers as commander in chief, there were several other events which aroused the ire of citizens. **Conscription**, the compulsory enrollment of persons into military service, was used by both sides. In the North, Congress passed the *Union Enrollment Act* or the *Draft Act of 1863* to supply the U.S. Army with troops. The *Act* allowed draftees to hire a substitute for $300. Poor Northerners, especially recent Irish immigrants, objected to this discrimination, and bloody riots broke out in New York City in the summer of 1863, injuring more than 1000 people.

CIVIL WAR ADVANTAGES

North	South
greater population diversified crop production 21,000 miles of railroads larger industrial capacity superiority in finances and munitions control of the seas	necessary to fight only a defensive war better trained commanders and troops fighting on home territory

Lincoln's issuing of the ***Emancipation Proclamation*** was another controversial action. While it did not free any slaves, it gave the North a "moral cause" for victory. African Americans had to serve in segregated units in Northern Army. They were not accepted as equals by all Union troops. African American troops received less pay and were issued inferior equipment.

☆ CAPSULE – CIVIL WAR ENGAGEMENTS

- **Manassas, VA (Bull Run) – July 1861**
  A Confederate victory under General "Stonewall" Jackson which shook the Union's confidence in its superior supplies and weapons.

- **Shiloh, TN – April 1862**
  Union troops moved up the Mississippi River, and forced the surrender of Memphis, New Orleans, and Baton Rouge. Most of the Mississippi came under Union control. (Grant's success at Vicksburg in 1863 later gave the North full control of the Mississippi)

- **Antietam, MD – Sept. 1862**
  A draw which temporarily stopped the Northern advance of the Confederate troops led by General Robert E. Lee, but enormous casualties were costly to the South.

- **Gettysburg, PA – July 1863**
  Heavy casualties on both sides, but a Union victory by General George Meade over the Confederate forces of Lee. A turning point in that Confederate troops retreated to the South, and the Confederate hope of recognition and aid from European nations was abandoned.

- **Atlanta-Savannah, GA – May-Dec. 1864**
  The Union's General William T. Sherman laid siege to Atlanta, and afterward undertook a "March to the Sea" to Savannah. Enroute, Sherman plundered the land, tore up railroads, and destroyed property.

- **Richmond, VA (Appomattox Courthouse) – April 1865**
  General Lee's Confederate forces, outnumbered and surrounded by Northern troops, surrendered to Union Commander Ulysses S. Grant. This ended the Civil War.

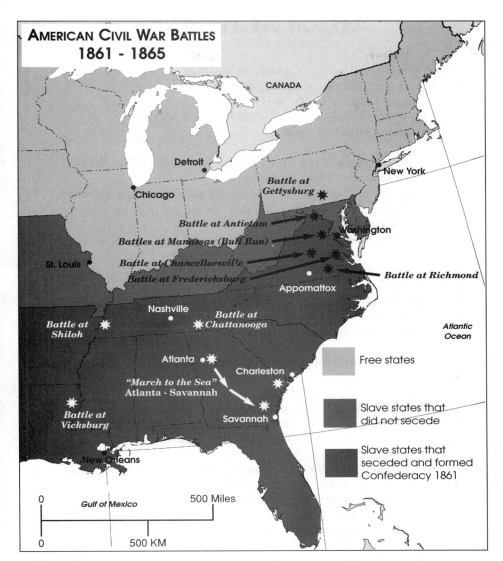

American Civil War Battles 1861 - 1865

CANADA

Detroit

Chicago

New York

Battle at Gettysburg

Battle at Antietam

Battles at Manassas (Bull Run)

Washington

St. Louis

Battle at Chancellorsville

Battle at Fredericksburg

Battle at Richmond

Appomattox

Nashville

Battle at Chattanooga

Battle at Shiloh

Atlantic Ocean

Atlanta

Charleston

"March to the Sea" Atlanta - Savannah

Battle at Vicksburg

Savannah

Free states

Slave states that did not secede

Slave states that seceded and formed Confederacy 1861

New Orleans

Gulf of Mexico

0   500 Miles

0   500 KM

SUMMARY

From its beginnings under Washington to the secession crisis under Lincoln, the young nation tested the durability of its new constitutional structure. Compromise is essential in a diverse democratic republic, but at the close of this era, moderates failed to make compromises work. Extremists on both sides came to the forefront, until war between the states was inevitable. Though the Union won the resulting Civil War, it came at a great cost. Suffering on both sides was immense. Just a week after the Confederate surrender in April 1865, President Lincoln was assassinated by Southern sympathizer John Wilkes Booth. The War concluded with great sadness among the victors, bitterness for the defeated South, and an uncertain future for the 3.5 million former slaves.

LESSON ASSESSMENT

MULTI-CHOICE

1 Which presidential action is an example of the unwritten constitution?
   1 appointing justices of the Supreme Court
   2 granting pardons for federal crimes
   3 submitting a treaty to the Senate for ratification
   4 consulting with the Cabinet

2 One of the purposes of the financial plan devised by Treasury Secretary Alexander Hamilton was to
   1 reduce the cost of American products sold in foreign countries
   2 provide a sound currency for the new nation
   3 eliminate tariffs on foreign imports
   4 create a system of state controlled banks

3 Which foreign policy did George Washington support?
   1 sending American troops to help in the French Revolution
   2 expansion of the United States into Canada
   3 forming alliances with European countries
   4 adopting a position of neutrality

4 Why was the Supreme Court decision in *Marbury v. Madison* (1803) so influential?
   1 The power of the executive branch was increased.
   2 The Court assumed the power to declare laws unconstitutional.
   3 The meaning of the elastic clause was narrowed.
   4 Congress was given the power to pass Constitutional amendments.

5 Which pair of events are examples of contradictory interpretations of the *Constitution of the United States*?
   1 Washington's neutrality policy and Washington's opposition to the Whiskey Rebellion
   2 Hamilton's support of the Bank of the United States and Hamilton's efforts to sell bonds
   3 Jefferson's opposition to the Bank of the United States and Jefferson's purchase of Louisiana
   4 Lincoln's appointment of Ulysses Grant and Lincoln's *Emancipation Proclamation*

6 As a result of the Monroe Doctrine (1823), the United States was able to
   1 form military alliances with European nations
   2 increase trade with Africa
   3 expand its influence in the Western Hemisphere
   4 colonize much of South America

7 What was a major impact of many of the Supreme Court decisions under Chief Justice John Marshall?
1 strengthening of the powers of the federal government
2 restrictions on big business
3 reduction of racial discrimination
4 expansion of the rights of the accused

Directions: Base your answer to question 8 on the chart at the right and on your knowledge of social studies.

VOTING EXPANDS		
YEAR	POPULAR VOTE	TOTAL POPULATION VOTING (%)
1824	356,000	3.3 %
1828	1,155,000	9.5 %
1840	2,404,000	14.1 %

8 What is one reason for the increases indicated in the chart?
1 immigration declined during the period
2 most property requirements to vote were dropped
3 women were allowed to vote
4 the number of major political parties expanded from two to four

Directions: Base your answer to question 9 on the chart at the right and on your knowledge of social studies.

House Vote on the Tariff of 1828 (Tariff of Abominations)		
Section	For	Against
New England	16	23
Middle Atlantic	55	11
West (OH, IN, IL, MO)	17	1
South	3	50
Southwest (TN, KY)	12	9

9 What two sections were most clearly for the tariff?
1 New England and the South
2 Middle Atlantic and the West
3 South and West
4 New England and Middle Atlantic

10 Before the Civil War, one example of increased democracy was
1 the emergence of the national nominating conventions
2 the granting of the right to vote to women
3 the direct election of Supreme Court judges
4 the passage of the amendment which abolished all poll taxes

11 The Second Great Awakening and the attraction of the Mormons and Shakers indicated
   1   widespread displeasure with the American political system
   2   attempts by some groups to break away from the United States
   3   general support among Americans for slavery
   4   the desire to seek new directions in religion

Directions: Base your answer to question 12 on the quotation below and on your knowledge of social studies.

"We hold these truths to be self-evident: that all men and women are created equal; that they are endowed by their Creator with certain inalienable rights; that among these are life, liberty, and the pursuit of happiness..."

– *Declaration of Sentiments ...,* 1848

12 The document that served as the most direct model for this resolution was the
   1   *Articles of Confederation*
   2   *Emancipation Proclamation*
   3   *Constitution of the United States*
   4   *Declaration of Independence*

13 With which movement are William Lloyd Garrison, Frederick Douglass, and Harriet Tubman associated?
   1   educational reform
   2   women's suffrage
   3   abolition
   4   prison reform

14 The *Missouri Compromise* and the *Compromise of 1850* were both attempts to
   1   abolish the electoral college
   2   increase voting rights among minority groups
   3   stop foreign governments from interfering in slavery
   4   settle disputes over slavery and the admission of new states

15 The Supreme Court's *Dred Scott v. Sanford* (1857) decision outraged people and strengthened the abolitionist movement because it said that
   1   importation of slaves could be resumed
   2   slavery must be abolished in all federal territories
   3   Congress could not forbid slavery in the territories
   4   freed slaves could not vote

16 By the time of the Civil War, slavery had nearly disappeared in the North mainly because
1 slave rebellions in Northern states had forced the end of slavery
2 slavery did not fit the economic interests of the North
3 the *Constitution of the United States* required the end of slavery in Northern states
4 ending the slave trade resulted in a shortage of slaves in America

17 Which argument did President Abraham Lincoln use against the secession of the Southern states?
1 Slavery was not profitable.
2 The government was a union of people and not of states.
3 The Southern states did not permit their people to vote on secession.
4 As the commander in chief, he had the duty to defend the United States against foreign invasion.

18 What was the most important advantage the North had during the Civil War?
1 unified support for the war effort
2 superior military leadership
3 economic aid from Great Britain and France
4 more human resources and war material

19 The *Emancipation Proclamation* helped Lincoln and the Union during the Civil War by
1 giving the Union a moral cause for victory
2 freeing all slaves in the United States
3 banning the importation of new slaves into America
4 convincing Britain and France to send troops to help the Union cause

20 During the American Civil War, African Americans in the North
1 were forbidden to fight for the Union
2 fought for the Union, but usually in segregated units
3 fought side by side with other Union troops in all battles
4 were used in supply operations for the North, but did no fighting

THEMATIC ESSAY

Directions: Write a well-organized essay that includes an introduction, several paragraphs explaining your position, and a conclusion.

Theme:

> ### Controversial Presidential Actions
>
> Between 1789-1865, American Presidents undertook a number of actions that were considered controversial at the time.

Task:

> Using your knowledge of United States history and government, write an essay in which you
> - identify *three* (3) Presidents and a controversial action of each
> - discuss the reasons for the controversy
> - explain how the Presidential action was intended to be beneficial to the country

Suggestions:

You may use any controversial Presidential action in the time period indicated from your study of U.S. history and government. Some suggestions you might wish to consider include: Washington's *Proclamation of Neutrality*, Jefferson's purchase of Louisiana, Jefferson's *Embargo Act*, Jackson's Bank Veto, Lincoln's *Emancipation Proclamation*. **You are *not* limited to these suggestions**.

PRACTICE SKILLS FOR DBQ

Directions:

The following task is based on the accompanying documents. The documents may have been edited for the purposes of this exercise. The task is designed to test your ability to work with historical documents. As you analyze the documents, take into account both the source of the documents and the author's point of view.

Historical Context:

In the period from 1789 to 1860, there were a number of times that interpretation of parts of the Constitution proved controversial.

Part A – Short Answer

The documents that follow present views of the *Constitution of the United States*. Examine each document carefully, then answer the scaffold question(s) that follow.

Document 1

Question for Document 1

1a What is being done to the Constitution by the people in the picture?

1b How did Alexander Hamilton view the action being taken?

Document 2

> "The power of Congress, then, comprehends [includes] navigation within the limits of every state in the Union, so far as that navigation may be, in any manner, connected with commerce with foreign nations, or among the several States, or with Indian tribes."
>
> – *Gibbons v. Ogden*, 1824

Question for Document 2

How did this interpretation of the Constitution increase the powers of Congress?

Part B – Essay Response

Task: Using only the *two* documents, write one or two paragraphs describing how Constitutional interpretations affected American society between 1789-1860.

State your thesis:
- use only the information in the documents to support your thesis position
- add your analysis of the documents
- incorporate your answers from the two Part *A* scaffold questions

_____

_____

_____

_____

Additional Suggested Task:
From your knowledge of United States history and government, make a list of additional examples of the interpretation of the Constitution by the executive branch or the courts during the time period 1789-1860.

_____

_____

_____

_____

_____

_____

_____

_____

_____

_____

_____

_____

_____

★ **LESSON**

4

PAGE 119

INDUSTRIALIZATION OF THE UNITED STATES

The Brooklyn Bridge, NYC – built 1869-1883
(PhotoDisc ©1995)

INDUSTRIALIZATION OF THE UNITED STATES

THE RECONSTRUCTION ERA

The Civil War ended with a loss of over a half million lives and a Union victory. Important questions faced the nation:

- How to deal with the former Confederate leaders?

- What should be the economic and political fate of the freed slaves?

- How to bring the former Confederate southern states back into the Union?

- What would be the role of the federal government in these and other questions?

The resulting struggles to answer these questions led one historian to call the Reconstruction Era "America's Unfinished Revolution."

POLITICAL STRUGGLES OVER RECONSTRUCTION

Reconstruction (1865-1877) refers to the rebuilding of the nation after the Civil War. The two main political tasks were readmitting the southern states back into the Union and granting rights to the newly freed slaves.

Even before the Civil War ended, Congress claimed authority over Reconstruction planning. President Lincoln vetoed Congress' *Wade-Davis Bill* (1864), which called for harsher treatment of the former Confederate states. The President led Reconstruction planning, although certain members of Congress felt him too lenient. After Lincoln's assassination in 1865, the conflict over Reconstruction control deepened between Congress and Lincoln's successor, President Andrew Johnson. By late 1865, Congress took control of Reconstruction planning.

Basic Belief

The Union had not been broken since the Confederate states did not have the constitutional authority to secede. Therefore they should not be treated harshly.

Basic Provisions

- granted pardons to Southerners who took a loyalty oath to the Union
- when 10% of those who voted in 1860 took a loyalty oath, the state would be readmitted to the Union (**10% Plan**)
- high ranking Confederates would not be allowed to vote

Status of Former Slaves

Working with the President, Congress created the **Freedmen's Bureau** which:

- provided relief supplies (food, clothing, shelter, and medical supplies) to both African American and white refugees
- provided a local court system
- negotiated contracts between freedmen and employers
- established thousands of schools across the South (notable achievement)
- initially resettled freedmen on confiscated lands (most land later returned to former owners)

Relations with Congress

- Lincoln vetoed the *Wade-Davis Bill,* Congress attempt to control Reconstruction planning, but showed willingness to work with Congress
- approved Secretary of War Stanton's policy for temporary military authority and provisional governments to be set up in the South

Basic Belief
Generally followed Lincoln's plan.

Basic Provisions
- President granted amnesty to most Southerners who took loyalty oaths to the Union.
- States needed to draw up new state constitutions that prohibited slavery and secession.
- States had to ratify the Thirteenth Amendment which prohibited slavery.

Status of Former Slaves
White, pre-war leaders regained power in the southern states. **Black Codes** (segregationist employment contracts and legal status restrictions) blocked the expansion of civil rights for African Americans and angered northern reformers.

Relations with Congress
As Radical Republicans took control of Congress, President Johnson's policies and leadership lost support. Congress passed measures to silence and restrict the President, including the *Tenure of Office Act* (1867), which resulted in the impeachment of President Johnson.

JOHNSON AND THE RADICAL REPUBLICAN CONGRESS

There was a brief period of cooperation between President Johnson and Congressional leaders in the aftermath of Lincoln's assassination. However, it soon gave way to tense relations. When Johnson tried to remove Radical Republican Secretary of War Edwin M. Stanton without Senate approval, he technically violated the *Tenure of Office Act* (1867). The House of Representatives impeached Johnson in 1868 in the last few months of his term. The Senate vote for removal from office was one vote short of the necessary two-thirds vote after a three month trial. The acquittal established the precedent that removal from office should only occur in serious situations. Repealed in 1887, the *Tenure of Office Act* was declared unconstitutional by the Supreme Court in 1926.

Radical Leader:
**Congressman
Thaddeus Stevens**

Basic Belief

Radical Republicans believed the Union had been broken and the Confederate states had committed state suicide. Therefore, the South should be treated harshly, as conquered territories.

Basic Provisions

In late 1865, Radical Republican leaders in Congress swept aside Johnson's work and took over Reconstruction planning. Their clearly defined goals included:

- establish democracy in the South
- ensure voting and civil rights for all, including African Americans
- confiscate and redistribute land ("40 acres and a mule")

Not all these ideas became part of the final congressional Reconstruction plan. The Republican controlled Congress finally passed the Military Reconstruction Plan of 1867. Its provisions included:

- military control of the South until new governments established
- right to vote for former slaves in state elections
- mandatory ratification of the Fourteenth Amendment for each southern state
- ratification of a congressionally approved state constitution for each southern state

Status of Former Slaves

Republican controlled Southern governments led to some improvements. African Americans supported the party of Lincoln and, in many cases, won elected office themselves, but had little role in party politics. **Carpetbaggers** referred to Northerners who came south to help in Reconstruction and scalawags referred to supportive white Southerners. Violence was used to keep African Americans from exercising their right to vote.

POST CIVIL WAR AMENDMENTS

During the Reconstruction years, three amendments to the *Constitution of the United States* were ratified. Ironically, the mandatory approval of the Southern states was necessary for ratification.

- **Thirteenth Amendment** (1865) abolished slavery in the United States.

- **Fourteenth Amendment** (1868) stated: *a*) all persons born or naturalized in the United States are citizens; *b*) prohibited the states from limiting citizens' privileges and immunities or depriving them of due process or equal protection of the laws; *c*) declared the Confederate debt null and void; *d*) reduced the power and rights of former Confederate officials.

- **Fifteenth Amendment** (1870) prohibited states from denying the right to vote on account of race, color, or previous condition of servitude.

Through these amendments, African Americans elected many African Americans to public office (including fourteen Congressmen and two United States Senators).

SOUTHERN RESPONSE TO RECONSTRUCTION REFORMS

In response to these changes, organized efforts to limit the political, social, and economic role of the African American developed. Congress passed the *Amnesty Act* in 1872 which pardoned most of the remaining Confederates, removing the last barrier to their regaining political strength. Southern states passed a number of restrictive laws.

- **Poll taxes** of one or two dollars were assessed on those wishing to vote. Lack of payment meant no voting.

- **Literacy tests** often involved interpreting difficult legal documents to prove the ability to read before one could vote.

- **Grandfather clauses** exempted whites whose grandfathers had been eligible to vote before the Civil War from taking literacy tests.

- **Jim Crow laws** formalized segregation. Segregation by law or statute is known as **de jure segregation**.

Groups such as the **Ku Klux Klan** launched terrorist campaigns to deprive African Americans of social and political equality. Klan activities prompted Congress to pass two *Force Acts* and an Anti-Klan law in 1870 and 1871. Despite federal authority to take action against the Klan, few convictions resulted. Nevertheless, the federal intercessions forced the Klan underground.

NATIONAL POLITICAL SCANDALS DURING THE GRANT ERA

- **Gold Market Scandal** – In 1869, financial speculators Jay Gould (1836-1892) and Jim Fisk (1834-1872) sought to dominate the gold market by purchasing all available gold and selling it at higher prices. Through Grant's brother-in-law, they convinced the President it would be unwise for the Treasury Department to sell any United States gold. Grant initially agreed, but when he reversed his position, the price of gold fell so low a financial panic resulted.

- **Credit Mobilier Scandal** – Attempts of the Credit Mobilier Company, involved with the building of the transcontinental railroad, to block a congressional investigation into its swindling of millions of dollars from stockholders.

- **Salary Grab Act Scandal** (1873) – Congress doubled the pay of the President and raised its own salary 50% for the previous two years. It was later repealed.

- **Whiskey Ring Scandal** (1873-1877) – Revenue collectors and liquor distillers cheated the federal government out of tax revenue.

- **Indian Service Scandal** (1876) – Government officials accepted bribes in assigning trading posts in Indian territory.

War hero **Ulysses S. Grant** became the first president elected after the end of the Civil War. A better warrior than president, his administration became known for political scandals and corruption.

Corruption occurred more frequently at the state and local level. One instance revolved around the infamous **Tweed Ring** in New York City. Political boss William Marcy Tweed embezzled some 200 million dollars through kickbacks, rent padding, and other schemes.

Political cartoonist **Thomas Nast** (1840-1902), a German immigrant, attacked political corruption. His cartoons attacking Boss Tweed helped to turn public opinion against Tweed. Nast popularized the political cartoon in America.

THE END OF RECONSTRUCTION

By the mid 1870s, Reconstruction was gradually ending. Radical leaders had died or left office, reformers had lost momentum, and others looked to the industrial future.

Democratic candidate and reform governor of New York, **Samuel Tilden** (1814-1886), won the popular vote over Republican candidate and reform governor of Ohio, **Rutherford B. Hayes** (1822-1893). However, he was one electoral vote shy of securing the presidency. The electoral votes from four states were disputed. Congress appointed a **bipartisan** (both Republicans and Democrats) electoral commission which granted the disputed votes to Hayes ensuring his victory.

Historians speculate that a deal was struck to give Hayes the presidency. Democrats agreed to Hayes' victory if Republicans agreed to removing federal troops from the South, appointing a southerner to the Cabinet, and granting federal money to southern railroads. This is often referred to as the Compromise of 1877.

Removal of most Union troops from the South occurred within one year of the end of the Civil War. Military occupation, a part of the Radical Reconstruction program, ended in the spring of 1877. The last Radical state government fell and **redeemer governments** (southerners who took power back from the carpetbaggers) regained political power at the expense of African Americans.

THE SUPREME COURT AND THE FOURTEENTH AMENDMENT

The Fourteenth Amendment guarantees equal protection of the laws and due process of the laws to all citizens. Decisions of the Supreme Court in the late 19th century narrowly defined the extent of these protections. Its precedents remained in effect until the 1950s and 1960s.

The **Civil Rights Cases** (1883) declared unconstitutional the *Civil Rights Act* of 1875 which outlawed segregation. The Court stated that the federal government had no jurisdiction over the behavior or private groups in race relations.

The constitutionality of Jim Crow legislation was at the heart of the case of *Plessy v. Ferguson* (1896). Homer Plessy, a mulatto, challenged a Jim Crow law of Louisiana requiring railroads to provide separate accommodations for African American and white passengers. He appealed his arrest and conviction to the Supreme Court. The Court debated this constitutional question: Did the Tenth Amendment concept of reserved rights of states allow them to pass segregation legislation if it contradicted the equal protection guarantees of the Fourteenth Amendment? The Court ruled against Plessy.

The Supreme Court's ruling in *Plessy v. Ferguson* upheld the constitutionality of de jure segregation. The Court did not consider whether the conditions or facilities were equal. It did not see separation as fundamental violation of equal treatment. This judicial precedent remained in effect until the ***Brown v. Board of Education of Topeka, Kansas*** (1954) decision.

ROLE OF AFRICAN AMERICANS – THE DEBATE

W.E.B. DuBois
(Library of Congress)

While the major parties generally ignored the issue of social equality for African Americans during the last quarter of the 19th century and the beginning of the 20th century, clear voices emerged from the African American community itself. They addressed the proper role of African Americans in society, although in different terms. Two of the key African American leaders were Booker T. Washington and William E.B. DuBois.

ROLE OF AFRICAN AMERICANS – THE DEBATE

Booker T. Washington (1856-1915)	William E. B. DuBois (1868-1963)
Background: former slave and self-made man	**Background:** middle class New Englander with a Ph.D. from Harvard University
Beliefs: • ignore racial discrimination • called for realistic accommodation in a speech known as the 1895 *Atlanta (Exposition) Compromise* • economic and property rights first, political equality would result gradually • need for African Americans to dignify common labor and work from the bottom up	**Beliefs:** • supported education, access beyond vocational education • rejected B.T. Washington's accommodation theory in *The Souls of Black Folk* (1903) • favored a more militant approach to securing immediate equal voting and economic rights and an end to segregation
Founded: • Tuskegee Institute in 1881, a vocational school and leading college for African Americans	**Founded:** • Niagara Movement in 1905 to increase agitation for equal rights • National Association for the Advancement of Colored People (NAACP) in 1909 in conjunction with other reformers including Jane Addams

NEW POLITICAL ALIGNMENTS	
Republicans	**Democrats**
• won majority of post-war presidential elections • major support from northern industrialists, urban workers, western farmers, veterans, newly franchised African Americans	• major support from the South - Solid South refers to the consistent and overwhelming Democratic majorities in elections for over a century • support from industrialists and workers who did not support Republican policies such as high tariffs

NEW POLITICAL ALIGNMENTS

Except for the Radical Republicans' agenda, reform did not dominate the agendas of either the Republicans in general nor the Democrats after the Civil War. The two parties sought to appeal to a number of interest groups.

THE RISE OF AMERICAN BUSINESS, INDUSTRY, AND LABOR (1865-1920)

Even before the Civil War broke out, important changes could be seen emerging in the American economy. The rise of the factory system had moved the place of production from the home to the factory which utilized new machinery, new power sources, and more unskilled than skilled labor. These changes occurred in England much earlier due to a variety of factors. But in both countries, although at different times, the textile industry led the move to mechanization.

RAPID INDUSTRIALIZATION OF THE NORTH

In the early 19th century, the Industrial Revolution came to America. New England's swift moving streams and rivers provided the water power to run early factories. The North's abundance of natural resources attracted factory and mill owners. Development of transportation networks, including the canal system and railroads, encouraged development.

By the Civil War, manufacturing and shipping dominated the North. Agriculture dominated the western and southern regions of the United States. The primary southern crop and export was cotton. The western economy had more diversified agriculture and the beginnings of a manufacturing area.

☆ CAPSULE – GROWTH IN IRON AND TEXTILES

Iron Industry

- By the mid-1800s key developments allowed the growth of the iron and steel industry in the United States.

- Transportation of ore became easier with the 1855 completion of the Sault Sainte Marie Canals (also called the Soo Canals) connecting Lake Superior and Lake Huron.

- High grade ore was found in the Mesabi Range in northeast Minnesota area (c. 1880s).

- Better production methods resulted from the Bessemer/Kelly process for converting iron to steel. Iron impurities were burned off resulting in stronger, more durable steel. Implemented in Pittsburg factories in the mid-1800s, it spread rapidly.

- As production increased, industry developed more machinery to shape and roll the steel, thereby increasing its usefulness.

Textile Industry

- The first textile mill in the United States thanks to Samuel Slater's smuggled plans (1790) and the invention of the cotton gin (1793) signaled the growth of the American textile industry.

- New England's water power fueled the textile industry in the U. S.

- In 1813, Francis Cabott Lowell (1775-1817) established the first factory to house all textile operations (from thread to cloth) under one roof. Lowell's system included the large scale employment of young women (initially mostly New England farm daughters) housed dormitory style. The system hit its peak in the 1830s. The system died out with the loss of the Southern cotton supply during the Civil War.

In the post-Civil War period, rapid economic change continued in the North. It became more industrialized, with the number of non-agricultural workers and factories increasing dramatically. By 1900, over 60% of American workers were involved in non-agricultural jobs. This was a marked shift from just 60 years earlier. **Real wages** (amount of goods and services income buys) rose from 1860 to 1890, but working conditions included 10-12 hour work days and six day work weeks. Child labor, low wages, and little or no safety precautions were the norm. From 1875-1900, the United States enjoyed a **favorable balance of trade** – exporting more goods than it imported. Immigration, unrestricted for most of the 19th century, provided a constant supply of cheap labor.

THE CIVIL WAR'S EFFECTS ON THE ECONOMY AND POLITICS OF THE SOUTH

The aftermath of the Civil War profoundly effected the South as well. Widespread devastation created tremendous problems. After Radical rule ended (1877), the Southern governments became dominated by industrialists, merchants, and bankers. The **New South** refers to the growing industrialization after the Civil War. However, much of this industrial growth was tied to agricultural products. Many Southern industries were subsidiaries of northern firms and depended upon Northern banks for capital.

The devastation caused by the Civil War caused a significant change in Southern agriculture. The number of property owners remained stable while the number of farms doubled and the acreage per farm decreased. Tenant farming or **sharecropping** predominated.

To escape the sharecropping system, a "new form of slavery," many African Americans moved west, such as this 1885 homesteading family.
– Nebraska State Historical Society

AMERICAN CAPITALISM

There was no central agency or program directing America's great economic change. Industrialization was driven by **capitalism**. This is an economic belief that the means of production must be privately owned and decisions must be made freely by individuals and businesses.

Capitalism is a dynamic way of making economic decisions. It is based on continued growth and improvement of living standards. Capitalism is fast-moving but it is not orderly, however. Thousands of businesses are growing at once. Each one is making different decisions daily. The change is fast, uneven, and unpredictable. As a result, America went through "economic growing pains" in the late 19th century. Some people were hurt in this change. Most saw life change for the better amid the smoke of the factories.

Capitalism works in a **market** structure. Producers and consumers freely interact. Orders and requests go back and forth. Those "market signals" help businesses estimate what to produce, who will produce it, how to produce it, and how to distribute the rewards. Consumer demand and cost of resources guide business production decisions. Ideally, there would be little interference in the interaction between consumers and producers from the government. The free flow of decisions results in the supply of goods and services available to meet demand.

For a capitalist free market system to show progress, production has to be efficient. Production is also linked to borrowing, accumulating, and reinvesting the money **(capital)** gained in the market. If production expands, the economy as a whole grows. If there is growth, then the quality of life improves. Theoretically, a capitalist structure also depends on a friendly, but unrestrictive role by government **(laissez-faire)** and open competition.

Before the Civil War, most American businesses were too small to have much excess money for capital investment. Expansion money came from Europeans. During the Civil War, demand for war goods generated more profits and investment capital began to come from Americans themselves. This new reservoir of "home-grown" capital fueled the great industrial expansion after the Civil War.

In return for the lease of the land, a sharecropper would turn over a portion of his crops (usually one-third for land and one third for the use of tools). This system perpetuated the plantation system. Most former slaves became sharecroppers or tenant farmers, experiencing limited economic opportunity. By 1920, over two-thirds of Southern farmers, both African American and white, were sharecroppers.

Since currency was in short supply in the post-war South, farmers borrowed on their expected harvest to secure needed credit. This is known as the **crop lien system**. High prices caused the farmers to go deeper into debt. Most farmed cotton as a single cash crop. As cotton production increased, prices dropped causing further hardship.

BUSINESS ORGANIZATIONS

In an effort to deal with America's business expansion and a roller coaster business cycle (boom periods followed by depressions or panics), businesses began to develop new methods of organization and combination in the late 19th century. Increased profits resulted from large-scale production (**economies of scale**) and lowered per item costs. Businessmen sought new ways to increase their profits and productivity. Mergers seemed to be the answer, but as business combinations grew, the openness of competition was compromised.

Pools resulted when a number of similar companies in the same industry (e.g., railroads) voluntarily entered into agreements to break competition by manipulating prices and output. Pool members often violated these agreements to hurt co-conspirators. Pooling was eventually outlawed.

FORMS OF BUSINESS ORGANIZATION

Form	Advantages	Disadvantages
Proprietorship	• owner close to customers and workers • has total control of management • receives all profits	• owner assumes all risks • limited capital available • one manager's perspective
Partnership	• more capital can be raised • risks are shared • more management perspective	• profits must be shared • unlimited liability for owners • dissolves if one partner leaves

Proprietorships and partnerships were the most common forms of business organization prior to the industrial revolution since most businesses were small scale operations.

Form	Advantages	Disadvantages
Corporation	• increased capital through sale of shares (stocks) • losses limited to investment • increased number of managers • ownership transferable • larger growth potential • research facilities possible • risks shared	• state & federally regulated • subject to corporate taxes • management removed from customers & workers

Corporations allowed nationwide operations, more efficient access to wider sources of capital, and gave protection to investors. Since corporations are chartered as "legal persons" and regulated by state authorities, they can own property, lend and borrow money, sue and be sued, and pay taxes.

Mergers among the strongest companies in a field resulted in monopolies when merged companies became so large that they could undercut all competition. The Justice and Commerce Departments and the Federal Trade Commission later monitored mergers to prevent monopolies from forming.

Trusts became a common form of combination. Chartered by a state, trusts had a board of directors which held the stock or trust certificates of its members. This arrangement allowed increased control over individual members' activities. Shareholders shared in the dividends, but exercised no say in the company. Trusts were later outlawed.

After the passage of the *Sherman Anti-Trust Act* in 1890, combinations such as pools, trusts, and mergers were regulated by the government. As a result, other forms of combination developed. **Interlocking directorates** occur when one or more persons serve on the board of directors of several corporations. **Holding companies** control one or more companies by holding a controlling number of voting shares in these companies. It took many years, but eventually even these behaviors were monitored by government agencies.

HORATIO ALGER AND THE AMERICAN WORK ETHIC

Early America's Calvinist / Puritan virtues included hard work, a shunning of vanity, and an emphasis on self-reliance. In the late 19th century, this "Puritan work ethic" was compatible with the ideas of laissez-faire economics. **Horatio Alger** (1834-1899) popularized these ideas in his books. Alger's rags-to-riches stories featured heroes who achieved great wealth through hard work, honesty, and thrift.

INVENTORS AND INNOVATORS OF THE INDUSTRIAL ERA	
Name	**Innovation**
Henry Bessemer/William Kelly 1850s	Bessemer/open hearth steel processes
George Pullman 1864	railroad sleeping car
George Westinghouse 1868	air brake
Great Atlantic & Pacific Tea Co. 1869	apply department store retailing techniques to food
Aaron Montgomery Ward 1870s	catalog shopping for rural customers
Alexander Graham Bell 1876	telephone
Thomas Alva Edison 1876	first industrial research laboratory; phonograph; incandescent light bulb

☆ Capsule – Representative Entrepreneurs

Much of the investment capital for business development before the Civil War came from adventurous Europeans. The infusion of domestic investment capital, accumulated during the Civil War, led to massive growth and expansion. The business leadership and the daring of business entrepreneurs, who organized new businesses and organized the large sums of money to start them, encouraged the growth of big business.

Andrew Carnegie (Steel)

A classic rags-to-riches story, Scots immigrant Andrew Carnegie (1835-1919), began his career in the railroad industry. Seeing enormous financial potential, he entered the steel business. The company he created sought to control the business from the supply of raw materials to production to distribution. This control over all aspects of an industry is called vertical integration. By 1900, Carnegie Steel Company produced over one-half of the nation's steel. In 1901, Wall Street financier J. P. Morgan bought out Carnegie and formed the United States Steel Company. Carnegie retired and spent over $450 million on libraries and other philanthropic works.

John D. Rockefeller (Oil)

Rockefeller (1839-1937) entered the oil refining business in 1859. Using a variety of business tactics, often ruthless, he sought to eliminate the wastefulness and increase the profitability of the oil refining business. By 1880, Rockefeller controlled nearly all U.S. oil shipping and refining facilities. This control over a limited aspect of one industry is called horizontal integration.

Rockefeller also acquired interest in related businesses, such as barrel making, pipelines, railroads, and oil storage facilities. He created the Standard Oil Trust in 1882 only to be dissolved ten years later by the Ohio Supreme Court. Standard Oil Company of New Jersey, a holding company, replaced the trust. This was dissolved by the U.S. Supreme Court in 1911 and separated into 34 units. John D. Rockefeller retired in 1896, the richest man alive. He then engaged in philanthropic endeavors, including creation of the Rockefeller Foundation.

J. Pierpont Morgan (Money and Banking)

Born into a banking family, J. P. Morgan (1836-1913) was an investment banker. Early in his career he help channel European capital into American enterprise. Morgan came to head the money trust which virtually controlled the American economy. After the Civil War, he began investing in railroads and by the early 20th century, he and his group held over 300 directorships in over 100 companies worth more than $22 billion. J. P. Morgan & Company lent the United States government $65 million in gold in 1895. In 1901 he bought out the Carnegie Steel Corporation and merged it with others to form U. S. Steel, the world's first billion dollar corporation. Morgan believed in combinations rather than free competition. He helped to create great trusts, including one ordered broken up by the Supreme Court in *Northern Securities v. the United States* (1904) during President Theodore Roosevelt's administration.

Henry Ford (Automobiles)

Henry Ford (1863-1947), a mechanical genius, created the Ford Motor Company in 1903. In 1908, he designed the Model T, a durable, economical automobile. Using assembly line and mass production techniques, he produced a car the average American could afford. Like Rockefeller and Carnegie, Ford sought to control the total enterprise from raw materials to distribution of the final product. Although Ford paid high wages, he tolerated no opposition and refused to recognize labor unions.

Henry Ford in Quadmobile

Courtesy of
Henry Ford Museum
and Greenfield Village
http://www.hfmgv.org

LAISSEZ-FAIRE

Laissez-faire implies little or no government regulation of business beyond providing an atmosphere conducive for business development. This would include maintaining a stable currency and providing a stable government. In 1776, Scots philosopher **Adam Smith** explained capitalism in his book, *An Inquiry into the Nature and Causes of the Wealth of Nations*. The economic principles of capitalism supported the industrial revolution. These principles included private ownership of the means of production, the profit motive, competition, free enterprise, and the setting of prices in the market place through supply and demand. As Smith noted in *The Wealth of Nations*, free enterprise, not the government, determines the answers to basic economic questions – what to produce, for whom to produce it, how to combine the scarce resources for production. The law of supply and demand, not government planners, reflects the interaction of the free choices of consumers and producers in the marketplace.

Starting with Alexander Hamilton's financial program of the 1790s, the federal government supported and promoted American business. The guarantees of the Fourteenth Amendment, as interpreted by the Supreme Court, protect individuals and corporate persons. During the late 1800s, industrialists and economists supported this position.

REACTION AGAINST BIG BUSINESS PRACTICES

Industrial leaders commanded vast power and control over resources, production, and distribution. As corporate power grew, critics began to question business practices and their restrictive control of America's resources. Their behavior began to alter the interactive free choice of consumers and producers. Newspapers publicized corrupt business practices. But not all looked at these business leaders negatively. Historians have called them both "robber barons" and "captains of industry" – depending on the writer's point of view (see chart below).

CALLS FOR GOVERNMENT CONTROL

At the end of the 19th century, many Americans criticized the tactics of big business. The public looked increasingly to the passive government to reassert itself against mounting abuses in the industrial society. Although Adam Smith warned against the unnecessary interference of

ROBBER BARONS OR CAPTAINS OF INDUSTRY?

Robber Barons (Negative view of industrialists)	Captains of Industry (Positive view of industrialists)
exploited workers	created new products
engaged in unscrupulous business practices	created highly efficient industries
engaged in political corruption	donated to charities
discouraged competition (monopolists)	

government in the marketplace in *The Wealth of Nations*, he also warned against monopolistic business practices. As the United States industrialized, one of Smith's negative market forces – government regulation – had to be used to restrain the other (monopoly).

Individual states began taking action, especially to aid farmers. In the 1870s, railroad shippers took advantage of the farmers of western and prairie states by charging high freight rates to get their goods to market. These states enacted laws to regulate railroad abuse, but the railroad owners challenged these Granger laws in the courts.

Although Congress – especially the Senate – was strongly influenced by business and lobbies, some strong federal actions under Article I, Section 8's **Commerce Clause** did occur in the period after the Civil War.

- *Munn v. Illinois* (1877) upheld the Illinois Granger law. The Supreme Court reasoned that the state government could use its police powers to regulate private business in the public interest. This set a major precedent.

- *Wabash RR. v. Illinois* overturned the *Munn* ruling in 1886. The Court said states could regulate railroads only <u>within</u> their boundaries. The *Wabash* ruling said Congress alone could regulate interstate commerce. Farmers and the public looked to Congress for action.

- *Interstate Commerce Act* (1887) set up the Interstate Commerce Commission to regulate railroad rates and prohibit railroad pools. Court challenges limited the effectiveness of the ICC's power, but it established the precedent for federal regulation of interstate commerce.

- *Sherman Anti-Trust Act* (1890) outlawed monopolies and forbade trust, pool, or other combinations in restraint of trade. Again, the courts refused to uphold its enforcement, and corporations developed new methods of combination to circumvent the regulation.

THE RISE OF LABOR ORGANIZATIONS

As companies grew in size, management became distanced from its workers. Frequent cost cutting led to deteriorating conditions for millions of workers. Division of labor and mechanization made work monotonous. **Sweatshop** conditions (factory in which employees work long hours at low wages under poor conditions) became common. Factory work was hazardous and poorly trained workers on the edge of exhaustion were susceptible to accidents. Ten hour work days, and six day work weeks were common. Children and women worked for lower wages than men.

To gain better conditions, employees slowly organized unions. Workers gradually realized the strength of acting together. They sought **collective bargaining** (workers uniting to seek common demands instead of doing it individually).

In the industrial era, labor organizations developed rapidly. **Craft unions** organized workers by a particular skill and **industrial unions** organized all workers in a particular industry. Despite the significant impact of the union movements, only a small percentage of the work force was actually unionized. By 1900, only one million workers were union members out of a work force of 27.6 million. However, the knowledge of the gains made by unions became nationwide models for decent working conditions that employees pressured employers to emulate.

EFFORTS AT CREATION OF NATIONAL LABOR UNIONS
Knights of Labor, 1869/Uriah Stephens, 1880s/Terence Powderly
Membership: admitted all workers - regardless of race, creed, color, gender, or national origin - except doctors, lawyers, bankers, and those who sold liquor; membership increased under Powderly - female (80%) and immigrants
Goals: basic reforms including eight hour work day, no child labor, equal pay for men and women, establishment of cooperatives, preferred boycotts to strikes
Success: peaked in 1886 then rapidly declined; a series of unsuccessful strikes, failure of cooperatives, and the Haymarket Riot in 1886 turned public opinion against them; they lost membership to the AFL
American Federation of Labor (AFL), Samuel Gompers (1850-1924)
Membership: organized along craft lines accepting only skilled workers
Goals: basic reforms including eight hour work day, no child labor, equal pay for men and women, establishment of cooperatives, preferred boycotts to strikes
Success: greatest success in organizing skilled workers; had 1 million members by 1901; local units set their own course of action, while the national organization lobbied for legislation and handled the general direction of the union.
International Ladies Garment Workers Union (ILGWU) 1900/later affiliated with the AFL
Membership: industrial union within the garment industry; primarily female (80%) and immigrant
Goals: sought to improve sweat shop conditions in garment industry
Success: uprising of the 20,000 – a general strike called by shirtwaist workers in 1909 – and the safety campaign after the tragic Triangle Shirtwaist Company Fire in 1911 won public support

Organized labor generally supported free, public education as a cornerstone of democracy. They stressed the inclusion of practical as well as liberal arts. Compulsory school attendance was another goal. Fewer children in the work force meant less job competition. Immigrants, women, and African Americans were denied admittance to many early unions.

THE RADICAL FRINGE

Opponents of capitalism such as socialist Karl Marx of Germany believed that large scale means of production should become the property of the community. The **Industrial Workers of the World** (IWW or "Wobblies'") wanted to seize industries without the control of either the capitalists or the politicians. The IWW emerged from the western mining struggles in 1905. The Wobblies emphasized worker solidarity and endorsed strikes and sabotage. Socialist IWW leaders emphasized class struggle. They included radical leaders such as Big Bill Haywood, Elizabeth Gurley Flynn, and Eugene V. Debs. The IWW rapidly declined in 1917, due in part to the American public's negative reaction to the Marxist – socialist – communist takeover in Russia's Bolshevik Revolution.

MAJOR STRIKES

In an effort to secure their demands, unions went on **strike** – a stoppage of work by employees in support of demands made on their employer, such as for higher pay or improved conditions. Several major strikes in the late 19th and early 20th centuries erupted into violent confrontations. They aroused public fear and had the effect of decreasing public support for the union movement.

- **The Great Railway Strike** (1877)
  Railroad worker pay cuts led to the first interstate workers strike. Public sympathy diminished as looting and rioting increased. President Hayes sent in federal troops to help end the strike. The strike failed, but demonstrated the potential power of national action.

- **The Homestead Strike** (1892)
  An AFL affiliated union went on strike to protest pay cuts at the Carnegie plant in Homestead, Pennsylvania. Company President Henry Clay Frick refused to back down and called in private guards. State militia also helped put down the violence. The strike and the union collapsed. Other steel mills refused to recognize unions in the steel industry until the United Steelworkers Union emerged in the 1930s.

- **The Pullman Boycott** (1894)
  Pullman workers suffered severe wage cuts as a result of the Panic of 1893, but the company store did not lower its prices. The American

★ CAPSULE – LABOR RELATIONS

Key Terms

- **collective bargaining** – process of negotiating a contract between a union and an employer. Way most labor-management agreements are decided.
- **mediation** – disinterested third party seeks to work out an agreement between labor and management. Recommendations are non-binding.
- **arbitration** – both parties bound to follow the decision of a disinterested third party.

Powerful Weapons

Unions	Management
• **strike** – stoppage of work by employees in support of demands made on their employer	• **lockout** – keeping workers out of the job site
• **boycott** – abstaining from using, buying, or dealing with a company as an expression of protest	• **scabs** – hiring substitute workers or thugs to break the strikes
• **strike fund** – union money distributed to workers to sustain them during a strike	• **injunction** – court order to stop strike
• **picketing** – group of persons stationed outside a place of employment, usually during a strike, to protest and discourage entry by nonstriking employees or customers	• **yellow-dog contract** – workers pledge not to unionize as condition of employment
• **publicity** – issuing statements in the media on the unfairness of working conditions	• **blacklist** – employers circulate lists of undesirable workers who led strikes

Railway Union, headed by **Eugene V. Debs** (1855-1926), organized a boycott which tied up delivery of the U.S. mail. Federal troops and an injunction ended the national boycott. Debs went to jail.
Management used provisions from the *Sherman Anti-Trust Act* to limit the power of unions to strike.

- **The Lawrence Textile Strike** (1912)
  This was the IWWs most notable and successful strike. Wage cuts and speed-ups for skilled and unskilled Lawrence workers led to the strike. The company's settlement met virtually all union demands, including wage increases and overtime pay.

Society Adjusts to Industrialization

Urbanization, immigration, and the end of the American frontier left their mark on American life. Cities grew rapidly. By 1900, New York, Chicago, and Philadelphia each had more than 1 million inhabitants.

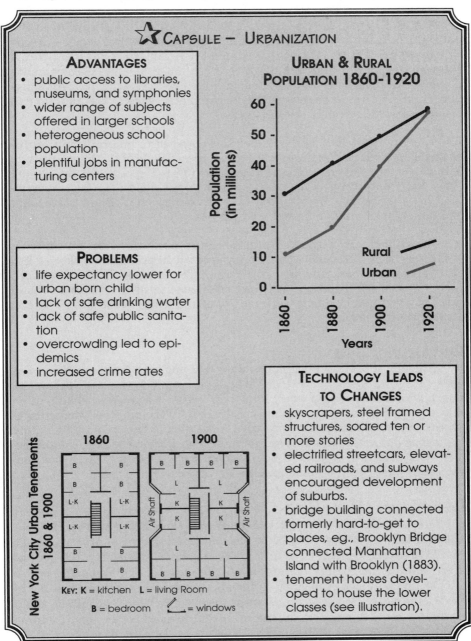

☆ Capsule – Urbanization

Advantages

- public access to libraries, museums, and symphonies
- wider range of subjects offered in larger schools
- heterogeneous school population
- plentiful jobs in manufacturing centers

Urban & Rural Population 1860-1920

Problems

- life expectancy lower for urban born child
- lack of safe drinking water
- lack of safe public sanitation
- overcrowding led to epidemics
- increased crime rates

New York City Urban Tenements 1860 & 1900

1860   1900

Key: **K** = kitchen   **L** = living Room
B = bedroom   = windows

Technology Leads to Changes

- skyscrapers, steel framed structures, soared ten or more stories
- electrified streetcars, elevated railroads, and subways encouraged development of suburbs.
- bridge building connected formerly hard-to-get to places, eg., Brooklyn Bridge connected Manhattan Island with Brooklyn (1883).
- tenement houses developed to house the lower classes (see illustration).

AMERICAN SOCIETY IN THE GILDED AGE (1877-1900)

Mark Twain (Samuel Clemens, 1835-1910) called the industrial era "the Gilded Age." Rather than a golden age, Twain and other critics saw the coating of glittering fortunes and new technologies as thinly covering the ruthless exploitation of workers, consumers, and constituents.

During the Gilded Age, Charles Darwin's scientific theory of evolution and natural selection was applied to the industrial experience by British and American philosophers. Under the idea of **Social Darwinism**, power and wealth go to those most capable. Government's laissez-faire policies complemented this idea of industrial natural selection. Supporters said people should be completely free to accumulate and dispose of wealth as they see fit.

Some industrialists of the Gilded Age engaged in philanthropy. Multi-millionaire Andrew Carnegie wrote that it is the duty of the wealthy to help those less fortunate than themselves (*The Gospel of Wealth*, 1900). However, philanthropy was a matter of personal choice. Carnegie distributed his vast fortune by building libraries across the United States and founding educational and peace institutions.

The Gilded Age witnessed **conspicuous consumption** on the part of the very rich. Those who had money spent it in pretentious ways. They built elegant homes and massive "summer cottages" in Newport, RI. They filled these dwellings with ostentatious furnishings and works of art. They adopted eloquent clothing styles and threw elaborate parties to display their wealth.

THE WORKING CLASS

Although the working class standard of living rose for many, there was a struggle to survive on low wages of unskilled workers (av. = $5. per week). There was widespread poverty in urban areas. Entire households often worked to bring in money for essential items. Working class women comprised 15-20% of the American work force during the late 1800s. Many worked as domestics and approximately 25% of working women sought factory work. Extra money could be made taking in boarders. Most new conveniences were beyond the financial reach of the working class.

THE GROWING MIDDLE CLASS

The middle class benefited from American industrialization. Managerial jobs increased and the standard of living rose. Approximately $1000 year ($20 per week) could provide a comfortable living. (Of course, there was no income tax at this point.) The increased purchasing power of consumers fueled American industrial growth. Freed from the incessant demands of farm life, there was more leisure time. It could be spent watching spectator sports, engaging in outdoor activities, or attending theatre performances and concerts.

Middle and upper class women aspired to the "Victorian ideal" of the woman as the light of the home. Labor saving devices allowed middle class women more free time. Many middle class women became involved in reform movements. Some sought employment as teachers and social workers.

THE POPULAR PRESS AND LITERATURE

The massing of people in urban centers and a surge of technological changes encouraged the publishing industry. Newspapers increased in readership. Joseph Pulitzer (*New York World*) and William Randolph Hearst (*New York Journal*) popularized their papers by sensationalizing news. This "yellow journalism" exploited scandals, disasters, and crimes. Low priced adventure paperbacks called "dime novels" became the popular reading material in the United States.

Regional literature captured the lifestyle and flavor of different regions of the United States by using local expressions or dialects. Joel Chandler Harris' "Uncle Remus Stories" romanticized the old South. Hamlin Garland wrote realistically about harsh conditions on the Great Plains. Mark Twain's sometimes sarcastic writings entertained many.

CHANGING PATTERNS OF IMMIGRATION

The United States is a nation of nations. With the exception of the Native Americans, everyone in the United States can trace their families back within 400 years to one or several immigrants or forced migrants.

THE PROCESS OF BECOMING AN AMERICAN

Immigrants adapted to American culture by learning the new language, customs, and traditions. This process is called **acculturation**. Street life, work, schools, immigrant newspapers, ethnic organizations, and the naturalization process helped immigrants acculturate. Assimilation occurs when an immigrant blends into the society. **Assimilation** is much more difficult to attain than acculturation and seldom happens in the first generation.

THEORIES OF AMERICANIZATION
• **Homogeneous Culture Theory** is based on newcomers being changed into English-speaking and -acting Americans.
• **Melting Pot Theory** holds that all immigrants are different, but are transformed (melted) into a new homogeneous, yet ever-changing society.
• **Cultural Pluralism Theory** emphasizes the diversity of the inhabitants of the United States, but recognizes a common center of political and economic institutions, including language. Synonyms include: cultural symphony, cultural mosaic, and "salad bowl."

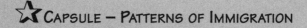

★ CAPSULE – PATTERNS OF IMMIGRATION

COLONIAL PATTERNS (1609-1776)

- from the arrival of the earliest European settlers to the United States declaring its independence, certain characteristics of this wave of immigrants emerge
- English settlers numbered the most
- Scots-Irish, Germans, Swedes, and Dutch arrived in significant numbers
- some half million Africans were forced to migrate to the American Atlantic colonies
- some fled for religious persecution (e.g., Pilgrims, Puritans, English Catholics, Spanish and Portuguese Jews, French Huguenots)
- some fled political persecution (e.g., German and Scots-Irish dissenters)
- some fled famine and war
- some came as indentured servants or redemptioners

ETHNIC & GEOGRAPHIC DISTRIBUTION
Circa 1870

- total Continental U.S. Population - 39,818,440
- almost even male-female split (slight male edge)
- almost 5 million non-whites (4.8 million African Americans, Indians, Chinese, and very few others)
- 12.3 million people in the Northeast, 13 million in the North Central States, 12.3 million in the South, and approximately 1 million in the West
- vast majority of Americans (approx. 82%) of Northern and Western European ancestry

EXAMPLES OF CONTRIBUTIONS

- building transportation systems – Chinese, Irish, Italians, Slavs (railroads, roads, canals)
- mining – Welsh, Poles, Slavs
- textiles/garment trades – English, Jews
- optical equipment – Germans
- chemical industry – French
- stone masons / sculptors – Italians

"OLD IMMIGRANTS" PATTERN (1776-1890)

- arrived prior to 1890
- western frontiers wide open
- most from Northern and Western European countries (majority from Ireland, Scandanavia and Germany)

"NEW IMMIGRANTS" PATTERN (1890-1920)

- arrived after to 1890
- settled in urban centers; formed ethnic ghetto neighborhoods
- western frontiers closing
- most from Southern and Eastern European countries (majority from Poland, Italy and Russia)
- fled economic depravation; responding to promise of industrial employment
- fled religious persecution (E. European Jews fled pogroms of Russians and Austrians)

IMMIGRATION TO THE UNITED STATES 1820-1930

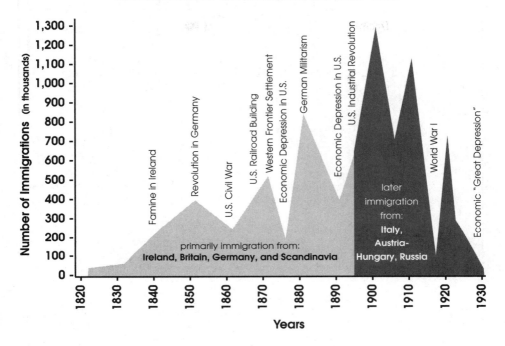

ANTI-IMMIGRATION REACTIONS

The United States has experienced frequent bouts of nativist or anti-immigrant sentiment. Before the Civil War, minor political parties, especially the **American Party** (or the **"Know Nothings"**) of the 1840s and 1850s, spoke strongly against immigration. This was a viciously anti-Catholic movement, and it increased in strength as large numbers of Catholics, especially the Irish and Germans, began to enter the country. The Know Nothings sought to restrict immigration and limit office-holding by naturalized citizens. To this day, nativist reaction is connected to fear of economic competition. Many poor immigrants often take low paying jobs to survive.

After the Civil War, nativist reaction (xenophobia) developed again over fears of job competition, concern that new immigrants would not assimilate, and the belief that they were mentally and physically inferior to earlier immigrants. Stereotyping occurred. After 1890, many groups called for immigration restrictions. The Ku Klux Klan and the **American Protective Association** sought to limit Catholic immigration. Catholic opponents believed with an increasing Catholic population, the Pope would be determining American policies. Nativists were also anti-Semitic (anti-Jewish), anti-Asian, anti-minority. Eventually this agitation led to federal laws that restricted immigration.

Chinese Exclusion Act (1882)

Nativists labeled Chinese on the West Coast a "yellow peril." Anti-Chinese groups portrayed them as strikebreakers, cheap labor, and possessing a culture unlikely to assimilate. State and local governments passed discriminatory laws. California's representatives urged Congress to take stronger action. Congress passed a law prohibiting Chinese immigration for ten years (later renewed).

Gentlemen's Agreement (1907)

Nativist actions in California prompted President Theodore Roosevelt to negotiate an immigration plan with the Japanese government. Japan denied passports to Japanese workers headed to the United States. San Francisco promised to desegregate its schools. Anti-Japanese agitation continued, but Japanese immigration ceased.

Literacy Test Act (1917)

Despite previous vetoes, the *Literacy Test Act* became law in 1917. Immigrants had to demonstrate literacy in their own language or English before receiving a visa. It kept out very few immigrants.

Emergency Quota Act (1921)

This act for the first time sharply limited the number of immigrants allowed into the United States. Fear of communists and revolutionaries and disillusionment in the aftermath of World War I led to its support. Each country had a quota based at 3% of the number of each nationality living in the United States in 1910. Immigration was limited to 350,000 a year.

National Origins Quota Act (1924)

Further limited immigration by decreasing the quotas allowed each nation. Using 1890 as the base year biased allotments towards Western and Northern European countries. It prohibited Asian immigration.

National Origins System (1929-1965)

Lowered allowable immigration to 150,000 a year and continued national origins system quotas.

SETTLING THE AMERICAN FRONTIER
(1850-1890)

From the colonial period, American settlers moved westward, expanding first the colonial, and later national boundaries. The Manifest Destiny of the first half of the 19th century led to increased settlement in the second half of the century. Settlement led to increased conflict with Native Americans.

From the 1850s-1890s, western development focused on the land between the Mississippi River and the Pacific Coast, although

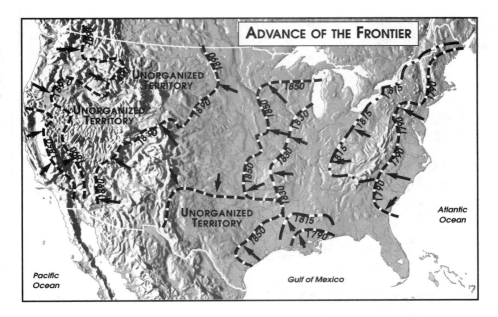

ADVANCE OF THE FRONTIER

Washington and California had been settled before the Civil War. Economic opportunity beckoned in the West. Railroad development, lumbering, and mining employed many and profited some greatly. Some ventures prospered, such as Montana's Anaconda Copper Mine, while most fared worse. Cattle ranching drew thousands, including future President Theodore Roosevelt. Oil development spread westward. The largest oil strike of the era occurred at Spindletop, Texas (1901). In 1890, the federal government declared the frontier officially closed. This marked the end of an era of the availability of cheap or free land.

From the middle to the end of the 19th century, several events encouraged the settlement of the land west of the Mississippi River, including:

- The *Homestead Act*, passed by Congress in 1862 offered one hundred and sixty acres of free federal land to any homesteader who would work and live on it for at least five years. Thousands took advantage of this offer. Young veterans of the Civil War were especially attracted to a new life in the west after seeing so much destruction to their family lands in the east.

- **Growth of the railroad industry** and completion of the transcontinental railroad made getting to the west easier and made it possible to ship more food eastward to America's great urban industrial cities. Chicago became a major terminal for cattle shipments and center of America's meat-packing industry. Omaha, Kansas City, Cheyenne, Los Angles, Portland, and Seattle became bustling transportation terminals and commercial centers.

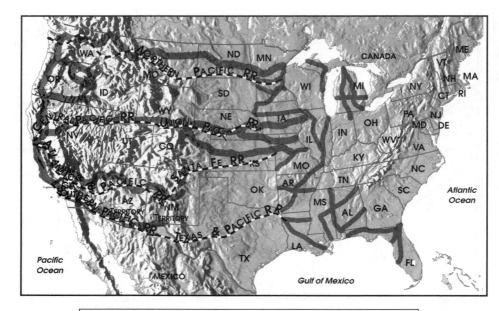

RAILROAD LAND GRANTS AND SOME MAJOR WESTERN RR LINES

THE LAND GRANTS

The area of the land grants shown on the map is exaggerated in order to show the extent of the lands given to the railroads. The typical grant included a 10-mile wide swath with a RR track right-of-way through the granted land. The American RRs received 131 million acres from the federal government and 49 million acres from the states.

- **Generous land grants** from Congress to the railroads made them agents of development, for they sold land to settlers. Railroads joined many western states in opening immigration bureaus in European countries. Railroad agents often met immigrants disembarking in eastern cities with offers to move west.

TURNER'S FRONTIER THESIS

In 1893, American historian **Frederick Jackson Turner** proposed a controversial thesis in his work, *The Significance of the Frontier in American History*. He argued that the frontier was the chief influence in shaping the American character.

Turner said the abundance of cheap land fostered: social and political equality, a rise in nationalism and optimism, a safety valve for unemployed industrial workers, and economic independence. Critics now say Turner's frontier thesis was too simplistic. They argue a number of factors shaped the American character besides the frontier, including European influence and industrialism.

NATIVE AMERICANS
AND THE STRUGGLE ON THE FRONTIER

Native Americans had a close relationship with nature. Many groups engaged in farming. They altered their environment by using fire for scrub removal, communication, and farming practices. Native Americans often made full use of the supplies nature provided. The buffalo provided virtually everything the native people of the Great Plains needed. Still, Native Americans suffered from seasonal scarcity of food supplies.

As more and more white settlers came to the New World, problems developed. Native Americans understood communal ownership of land, not the European idea of private ownership of land. Such cultural differences caused problems. Native Americans lost control of their land due to lack of immunity to European diseases, less developed technology, and less complex military and political organizations.

GOVERNMENT ACTION

During the colonial period, the British had tried to diminish hostilities between the settlers and the Native Americans by passing the **Proclamation of 1763** in the aftermath of the French and Indian War. It prohibited colonial settlement west of the Appalachian Mountains, reserving that area for the Native Americans. It failed. After the Revolutionary War, conflicts continued.

UNITED STATES GOVERNMENT RELATIONS WITH NATIVE AMERICANS

Northwest Ordinance (1787)

Congress set up governing rules for the area from the Great Lakes to the Ohio and Mississippi Rivers. This law said that the U.S. government would treat Native Americans in good faith. It would never take land without their permission. In reality, it proved meaningless.

Indian Removal Act (1830)

Congress authorized President Jackson to negotiate treaties and send the U.S. Army to move remaining eastern Indians to west of the Mississippi River. By the 1840s, few Native Americans lived east of the Mississippi River.

Treaties (some 370 between 1778-1871)

These agreements ceded tribal lands to the federal government. They were repeatedly broken or significantly changed. Congress finally abandoned the use of formal treaties in 1871. By this time most tribal land was gone and most Native Americans lived on reservations as wards of the federal government.

– continued page 150

The Cherokee Cases
(*Cherokee Nation v. Georgia*, 1831 and *Worcester v. Georgia*, 1832)

As American settlement in Georgia pushed into desirable Cherokee lands, their leaders objected. They took their case to the Supreme Court several times. Chief Justice John Marshall ruled that the Cherokee nation was a "dependent state" but that the Court had no constitutional jurisdiction to stop Georgia. He also said that only the federal government, not the states, had power over Indian nations. However, the President and Congress took no action to support the Cherokees' claims. Rather, under the *Indian Removal Act*, a forced march of thousands of Southeastern Indians in 1838-39 to areas west of the Mississippi is remembered as the "Trail of Tears." Approximately 25% of the 15,000 Cherokee people moved died along the way.

Indian Wars (1850-1890)

From the 1850s to the 1890s, a series of Indian Wars broke out as settlement pressed westward. Mineral discovery, including gold at Pike's Peak, Colorado in 1858, and the movement of homesteaders increased the disruption of the Indians' lifestyle and livelihood. Conflict increased. Some groups moved to government reservations with little protest. Others, such as the Nez Perce and the Apaches resisted. Despite winning some battles – including the defeat of General George Custer by Chief Sitting Bull at Little Bighorn in 1876 – Native Americans did not win in the end. The last battle occurred at Wounded Knee, South Dakota in 1890, when a band of Sioux was killed by U.S. Army troops.

Dawes General Allotment Act (1887)

Helen Hunt Jackson's 1881 book, *A Century of Dishonor*, brought attention to the plight of the Indians. In response to calls for reform, Congress passed the *Dawes Act*. Each Indian family head would be allotted a 160-acre farm from reservation land. American citizenship would be granted when they became "civilized." Surplus reservation land would be sold. The *Act* did not work. The government's offer of poor land to Indians unused to farming added up to failure. Native Americans lost over one-half of their reservation land under this act.

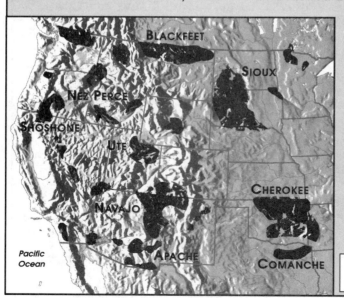

POST CIVIL WAR
INDIAN RESERVATIONS

THE MINING FRONTIER

The California gold rush of the 1850s lured many to the West. As the California rush ended, many prospectors explored other areas of the West. Nevada and Colorado land yielded rich strikes of silver and gold. Abandoned mines and "ghost towns" signaled an end to successful mining. By 1890, as silver and gold strikes diminished, industry's need for other metals including copper, lead, and zinc increased.

THE CATTLE FRONTIER

The Spanish introduced cattle ranching to the Americas. It quickly spread to other European settlers. A rancher could maximize his holdings by buying land that bordered public (government owned) land. He then had access to an enormous range for his cattle, known as the open range. However, cattle ranching in the American West declined after its peak in the late 1880s due to

- overgrazing, disease, severe winters, and falling prices which forced most ranchers out of business

- railroad development that cut through cattle grazing lands

- homesteaders who sought to farm former grazing lands; the development of barbed wire allowed vast tracts of land to be inexpensively enclosed, cutting down on the open range

Since frontier towns usually lacked organized police forces to keep order and violence erupted frequently over land and mining claims, vigilante groups formed. Sometimes these unauthorized secret citizen groups maintained order. More often, vigilantes instigated mob violence and often threatened the peace and safety of people.

THE FARMING FRONTIER

The last western lands settled were the grasslands of the trans-Mississippi West, the Great Plains. A harsh, extreme climate, lack of trees for fuel and lumber, and tough sod led earlier travelers to refer to the Great Plains as the "Great American Desert."

FARMING THE WEST
• Settlers used the sod to build homes ("soddies").
• Settlers burned buffalo and cattle manure for heat.
• Windmills provided much needed water, although dry farming techniques were used as well.
• Reliable steel plows cut through the tough sod.
• Mechanical reapers allowed for quick harvesting with few people.
• Government policies also encouraged settlement. Besides the *Homestead Act*, the *Morrill Land Grant Act* of 1862 provided for the sale of federal land to fund agricultural colleges and quicken the pace of scientific development.

Despite these changes, the floods, droughts, and blizzards brought by weather extremes and insects caused problems. The loneliness of prairie life became a common complaint, especially for women maintaining home and nurturing children. Churches and clubs provided social contact.

Beginning in the 1870s, mail order houses, such as **Montgomery Ward** and **Sears, Roebuck and Co.**, brought manufactured goods of the industrial age to rural areas.

The American farmers made money during the Civil War years feeding the Union armed forces and the industrial cities. However, in the decades following the War they complained of low agricultural prices, high industrial prices, high railroad charges, and lack of credit.

FARMERS TAKE ACTION

After the Civil War, America's farmers began to organize an "agrarian crusade" to demand action from the states and the federal government to counteract their problems. The Grange Movement was founded in 1867. Formally known as the National Grange of the Patrons of Husbandry, it started as a series of farm clubs. The farmers became politically active by electing their own candidates to state and local political office. State laws passed to regulate railroads were called "Granger Laws." The Grange supported farmers acting together to purchase major equipment and buying and selling in groups to avoid middleman costs. These cooperatives were generally unsuccessful due to lack of organization and training.

AGRICULTURAL PROBLEMS FOLLOWING THE CIVIL WAR
• **overproduction** – result of improved methods and more farmland
• **falling agricultural prices** – result of overproduction and foreign competition
• **high middleman charges** – costs for grain storage elevators, packing houses, wholesale distributors ,and especially railroad freight rates increased the cost of farm goods for consumers
• **tight credit policies** – banks reluctantly loaned to farmers; often at high rates
• **high industrial prices** – blamed on high tariff policies and the growth of monopolies

RAILROADS FIGHT BACK

From 1876-1900, farm state legislatures tried to regulate the railroads, viewed as the biggest enemy of farmers. The railroad companies challenged Granger laws as far as the Supreme Court. The basic legal issue involved: Did the states (government) have the right to regulate a private business for the public good?

FARMERS V. RAILROADS: KEY CASES

- *Munn v. Illinois* (1877)
  The Supreme Court ruled that states could regulate private property engaged in the public interest (the Grange laws were upheld).

- *Wabash, St. Louis, and Pacific R.R. v. Illinois* (1886)
  The Supreme Court changed its Munn ruling. It said that states could regulate the railroads only within their boundaries (only Congress could regulate interstate commerce).

- *Chicago, Milwaukee & St. Paul R.R. Co. v. Minn.* (1889)
  The Supreme Court overturned a Minnesota law which denied the right of businessmen to appeal freight rates set by the state government.

THE NATIONAL GOVERNMENT RESPONDS

The outcome of the *Wabash* decision shifted responsibility for interstate railroad regulation to Congress. In 1887, Congress passed the *Interstate Commerce Act* which called for railroad rates to be "...fair and reasonable." The Interstate Commerce Commission (ICC) was created to investigate any alleged violations of the prohibitions on pools, rebates, and rate discrimination.

POPULISM

As the Grange declined in power, other "farm parties" appeared. The most significant political party, the Populist or People's Party developed in 1892. Speakers encouraged farmers to "raise less corn and more hell."

Farmers believed that not enough money in circulation was the source of their problems. They wanted inflation to make their existing debts worth less. Until 1873, the United States was on a bimetallic standard. The value of gold and silver determined the value of money. In 1873, however, silver prices rose. Congress passed a law stopping the issuance of silver coins. The farmers felt the single gold standard would make money even harder to get. They called the Congressional action "the Crime of '73." The farmers campaigned for the free coinage of silver. They wanted the government to back money with cheaper silver instead of gold. They believed this would increase the amount of money in circulation and end their economic woes.

THE POPULIST PARTY PLATFORM
• more government control of the railroads • graduated income tax • secret ballot • direct election of Senators • 8-hour work day • government ownership of telephone and telegraph • restriction of immigration • free and unlimited coinage of silver at the rate of 16:1

As a third political party, the **Populist Party** had mixed success. In the 1892 presidential election, it garnered one million popular votes and 22 electoral votes. It was the best third party showing since Republicans in 1856. In the 1894 congressional elections, the Panic of 1893 depression conditions worsened and the Populists elected six Senators and seven Representatives.

The Populist Party reached its zenith in the 1896 presidential election. The Populists supported Democratic candidate **William Jennings Bryan** (1860-1925). A magnificent orator, Bryan awed audiences with his anti-Republican/business interest "Cross of Gold" speech. The Democrats courted the farmer by supporting free coinage of silver. The Republicans chose **William McKinley** (1843-1901) and supported high tariffs, the gold standard, and no free coinage of silver. After a hard-fought campaign, McKinley won the Northeast, Midwest, California, and Oregon by narrow margins. Bryan won the less populous South and the West by large margins, but lost the election in the electoral college. Congress adopted the singular gold standard in 1900.

SUMMARY

As the 20th century approached, tremendous changes propelled the United States into a world role. There was a growing urban population. Americans moved from the farms to the cities. Millions of immigrants settled in the cities. The 1920 census registered over 50% of the nation's population living in cities and town having over 2,500 people. Urbanization and industrialization went together.

There was also the growing role of American business. The West and domestic markets took most business energy in the late 1800s. America's rich supply of natural resources, growing labor force, and wealth of inventions soon had American business looking beyond the borders of the United States, first to the Western Hemisphere, and then to Asia.

Some Americans believed there were better ways to achieve progress. They criticized industrialization and offered various ideas for reform. In *Progress and Poverty* (1879), Henry George sought a single tax on land to replace all other taxes and end poverty. In *Looking Backward* (1888), Edward Bellamy (1850-1898) supported socialism. Henry Demerest Lloyd, an early "muckraker," proposed a similar plan to Bellamy's in his book, *Wealth Against Commonwealth* (1894) where he criticized the ruthless tactics of John D. Rockefeller and other industrialists.

LESSON ASSESSMENT

MULTI-CHOICE

Directions: Base your answer to questions 1 and 2 on the poem below and on your knowledge of social studies.

Wide open and unguarded stand our gates...
And through them presses a wild motley throng -
Men from the Volga and the Tartar steppes,
Featureless figures of the Hoang-Ho,
Malayan, Scythian, Teuton, Kelt, and Slav,...
O Liberty, white Goddess! Is it well
To leave the gates unguarded?...

– Thomas Bailey Aldrich, 1885, from *Unguarded Gates*

1 The author most clearly expresses the idea that
   1 the existing immigration restrictions are adequate
   2 immigration restrictions are needed
   3 unrestricted immigration should be the United States' policy
   4 the Chinese Exclusion Act is wrong

2 Which concept does this poem reflect?
   1 nativism   3 socialism
   2 imperialism   4 nationalism

Directions: Base your answer to question 3 on the chart below and on your knowledge of social studies.

PRESIDENTIAL VETOES & CONGRESSIONAL OVERRIDES		
	VETOES	**OVERRIDES**
All Presidents (1789-1865)	36	6 (16.6%)
Andrew Johnson (1865-1869)	21	15 (71.1%)

3 Which statement does the information in the chart best support?
   1 Presidents through 1869 never disagreed with Congress.
   2 President Andrew Johnson followed the veto pattern set by earlier Presidents.
   3 President Andrew Johnson enjoyed Congressional support for his policies.
   4 Congress did not support the leadership of President Andrew Johnson.

Directions: Base your answer to question 4 on the map below and on your knowledge of social studies.

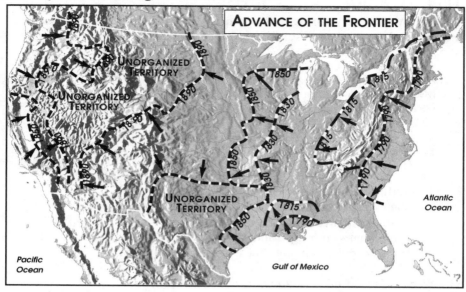

ADVANCE OF THE FRONTIER

4 Which statement is best expressed by the information in the map?
1   The movement of the frontier in the United States proceeded from west to east until 1890.
2   It took until 1815 for the frontier to move west of the Mississippi River.
3   The settlement of California and the Pacific Northwest occurred before that of the Great Plains.
4   The general movement of the frontier occurred from south to north before 1850.

Directions: Base your answer to questions 5 and 6 on the quotation below and on your knowledge of social studies.

"This, then, is held to be the duty of the man of wealth: To set an example of modest ... living...to consider all surplus revenues which come to him simply as trust funds, ...the man of wealth thus becoming the mere trustee and agent for his poorer brethren, bringing to their service his superior wisdom, experience, and ability to administer, doing for them better than they would or could do for themselves..."

– Andrew Carnegie, *Wealth*, 1889

5 Carnegie would most likely support
1   increased federal taxes to provide programs for the poor
2   philanthropy on the part of the wealthy
3   the view of industrialists as "robber barons"
4   federal government takeover of settlement houses

6   This quotation from Carnegie is best supported by the late 19th century belief in
    1   Social Darwinism   3   isolation
    2   socialism   4   imperialism

7   According to the theory of laissez-faire economics, prices should be determined chiefly by
    1   government regulations
    2   supply and demand
    3   leaders of business and government
    4   negotiations between labor and management

8   During the period 1850-1900, the federal government encouraged the westward settlement of the United States by
    1   making low-interest loans to settlers
    2   paying western farmers to plant certain crops
    3   giving free land to homesteaders
    4   honoring Native American territorial claims

9   Which was the major reason for the slow growth of labor unions in the United States during the 19th century?
    1   lack of public and legal support for union activities
    2   language and cultural barriers among workers
    3   existence of adequate wages and good working conditions
    4   rejection of unionization by skilled workers

10 Following the Civil War, which development most helped the settlement of the western United States?
    1   movement of former slaves into the new territories
    2   peaceful resolution of territorial claims with Native Americans
    3   restrictions on immigration
    4   expansion of the railroad systems

Directions: Base your answer to question 11 on the quotation below and on your knowledge of social studies.

"Many, if not most, of our Indian wars have had their origin in broken promises and acts of injustice on our part."

11 The speaker would most likely agree that Native American treatment by the United States government was based on
    1   desire for territorial expansion
    2   prejudice towards Native American religious practices
    3   congressional takeover of Reconstruction planning
    4   refusal of Native Americans to take part in treaty negotiations

12 The primary reason that the United States did not restrict immigration before the 1880s was that
1 nativist protest groups supported unrestricted immigration
2 internal movement and industrialization needed an expanding population
3 the *Constitution of the United States* left immigration policy up to the states
4 very few people immigrated to the United States

13 Which characteristic most accurately applies to the United States at the end of the 19th century?
1 There was nationwide demand to grant civil rights to Southern African Americans
2 Business organization shifted from large corporations to small businesses.
3 Labor unions organized over half of the industrial workers in the United States.
4 There was a general movement from rural, agrarian life to urban, industrial life.

14 What occurred to southern agriculture with the end of slavery at the conclusion of the Civil War?
1 corn, rather than cotton became the staple crop
2 profit increased with the introduction of wage labor
3 division of large plantations into small tenant farms
4 factories replaced farming in the southern economy

15 The *Chinese Exclusion Act* (1882) and the *Gentlemen's Agreement* (1907) were early actions of the federal government that led to
1 the development of democracy in Asia
2 moderate reductions in the number of imported goods
3 the establishment of naval bases in the Pacific Ocean area
4 severe limits on immigration from Asia

16 The best evidence that the Civil War greatly increased the power of the federal government over the states was the
1 reelection of Abraham Lincoln in 1864
2 passage of the black codes
3 impeachment of President Andrew Jackson
4 ratification of the Thirteenth, Fourteenth, and Fifteenth Amendments

17 The philosophies of Booker T. Washington and W.E.B. DuBois differed most with regard to the
1 effects of Reconstruction upon the South
2 need for education to improve the condition of the African American
3 best response of African Americans to racial segregation
4 support for American foreign policy towards Africa

18 Jim Crow laws passed in the South during the late 19th century were designed to
    1   guarantee civil rights to African Americans
    2   create a system of legal segregation
    3   enforce the Fourteenth Amendment's protections
    4   guarantee a job to every able bodied worker in the South

19 A major purpose of the Granger movement of the early 1870s was to
    1   eliminate the abuses of the railroads
    2   support the policies of laissez-faire economics
    3   correct injustices in the civil service system
    4   reduce the importance of manufactured goods

20 The *Dawes Act* of 1887 granted farmland to Native Americans as part of a plan to
    1   give them enough space to raise buffalo
    2   assimilate them into American society
    3   preserve tribal cultural traditions
    4   promote peace among warring tribes

THEMATIC ESSAY

Directions: Write a well-organized essay that includes an introduction, several paragraphs explaining your position, and a conclusion.

Theme:

> **Economy, Agriculture**
>
> United States economic growth and development from 1865-1900 had a tremendous impact on American agriculture.

Task:

> Using your knowledge of United States history and government, write an essay in which you
> • Describe a positive and negative effect of United States economic growth and development on American agriculture during the period 1860-1900.
> • Discuss how American farmers dealt with the negative effects.

Suggestions:
    You may use any effects on agriculture from your knowledge of this period and United States history and government. Some suggestions

you may wish to consider include: mechanization, tenant farming, railroads, agrarian crusade, Great Plains, the *Homestead Act*. **You are *not* limited to these suggestions**.

PRACTICE SKILLS FOR DBQ

Directions:

The following task is based on the accompanying documents. The documents may have been edited for the purposes of this exercise. The task is designed to test your ability to work with historical documents. As you analyze the documents, take into account both the source of the documents and the author's point of view.

Historical Context:

During the Era of Industrialization, great changes occurred in the workplace.

Part A – Short Answer

The documents that follow present views of the workplace in the industrial era. Examine each document carefully, then answer the scaffold question(s) that follow.

Document 1

> **Q**(uestion): "State the differences between the conditions under which machinery is made now and those that it existed under ten years ago."
>
> **A**(nswer): "Well, the trade has been subdivided and those subdivisions have been again subdivided, so that a man never learns the machinist's trade now. Ten years ago he learned, not the whole of the trade, but a fair portion of it. Also, there is more machinery used in the business, which again makes machinery ... one man may make just a particular part of a machine and may not know anything whatever about another part of the same machine. In that way machinery is produced a great deal cheaper than it used to be ... 100 men are able to do now what it took 300 or 400 men to do fifteen years ago..."
>
> – John Morrison, "Testimony of a Machinist," 1883
> (Source: *Report of the Committee of the Senate upon the Relations between Labor and Capital*, 48th Congress, 1885)

Question for Document 1

What was a major change in the machinist's trade from 1875 to 1885?

Document 2

"The opinion of the committee presented in its preliminary report, that large numbers of children were employed in manufacturing places contrary to law, has been amply confirmed by its further and fuller investigations...These children were undersized, poorly clad and dolefully ignorant, unacquainted with the simplest rudiments of a common school education, having no knowledge of the simplest figures and unable in many cases to write their own names in the native or any other language... The following testimony of Eva Lunsky, 16, supports this position:

Q. "Do you know when the 4th of July is?"
A. "No, sir."
Q. "Do you know the names of the summer months?"
A. "No, sir."
Q. "What month is this; do you know what month this is?"
A. "No, sir."

– Report from a New York State legislative committee hearing, 1896

Question for Document 2

What problem was this New York State legislative committee investigating?

Part B – Essay Response

Task: Using only the two documents, write a one or two paragraph discussion of the impact of work place changes during the second half of the 19th century.

State your thesis:

- use only the information in the documents to support your thesis position
- add your analysis of the documents
- incorporate your answers from the two Part A scaffold questions

_____

_____

_____

_____

Additional Suggested Task:

From your knowledge of United States history and government, make a list of additional ways industrialization changed U.S. society.

_____

_____

_____

_____

_____

_____

_____

_____

_____

_____

_____

_____

_____

_____

_____

_____

_____

_____

_____

_____

_____

_____

_____

_____

_____

THE PROGRESSIVE MOVEMENT AND THE GREAT WAR

The Statue of Liberty was a gift from the French to the American people and was designed (1870-75) by the French sculptor Frédéric Auguste Bartholdi. It was completed in Paris in 1884 and unveiled in New York Harbor on Oct. 26, 1886.   (PhotoDisc ©1995)

THE PROGRESSIVE MOVEMENT AND THE GREAT WAR

REVIEW:
REFORM TRADITION IN AMERICA

Reform is part of the American tradition. Throughout United States history, Americans, individually and in groups, worked to improve the quality of American life through private or government action. Some reform movements focused on narrow issues while others drew a broad range of causes together.

THE PROGRESSIVE ERA:
REFORM PRESSURES IN THE INDUSTRIAL AGE

By 1890, some people began to believe that industrial achievement had occurred at great human cost and the waste of natural resources. Economic and social inequities, political corruption, and technological change were among the factors contributing to this view.

- **Economic depression** –- The Panic of 1893 led to the worst depression of the 19th century. Four million people lost their jobs.
- **Impact of developing technologies** – Mechanization, the factory system, and growth of a management class distanced the workers from their bosses and consumers from workers. Working conditions deteriorated leading to labor unrest and violence. Development of the telegraph, telephone, teletype and publishing technologies made it possible for reformers to exchange information and coordinate activities.
- **Monopolies** – Growing monopolization limited competition hurting consumers and laborers.
- **Inequities of Wealth and Poverty** – While the "Gilded Age" resulted in incredible wealth for a few, for many it was a time of grinding poverty. The gap between the lifestyles of the rich and poor grew enormously.
- **Urban Living Conditions** – Poverty, crime, growth of slums, and poor sanitation led to calls for reform.
- **Political Corruption** – The rise of urban political machines and bossism contributed to political corruption at all levels of government.
- **End of the Frontier** – The end to free or cheap land and the indiscriminate use of natural resources led to calls for protection of the nation's natural treasures and resources.

☆ CAPSULE – SOME REFORM MOVEMENTS PRIOR TO 1890

American Revolutionary Era

- first democratic republic since ancient times
- nobility prohibited
- primogeniture outlawed
- land reform increased eligible voters
- growing support for public education
- elimination of slavery in the North

Abolition Movement

- anti-slavery crusade of 1830s-1860s
- sectional issue favored by the North
- slavery issue helped to bring on Civil War
- slavery abolished with Thirteenth Amendment (1865)
- Key figures: Frederick Douglass, Harriet Tubman, Angelina and Sarah Grimke, and William Lloyd Garrison

Early Women's Rights Movement

- initially tied to the abolition movement
- sought to change femme covert status of married women by seeking legal and political rights
- Seneca Falls Convention (1848) issued the *Declaration of Sentiments*
- success of abolition resulted in no similar gains for women
- focus on achieving the vote in the 1850s - in the 1860s the movement split on tactics; 1869 Wyoming Territory gave women the vote; 1872 Victoria Woodhull (1838-1927) became first female presidential candidate; 1878 Anthony's group proposed a right-to-vote amendment
- Key figures: Elizabeth Cady Stanton, Lucretia Mott, Susan B. Anthony, Lucy Stone

Civil Service Reform

- dates to President Andrew Jackson's "spoils system" of the 1830s
- reformers wanted jobs granted based on merit, not patronage
- President Garfield's assassination in 1881 acted as a catalyst for change
- *Pendleton Act* (1883) created a civil service commission to administer civil service examinations and make appointments based on scores (basis for today's system).

CHARACTERISTICS OF THE PROGRESSIVE ERA

The problems of the industrial era raised the fears and social concerns of the growing middle class and the upper-middle class. The **Progressive Era** refers to the reform response to these problems during the period 1900-1917. Characteristics of this period include:

- **Rising power and influence of the middle class** – A well-educated group among the middle class (businessmen, lawyers, social workers, doctors, clergy, educators) became the core of the Progressive movement. Primarily urban, this rising middle class had the moral training that stressed a "Christian duty" to help those less fortunate, and often the leisure time to devote to reform efforts.
- **Wide variety of reform efforts** – Problems ranging from political corruption, trusts, taxation, railroad rates, vice, working conditions, women's suffrage, civil rights for African Americans to Prohibition became calls for reform. Diverse issues attracted diverse supporters who were not always in agreement with each other. Some reforms focused on a single issue while others favored a broader approach.
- **Need for people to take action** – Reformers called for social activism. People needed to get out, work for, and demand reform from government and other agencies. Some Protestant church leaders became agents of social reform through the **Social Gospel** movement working to aid the urban poor.
- **Optimistic mood** – Progressives believed something new and hopeful was being created.
- **Belief in science and government** – Although they rejected party politics, Progressives believed science and technology could be used to solve problems and government must provide the leadership to do so.
- **Belief in capitalism** – Progressives supported the capitalist system and rejected radical socialistic reforms.
- **Desire to expose evils** – The public must be given information on corruption and abuse so they could act accordingly.
- **Relatively prosperous economy** – The recovery, after the Panic of 1893, led the rising middle class to express their concerns.
- **New generation of politicians** – Politicians, such as Robert LaFollette, Theodore Roosevelt, Woodrow Wilson and Louis Brandeis, who came-of-age with industrialism, began to take prominence.
- **Increasing role for women in politics** – The conditions of labor, education, child welfare, and consumerism attracted large numbers of middle class women to reform efforts. Women's suffrage was a major goal.
- **Spread from city level to state and national levels** – Local reform efforts at the city level spread to include state reform action. Eventually national reform efforts succeeded.

Despite its emphasis on reform, not all benefited from Progressive Era reforms. African Americans, workers, and farmers generally did not.

COMPARING THE POPULISTS AND THE PROGRESSIVES

Populists	Greater voter participation End to government corruption Limit the control of monopolies	Progressives
sought reform in the 1890s usually farmers or factory workers reforms included major change to the capitalist system, inc. government ownership of the railroads		Sought reform 1900-1917 Primarily urban, middle class movement Sought regulation of worst abuses of capitalism, but not a fundamental change to the system

INFLUENCE OF THE MUCKRAKERS

A variety of individuals and groups responded to the call to expose society's evils and take action. Reform writers, journalists, photographers, and editors exposed the evils of big business by investigating charges of corruption and abuse. Theodore Roosevelt's comments nicknamed these people **muckrakers**. The widely published articles and novels spurred the public to call for government action. Numerous state and national laws were passed. These included the ***Meat Inspection Act*** (1906), which used the interstate commerce clause to subject all meat crossing state lines to inspection by federal employees and the ***Pure Food and Drug Act*** (1906), which used the commerce clause to forbid the sale of adulterated goods or those fraudulently labeled. Muckraking journalism faded after the election of 1912, but today's investigative journalists follow the muckraking tradition.

CRUSADING WRITERS

Muckraker	Work	Subject
Jacob Riis	*How the Other Half Lives* (1890)	tenement conditions
Ida Wells	*A Red Record* (1895)	lynching statistics
Frank Norris	*The Octopus* (1901), *The Pit* (1903)	railroad abuses, wheat exchange
Ida Tarbell	*History of Standard Oil Company* (1904)	ruthless tactics in oil industry
Lincoln Steffans	*The Shame of the Cities* (1904)	corruption in urban politics
Upton Sinclair	*The Jungle* (1906)	problems in the meat-packing industry

OTHER PROGRESSIVE CONCERNS AND REFORMERS

Besides the muckrakers, many private individuals and organizations became agents of social reform during the Progressive Era.

To aid the urban poor (often immigrants), **Jane Addams** (1860-1935) and others established **settlement houses** in slum neighborhoods. Their offerings included adult education classes, child-care, clinics, and Americanization classes. In 1889 Addams established Hull House in Chicago. This idea started in England and spread to urban America. The writing of Jacob Riis (1849-1914) spurred housing reform.

Jane Addams comforts settlement children.
(Courtesy of *Ladies' Home Journal* "100 Most Important Women of the 20th Century," Meredith Corp ©1999)

Suffrage was the key goal for the **women's rights** movement. In 1890, the more radical women's group led by **Susan B. Anthony** merged with the more moderate group led by **Lucy Stone** and her husband to form the **National American Woman Suffrage Association** (NAWSA). These new **suffragists** took direct action through marches and demonstrations. Quaker **Alice Paul** lost support because of her more militant tactics learned from the "suffragettes" of England. Moderate **Carrie Chapman Catt** (1859-1947) revived the NAWSA. By 1919, fifteen states granted female suffrage. The active role of women during World War I aided their quest for national suffrage. In 1920, ratification of the **Nineteenth Amendment** granted all American women the right to vote.

Based on her nursing experience with immigrant mothers in New York City, **Margaret Sanger** (1879-1966) promoted the use of birth control. Her actions violated existing obscenity laws and brought her into conflict with the law. In 1921, she organized the American Birth Control League that later became the Planned Parenthood Federation of America in 1942.

The start of World War I in Europe led many, including Jane Addams (who won the Nobel Peace Prize in 1931 for her efforts in the peace movement), to support **pacifism** (opposition to war). **Jeannette Rankin** (1880-1973) of Montana became the first female member of the House of Representatives. She voted against United States entry in World War I, later casting the lone dissenting vote against U.S. entry into World War II.

The policies and programs of Booker T. Washington and William E.B. DuBois divided the movement for **racial equality and justice** (See Lesson 4). The number of lynchings in the South grew during the late 19th and early 20th century. Journalist **Ida Wells** (1862-1931) compiled lynching statistics and attacked discrimination in her writings. Southern Senators **filibustered** (use of unlimited debate to a block a vote) anti-lynching bills. Jamaican-born **Marcus Garvey** (1887-1940) founded the Universal Negro Improvement Association in 1914. The UNIA sought to create free and independent nations in Africa. Garvey hoped that African Americans would help populate these nations. Garvey became one of the first African American nationalists. He was jailed for mail fraud and later deported.

The **temperance** movement's goals moved from moderate use of alcohol to **prohibition**. Critics, like the National Prohibition Party (1869), the Women's Christian Temperance Union (1874), and the Anti-Saloon League (1895) believed drinking led to crime, poverty, and vice. The **Eighteenth Amendment** (1919) banned the sale, manufacture, and distribution of alcohol.

B'nai B'rith, a fraternal organization founded in the 1840s, fought discrimination and prejudice against Jews. In 1913, Progressive Era American Jews formed the **Anti-Defamation League** (ADL), which broadened its scope to seek an end to religious and racial prejudice.

PROGRESSIVISM INFLUENCES AMERICAN POLITICS

Urban middle class reformers influenced changes at every level of American government starting at the municipal and state levels. The reformations of the state of Wisconsin acted as a model for other states to follow.

THE WISCONSIN IDEA: MODEL FOR STATE REFORM
• work of governor and university professors • railroad regulation • regulatory commissions • tax reform • direct primary • state civil service reform • workmen's compensation laws

PROGRESSIVE STATE REFORMS
Initiative – process where voters can suggest new laws and amendments
Referendum – people allowed to vote directly on legislation
Recall – process where voters can remove officials from office before their term is up
Secret Ballot – (also known as the Australian Ballot) voters could make their choices in privacy

"GRASS ROOTS" PROGRESSIVISM

Municipal Reform

- City reform attacked bossism and political machines by calling for civil service reform.
- The city commission system replaced mayors and councils with elected commissioners who made and enforced laws.
- Under the city manager system, elected city council members appointed a professional manager, not a politician, to direct the government.

State Reform

- Reformers sought to control the power of the political machines at the state level. Progressive governors provided leadership, including **Robert LaFollette** (1855-1925) of Wisconsin (see chart on page 169), **Woodrow Wilson** (1856-1924) of New Jersey, and **Theodore Roosevelt** (1858-1919) of New York.
- Goals often differed by region (West - railroad regulation, South - anti-big business, North - political corruption and labor conditions).
- State police powers were used to regulate the health and safety of citizens, including requirements for factory inspections, workmen's compensation insurance, minimum employment age, maximum hours for child labor (8-10 hours per day), limits on working hours for women, and old age pensions.
- In reality, many of these reforms proved difficult to enforce. Strong opposition came from the courts and big business. U. S. Supreme Court rulings in *Lochner v. New York* (1905) and *Muller v. Oregon* (1908) illustrate a range of opinion. In *Lochner* the Court ruled unconstitutional a New York law limiting bakers' hours to ensure the health of the bakers and safety of the consumers. The Court reasoned that the law violated the Fourteenth Amendment's due process rights of the bakers to work more than 10 hours a day. Three years later, in *Muller*, the Court upheld an Oregon law limiting women workers to 10 hours a day. **Louis Brandeis**, Oregon's lawyer, used scientific data and statistics to argue Oregon's case. Two important precedents were set by this case: use of non-legal data as evidence (Brandeis brief) and certain circumstances supported use of a state's police powers.

NATIONAL REFORM

Progressive Era presidents included the first three presidents of the 20th century – **Theodore Roosevelt** (after McKinley's assassination in 1901), **William Howard Taft**, and **Woodrow Wilson**.

TEDDY ROOSEVELT'S PROGRESSIVISM

President Theodore Roosevelt believed a strong and forceful presidency should act as the "steward" of the people's general welfare. The public good must be the primary interest of the President. The conservative President

Roosevelt also believed that trusts were a necessary evil and here to stay, but their worst abuses should be controlled. He called on government and especially business to give the people a "Square Deal."

Coal miners in Pennsylvania went on strike (Anthracite Coal Strike 1902) demanding higher pay, shorter working hours, and union recognition. Coal mine owners, wishing to break the union, refused to negotiate. President Roosevelt called the two sides together as the strike lengthened, threatening the nation's supply of winter fuel. When the talks broke down, Roosevelt threatened to use troops to mine the coal. The owners agreed to binding arbitration, which gave workers some of their demands. Roosevelt's popularity increased.

Theodore Roosevelt, 26th President of the U.S. (White House Historical Association, National Geographic Society)

Failure to get Congress to create stronger anti-trust legislation in 1902 led President Roosevelt to use the *Sherman Anti-Trust Act* of 1890 to challenge trusts not acting in the public interest ("bad trusts" not "good trusts"). In 1904, in ***Northern Securities Co. v. United States***, the Supreme Court ordered the breakup of the railroad monopoly in the Pacific Northwest belonging to J.P. Morgan and James J. Hill. The Roosevelt administration took "**trust-busting**" action against over forty other American trusts.

WILLIAM HOWARD TAFT'S PROGRESSIVISM

Theodore Roosevelt supported Secretary of War William Howard Taft's (1857-1930) bid for the Presidency in 1908, but Taft lacked Roosevelt's charisma and dynamic view of the Presidency. Despite the growing concern of the progressive wing of the Republican Party over his tariff policies and dismissal of forester Gifford Pinchot, Taft's administration engaged in reform. Controversy within the Republican Party led Theodore Roosevelt to reenter national presidential politics in 1910.

During Taft's Administration, the Justice Department sued twice as many trusts as under the Roosevelt Administration. In 1911, the Supreme Court ordered John D. Rockefeller's Standard Oil Company

PROGRESSIVE CONGRESSIONAL LEGISLATION 1900-1910	
Actions	**Impact**
Commerce Department (created 1903)	collected information necessary to enforce anti-trust legislation
Elkins Act (1903)	expanded powers of the Interstate Commerce Commission (ICC) and made rebates illegal
Meat Inspection Act (1906) and *Pure Food and Drug Act* (1906)	provided consumer protection
Hepburn Act (1906)	strengthened the *Elkins Act* and gave the ICC more power to regulate railroad rates (subject to court approval); broadened its control of interstate commerce, including oil pipelines, railroad terminals, and sleeping car companies
Conservation Actions	influenced by naturalists such as John Muir (1838-1914), who helped convince Congress to establish Yosemite National Park in 1891, President Roosevelt sought a plan for resource management and the protection of America's natural treasures
Newlands Reclamation Act (1902)	set aside money from the sale of western lands for irrigation and created the National Forest Service under the control of conservationist Gifford Pinchot (1898-1910)
Antiquities Act (1906)	provided that sites of historic or scientific interest be placed under national protection, including Niagara Falls and the Grand Canyon
Forest Preserves	added 150 million acres to national forests and preserves - using existing presidential authority

breakup (***Standard Oil Company of New Jersey v. United States***, 1911). Under the Supreme Court's "rule of reason," trusts were not automatically condemned. Instead, their actions had to be analyzed to see if they were engaged in "unreasonable restraint of trade." Also, under Taft, the *Mann-Elkins Act* (1910) gave the ICC the power to regulate telephone and telegraph communication.

THE 1912 PRESIDENTIAL ELECTION

The 1912 presidential election turned out to be a three-way race among candidates with progressive credentials. The Republican Party split. When the Republican Party convention supported the more conservative Taft for reelection, Theodore Roosevelt and his reform-minded supporters left the Party and formed the Progressive or "Bull Moose"

1912 Presidential Election Results

Candidate & Party	Popular Vote	Percent of Popular Vote	Electoral Vote
Woodrow Wilson (Democratic)	6,296,547	41.9	435
Theodore Roosevelt (Progressive)	4,118,571	27.4	88
William H. Taft (Republican)	3,486,720	23.2	8
Eugene V. Debs (Socialist)	900,672	6.0	0
Eugene W. Chafin (Prohibition)	206,275	1.4	0

Party. Roosevelt called for a New Nationalism. The Democrats nominated Woodrow Wilson, former president of Princeton University and governor of New Jersey, and his progressive program, which would be called the New Freedom.

The Republican split allowed Wilson to win a slim plurality of the popular vote and an overwhelming electoral majority. Wilson became the first Democratic president in 20 years. He was reelected in 1916.

WOODROW WILSON'S PROGRESSIVISM

President Wilson was an active reformer who worked energetically to enact his program. There were a number of significant reforms during his administration (1913-1921).

Despite Congressional opposition, Wilson secured the passage of the *Underwood Tariff Act* (1913), the first great reduction in tariffs since 1857. Reformers saw reduced tariffs as a way into increase foreign competition and limit the power of trusts.

TWO APPROACHES TO PROGRESSIVE REFORM

New Nationalism
Theodore Roosevelt
- supported high tariffs
- most trusts acceptable, but needed regulation
- vigorous government action against society's problems

greater political democracy

social and economic reforms

New Freedom
Woodrow Wilson
- supported lower tariffs
- breakup trusts to restore competition
- revise nation's monetary system

Woodrow Wilson during the 1912 presidential campaign against William Howard Taft and Theodore Roosevelt. (Library of Congress)

Congress passed the *Federal Reserve Act* (1913) to take power away from eastern banking interests and bring financial stability to the nation. The *Act* created the Federal Reserve System or "Fed." This government controlled banking system allowed for an elastic currency (one that could expand or contract as the economy required).

Populist-inspired tax reform was achieved with the ratification of the **Sixteenth Amendment**. It established a direct progressive income tax, called the graduated income tax (tax rate increased as income increased), in which "the more you make, the more you pay."

Presidential support encouraged Congress to pass the *Clayton Anti-Trust Act* (1914) which strengthened the *Sherman Anti-Trust Act* of 1890 by listing business abuses, including rebates, certain interlocking directorates, and exclusive sales contracts. The *Clayton Act* exempted labor unions and agricultural cooperatives, but hostile court decisions effectively ignored these exemptions. Congress also created the **Federal Trade Commission** in 1914. It investigated monopolistic practices, including adulterating foods, misleading advertising, spying and bribery, and could issue "cease and desist orders" when such practices were found.

Two anti-child labor laws were passed in an attempt to end child labor, but were declared unconstitutional by the Supreme Court.

Women achieved the right to vote (women's suffrage) with the ratification of the Nineteenth Amendment in 1920.

PROGRESSIVE ERA AMENDMENTS	
Sixteenth Amendment (1913) . . . . .graduated income tax	
Seventeenth Amendment (1913) . . . . .direct election of U. S. Senators	
Eighteenth Amendment (1919) . . . . .prohibition	
Nineteenth Amendment (1920) .women's suffrage	

WORLD WAR I AND ITS EFFECTS ON DOMESTIC REFORM

By 1916, the Progressive movement had run its course. The Eighteenth and Nineteenth Amendments had gone to the states for ratification, although they would take effect after World War I. For the most part, public concern shifted to the growing conflict in Europe. Eventually, American participation in World War I required coordination of the government and cooperation by all involved. Many government business regulations were dropped or relaxed to stimulate war production. Domestic issues were largely set aside, and some lost support altogether. As America entered its first transatlantic conflict, the enemy was no longer corruption and inequality at home, it was now "over there."

CHANGING FOREIGN POLICY

INDUSTRIALIZATION AND GLOBAL COMMERCE

During the second half of the 19th century, expansion of industry prodded the United States to look beyond its borders for markets and raw materials. American industry experienced tremendous growth in the decades after the Civil War. Americans with surplus capital looked beyond North America for new places to invest. They looked overseas for new markets and new sources of raw materials. The "close" of the frontier in 1890 indicated to many that it was time to expand abroad. Pursuing these policies, government and business leaders hoped to strengthen America's position as a leading industrial nation.

Led by Britain and France, European nations rushed to gain control of colonies in the second half of the 19th century. Nearly all of Africa, India, and Indo-China came under the domination of Europe. The Europeans attempted to justify their conquests by claiming it was the "White Man's Burden" to bring the benefits of western civilization to less developed regions.

Early in the 19th century, American Christian missionaries ventured into various parts of Asia and the Pacific to find converts. Hawaii was of particular interest to New England Congregationalists. By the close of the 19th century, many Americans came to believe that it was the "divine mission" of the United States to spread the benefits of democracy, liberty, and Christianity to the less civilized. A number of authors, including the **Rev. Josiah Strong**, (*Our Country*, 1885) popularized the belief that it was the duty of Americans to uplift the less fortunate. Such popular ideas made it easier for Americans to accept an imperialistic role for the United States.

Between 1870 and 1900, the value of American agricultural and industrial exports more than tripled. The ever-increasing output of factories and farms could not be consumed within the nation. American merchant and naval fleets were strengthened and modernized to give the nation a greater role in international commerce.

There was a military viewpoint on expansion, too. In 1890, **Captain Alfred Thayer Mahan** (1840-1914) of the U.S. Naval War College, authored *The Influence of Sea Power Upon History, 1660-1783*. Mahan's book tried to show that throughout history, nations with sea power dominated the world. Mahan urged that it was time for Americans to "look outward" for naval bases, markets, and raw materials. Modernization of the Navy was already underway. By 1900, the U.S. Navy was ranked third in the world.

The increased speed of steamships made overseas trade more profitable, and the need for coaling stations forced Americans to take an interest in Pacific Islands. Trans-oceanic telegraph cables brought the hemispheres closer together. Continued industrial growth required new sources of raw materials and improved military weapons made conquest easier.

THE TARIFF CONTROVERSY:
FREE TRADE V. PROTECTIONISM

One of the more hotly debated political issues of the 19th century was the tariff. **Protectionists**, usually Republicans and their business backers, argued that high tariffs protected the wages and jobs of workers as well as the profits of capitalists. **Free Trade** supporters advocated lower tariffs (and eventual elimination of all tariffs). They were often Democrats and claimed that high rates raised the price of manufactured goods for consumers, benefited only a few, and interfered with America's ability to sell goods overseas. The tariff rose and fell depending on the party in power.

MANIFEST DESTINY AND EXPANSION TO THE PACIFIC

In the first part of the 19th century, Americans made their way across the continent spurred on by the belief in Manifest Destiny, that America had a "divine mission" to conquer the entire continent. The annexation of Texas, settlement of the Oregon dispute, and the spoils of the Mexican War brought the Americans to the Pacific by 1850. The new west coast ports increased interest in Far Eastern trade.

JAPANESE CONTACTS (1857-1900)

Japan had isolated itself in the mid 17th century, having little to do with western civilization. In 1853, disputes over American whaling rights and interest in trade led to a visit by Commodore **Matthew C. Perry** (1794-1858). He persuaded the Japanese to open several ports to American commerce. This was soon followed by European powers making similar demands. The Japanese were impressed by modern technology and military power of the westerners. By 1900, Japan had a modern government, a thriving textile industry, and rapidly growing heavy industries. Japan also modernized its military and began its own era of imperialism.

THE CHINA TRADE:

Despite a distance of over 12,000 miles, American east coast merchants carried on a profitable trade with China from the 1780s. In the mid-1800s, the speed of American clipper ships and the addition of the Pacific ports contributed to an increase in the China trade prior to the Civil War.

Americans were interested primarily in trade and missionary activity. However, European imperialists annexed territory and established economic control (spheres of influence) over large parts of China toward the end of the 19th century.

In 1900, groups of nationalistic Chinese protested the foreign dominance of their country. Surreptitiously encouraged by their government, these groups went on a violent rampage, killing foreigners and destroying foreign owned property. The uprising became known as the **Boxer Rebellion**. After several months, an international military force, which included U.S. troops, ended the rebellion.

With the foreign spheres of influence threatening U.S. trade in China, Secretary of State **John Hay** sent two notes to major powers with trading interests in China. In these 1899 and 1900 communications, Hay declared principles which became known as the **Open Door Policy**. Hay wanted equal opportunity for all nations in trade, investments, and profits. The second note warned the imperialistic nations of Europe and Japan not to annex any Chinese territory.

ACQUISITION OF HAWAII

American interest in Hawaii began with missionary activities early in the 19th century. Sugar growers flocked to the islands in the 1870s. Americans gradually dominated affairs. In 1893, American settlers overthrew Queen **Liliuokalani** and requested annexation by the United States. Five years later, the fighting in the Philippines during the Spanish American War convinced President William McKinley and Congress that Hawaii was needed to send supplies and men across the Pacific. Congress declared Hawaii a U.S. territory in 1898 and an important mid-Pacific naval base was established at Pearl Harbor.

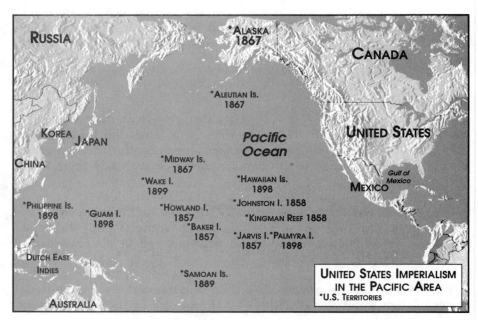

Chief organizer, Lieutenant Colonel Theodore Roosevelt, poses with the Rough Riders who fought in the battle of San Juan Hill, Cuba, 1 July 1898
(Library of Congress)

Causes

- harsh treatment of Cubans by Spanish rulers

- American investors loss of profitable agricultural trade (sugar cane, tobacco)

- yellow journalism – false and exaggerated stories published by American newspapers

- explosion of the battleship *Maine* (incorrectly blamed on the Spanish)

Results

- Spain gave up Cuba (placed under American supervision)

- Spain gave Puerto Rico and Guam to the United States

- United States paid $20 million to Spain for the Philippines

THE SPANISH AMERICAN WAR

In 1898 with the American public clamoring for war, McKinley requested a recognition of Cuba's independence and a declaration of war, which Congress passed on 25 April. The fighting lasted until August. Serious deficiencies in the nation's military preparedness were exposed. Poor planning, rotten food, and unsanitary conditions killed many more than combat. In the *Treaty of Paris*, concluded on 10 December 1898, a humiliated Spain yielded to American imperialism. The Spanish ceded Puerto Rico, Guam, and the Philippine Islands. Cuba was given independence but agreed to cede territory for U.S. naval stations.

The Spanish American War established the United States as a major power in the Far East and the dominant power in the Caribbean. Although Filipino nationalists fought a bitter four-year struggle for immediate independence, the United States clung to the archipelago, because it seemed a portal to the China market.

THE DISCOMFORT OF IMPERIALISM

Some Americans felt uneasy about having colonies. The **Anti-Imperialist League** campaigned against annexing the Philippines, Guam, and Puerto Rico. Prominent "anti-imperialists" included Jane Addams, Andrew Carnegie, Mark Twain, Samuel Gompers, and educator John Dewey.

The imperialists proclaimed the vigorous new mission of the United States was to spread democracy, western civilization, and Christianity. They emphasized the need to challenge the imperialistic nations already in the Pacific. In February 1899, the Senate ratified the *Treaty of Paris*. America establish its own empire barely a century after it declared its own independence from the British Empire.

☆ CAPSULE – UNITED STATES EMPIRE

CUBA – A U.S. PROTECTORATE
For nearly a generation after the overthrow of the Spanish, Cuba existed as a satellite of the U.S. Some highlights of that period include:
- 1898 – The *Teller Resolution* made Congress promise not to annex Cuba.
- 1901 – The *Platt Amendment* set up terms for withdrawal of U.S. occupation troops and granted a modified independence. The agreements made Cuba an informal U.S. protectorate.
- 1934 – Congress repealed the Platt Amendment and gave the Cuban people total independence.

PUERTO RICO
After the Spanish-American War, Puerto Rico became a U.S. colonial possession and eventually received special status as a commonwealth. Key steps in this evolution include:
- 1900 – The *Foraker Act* granted territorial status to Puerto Rico, with limited self-government.
- 1917 – The *Jones Act* extended American citizenship to residents.
- 1952 – Commonwealth status permitted residents to elect their own legislature and governor, but they were not represented in Congress nor in the Electoral College. (Puerto Rico could become a state if the Puerto Rican people desired and the U.S. Congress approved.)

PHILIPPINES
Located over 7,000 miles from the U.S. mainland, the United States had difficulty governing the Philippines as a colony.
- 1899-1902 – Americans troops crushed Emilio Aguinaldo's rebels in a bloody four-year guerrilla war for independence.
- 1902-1942 – During U.S. control of the islands, sanitation programs, economic development, literacy, and democratic ideas were all put in place.
- 1942 – Japanese forces overran Philippines and forced Americans out.
- 1946 – After liberating the Islands from the Japanese in World War II, the *Tydings–McDuffie Act* freed the islands in 1946.

Map caption/labels:

UNITED STATES IMPERIALISM IN THE CARIBBEAN SEA 1898-1917

UNITED STATES | Atlantic Ocean
Gulf of Mexico
BAHAMAS IS. (BR)
VIRGIN IS. PURCHASED FROM DENMARK, 1917
CUBA
DOMINICAN REPUBLIC
GUADELOUPE (FR)
GUANTANAMO U.S. NAVAL BASE 1903
HAITI
MARTINIQUE (FR)
BARBADOS (BR)
BRITISH HONDURAS
JAMAICA (BR)
PUERTO RICO U.S. POSSESSION AFTER 1898
TRINIDAD (BR)
MEXICO
HONDURAS
GUATEMALA
NICARAGUA
VENEZUELA
Pacific Ocean
EL SALVADOR
COSTA RICA
BRAZIL
U.S. ACQUIRED CANAL ZONE, 1903 PANAMA CANAL COMPLETED, 1914
COLOMBIA

LATIN AMERICAN AFFAIRS

INFLUENCE OF THE MONROE DOCTRINE (1823–1898)

In an 1823 speech to Congress, President James Monroe stated that

- the United States opposed European nations establishing any new colonies in the Western Hemisphere

- the United States would follow a policy of minimal involvement in European politics

With only one exception, there were no significant challenges to the Monroe Doctrine for almost seventy-five years. (During the Civil War, an indirect attempt by France to control Mexico through a puppet emperor – the Maxmillian Affair of 1864-1865 – was condemned by the United States and eventually abandoned by the French.)

United States influence and intervention in the domestic affairs of many Latin American nations grew tremendously in the decade following the Spanish–American War. By 1900, United States policy makers dreamed of creating an "American Lake" in the Caribbean. They felt they were meeting the strategic and economic demands of the nation. However, many Latin American nations harbored increasing resentment toward U.S. meddling in their affairs.

In 1895, Britain refused to submit a boundary dispute between Venezuela and British Guiana to arbitration. The United States intervened. Secretary of State Richard Olney warned Britain to reconsider, claiming that "the United States is practically sovereign on the [South American] continent." Hostilities were averted when Britain finally agreed to arbitration of the disputed area.

In 1905, President Theodore Roosevelt went further. He stated that in cases of "chronic wrongdoing," the United States would use "international police power" in Latin America. This became known as the **Roosevelt Corollary** to the Monroe Doctrine. It was applied in 1905 to the Dominican Republic when it was unable to repay debts to European nations. To keep Europe out of the Americas, the United States took over the economy of the Dominican Republic and supervised the debt repayment.

ROOSEVELT'S "BIG STICK" POLICY

Even before becoming President, Theodore Roosevelt was an advocate of an aggressive foreign policy. He felt it was important for the United States to wave a "big stick" – make a strong show of force in foreign affairs. He believed the policy would keep Europeans out of the Western Hemisphere and bring the Latin American nations in line with U.S. wishes.

During Roosevelt's administration, the "big stick" was used in Cuba to end a rebellion (1906), and in Venezuela (1902) and the Dominican Republic (1903-1905) to collect debts. Although many Latin American nations were poorly governed, they nonetheless resented the "big stick" policies, and similar interventions by later presidents.

TAFT AND DOLLAR DIPLOMACY

In the same vogue as Roosevelt, President William Howard Taft expanded America's "international police power" in Latin America. Nicaragua, Haiti, and the Dominican Republic were all occupied by U.S. military forces in order to protect American investments and loans. Taft's approach was called "Dollar Diplomacy" by critics and met with considerable protest in Latin America, but it was enthusiastically supported by American business interests.

WILSON AND THE MEXICAN REVOLUTION

In 1910, Mexican rebels launched a revolution against dictator **Porfiro Diaz**. It began nearly a decade of civil war in that country. American businessmen watched with concern as the government changed hands several times, and threatened to end foreign investment.

☆ CAPSULE – PANAMA CANAL: ACQUISITION AND CONSTRUCTION

In the 1850s, American Settlement of California aroused interest in a Central American canal connecting the Atlantic and Pacific. The 13,000 mile water route from New York to California would be cut in half with a canal. With the addition of territories in the Caribbean and the Far East, a canal became a vital strategic and commercial necessity for the United States.

In 1901, the United States paid a French canal company 40 million dollars for the land rights in Panama. Later, the U.S. negotiated a treaty with Colombia, which controlled Panama at the time. When the Colombian senate refused to ratify the treaty, U.S. naval ships helped Panamanian rebels stage a revolt that led to independence.

Immediately afterwards, President Roosevelt finalized a Panamanian treaty. As part of the agreement with Panama, the United States took title to a ten mile wide strip of land and paid Panama annual rent for its use. In 1914, after ten years of construction, the two oceans were joined.

In contrast to the poverty of most Panamanians, a small, affluent American community resided in the Panama Canal Zone. Panamanians' growing resentment to the U.S. ownership erupted into riots in 1964. After years of negotiations, a 1977 treaty provided for the gradual return of the area to Panama.

President Wilson applied a policy of "Watchful Waiting." He resisted calls for American military intervention, but also refused to recognize a Mexican government with questionable authority. This worked for a time, until Mexican rebel **Pancho Villa** (1878-1923) crossed the border and killed American citizens in 1916. U.S. troops led by General **John Pershing** (1860-1948) pursued Villa into Mexico. Order was finally restored to Mexico after 1917, but Villa was never captured.

WORLD WAR I INVOLVEMENT: 1914-1920

The United States struggled to stay out of European affairs in the 19th century. However, its change of status to an industrial giant at the end of the century made it more important in global affairs. The expansion of overseas trade increased its contacts with other countries, especially in Europe. By 1914, a complex series of events drew Europe into a general war.

When Europe became involved in World War I, the U.S. wanted no part of the conflict. In 1914, President Wilson issued a proclamation of neutrality. However, as neutrals, U.S. merchants wanted to continue trading with both sides.

At the start of hostilities, Britain attempted to choke off Germany by blockading the European coasts. To retaliate, Germany used submarine warfare against enemy shipping in the Atlantic. This threatened the shipping rights of neutral nations. Traditional rules of warfare, which required enemy ships to identify themselves before sinking a merchant ship, were impossible for the submarine, which needed to remain underwater to be effective. This **unrestricted submarine warfare** killed many innocent people. The most deadly attack occurred against the *Lusitania* (7 May 1915), when over 1,000 lives were lost. Germany, though widely condemned, defended actions as the only way to break the British blockade.

In the new approach to warfare, the label of neutrality lost its meaning. American ships were attacked. One side or the other felt the goods that Americans

BACKGROUND CAUSES OF WORLD WAR I

- **Economic Competition** – industrialized nations competed for markets and raw materials
- **Nationalism** – groups ruled by other nations struggled for independence (e.g., Serbs ruled by Austria)
- **Entangling alliances** – groups of nations (Triple Alliance – Germany + Austria + Italy versus Triple Entente – Britain + France + Russia) allied themselves to balance the power of others
- **Military competition** – European nations tried to build bigger and better armies and navies than their rivals (submarines, tanks, poison gas, artillery, machine guns, and airplanes made warfare much more deadly)
- **Imperialism** – European nations, in need of raw materials, confronted each other for colonies in Asia and Africa

supplied were helping the enemy. The British controlled the surface of the Atlantic and blocked American ships from trading with Germany. The Germans' submarines threatened shipping to Britain from under the waves. President Wilson protested, and the attacks stopped for a while.

The mindset of neutrality proved hard to maintain domestically, too. The United States was still a nation of immigrants. There were many who were emotionally supporting one side or another in the European conflict. Wilson urged the people to keep a neutral outlook, but there were cultural forces at work. America's heritage was British. The belief in democracy shifted people's sympathy toward Britain and France as opposed to the **autocracy** of the Central Powers. There was greater trade and investment with the Allies than with the Central Powers. These factors combined to influence the nation's thinking.

> ### KEY ELEMENTS OF WILSON'S FOURTEEN POINTS
>
> Early in 1918, President Wilson announced America's war aims and proposed a plan for world peace that included the following ideas:
>
> * an end to secret diplomacy
> * freedom of the seas
> * free and open trade
> * reduction of armaments
> * consideration for native populations in colonial areas
> * self-determination for subject nationalities of Europe, including Poland, Czechoslovakia, and Alsace-Lorraine
> * a general association of nations to protect the political independence and territorial integrity of all nations

Early in 1916, Wilson demanded an end to Germany's random sinking of merchant ships. The German government agreed to halt these attacks when they issued the ***Sussex Pledge*** (May 1916). A few months later, Germany renewed its unrestricted submarine warfare and sank four American merchant ships. The ***Zimmerman Note*** (March 1917) angered Americans when British intelligence announced a purported plot by minor German diplomats to persuade Mexico to declare war against the United States.

By 1916, the War in Europe **stalemated** (no decisive victories for either side). The loss of life and the economic costs mounted, but no one could win. Desperate, the British resumed **seizing** American ships, but the German's U-boats stepped up the torpedoing of American ships. The killing and destruction by the Germans finally drove Wilson to ask Congress for a declaration of war in April of 1917.

As was often the case in its history, the United States was poorly prepared to wage war. Congress had not seen much reason to build up the armed forces while the nation was neutral. The army was small and short of supplies. In 1916, Congress authorized a slight increase in manpower and equipment. Men volunteered, but nearly 3 million were drafted under the *Selective Service Act* of May 1917.

General **John J. Pershing** (1860-1948) began organizing, equipping, and training 42 divisions. Pershing and some administrative units of the **AEF** (American Expeditionary Force) arrived in Europe in June, only two months after the declaration of war.

Earlier in 1917, civil war and then revolutions in Russia forced the Tsar to abdicate. Russia surrendered to Germany and dropped out of the War just as America was coming into it.

With Russia out of the War, German commanders Hindenberg and Ludendorff shifted thousands of troops to the Western Front, severely pressing Britain and France. However, the United States had a substantial fighting force on European soil by the spring of 1918. The AEF helped to stop the German advances at St. Mihiel, Chateau-Thierry, and Belleau Wood. Near the end of the War, American troops suffered heavy casualties leading the Allied counteroffensive at Argonne Forest. America suffered 116,000 war deaths and 204,000 were wounded. All told, "the Great War" took 8.5 million lives worldwide, and twice as many were wounded. Germany surrendered as the Allies neared the German border in November 1918.

For those that did not serve in uniform, there were high-paying defense plant jobs. Women, immigrants, and African Americans easily found work. Because labor was in short supply and demand was high, wages rose. There were some strikes, but if they slowed the war effort, the strikers were arrested.

Domestic Opposition to the War

At home, the government kept socialists, communists, and anarchists under close surveillance during the War. Socialist-Labor Party leader Eugene Debs spoke out in protest against what Socialists called "the capitalist war" and was convicted under the *Espionage Act* and given a ten year prison sentence. (He was pardoned by President Harding in 1921.)

The Industrial Workers of the World (see Lesson 4) organized a number of strikes in important industries during the War, delaying government production schedules. IWW leader "Big Bill" Haywood, and over 100 other "Wobblies," received jail sentences of up to 20 years for hindering the war effort. **Emma Goldman**, an anarchist from Russia, opposed militarism and the use of force. She received a two year jail sentence for speaking out against the draft, and was later deported to Russia.

In *Schenck v. the United States* (1919), the Supreme Court upheld the government's treatment of war protesters. It said the government could suppress freedom of speech when there was a "clear and present danger" to the society.

A number of women's organizations opposed war in general and American entrance into the League of Nations in particular. Representative **Jeannette Rankin** (MT) voted against the declaration of war against Germany, and organized American Women Opposed to the League of Nations. Another group, the **Women's International League for Peace and Freedom** opposed the League of Nations because it still permitted war in certain cases. They also protested the use of income tax monies for military purposes.

THE PARIS PEACE NEGOTIATIONS

In 1919, the major powers gathered in Paris for an international peace conference. Wilson, Prime Minister **David Lloyd George** (Britain), Premier **Georges Clemenceau** (France), and Premier **Vittorio Orlando** (Italy) controlled the conference.

President Wilson hoped to negotiate a fair and just peace based on his *Fourteen Points*, but rivalries among the European nations stood in his way. He discovered that secret treaties had been made at the start of the War. Wilson got his idea of a League of Nations incorporated into the Treaty, but he could not get the other nations to adopt other points.

After several months, the *Treaty of Versailles* was completed. It dissolved the German, Austro-Hungarian, and Ottoman Empires. In the Treaty, the European powers required disarmament, huge **reparations** (financial payments for damages), and territory from Germany. Also, the League of Nations took over administration of Germany's colonies. Historians generally agree that Wilson did the best he could under the circumstances, at least in softening some of the Allies' more extreme demands.

☆ CAPSULE – GREAT RED SCARE: 1918-1919

World War I propaganda and fear made Americans suspicious of subversive activities. Intolerance spread to any group that reflected foreign influences (immigrants, Catholics, Jews, African Americans, radicals). The tension continued into the 1920s. In times of emotional stress, individual rights can be trampled.

One example of this tension was in labor relations. The post-war depression of 1919-1920 caused nearly 3,600 strikes. Workers became frustrated as state and federal courts issued orders arresting strike leaders and breaking the strikes.

Some radical labor leaders urged American workers to follow the lead of Russia. Lenin and the Bolsheviks had just taken power there and set up a communist state, later called the **Union of Soviet Socialist Republics** (U.S.S.R.). Many Americans were not sorry to see an end to the autocratic rule of the Tsar, but some believed that the Bolsheviks' next move would be in the United States.

In the spring of 1919, a series of terrorist bombings took place nationwide. Mail bombs were sent to such prominent individuals as J.P. Morgan, John D. Rockefeller, and Supreme Court Justice Oliver Wendell Holmes, Jr. Employers played on public fears. Some even blamed the small Communist and Socialist Parties in America for the disruptive strikes. While the threat of a communist takeover in America was remote, the hysteria of the **Red Scare** made it seem real. Newspapers blamed radicals for the country's turmoil. Some states passed "criminal syndicalism" laws, which made it unlawful to advocate violent change.

During the Great Red Scare, Wilson's Attorney General, A. Mitchell Palmer, launched raids on the headquarters of radical groups in 33 cities. In the **Palmer Raids**, over 3,000 people were rounded up. Many were held without bail and denied access to lawyers. Over 550 aliens among them were eventually deported.

The Granger Collection

The President knew the U.S. Senate had to ratify any treaty he signed in Paris. Yet, he had barely consulted with the Senate during the negotiations. The nation was weary of war and reform. There were Senators such as **William E. Borah** and **Henry Cabot Lodge**, who opposed the League of Nations. They said the people did not want any more involvement in Europe. They were espe-

cially opposed to American entrance into the League of Nations, which would require the United States to support the European members against acts of aggression.

Wilson stubbornly refused to compromise. He toured the country trying to get the people to put pressure on their Senators. Wilson suffered a stroke during the tour. It crippled the President for the rest of his life. The Senate took several votes on the Treaty, but in the end, the Senate rejected the *Treaty of Versailles*. Later, the United States signed separate peace treaties to end the War.

SEARCHING FOR PEACE AND ARMS CONTROL: 1919-1930

THE WASHINGTON NAVAL ARMS CONFERENCE

While rejecting participation in the League of Nations, U.S. leaders still wanted to avoid new wars. During the War, the United States and other nations embarked on costly shipbuilding programs. In 1920, the growing demands for disarmament, coupled with questions about colonies and mandates in the Pacific, led to support for a meeting of the great powers.

In 1921-1922, President Harding's Secretary of State, **Charles Evans Hughes** (1862-1948), sponsored the **Washington Conference on Naval Armaments** to address disarmament and peace issues. The U.S., Great Britain, Japan, France, and Italy produced a *Five Power Naval Armaments Treaty* (1922). It put a 10-year moratorium on the construction of major ships (10,000 tons or more – battleships, cruisers). It also limited the gross tonnage of these ships that each nation could maintain to a 5-5-3-1-1 ratio. No limits were placed on smaller ships (destroyers, subs), and Japan continued to build these at a rapid pace.

While there was no enforcement machinery for the *Five Power Treaty*, the spirit of the Washington Conference slowed the arms race – at least temporarily. Due to the expense of World War I, most nations did not have the resources to devote to military construction. To meet the tonnage limit, Britain and the U.S. even scuttled some existing ships and some under construction (66 and 30 respectively). In 1930, the Washington agreement was expanded to other classes of ships at the 1930 London Naval Conference, but the system fell apart with the rise of militarism later in the that turbulent decade.

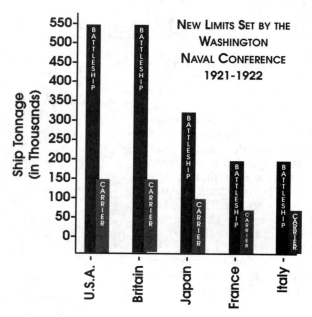

New Limits Set by the Washington Naval Conference 1921-1922

WAR DEBTS

Despite shunning the League, U.S. diplomats remained active in other areas in the 1920s. During the Great War, the United

States government had loaned the Allies over 10 billion dollars, and expected repayment after the War. High tariffs restricted trade during the 1920s, and foreign governments found it difficult to raise money. The United States extended payment time and lowered interest rates, but much of the debt was still outstanding in 1930. The American government still demanded payment in full, and eventually denied further loans to those still in arrears. No further payments were made, however, and the issue was eventually dropped as the Great Depression deepened.

KELLOGG–BRIAND PACT (1928)

In 1928, diplomats from the United States and France produced the *Kellogg-Briand Pact*. Over 60 nations pledged to outlaw war and settle disputes by peaceful methods. The *Pact* had the backing of the League of Nations, but like other agreements of this time, it had no enforcement apparatus and could not be implemented.

THE WORLD COURT

To settle international disputes, the League of Nations established an independent **World Court** in 1920. Presidents Harding and Coolidge supported U.S. membership but the Senate once again feared foreign entanglements. President Franklin Roosevelt tried again in the 1930s, but to no avail. By that time, the Senate reflected the deepening isolationist sentiments of the American public in the 1930s.

SUMMARY

America entered the 20th century bursting with a great industrial energy. Progressive reformers launched assaults on the abuses of big business and government corruption. They changed banking and trade, created safer and better working conditions, broadened voting rights, and even saw victory in controlling the use of alcohol. However, each new commercial regulation and government commission chipped away at laissez-faire.

America's new power was exerted overseas, too. It built its naval power, acquired colonies, and developed worldwide trade. World War I officially brought the United States into the realm of European power politics. Yet, the rejection of the *Treaty of Versailles* and the League of Nations showed that Americans were uncomfortable as a world power. The Red Scare showed a public suspicious of the Old World.

LESSON ASSESSMENT

MULTI-CHOICE

Directions: Base your answer to question 1 on the poem below and on your knowledge of social studies.

> Mary had a little lamb
> And when she saw it sicken
> She shipped it off to Packingtown
> And now it's labeled chicken.
>
> – New York newspaper, 1906

1 The author of this verse mostly likely supported
  1 the passage of laws restricting child labor
  2 a reduction in railroad rates
  3 consumer legislation
  4 compulsory school attendance

2 In the United States, the term "muckraker" has been used to describe authors whose writings deal mainly with
  1 criticizing the government's social welfare policies
  2 advancing socialistic policies
  3 publicizing constitutional issues dealing with minority rights
  4 exposing social conditions in need of reform

3 Progressives favored the direct election of Senators because the Progressives wanted
  1 political machines to become more powerful
  2 state legislatures to become more powerful
  3 the power of Congress to increase
  4 political corruption to lessen

4 A basic function of the Federal Reserve System is to
  1 increase the federal supply of gold
  2 increase federal revenue
  3 regulate the amount of money and bank credit available
  4 provide the nation with additional commercial banks

5 In the late 1890s and the early 1900s, the public became aware of the poor housing conditions and the economic distress of many immigrant urban dwellers through the
  1 writings of Harriet Beecher Stowe
  2 activities of the pacifist movement
  3 photographs of Jacob Riis
  4 campaign platform of the Know-Nothing Party

6   A major reason for the success of the Progressive movement is that its proposals
1   received support from both major political parties
2   focused on reforms in agriculture
3   avoided clashes with big business
4   concentrated solely on labor reform

7   The *Sherman Anti-Trust Act* and the *Clayton Anti-Trust Act* were both designed to
1   establish safe working conditions in factories
2   promote fair competition in business
3   force industry to use natural resources wisely
4   decrease federal income taxes on corporations

8   President Theodore Roosevelt's policy regarding big business was to
1   replace private ownership with public ownership
2   encourage a laissez-faire attitude toward business
3   support the deregulation of business
4   distinguish between "good" and "bad" trusts

9   In the early 20th century, a major goal of Robert M. LaFollette and other Progressives was to
1   start a civil rights movement for African Americans
2   increase opportunities for citizen participation in government
3   build support for imperialistic ventures in Latin America
4   bring recognition to American artists and authors

10 A graduated or progressive income tax is based on the idea that tax rates should
1   be the same for all individuals and businesses
2   be adjusted to achieve a balanced federal budget
3   rise as individual or business incomes rise
4   increase more rapidly for business profits than for personal incomes

11 Which action could the Federal Reserve System take to reduce the problem of recession?
1   lowering spending on social programs
2   lowering interest rates
3   raising tariffs on imports
4   raising federal income taxes

12 The national effort to ratify the women's suffrage amendment was strengthened by
1   the economic opportunities created by World War I
2   public outrage over corruption in the federal government
3   a backlash against the adoption of national Prohibition
4   active support from the nation's business leaders

Directions: Base your answer to question 13 on the cartoon at the right and on your knowledge of social studies.

13 The issue depicted in the cartoon was resolved later in the 20th century by
1 a Supreme Court decision
2 an act of Congress
3 a constitutional amendment
4 an executive order

14 At the end of the 19th century, a major objective of United States foreign policy was
1 continental expansion
2 breakup of the British Empire
3 development of an overseas empire
4 incorporation into the European balance of power

Directions: Base your answer to questions 15 and 16 on the speakers' statements below and on your knowledge of social studies.

SPEAKER A: These poor, uncivilized, unchristianized people need our assistance if they are to be uplifted from their ignorance to a point at least approaching our level of accomplishment.

SPEAKER B: These islands would certainly make excellent coaling stations for our great naval fleet which is growing each year as Congress approves additional funds for construction of new ships.

SPEAKER C: We threw off the yoke of British imperialism in 1783. What right have we, the great democratic republic of the modern world, to deny another people, halfway across the globe, of their sovereignty?

SPEAKER D: We have no alternative but to accept the Philippines as our own. God would not forgive us if we rejected his obvious faith and trust in our nation. Democracy must be carried to the four corners of the globe.

SPEAKER E: Were our economic rivals to obtain the Philippines, it would be a commercial disaster for our nation. We entered the race late, but we must not fall behind now.

15 Which two historical figures would be most in agreement with Speakers *A* and *B*?
   1 Andrew Carnegie and Mark Twain
   2 William McKinley and Theodore Roosevelt
   3 Jane Addams and Emma Goldman
   4 Samuel Gompers and Emilio Aguinaldo

16 Speaker *C* reflects the sentiments voiced by
   1 yellow journalists
   2 loose constructionists
   3 anti-imperialists
   4 protectionists

17 Which 1890s headline is the best example of "yellow journalism"?
   1 ***President Supports Child Labor Legislation***
   2 ***McKinley Asks Congress to Annex Hawaii***
   3 ***Populists Demand Graduated Income Tax***
   4 ***Spanish Authorities Butcher Innocent Cubans***

18 The main reason the United States developed the Open Door Policy was to
   1 allow the United States to expand its trade with China
   2 demonstrate the positive features of democracy to Chinese leaders
   3 aid the Boxer rebels in overthrowing the Chinese Empress
   4 encourage Chinese workers to come to the United States

Directions: Base your answer to question 19 on the map at the right and on your knowledge of social studies.

19 The situation shown in the map threatened the United States policy of
   1 manifest destiny
   2 intervention
   3 imperialism
   4 neutrality

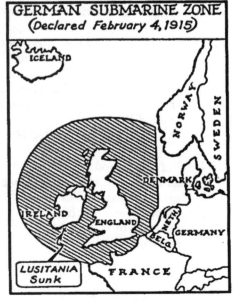

GERMAN SUBMARINE ZONE
(Declared February 4, 1915)

ICELAND
NORWAY
SWEDEN
DENMARK
IRELAND
ENGLAND
NETH.
BELG.
GERMANY
LUSITANIA Sunk
FRANCE

20 President Theodore Roosevelt's policies toward Latin America were
evidence of his belief in
1 non-involvement in world affairs
2 intervention where American interests were threatened
3 complete sovereignty for all nations
4 preserving European interests in the Western Hemisphere

21 Just prior to World War I, the nations of Europe believed that the
balance of power could best be maintained by
1 a system of alliances
2 an international court
3 increases in tariff barriers
4 open agreements, openly arrived at

22 The *Fourteen Points* proposed by President Wilson inspired hopes for
a fair settlement of World War I because this program called for
1 an agreement among nations to establish military alliances
2 the return of Europe to its pre-war political status
3 economic sanctions against the Central Powers so they would be
powerless to start another war
4 a world peace organization to guarantee political independence
for all nations

23 The "clear and present danger" ruling by the Supreme Court in
Schenck v. the United States (1919) confirmed the idea that
1 annexing foreign territory is unconstitutional
2 racism in the United States is illegal
3 interstate commerce must be regulated by state governments
4 constitutional rights are not absolute

24 Which factors were the major cause of the Red Scare and the Palmer
Raids that followed World War I?
1 the success of the Communist Party in congressional elections
2 the revival of the Ku Klux Klan and the passage of prohibition
3 the Bolshevik Revolution in Russia and terrorist bombings in the
United States
4 the failure of the United States to join the League of Nations

25 During the period between World War I and World War II, which
general theme was the strongest sentiment in U.S. foreign policy?
1 overseas expansion
2 global peacekeeping
3 militarism
4 isolationism

THEMATIC ESSAY

Directions: Write a well-organized essay that includes an introduction, several paragraphs explaining your position, and a conclusion.

Theme:

> **Foreign Policy Change**
>
> Nations design their foreign policies to protect and promote their vital interests. At the beginning of the 20th century, United States foreign policy underwent a number of significant changes.

Task:

> Using your knowledge of United States history and government, write an essay in which you
> * identify *two* (2) of the changes in U.S. foreign policy at the beginning of the 20th century
> * discuss the motivations and background for each change
> * explain how each change reflected the vital interests of the U.S. at that time

Suggestions:

You may use your knowledge of any of the changes in United States policy in the late 19th and early 20th centuries. Some suggestions you may wish to consider include: annexation of overseas colonies, expansion of trade, intervention in internal affairs of other nations, or involvement in international conflicts. **You are *not* limited to these suggestions**.

PRACTICE SKILLS FOR DBQ

Directions: The following task is based on the accompanying documents. The documents may have been edited for the purposes of this exercise. The task is designed to test your ability to work with historical documents. As you analyze the documents, take into account both the source of the documents and the author's point of view.

Historical Context:

During the late 19th and early 20th centuries, Americans began to take a closer look at the effects of the industrial system.

Part A – Short Answer

The documents that follow present different views of muckrakers. Examine each document carefully, then answer the scaffold question that follows it.

Document 1

"Perhaps no other single force was more responsible for the success of the progressive movement than the group of popular writers that emerged to write for the fast flourishing muckrake magazines. Nothing was too holy for their prying eyes, no institution too sacred for their debunking pens. If at times they bordered on the sensational, they at least exposed a picture of American politics and social conditions that had never before been revealed. The American public gasped with consternation and anger at what they saw."

– George Mowry, *Theodore Roosevelt and the Progressive Movement*, 1946

Question for Document 1

What role did these "popular writers" play in the Progressive Movement?

Document 2

"The muckrakers had much in common with the political cartoonists. Their villains made convenient, easily recognizable symbols. Evil could be personified as the Monster Trust, the Self-serving Politician...Such an approach...seldom got to the heart of social problems. In their indignant style muckrakers told Americans what was wrong with their society, but not how the problems arose nor what could be done...[Upton] Sinclair [in *The Jungle*] had pointed an accusing finger at the [meat]packers without offering any specific suggestions for cleaning up the meat industry."

– James Davidson and Mark Lytle, "USDA Government Inspected," *After the Fact*, 1986

Question for Document 2

What was a drawback or problem to the muckrakers' style of writing?

Part B – Essay Response

Task:

Using only the two documents, write one or two paragraphs explaining the role of muckrakers in the Progressive Movement (1900-1917).

State your thesis:

- use only the information in the documents to support your thesis position
- add your analysis of the documents
- incorporate your answers from the two Part *A* scaffold questions

_____

_____

_____

_____

Additional Suggested Task:

From your knowledge of United States history and government, make a list of additional examples of muckraker activity in the Progressive Reform Era.

_____

_____

_____

_____

_____

_____

_____

_____

_____

_____

_____

_____

_____

_____

_____

ECONOMY: PROSPERITY – THEN, THE GREAT DEPRESSION

Pre-WW II upper middle class vacationers motor to a summer resort in their 1937 GM Pontiac Sedan. (Retro-Americana, ©PhotoDisc)

ECONOMY: PROSPERITY – THEN, THE GREAT DEPRESSION

WAR ECONOMY AND PROSPERITY

The extreme economic fluctuations in the 1920s and 1930s were partly due to World War I devastation. In America, there was a short recession as industry converted to peacetime production – elsewhere it was longer. Then came a dizzying boom of prosperity in the 1920s, followed by the greatest collapse in modern history, and a long, anguished recovery, spurred by World War II production. Wars were not the only cause of the instability. It also resulted from actions and inactions of governments, business leaders, and private individuals. Out of the massive economic collapse that came in the 1930s, there arose dictatorships that plunged the world into the nightmare of the Second World War.

WAR ECONOMY

After declaring war in 1917, Congress granted President Woodrow Wilson the power to mobilize the American Expeditionary Force (AEF) to Europe. In the process, Congress temporarily converted the United States into a partial **command economy**.

The basic U.S. economic system is a **market economy**. In a market, the aggregate (total) decisions of businesses and consumers – supply and demand – give the economy its general direction. There is minimal governmental interference (laissez-faire). In a command economy, governmental authorities plan and make the basic economic decisions for the public.

GOVERNMENT BOARDS AND CONTROLS

During World War I, the United States government began to command substantial sectors of the economy under its wartime authority. Wilson created a **Council of National Defense**. The Council consisted of cabinet officers and civilian advisors who set up agencies to organize economic forces of the home front. To run the agencies, Wilson recruited experienced public servants such as **Herbert Hoover** and private sector leaders, such as Wall Street financier **Bernard Baruch** and AF of L president Samuel Gompers. The government commandeered the railroads and the shipping industries. News releases, posters, and slogans reminded the public that it was part of the war effort.

Under the *Selective Service Act* of 1917, Congress drafted nearly three million men by the end of the War. Congress also raised taxes and authorized bond drives to pay for the War. Of course, private businesses profited from supplying war matériel to the government. The chart below indicates the extent of the government's management of the American economy during World War I.

The combined effect of the draft and volunteer enlistment shrank the labor force. The labor shortage triggered a rise in wages (supply and demand). This increased the migration of African Americans to Northern manufacturing cities from the segregated South. Wartime industrial production absorbed nearly half a million African Americans.

Women filled some of the gaps in the ranks of labor, too. They worked in factories and at many other jobs previously reserved for men. With husbands being drafted, many married women entered the job market due to lack of family income.

As World War I drew to a close, nearly 3,600 strikes broke out nationwide. A wave of fear generated by radical labor groups made the situation worse. Radical political leaders urged American workers to follow the lead of the Bolsheviks who had just taken power in Russia. The rash of

U.S. Government Command During WW I	
Federal Agencies	**Economic Sectors Managed**
War Industries Board	allocated raw materials; supervised war production
War Labor Board	mediated labor disputes to prevent strikes
Shipping Board	built transports for men and materials
Railroad Administration	controlled and unified R.R. operations
Fuel Administration	increased production of coal, gas, and oil; Eliminated waste
Food Administration	increased farm output; public campaigns to conserve supplies
Raising Funds for the War effort	increased income and excise taxes; "Liberty Bond" and "Victory Bond" Drives

strikes plagued employers and played on public fears. Business leaders condemned all strikes as revolutionary, although most had simple economic goals of higher wages and better working conditions. These tense labor events led to the Great Red Scare and the Palmer Raids (see Lesson 5).

RECONVERSION 1918-1920

As the War ended, the government demobilized. It dropped its demand for war matériel. This caused a general **economic contraction** (decline). As the country went into this sharp depression (1919-1920), production cuts led to plant closings and widespread unemployment. Labor unions began a long series of bitter and sometimes violent strikes.

However, economic resources held back in the war economy were freed when the economy returned to a market structure. There were vast profits made during the War, and businessmen invested in response to civilian workers and returning servicemen cashing in war bonds and spending on homes, autos, and other consumer goods. Sending food and other goods to help Europeans rebuild their countries also stimulated demand. It took just over a year for all of this increased demand to pull the economy out of the post-war conversion depression.

THE ROARING TWENTIES

The conversion years of 1919 through 1921 were uneasy, anxious years. Americans entered the new decade disillusioned with world politics. Postwar depression made life hard. There was a terrifying influenza epidemic. Race riots plagued Chicago. Bombings and government raids against radicals, socialists, and anarchists heightened the tension.

Most Americans yearned to put the anxiety behind them. In the election campaign of 1920, Republican candidate Warren Harding voiced their yearning with his "return to normalcy" phrase. He tapped their desire to restore the American Dream – to seek personal satisfaction, material wealth, and a trouble-free life.

At home, Americans did their best to forget the War and the problems in Europe. Most people wanted to forget political affairs altogether and to enjoy the promise of American prosperity. They seemed to be rejecting Progressivism, Wilsonian idealism, and internationalism.

Harding - Change in Government

Inept but personable, Warren Harding did not see the presidency as pro-active in the way that Theodore Roosevelt and Woodrow Wilson had seen it. He was a passive chief executive, preferring to let Congress take political leadership. Lobbyists and special interest groups had easy access to Congress. They were able to gain influence with senators and representatives – and corruption increased.

Warren G. Harding
29th U.S. President
(White House)

In the White House, President Harding generously (and naively) gave jobs to cronies of the "Ohio Gang" – the political bosses that advised him. Having political hacks steer government agencies is a recipe for trouble. A number of unsavory scandals began to bubble. The scandals perplexed Harding. Just as the news of the scandals began to emerge, President Harding died from an embolism (blocked blood vessel) during a trip to Alaska in August 1923.

Consumerism

After the brief post-War economic contraction of 1919-1921, American business revived by taking advantage of new production and distribution ideas developed during the War. The focus shifted to the consumer market. Business improved on assembly-line patterns set up earlier in the century by Henry Ford. Electricity became more available as a result of expanded war production. It changed factory production (more economical and efficient power) and working hours (better lighting for night shifts). Mass advertising campaigns became widespread.

The Harding Scandals	
Scandal	**Details**
Teapot Dome	Secretary of the Interior Albert Fall and Navy Secretary Frank Denby accepted bribes for leasing government oil reserves in California and Wyoming to private oil companies.
Veterans Bureau	Veterans Bureau Director "Colonel" Charles Forbes (an army deserter) was convicted of taking cuts on hospital construction and mishandling funds for hospital supplies.
Alien Property	The Custodian of Alien Property was found guilty of conspiracy for selling captured German patents to chemical companies.
Justice Department	Attorney General Harry M. Daugherty – Harding's campaign manager – was dismissed when a Senate committee indicted him for illegal sale of liquor permits and criminal pardons.

☆ CAPSULE – THE AUTO REVOLUTION

Most symbolic of the mass consumer society was the automobile. In 1916, Congress authorized federal dollar for dollar matching of state expenditures for roads. In the 1920s, cheap cars became more and more available – Ford was asking $290 for the Model T by 1925. In 1920, there was one car registered for every thirteen Americans; by 1930, there was one for every six people.

1924 Chrysler
four-wheel hydraulic brakes

1922 Essex
first inexpensive sedan

The price was still expensive for the middle class. To keep the market alive, manufacturers and banks popularized credit-buying. With the **installment plan**, they made it easy for consumers to borrow for a high priced item and then make small payments (with interest) over a period of time. Sales boomed; registration of autos tripled.

The auto changed middle class life dramatically. As road construction advanced, many Americans saw in the auto a chance to have their families live away from the noise, congestion, and fast pace of the cities. The auto allowed people to commute to work and live a more peaceful life in the open spaces of **suburbia**. The auto triggered a suburban real estate boom by the

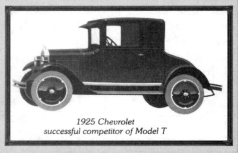

1925 Chevrolet
successful competitor of Model T

middle 1920s. Of course, low down payments and long-term mortgages fueled the speculative nature of this real estate boom. It became another staging ground for dishonest schemes.

THE REPUBLICAN PROSPERITY

In the 1920s, corporations streamlined their operations by mergers. Some mergers brought them into conflict with government anti-trust laws. However, Harding's administration tried to return to the laissez-faire attitude of the years before the Progressive Era. Government officials "looked the other way" when they should have been bringing anti-trust suits against many of these newly merged monopolies.

Calvin Coolidge
30th U.S. President
(White House)

(John) Calvin Coolidge (1872-1933) assumed the presidency on Harding's death in 1923. He believed firmly that business should control the leadership and prosperity of America. Harding's successor kept government out of the way of business as much as possible. Coolidge kept Harding's appointees to the Interstate Commerce Commission [ICC], the Federal Reserve Board, and Federal Trade Commission. They were laissez-faire men nominated by the "Ohio Gang" bosses that surrounded Harding. Even the Supreme Court announced that it would apply the "rule of reason" in anti-trust prosecutions. This meant the Court adopted a more lenient attitude toward business activities than it had in the Progressive Era.

Millionaire banker **Andrew Mellon** served as Secretary of the Treasury for both Harding and Coolidge. Mellon pressed the Republican-controlled Congress to stimulate business investment by reducing corporate taxes. Congress encouraged consumer spending by reducing personal income taxes.

Mellon also pressured Congress into passing enormously high protective tariffs (*Fordney-McCumber Act*, 1922 and the *Hawley-Smoot Act*, 1930). These acts were designed to shield American manufacturers from European competition as it recovered from the War. However, this protectionism backfired when the Europeans and Japanese reciprocated with their own high tariff duties against American goods.

THE SPECULATIVE BOOM AND SHALLOW PROSPERITY

Although the decade had a rocky start, Americans were optimistic throughout most of the 1920s. The increase in wealth was far less dramatic than commonly believed, but the optimism led many to blindly risk their life savings in stocks and real estate.

As a result, Wall Street boomed. Stock prices rose rapidly in the "Big Bull Market" of the Twenties. Many brokers accepted **margin** purchases (paying only a fraction of the stock's value). Some banks even allowed customers to borrow money just to buy the stocks on margin. Dummy corporations were even set up by stock brokers to buy and sell stocks to drive prices up artificially. The result of these schemes was highly overvalued stock prices. This artificially overinflated market floated on giddy optimism – much like today's bouts of "lottery fever."

At the time, there was no government oversight of the stock market. Unscrupulous characters set up deceptive stock schemes at will. Even with legitimate companies, real growth and productivity was nowhere near the prices of their stocks. People invested blindly, and the economy grew more unstable as the decade continued.

Corporations posted great gains – at least on paper. Investments seemed to be up, and technology did raise productivity. However, the prosperity had serious flaws. Workers were losing jobs to machines, and wages were stagnant. Middle class workers were supposed to be buying the cars, vacuum cleaners, washing machines, and toasters that corporations were churning out. Without increased wages, workers could not long sustain the level of consumer demand that manufacturers needed. After 1925, consumption slowly began tapering off, but investors did not heed the shrinking profit margins.

PROBLEMS ON THE FARM

Agriculture did not follow the pattern of industrial prosperity. During World War I, overseas demand for food created a boom for U.S. farmers. To feed our troops and allied forces, farmers mortgaged their farms to buy new machinery and greatly expanded production. After the War, American farmers continued to feed millions through the international relief effort headed by Herbert Hoover.

However, European farmers recovered by the mid-1920s. The overseas demand for U.S. agricultural products declined. American farmers still had to pay off machinery that they had purchased during the War. Their only recourse was to produce more, but the glut of production caused prices to drop as each new crop was harvested.

Even technology began to work against the farmers. Refrigeration and transportation improvements allowed larger farmers to compete in far-off markets. Smaller local farmers could not afford the improvements and began losing business. Congress kept tariffs high and many nations reciprocated with high tariffs of their own. This made it even harder for U.S. farmers to sell their surplus overseas. By the mid-1920s, farm bankruptcies became widespread.

©PhotoDisc

FEAR, EMOTION, AND BASIC RIGHTS

During World War I, propaganda and fear made Americans more suspicious of subversive activities. Intolerance against German sympathizers grew, but it also spread to any group that reflected foreign influences (immigrants, Catholics, Jews, African Americans, radicals). The fear and emotionalism of wartime continued in the economic and political turmoil of 1919-1920.

This anxiousness carried into the 1920s. The national mood was a strange blend of optimism, over confidence, and social uneasiness. There was excitement, but a subconscious discomfort as new inventions changed daily life at a rapid pace. Personal beliefs and long-held traditions were questioned. There was underlying social tension which showed itself in a variety of ways. In times of emotional stress, individual rights can be overlooked or ignored. In the 1920s, there were several disturbing examples of this.

- **Resurgence of the Ku Klux Klan (KKK)**
  A new version of the Klan (its predecessor had been outlawed in the South during Reconstruction) attracted thousands of Americans throughout the nation to its racist, anti-foreign teachings. The Klan was influential in pressuring Congress to pass a series of restrictive immigration acts. The tense years after World War I saw a renewal of the massive waves of immigrants. **Xenophobia** (emotion-ridden anti-foreign feeling) and anti-immigrant sentiment grew. Congress passed a series of restrictive acts in the 1920s, ending with the *National Origins Act* in 1929, which limited immigration with a prejudicial set of quotas aimed at restricting Southern and Eastern Europeans and Asians (see Lesson 4, page 146).

- **Sacco-Vanzetti Trial**
  Denial of due process and anti-immigrant sentiment were also issues in the trial of two Italian immigrants. Avowed anarchists, Sacco and Vanzetti were arrested by Massachusetts officials in 1925. They were tried for robbery and murder on weak, circumstantial evidence. By the time they were electrocuted in 1927, the case and its appeals had come to symbolize the atmosphere of repression in the country.

- **Scopes Monkey Trial**
  Also in 1925, the celebrated **Scopes Monkey Trial** focused the national spotlight on repression of ideas. In Tennessee, a young biology teacher was prosecuted for violating a state law forbidding the teaching of Darwin's theories of evolution. William Jennings Bryan successfully championed the views of fundamentalist groups trying to stop the teaching of evolution. Brilliant defense lawyer **Clarence Darrow** failed in his defense of the teacher. Later, the Supreme Court overturned Scopes' conviction and declared similar state laws unconstitutional (1968).

Prohibition: The Noble Experiment

The deep social divisions in the nation in the 1920s were also illustrated by passage of the **Prohibition Amendment** (the Eighteenth Amendment to the Constitution). For nearly a century, prohibitionists ("drys") campaigned against alcohol as a dangerous drug that de-

"Yes, it is a noble experiment."
Newspaper editorial cartoon depicting President Hoover's "Noble Experiment" – the prohibition of alcohol.

stroyed lives and disrupted families and communities. In 1846, they succeeded in getting the entire state of Maine to "go dry."

After the Civil War, groups such as the **Prohibition Party**, the **Womens' Christian Temperance Union**, and the **Anti-Saloon League** argued that it was the government's responsibility to free citizens from the temptation of drink by barring its sale and manufacture. They had spotty success in some counties and communities. Their campaign gained momentum in World War I with the need to conserve grain.

The Eighteenth Amendment was finally ratified in January 1919. Nine months later, Congress passed the *Volstead Act* to enforce the amendment. Prohibition cut the nation's alcohol consumption, but it also caused a substantial rise in crime. There were 300,000 convictions under the *Volstead Act*. Yet, **bootlegging** (illegal manufacture and transportation of alcoholic beverages), **speakeasies** (secret, illegal saloons), and **rum-running** (smuggling from Canada and Mexico) increased and became organized by criminals such as Chicago's Al Capone.

Prohibition became a major political issue of the 1920s. It tore the Democrats apart in the 1924 and 1928 presidential campaigns. Opponents of Prohibition ("wets") claimed government should not try to regulate social behavior. "Wets," such as New York's Governor and 1928 Democratic presidential candidate **Alfred E. Smith** (1873-1944), criticized the government for interfering with the citizen's personal choices. Even before the 1920s, there was no real agreement on what proper moral behavior was. However, in the rapidly changing society of the "Roaring Twenties," Prohibition slowly failed. Finally, in 1933, "the noble experiment" was repealed by the Twenty-first Amendment.

SHIFTING CULTURAL VALUES

In the 1920s, technology and science were rapidly transforming American culture. The genteel traditions of a rural, agrarian society fell away. A new, fast-paced urban society took hold.

A NEW GENERATION EMERGES

The younger generation was disillusioned by the bloody experience of the War in Europe. Young people seemed to openly reject the past and embrace the new life-style which placed material pleasure and personal wealth above patriotism or service to others. The rise of the entertainment industry, the popularity of the phonograph, the growth of night clubs, and the faster pace of ragtime and jazz music along with dances like the Charleston, showed a changing pace of life.

FEMALE EMANCIPATION

In the 1920s, a powerful combination of social factors broke down the old-fashioned Victorian ideals about the status of women. Broader educational opportunity for women gradually took hold in the industrial era. During the Great War, women put that education to use in playing new, vital economic roles. The Nineteenth Amendment – women's suffrage – gave them a new political status.

These changes in economic and political status created a feeling of female emancipation in the 1920s. Emancipation showed itself in new fashions: short skirts, slacks, and shorts. It also showed itself in the breakdown of old social restrictions: disappearance of chaperones, increasing participation in sports, and co-ed schools. The reevaluation of the role of women raised moral questions. It caused a more open discussion of sexual behavior, which often shocked and embarrassed the older generation. It changed thinking about marriage, and divorce rates rose in the 1920s.

NEW SOCIAL OUTLETS

In the 1920s, the middle class had more leisure time. Professional sports and the entertainment business grew in economic importance. Entertainment was no longer centered in the vaudeville theatres of the big cities. The film industry took movies into every town. By the decade's end, the "silents" gave way to "talkies." Over the air waves, radio shows aggressively promoted sponsors' products in nearly everyone's parlor.

At Last!
Six Tubes With One Control *Price* $140

Educational advances changed the publishing industry. Readership of newspapers and older popular magazines, such as *The Saturday Evening Post*, and *Colliers*, multiplied. Many new periodicals, including *Time*, *Newsweek*, *Reader's Digest*, *Life*, and *The New Yorker* flourished during the inter-war period.

The 1920s produced literature that reflected the unsettled mood of the times. Among the works portraying disillusion and frustration are those of novelists **F. Scott Fitzgerald** (*The Beautiful and the Damned*, *The Great Gatsby*), **Ernest Hemingway** (*The Sun Also Rises*), and **Sinclair Lewis** (*Main Street*, *Babbitt*), and poets and playwrights such as **T. S. Eliot** (*The Waste Land*) and **Eugene O'Neill** (*Emperor Jones*).

THE HARLEM RENAISSANCE

To escape the rigid Jim Crow segregation system of the South, many African-Americans moved north in the opening decades of the 20th century. In the freedom of the Jazz Age, a new cultural consciousness arose. African Americans wrote and sang in the 1920s, expressing their hopes and frustrations in the arts. The novels of **Langston Hughes** and **Jean Toomer**, along with the poetry of **Claude McKay** and **Countee Cullen**, and the music of **Duke Ellington**, **Louis Armstrong**, and **Bessie Smith** emerged from a movement known as the Harlem Renaissance.

THE GREAT DEPRESSION

ONSET OF THE DEPRESSION

To many Americans, the 1920s seemed like a golden age. The ideal of the "American Dream" seemed to have become a reality. However, by the end of the decade, there were plenty of warning signs of weakness.

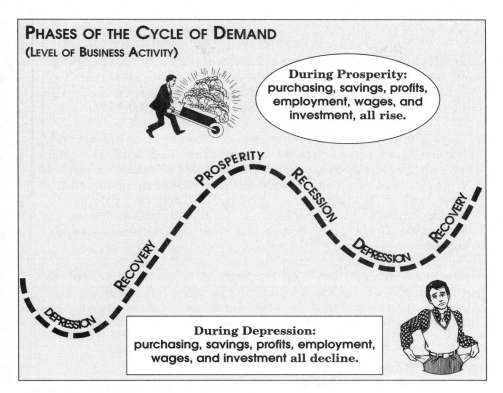

PHASES OF THE CYCLE OF DEMAND
(LEVEL OF BUSINESS ACTIVITY)

During Prosperity: purchasing, savings, profits, employment, wages, and investment, all rise.

PROSPERITY

RECESSION

RECOVERY

DEPRESSION

RECOVERY

DEPRESSION

During Depression: purchasing, savings, profits, employment, wages, and investment all decline.

WEAKNESSES IN THE ECONOMY

A large and diverse market economy naturally has ups and downs. Demand for goods and services, savings, investments, and employment are always changing. They can never be perfectly in line in a system that allows freedom of choice. Combinations of hundreds of factors cause the economy to soar at times and decline in others. The slightest change can cause chain reactions. The illustration above is a graphic representation of this **cycle of demand**, or what economists used to call the "business cycle."

Once the United States became industrialized and less agrarian, most Americans became painfully aware of the cycle of demand. In the late 19th and early 20th centuries, there were numerous recessions and several serious depressions – but the collapse of 1929-1932 was very different. It was much worse than ever before. Economists debate many reasons for this, but most of them accept the following as the key reasons.

- **Distribution of Wealth** – During the Twenties, the wealth flowed into the hands of only 5-10% of the population. American manufacturers overproduced massive amounts of goods. As the years went by, the number of people who could afford to buy goods actually declined.

The number of those who could consider themselves middle class stagnated.

- **Decline in Income** – Wages did not kept pace with the rising GNP (Gross National Product). Farmers, miners, and textile workers' incomes declined after the mid-1920s. Consumer purchasing began to slow. The number of poor Americans grew rapidly after 1925.

- **High Tariffs** – To make matters worse, after the stock market crash, businessmen's fear pressured Congress into raising tariffs even higher with the *Hawley-Smoot Act* (1930). It sealed off American markets from other nations. The other nations reciprocated by raising their own tariffs. U.S. trade declined. Without U.S. dollars circulating, buying American goods and paying debts to U.S. bankers became impossible. World trade dried up, and other national economies collapsed.

- **Government Inaction** – Government saw some of the signs of economic slowdown, but the Coolidge and Hoover administrations refused to tamper with income taxes and interest rates. The regulatory power acquired in the Progressive Era was not used actively.

THE STOCK MARKET CRASH

In the early and middle 1920s, businesses showed enormous profits. People rushed to buy shares in the "bull market" (rising stock prices). In the fall of 1929, business declines caused public confidence to falter. Edgy stockholders began to sell shares rapidly. The "bear market" (falling stock prices) accelerated down. Slimly financed "margin loans" for stocks were called in by brokers. Many investors could not pay. The wave of selling turned into a panic. The economy collapsed so rapidly – and completely – that it left the nation and the world in a state of shock.

Police stand guard outside New York's closed World Exchange Bank, 20 March 1931
–Herbert Hoover Presidential Library and Museum

Thirty-first President of the United States,
Herbert Hoover
– White House Historical Association

THE HOOVER RESPONSE

President **Herbert Hoover** (1874-1964) was a businessman and one of the most talented public administrators ever to be elected to the White House. After just seven months, his administration had to struggle with the worst economic catastrophe in history.

Like Harding and Coolidge, President Hoover believed in laissez-faire. He and his advisors felt the economy could repair itself as it had in the past. They did not want to start federal programs that took power from state and local governments. They thought that federal government interference destroyed individual freedom. At first, Hoover did little. He held White House conferences with business leaders. He encouraged them to increase production and raise wages, but little came of these meetings.

While there had never been a downturn such as this one, it became apparent to the press and the public that President Hoover's efforts were not aggressive enough. The economy spiraled downward. In 1932, the

HOOVER'S APPROACH TO THE GREAT DEPRESSION
• used White House conferences with business leaders to encourage increased production and wage hikes
• authorized some government spending to relieve suffering
• increased federal building projects to push some money into the economy
• suspended World War I debt payments to the U.S. by European nations
• set up the Reconstruction Finance Corporation (RFC) to give low-interest federal loans to save businesses from bankruptcy
• created the Federal Home Loan Bank to give low-interest federal loans to boost construction and decrease foreclosures

GNP was half of what it was in 1920. More than 5,000 banks had closed. Wages and prices continued to fall, and unemployment rose by nearly 20 percent.

Other groups began taking action. States and cities set up soup kitchens to feed the growing numbers of poor. However, with people out of work, the tax revenues of states and local governments shrank. They had no resources for welfare programs. They looked to the federal government for assistance, but little came.

LABOR FORCE AND UNEMPLOYMENT: 1929-1941 (NUMBERS IN MILLIONS)			
YEAR	LABOR FORCE	NUMBER UNEMPLOYED	PERCENT UNEMPLOYED
1929	49.2	1.6	3.2
1930	49.8	4.3	8.7
1931	50.4	8.0	15.9
1932	51.0	12.1	23.6
1933	51.6	12.8	24.9
1934	52.2	11.3	21.7
1935	52.9	10.6	20.1
1936	53.4	9.0	16.9
1937	54.0	7.7	14.3
1938	54.6	10.4	19.0
1939	55.2	9.5	17.2
1940	55.6	8.1	14.6
1941	55.9	5.6	9.9

Source: U.S. Dept of Commerce: Historical Statistics of the U.S.

Bewildered and shocked by the economic collapse, most people only half-heartedly expected government to act. With laissez-faire as the government's guiding principle, there had never been a tradition of large-scale government intervention. However, by 1932, people were clearly expecting more decisive leadership.

In June of 1932, destitute veterans sought a bonus promised to them by Congress. A veterans' **Bonus Army** demonstrated in Washington. Congress defeated the bonus bill. Hoover called out U.S. Army troops to disperse the veterans with bayonets and tear gas. It was a bad decision. The public was outraged.

Later that summer, as the Republicans were renominating Hoover, farmers tried to organize a general strike. Their attempt to withhold their produce to drive prices up collapsed in disillusion. Desperation was growing, and the people began to see Hoover's leadership as too timid.

FDR AND THE NEW DEAL:
RELIEF, RECOVERY, AND REFORM

In November, Hoover was soundly defeated at the polls. The nation elected the Democratic Governor of New York, **Franklin Delano Roosevelt**. In a **landslide vote** (overwhelming victory), "FDR," as the press began calling him during the campaign, won 59% of the popular votes and 88% of the electoral vote (472 to 59).

Franklin Roosevelt (1882-1945) was born to wealth at his family's estate in Hyde Park, NY. In his youth, he was attracted to the Progressive Movement because of his concern for human suffering. He won a seat in the New York State Senate in 1910, and President Wilson named him Assistant Secretary of the Navy in 1913. As a rising star in the Democratic Party, Roosevelt ran for vice-president on the Democratic ticket with James M. Cox in 1920. A year later, he was tragically paralyzed with polio and never regained the use of his legs. In 1928, he narrowly won election as Governor of New York to succeed his friend and mentor, Al Smith. As governor, FDR's willingness to try programs to help people cope with the Depression gave him national recognition.

THE NEW DEAL PHILOSOPHY

In the fall of 1932, Governor Roosevelt launched a vigorous campaign. He criticized Hoover's lack of action. Roosevelt was vague about his own programs, but he spoke of a different philosophy of government's role in the economy. He claimed that Hoover and the Republicans followed a "trickle-down theory." He claimed they believed in working from the top downward. He said they reasoned that, if government legislation protected the wealth of big corporations and the well-to-do, their continued investments would expand the economy and a better life would "trickle down" to workers and consumers in general.

Roosevelt and his advisors claimed a different view. They felt that government should use **pump-priming**: that government should take actions that would make the consuming public secure and optimistic. They believed in working from the bottom up – if government programs could increase consumer spending (demand), it would then generate business activity, foster confidence and investment, and keep the economy growing. Later, this idea would become part of a more complex formal theory of **demand management** in British economist **John Maynard Keynes'** (1883-1946) *General Theory on Employment, Interest, and Money* (1936). It challenged the classical approach to market economics and advocated an activist role for government.

FDR's APPROACH TO THE GREAT DEPRESSION: THE NEW DEAL'S "THREE Rs"
• **Relief**: actions to stop economic decline
• **Recovery**: actions to restart consumer demand
• **Reform**: actions to prevent additional serious economic decline

Action	Reason
Federal Emergency Relief Administration (1933)	gave federal money to states to help unemployed and poor
Civil Works Administration (1933)	gave the unemployed work on federal, state, and municipal road and clean-up projects
Agricultural Adjustment Administration (1933)	restored farmers purchasing power; paid farmers to reduce surplus production to raise prices
National Industrial Recovery Administration (1933)	set up plans for businesses on wages, prices, and working hours
Civilian Conservation Corps (1933)	environmental projects gave work to 16-30 year-olds
Federal Deposit Insurance Corporation (1933)	provided deposit insurance; made people confident in banks
Securities and Exchange Commission (1934)	regulated the trading of stocks and bonds
Social Security Administration (1935)	provided government pensions for older people
National Labor Relations Act (1935)	(Wagner Act) guaranteed workers collective bargaining process
Fair Labor Standards Act (1938)	set up a minimum wage of 40 cents/hour and controlled child labor

PERMANENT CHANGE

Amid the whirlwind of New Deal legislation, Roosevelt also led Congress to seek permanent reform of the economic system. The changes made life more secure and helped avoid many of the situations that had caused the Great Depression (see chart on page 218).

THE NEW DEAL OPPOSITION

Not everyone appreciated all the New Deal activity. For one thing, Roosevelt unbalanced the government's budget by **deficit spending** (spending more money than the government took in from taxes and tariffs). New Deal supporters hoped that a boost in income from programs such as the Civil Works Administration and Civilian Conservation Corps would "jump start" business activity and economic recovery.

Critics of the New Deal pointed out that with each step the government takes into the economy, some individual economic freedom is lost. Each program had a cost, government debt grew, and the taxpayer had to

---

☆ CAPSULE – NEW DEAL REFORMS

Banking

The *Glass-Steagall Banking Act* (1933) created the Federal Deposit Insurance Corporation (FDIC) to insure depositors against bank failures. It also required banks to undergo frequent examinations of their operations. The Federal Reserve Bank received more power to oversee banking in general.

Financial Structures

The Securities and Exchange Commission (SEC) was created to watch over the stock market.

Each depositor insured to $100,000

FDIC

FEDERAL DEPOSIT INSURANCE CORPORATION

Income Security

Based on earlier Progressive Era ideas and on the examples already adopted by many European nations, the *Social Security Act* (1935) created a system of insurance to assist people in coping with the loss of income due to old-age, unemployment, and physical handicaps.

Workers' Rights

The *Fair Labor Standards Act* (1938) secured reasonable working hours, basic conditions of safety, and a federal minimum wage. The *National Labor Relations Act* (or *Wagner Act*, 1935) established workers' rights to organize as a group to negotiate with employers (collective bargaining) and authorized the National Labor Relations Board to investigate contract labor problems and offer mediation of disputes.

CRITICISMS OF THE NEW DEAL

- growth in federal spending to finance the New Deal
- growth in federal debt to finance the New Deal unbalanced the budget
- growth of the federal bureaucracy – agencies and their staffs
- stretching of legislative and executive power

pay that debt. Critics were angry as government grew and the old idea of laissez-faire declined. They labeled the government programs "FDR's creeping socialism."

Opponents of the New Deal programs immediately launched legal challenges. By 1935, the Supreme Court was declaring key laws unconstitutional. The Court said that Congress had stretched its power over interstate commerce too far. It struck down the *Agricultural Adjustment Act (AAA)* in **United States v. Butler**, and the *National Industrial Recovery Act (NIRA)* in **Schechter Poultry Corp. v. United States**. The Court also ruled that New Deal laws on pensions, bankruptcy, and the minimum wage were questionable.

In the middle of the New Deal, conservative businessmen formed the American Liberty League to raise funds for conservative candidates. It was the main backing for Kansas Governor **Alf Landon** (1887-1987), the Republican Party's Presidential candidate in 1936. Landon won 17 million popular votes to FDR's 28 million, but he won only 8 electoral votes (2 states) to FDR's 523.

After his landslide re-election in 1936, FDR tried to make the Supreme Court friendlier to his programs. In his **Court Packing Plan**, Roosevelt proposed that Congress pass a law that would enable him to name additional federal judges for those over 70 years old who refused retirement. The Plan received nationwide criticism as attacking the principle of checks and balances. Congress rejected the Plan and FDR suffered his most devastating political defeat.

Opponents also denounced Roosevelt's decision to run for a third term in 1940. The action broke a precedent set 150 years before by George Washington. According to the Constitution, there was no limit on the number of presidential terms, but two terms had become a tradition and a part of the "unwritten constitution." Critics said FDR was undermining the constitutional principle of limited power. (In 1951, the *22nd Amendment* to the Constitution was adopted to limit presidents to two terms.)

⭐ CAPSULE – THE NEW DEAL AND SOCIETY

Group	Status
African Americans	• No action on discrimination in housing and jobs. In 1932, they made up nearly 20% of the unemployed. • Democratic leadership cautious on racial matters. Segregation was still strong in the North and the South. Southern legislators held key positions in Congress, and the success of the New Deal was largely in their hands. • **Works Progress Administration (WPA)** did have nondiscrimination clauses in its hiring regulations, but still by 1935, three times as many African Americans were on relief as whites. • African American leaders included: **A. Philip Randolph, Ralph Bunche, Robert Weaver**, and **Mary McLeod Bethune**, a director of the National Youth Administration.
Native Americans	• The ***Indian Reorganization Act*** (*Wheeler Act*, 1934) gave them greater control over their lands, and improved educational opportunities for their youth. • A special bureau was also created for reservation work under the Civilian Conservation Corps.
Women	• Women were brought into FDR's administration. Secretary of Labor **Frances Perkins** became the first female cabinet officer, and women were also appointed to judgeships and foreign service posts. • First Lady **Eleanor Roosevelt** used her considerable influence with the president, and her syndicated daily news column, "My Day," to press for more equal treatment for women under New Deal programs.

President Roosevelt's early cabinet. Frances Perkins is standing at far right.
Source: SSA History Archives

THE DUST BOWL

Farmers in general were suffering financially long before the collapse of 1929, but in 1932, nature turned tragically against them. A devastating drought that lasted more than four years in some areas hit the mid-section of the nation from Texas, Arkansas, and Oklahoma to the Dakotas. In the area which became nicknamed "the Dust Bowl," winds picked up the parched soil, and destitute farmers watched helplessly as it blew their fortunes away.

A million or more "Oakies" and "Arkies" packed up their families and possessions and hit the roads. These refugees from the Oklahoma and Arkansas Dust Bowl sought work in the agricultural regions of the West Coast. They often found rejection by western townspeople who feared their economic competition. John Steinbeck (1902-1968) wrote sympathetically about the tragedy in his classic novel, *The Grapes of Wrath*.

THE CULTURE OF THE DEPRESSION

The New Deal made a contribution to American cultural life. Programs were designed to assist creative artists. The Works Progress Administration (WPA) created theater and art projects. Artists worked on building murals and illustrations for federal publications. Dramatists and choreographers created new works that were performed throughout the nation under the **Federal Theater Project**. The WPA also supervised oral history projects, helping to preserve regional folklore. The New Deal also created a dramatic photographic record of rural life in the 1930s through the artistry of **Dorothea Lange** and **Walker Evans**.

Dorothea Lange Photo
"Depression Mother" Library of Congress

Entertainment in the 1930s reflected a desire for escapism. Hollywood films and daily radio shows catered to this desire and both experienced a golden era. Americans flocked to the movies to escape the Depression, watching Fred Astair and Ginger Rogers in glamorous formal wear dancing their cares away, or Dorothy (Judy Garland) flying over the rainbow in the *Wizard of Oz*, or Scarlett O'Hara and Rhett Butler (Vivian Leigh and Clark Gable) facing the problems of the Civil War South in *Gone with the Wind*. At home, they escaped from their dismal times with the comedy of George Burns and Gracie Allen, the music of Bing Crosby, melodramas, such as *Lights Out* and *Suspense*, or the many soap operas (*The Guiding Light*; *Ma Perkins*) that filled the airwaves.

POLITICAL EXTREMISM

In the troubled atmosphere of the 1930s, many groups gained popularity by trying to radically change the American system.

- **Communists** – The appeal of communism declined after the Red Scare of 1919. The economic breakdown of the Depression made the Communist Party of the U.S. especially attractive to intellectuals. However, leaders such as **William Z. Foster** and **Earl Browder** were loyal to international policies directed by the U.S.S.R. Their constant talk of radical revolution alienated many from the communist movement.

- **Socialists** – Socialist Party leader **Norman Thomas** criticized FDR for being too timid in using government to help the working class

- **Fascists** – Militant groups also emerged, promoting the type of dictatorial system that seemed to be working in Italy and Germany.

- **Other critics** – There were also antagonists that criticized the government for not doing enough. Doctor **Francis Townsend** led an old folks crusade for larger pensions and health care for the elderly. Louisiana's Senator **Huey Long** wanted more social programs and welfare aid for the poor and the farmer. The broadcasts of the "Radio Priest," **Fr. Charles Coughlin**, called for more socialist programs. Reaching back to the 19th century's Greenback Party platform, he suggested that the government print and distribute more money (intentional inflation). Coughlin wanted government to take over the banks as some European governments were doing.

SUMMARY

By 1938, the New Deal was losing momentum. At that point, the economy was inching upward, and government attention was being drawn to foreign events. Historians still argue about whether the New Deal was a success. Supporters feel that the New Deal had several positive impacts on American life.

- It preserved the free enterprise system by remodeling its weakest parts.

- It forged a new connection between the individual and government.

- It established the role of government as stimulater of economy.

LESSON ASSESSMENT

MULTI-CHOICE

1 During World War I, railroads were
    1 forced to operate at huge losses
    2 plagued by frequent strikes
    3 run by government agencies
    4 replaced by the trucking industry

2 In the election of 1920, Warren Harding's idea of a "return to normalcy" appealed to the voters' mood because they wanted
    1 a new reform movement in politics
    2 an end to frequent government scandals
    3 to play an influential new role in world affairs
    4 to pursue the "American Dream"

3 The economic boom and the financial speculation of the 1920s was caused in part by
    1 installment buying and an unregulated stock market
    2 the expansion of civil rights to women and minorities
    3 the mobilization of the economy for war
    4 increased government restrictions on big business

4 Reciprocation by Europe and Japan to high U.S. tariff policies resulted in
    1 lower prices on imported goods
    2 higher wages for most American workers
    3 declines in American exports
    4 increased consumption by the middle class

5 In the 1920s, the *Immigration Act* of 1924 and the Sacco-Vanzetti trial were typical of the
    1 rejection of traditional customs and beliefs
    2 increase in nativism and intolerance
    3 acceptance of cultural differences
    4 support of humanitarian causes

6 In the rapidly changing society of the 1920s, Prohibition slowly failed because
    1 isolationism cut down in the desire for imported products
    2 government enforcement of the *Volstead Act* was too strict
    3 political parties did not wish to take positions on temperance
    4 there was disagreement on proper standards of moral behavior

7 Which was an immediate effect of the accelerated use of new production techniques during the period from 1917-1929?
    1 a loss of commitment to the traditional work ethic
    2 a flood of consumer products on the market
    3 an increase in the rate of unemployment
    4 a sharp decline in business products

8   A condition of the 1920s that helped cause the Great Depression of
    the 1930s was
    1   over-speculation in Western lands
    2   over-dependence on foreign trade
    3   overproduction of goods by factories and farms
    4   overspending on social programs by the government

9   A characteristic of United States immigration laws passed during
    the 1920s is that they
    1   permitted unlimited immigration
    2   favored immigration from Eastern Europe
    3   prohibited immigration from the Western Hemisphere
    4   were more restrictive than prior laws

10 The growth of the automobile industry after World War I changed
    the United States economy by
    1   stimulating development of other new industries
    2   decreasing employment opportunities for assembly-line workers
    3   increasing the number of railroad passengers
    4   encouraging government operation of major industries

Directions: Base your answer to question 11 on the cartoon at the right and on your knowledge of social studies.

11 What is the main idea of the cartoon?
    1   Congress and the President were unable to cope with the Depression.
    2   The President and Congress constantly fought over Depression Era programs.
    3   President Franklin D. Roosevelt used a system of trial and error to improve the economy.
    4   President Franklin D. Roosevelt consistently adopted the Depression remedies proposed by Congress.

12 Because of the "Bonus Army" episode in 1932, President Hoover
1   lost public confidence
2   began to try new approaches to the economic crisis
3   suspended war debt payments for European nations
4   increased military spending to stimulate the economy

13 The power of labor unions increased during the New Deal mainly because
1   a new spirit of cooperation existed between employers and government
2   a shortage of skilled and unskilled laborers developed
3   management changed its attitude toward organized labor
4   federal legislation guaranteed labor's right to organize and bargain collectively

14 An immediate result of the Supreme Court decisions in *Schechter Poultry Corporation v. United States* (1935) and *United States v. Butler* (1936) was that
1   some aspects of the New Deal were declared unconstitutional
2   State governments took over relief agencies
3   Congress was forced to abandon efforts to improve the economy
4   the constitutional authority of the President was greatly expanded

Base your answer to question 15 on the cartoon at the right and your knowledge of U.S. history and government.

15 The main idea of the cartoon is that the passage of Social Security legislation would result in
1   the end of the free enterprise system
2   the bankruptcy of the federal government
3   a loss of individual identity
4   large-scale unemployment

16 Two important New Deal measures that were declared unconstitutional were the
1 Civilian Conservation Corps and the Works Progress Administration
2 *National Industrial Recovery Act* and the *Agricultural Adjustment Act*
3 *Fair Labor Standards Act* and the *National Labor Relations Act*
4 *Social Security Act* and the Home Owners Loan Corporation

17 The Works Progress Administration (WPA) embodied both the relief and recovery ideas of the New Deal, because it
1 hired the unemployed and stimulated purchasing
2 promoted the creative arts
3 restored public buildings
4 set production quotas for industry

18 The popularity of escapist novels and movies during the Great Depression is evidence that
1 the greatest number of jobs in the 1930s were in the entertainment field
2 American society did not try to solve the problems of the Great Depression
3 the Great Depression was not really a time of economic distress
4 popular culture is shaped by economic and social conditions

19 The New Deal confirmed a change in American political thinking because it advanced the principle that
1 a public office is a public trust
2 government intervention in business should be kept to a minimum
3 the government should play a significant role in solving social problems
4 the U.S. should not become involved in solving the problems of other nations

20 A major long-term result of the New Deal was that
1 state governments increased their power of taxation
2 the government established a "safety net" to protect the poor
3 the executive branch gave up much of its decision making power to Congress
4 Congress was required to balance the federal budget before instituting new programs

THEMATIC ESSAY QUESTION

Directions: Write a well-organized essay that includes an introduction, several paragraphs explaining your position, and a conclusion.

Theme:

> ### Altering the Quality of Life
>
> Actions by the federal government in the period between the two world wars had differing effects on groups in the society.

Task:

> Using your knowledge of United States history and government, write an essay in which you choose *three* (3) groups in American society between the two world wars. For *each* one chosen:
> • describe the existing economic, social, or political conditions experienced by the group, and
> • discuss the impact of a federal government action on the group.

Suggestions:

You may wish to focus on radical labor organizers, immigrants, farmers, Native Americans, industrial workers, women, bankers. **You are not limited to these suggestions.**

PRACTICE FOR DOCUMENT BASED QUESTION:

Directions:

The following task is based on the accompanying documents. The documents may have been edited for the purposes of this exercise. The task is designed to test your ability to work with historical documents. As you analyze the documents, take into account both the source of the document and the author's point of view.

Historical Context:

During the 1930s, the federal government's activities broke with long standing economic principles.

Part A – Short Answer

Analyze the documents and answer the questions that follow each document.

Document 1

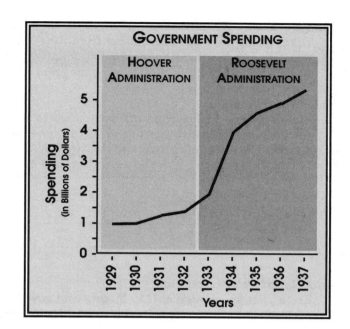

Question for Document 1

What change is taking place in government spending from 1929 to 1937?

Document 2

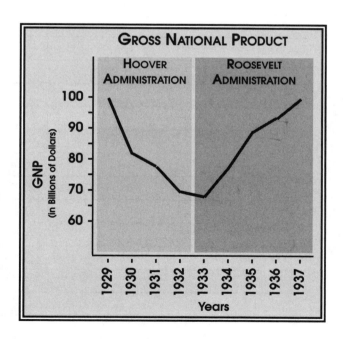

Question for Document 2

How do the GNP figures for the Hoover Administration differ from those for the early Roosevelt Administration?

Part B – Essay Response

Task: Using only the information from the documents, write a one or two paragraph discussion of why President Franklin D. Roosevelt's actions broke with past practices of the federal government.

State your thesis:
- use only evidence from the documents to support your response.
- add your personal analysis of the documents.
- incorporate your answers to the two Part A scaffold questions.

_____

_____

_____

_____

Additional Suggested Task:

From your knowledge of U.S. history and government, make a list of additional ways the New Deal broke with past practices of the federal government.

_____

_____

_____

_____

_____

_____

_____

_____

_____

_____

_____

_____

_____

_____

_____

NAZIS COME TO POWER (1933)
GOOD NEIGHBOR POLICY (1933)
U.S. RECOGNIZES U.S.S.R. (1933)

1935-

U.S. NEUTRALITY ACTS (1936-1939)

THE
UNITED STATES
IN AN AGE OF
GLOBAL CRISIS

AXIS PACT (1939)
WW II IN EUROPE (1939)

1940- **DESTROYERS FOR BASES** (1940)
ATLANTIC CHARTER (1941)
LEND-LEASE (1941)
U.S. ENTERS WW II (1941)

RATIONING (1942)

D-DAY (1944)

1945- **YALTA CONFERENCE** (1945)
HIROSHIMA (1945)
WW II ENDS (1945)

TRUMAN DOCTRINE (1947)

FAIR DEAL (1948)
MARSHALL PLAN (1948)
BERLIN AIRLIFT (1948-1949)

NATO (1949)

1950-

McCARTHY ERA (1950-1954)

On 9 August 1945, the United States dropped the 2nd Atomic Bomb of the War, "Fat Man." The photo is of the mushroom cloud as it rose over Nagasaki where 75,000 died from the bomb.
– U.S Air Force Photo

IN AN AGE OF GLOBAL CRISIS
RESPONSIBILITY AND COOPERATION

PEACE IN PERIL
(1933-1950)

ISOLATION AND NEUTRALITY

The Great Depression destroyed a very fragile structure of peace set up at Versailles in 1919 and world conferences in the 1920s. Peace depended on the smooth operation of the major nations' economies. The chaos, bitterness, and disillusionment of the Depression destroyed that delicate balance.

The enormous war debt and war reparations that Germany had to pay to Britain and France left its economy in shambles in the 1920s. The chaos of the economic collapse of the U.S. in 1929 surged outward like a tidal wave and shattered the German economy and others completely. Into the disarray in Germany stepped **Adolf Hitler** and the National Socialist Party (Nazis). A fringe minority up to this time, the chaos of the Depression gave the Nazis a new platform to insinuate themselves into power in 1933. They replaced a struggling parliamentary democracy with **fascism** – a system of government marked by centralization of authority under a dictator. It usually has stringent socioeconomic controls, suppression of the opposition through terror and censorship, and often a policy of belligerent nationalism and racism.

Italian Fascist leader Benito Mussolini and German Fuehrer Adolf Hitler parade together in Munich, 18 June 1940.   Photo credit: U.S. National Archives

Italy had turned to a fascist structure in the early 1920s. It concentrated economic power in state-directed arrangements under dictator **Benito Mussolini**. The aggressive tone and military buildup of these fascist regimes undermined the flimsy international peace structure.

After rejecting the *Treaty of Versailles* and League of Nations membership in 1919, American foreign policy followed a zig-zag course. Harding, Coolidge, and Hoover refused to commit any military power to peace-keeping. This stance reflected the anti-immigration and high tariff policies so characteristic of the anti-foreign mood of the 1920s.

In the 1920s and 1930s, many Americans felt comfortable with **isolationism**. They were fond of quoting Washington's *Farewell Address* (1796) in which the hallowed warnings of the first president deprecated foreign alliances. From then to Wilson's neutral stance throughout most of World War I, the advice of Washington appeared to have become a cornerstone of American policy. Isolationists also cited the *Monroe Doctrine* (1823). While it warned Europe to stop colonization of the Western Hemisphere, it also indicated a national disdain for involvement in European intrigues.

> "It is our true policy to steer clear of permanent alliances with any portion of the foreign world."
> – George Washington, *Farewell Address*, 1796

The isolationists' oversimplified view of the world was strengthened by the fact that in the 1930s, the two oceans still afforded reasonable protection. Japan's aggression in Manchuria in 1931, and similar moves by Italy and Germany in the mid-1930s, added even more strength to the isolationists' position that global involvement was a serious mistake.

Isolationists also pointed to the failure of the 1932-1934 **Geneva Disarmament Conference** and the *Nye Committee Report* to bolster their arguments. President Hoover had been enthusiastic about the disarmament conference, and FDR supported it, but it failed especially after Hitler began to rearm Germany. In 1935, North Dakota's Senator Gerald Nye released a report on his controversial "merchants of death investigation." The Nye Report claimed that U.S. bankers and manufacturers, seeking war profits in 1915-17, had effectively undermined President Wilson's neutrality position. Senator Nye found many financial arrangements had existed, but he found no evidence to connect them to government policies. However, the isolationist press ignored the lack of evidence. Their news articles led many Americans to conclude that the arms business had pushed America into World War I. The resulting outcry helped pave the way for the isolationist-leaning Congress to pass the *Neutrality Act of 1935*.

History shows that America always played a much more active role in world affairs than the isolationists believed. Involvements over territorial expansion and trading rights brought Americans into many conflicts with the Barbary States, Spain, France, Britain, Mexico, Germany, and even Tsarist Russia. Late 19th century industrial growth and tipping the balance in World War I had placed the United States among the world's great powers. No amount of wishful thinking about the past by isolationists could change these facts.

FDR VS. THE ISOLATIONISTS

In the mid-1930s, Franklin D. Roosevelt was primarily focused on domestic affairs, but he shared the Progressives' belief that America's rise to power had given it a major role to play in world affairs. FDR was an astute politician who understood the strength of the isolationists. Yet, he believed in seeking peaceful, economic solutions to problems. The President was troubled when militarism once again reared its head in Europe and Asia.

Roosevelt's Secretary of State, **Cordell Hull**, sought to boost American trade in world markets by a free trade policy. In 1934, the President and the Secretary pressed Congress for the ***Reciprocity Act*** (1934). This gave the President power to negotiate tariff rates with individual nations and gave government aid to American companies seeking more business abroad. While launching the New Deal at home, FDR signaled that he wished to break out of the isolationist stance of his predecessors. He launched two major diplomatic changes – the **Good Neighbor Policy** and **diplomatic recognition of the U.S.S.R.** (Union of Soviet Socialist Republics).

At the Pan American Union's Montevideo Conference in 1933, Secretary Hull pledged to end the long history of U.S. **interventionism** in the internal affairs of Latin American nations. Using the *Reciprocity Act,* he doubled the trade between the U.S. and Latin America by 1935.

Over many congressional protests, FDR officially gave diplomatic recognition to the communist regime in the Soviet Union in 1933. When the first ambassador to the U.S.S.R. arrived in Moscow however, he found Soviet dictator **Josef Stalin** more interested in negotiating a defense treaty against the rising threat of Japan than talking about trade.

Josef Stalin

STORM WARNING DIPLOMACY	
ACT	**PROVISION**
Neutrality Act of 1935	When the President proclaimed that a foreign war existed, no arms could be sold or transported on American ships to the nations involved. No Americans could travel on the ships of warring nations.
Neutrality Act of 1936	When the President proclaimed that a foreign war existed, no loans could be made to the warring nations.
Neutrality Act of 1937	No Americans could travel on ships of warring nations. All provisions of the above *Neutrality Acts* applied to civil wars.
Neutrality Act of 1939	Nations fighting aggression were allowed to buy war material from U.S. manufacturers on a "cash and carry" basis. President could proclaim "danger zones" and forbid U.S. ships to enter the danger zone.

THE NEUTRALITY ACTS (1935-1939)

In his second inaugural address in 1937, FDR did not even mention foreign affairs. At that point, the League of Nations and other peace arrangements were breaking down. Japan and Italy had already invaded foreign countries, and Germany was rearming in violation of the *Treaty of Versailles*. Yet, FDR knew he would stir up the country if he talked of America's role in the increasing dangers abroad. The country was in a pacifist mood and isolationists in Congress tried to insure non-involvement with a series of protective neutrality acts.

THE SPANISH CIVIL WAR: A TEST FOR ISOLATION

During the summer of 1936, a savage civil war erupted in Spain. It became a focus of international attention when Axis partners Mussolini and Hitler gave signifi-
cant aid to a right-wing, conservative coalition of army officers. The weak socialist-leaning Republican forces received aid from the Soviet Union. The army officers, led by "El Caudillo," **Francisco Franco**, were victorious and set up a fascist dicta-torship sympathetic to Hitler in 1939.

☆ CAPSULE – PRELUDE TO WORLD WAR II

Act	Response	Result
1931 Japan Invades North Manchuria	League of Nations reprimand; U.S. issues Stimson Doctrine, does not recognize Japan's claim to territory	Japan quits League of Nations, annexes Chinese conquests
1935 Italy Invades Ethiopia	U.S. passes *Neutrality Act*, no arms sales to belligerents. League of Nations reprimand	Italy conquers and annexes part of Ethiopia
1936 Germany Invades Rhineland Region	No response	Germans build fortifications along the Rhine River in violation of Versailles Treaty
1936 Germany & Italy back Franco in Spanish Civil War	U.S. broadens *Neutrality Acts* to include arms trade ban for civil war belligerents	Franco is victorious, becomes "silent partner" for Axis alliance
1937 Japan Invades China	FDR calls for "quarantine" of aggressor nations. League of Nations fails with trade embargo against Japan	Japan conquers and occupies most of N.E. China
1938 Germany Invades Austria	No response	Germany proclaims "Anschluss" – unification of Germany and Austria
1938 Germany Claims Czech Territory	Britain and France appease Hitler, allow Germans to take over the area at Munich Conference	Germany annexes Sudetenland region
1939 Italy Invades Albania	No response	Italy conquers and occupies Albania
1939 Germany & U.S.S.R. Invade Poland	Britain and France declare war; U.S. modifies *Neutrality Acts* to allow "cash and carry"	World War II begins

Fear of the Spanish conflict erupting into another major war led Congress to extend its earlier trade restrictions to include civil wars. In the *Neutrality Act of 1937*, FDR was able to gain some flexibility. Congress added a "cash and carry amendment" to allow belligerents to buy non-military goods in America as long as they made immediate payment and transported them in their own ships.

FDR's "Quarantine" Speech of 1937

In July 1937, Japan again attacked China. Roosevelt sensed that Americans wished to send aid, but the *Neutrality Acts* stood in his way. Japan's control of the Pacific made "cash and carry" too risky for Chinese ships. Early in October, FDR made his famous "quarantine speech" indicating that aggression must be stopped by peace-loving nations. Isolationists loudly denounced him, but it appeared that the public was beginning to change its mind as they watched aggression mount in the world. The rising sense of danger and the League of Nations' failure to act against aggression allowed FDR to act. He convinced Congress to increase defense spending for naval and air power.

Aggression Escalates

Neutrality legislation restricted President Roosevelt's diplomatic capabilities. As problems overseas escalated, Britain and France were not ready for the speed with which the pattern of aggression grew, and Roosevelt's hands were tied by Congressional limitations.

Appeasement at Munich (1938)

In 1938, Hitler demanded immediate German occupation of the predominantly German-speaking Sudetenland in western Czechoslovakia. No major nation in Europe was prepared to face the combined war machines of Nazi Germany and Fascist Italy. To try to resolve the Czech problem, a fateful international meeting was convened in Germany. At the Munich Conference (29 September 1938), France and Britain agreed to let Hitler take the Sudetenland in exchange for a pledge to cease further aggressive claims by Germany and Italy. Sadly, Britain's Prime Minister **Neville Chamberlain** claimed the world had purchased "peace with honor" by appeasing Hitler at Munich.

Publicly, Roosevelt reluctantly approved of the Munich Agreement. Privately, he told his Cabinet that such an **appeasement** (granting concessions to potential enemies to maintain peace) of the Axis dictators was shameful. FDR was aware that German diplomatic activities in Latin America were undercutting his Good Neighbor policy. With the time purchased by the Munich Agreement, Roosevelt worked intensely to cement friendly relations in Latin America.

WORLD WAR II BEGINS

The Munich appeasement bought very little time. In 1938, German troops took all Czechoslovakia. To balance the Axis' geographic power, France and Britain desperately tried negotiation with the Soviet Union.

Stalin, however, was suspicious of the anti-communist policies of the western democracies. In a shocking diplomatic move in late August 1939, the Soviet Union and Germany announced a mutual non-aggression treaty. This pact created a strange alliance between fascists and communists. It took pressure off Germany's eastern borders. It also gave both Hitler and Stalin a clear field to advance into Poland.

Hitler voiced demands for a return of German territory given to Poland after World War I. On 1 September 1939, just nine days after the Nazi-Soviet pact, Hitler launched his **blitzkrieg** (lightning war) against Poland. Bound by treaty to defend Poland, Britain and France declared war two days later. World War II began in Europe. While France and Britain mobilized, the massive German technological war machine rolled through Poland and conquered the country in three weeks.

Swiftly, the Soviets took a share of eastern Poland. They began annexing the tiny Baltic nations of Estonia, Latvia, and Lithuania, and then launched their own lightning invasion of Finland which fell in only four months.

The winter of 1939-40 was deceptively calm in Europe. In April of 1940, Hitler launched a Scandinavian blitzkrieg against Denmark and Norway (Sweden was traditionally neutral). In May, Hitler ignored the neutrality of the Netherlands and Belgium. German forces rolled through both before the month ended, leaving France exposed.

The Battle of France opened on 5 June, and Italy attacked from the south on 10 June. Paris fell to the Germans four days later. General **Charles DeGaulle**'s Free French government fled into exile in Britain. On 22 June, France's Field Marshal Henri Pétain surrendered to the Germans. In a matter three months, all of Western Europe except Great Britain had fallen to Hitler's war machine.

London in ruins after Hitler's blitz – the relentless series of air attacks and civilian bombing. (Photo credits: U.S. National Archives)

GRADUAL U.S. INVOLVEMENT

The velocity of the Axis offensive jolted America. Roosevelt rushed to set up defenses in the Western Hemisphere through the Pan-American Union and the Joint Defense Board with Canada.

Congress raised taxes for more military purchasing. It authorized the armed forces to absorb the National Guard, and it set up the nation's first peacetime draft. Fearing spy activities, Congress passed the *Smith Act* (1940) to monitor alien activities. The Act also made it illegal to advocate or teach the forceful overthrow of lawful government in the United States.

By the middle of 1940, the British stood alone under a relentless series of German air attacks. The *Neutrality Acts* of the late 1930s blocked Roosevelt's efforts to help them. Sensing that public opinion had changed in the rush of aggression in Europe, FDR took a bold step in September of 1940 in the **Destroyers-for-Bases Deal**. Stretching his power as Commander-in-Chief, he took fifty World War I navy

Children – orphaned, hungry, and homeless – following the German Blitz on London 1940. (Photo credits: U.S. National Archives)

ships and gave them to Britain in exchange for the use of naval base sites in Canada, Bermuda, and the Caribbean.

Roosevelt's worst fears came in that same month. Japan joined the Axis alliance. Roosevelt's reaction angered the Japanese. He authorized an **embargo** (stoppage) of iron and steel shipments outside the Western Hemisphere (except those to Britain).

Roosevelt's State of the Union Address in January of 1941 was his famous *Four Freedoms Speech* (freedom of speech, of worship, from want, and from fear). The four freedoms framed what became America's war aims.

★ CAPSULE – PEARL HARBOR: USS ARIZONA

On 16 March 1914, the New York (Brooklyn) Navy Yard laid down the keel to begin construction of battleship number 39, which would later be named **Arizona**.

In November 1918 the Arizona sailed for Europe to join Battleship Division Six serving with the British Grand Fleet, one week after the signing of the armistice.

During the years between the world wars, Arizona carried on with the routine of a Navy ship in peace time, conducting training, gunnery practice, fleet exercises, cruises and routine shipyard maintenance.

On 7 December 1941, Japanese aircraft attacked Pearl Harbor just before 8:00 AM, Sunday morning. The color detail was on deck in anticipation of raising the flag at the stern at 8:00. The Arizona came under attack almost immediately, and at about 8:10 received a hit by a 800-kilogram bomb. The majority of the crew members were either killed by the explosion and fire or were trapped by the rapid sinking of the ship. On 1 December 1942 the ship was stricken from the registry of U.S. Navy vessels.

In 1950 the tradition of raising and lowering the colors over the ship daily was started, and momentum gradually began to build toward providing a memorial for the ship and those who died on her. In 1960 construction began and the memorial was dedicated on Memorial Day, 1962.

Courtesy of: National Park Service and University of Arizona Library
http://www.cr.nps.gov/nr/twhp/ or http://www.library.arizona.edu/images.USS_Arizona.shtml

In that same speech, he called for a **Lend-Lease Act** by Congress, to allow the U.S. to lend and transfer arms and war supplies to Britain and other "victims of aggression." Lend-Lease overturned much of the 1930s neutrality legislation. It committed the United States to become what Roosevelt called the "Arsenal of Democracy." FDR extended the Navy's patrol region in the Atlantic and allowed merchant ships to arm themselves.

In June 1941, while still pounding Britain from the air, Hitler turned on his ally, Stalin, launching an all-out blitzkrieg against the U.S.S.R. Stalin appealed to the Allies for assistance. Within a few months, Roosevelt extended *Lend-Lease* to the U.S.S.R.

Roosevelt and Prime Minister **Winston Churchill** (1874-1965) met off the Canadian coast and drew up an informal set of anti-Axis war aims. Known as the *Atlantic Charter*, this document was eventually signed by 15 Allied nations, including the U.S.S.R. In 1945, it became the basis for the *United Nations Charter*.

THE U.S. IN WORLD WAR II

PEARL HARBOR

In 1940, Japanese-American relations reached a crisis stage. Japan wanted oil and rare metals in the Southeast Asia. France was the chief colonial power, but it had fallen to Hitler. U.S. Secretary of State Hull issued a steady stream of warnings to the Japanese, but they had no powerful enemies in Asia. (The British were fighting Hitler, the U.S. was officially neutral, and the Soviets had a non-aggression pact with Japan.) In July 1941, Japan attacked Thailand and the nearly defenseless French colonies. Diplomatic protests were issued by Hull, and FDR embargoed nearly all trade with Japan.

In the late fall of 1941, aggressive militarists under General Tojo took power in Japan. They planned a secret attack against several U.S. naval installations to devastate America. The majority of American seagoing power in the Pacific was located at the Pearl Harbor naval base in Hawaii. The American military strategists assumed it was far out of range for the Japanese. Their main concern was for the forces in the Philippines, which was still a U.S. possession.

Japan struck Pearl Harbor on 7 December 1941. The U.S. was caught unaware. Scholars agree this was not only due to the Americans' disorderly intelligence system, but to their weak analysis and communications. There were over 5,000 casualties that day. It was the single most costly defeat in American history. Six major battleships and many lesser vessels were rendered useless. The attack left Japan nearly unchallenged in East Asia and the Pacific. Congress declared war on Japan the next day.

Within a week, Japan's Axis partners declared war on the United States. All the internal debates about isolationism were put to rest. The attempts to stay out of Europe's problems had proven useless. America now had to face the full reality of World War II.

THE WAR IN EUROPE

Hitler had not been told by his Japanese allies of their plan to attack Pearl Harbor. He was angered because he had not yet disposed of Britain, and his attack on the U.S.S.R. was slowly unraveling. In declaring war in mid-December, he hoped the United States would focus on Japan in the Pacific and America's Lend-Lease aid to Europe would slow down.

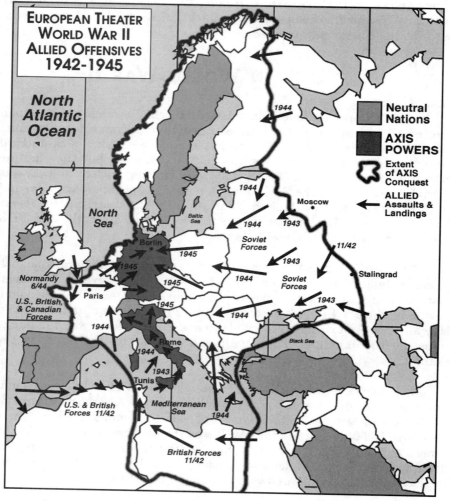

Roosevelt's strategy was the opposite of what Hitler had hoped. He ordered American commanders to temporarily "hold the line" in the Pacific and focus attention on the European theater of the War.

FDR's brilliant Chief of Staff, General **George C. Marshall**, sent his most talented assistant, General **Dwight D. Eisenhower**, to Europe as U.S. Commander. He was primarily a planner, conciliator, compromiser, and public relations figure. He succeeded in managing a vast mid-20th century wartime coalition. Eisenhower took the air war to the German homeland. He ordered bombing attacks by the Royal Air Force and U.S. Army Air Corps on strategic production centers.

General Marshall quickly sent aid to British forces in North Africa under General Bernard L. Montgomery. At El Alamein in Egypt, Montgomery defeated the Germans' legendary "Desert Fox," General Erwin Rommel. In November 1942, U.S. forces landed in North Africa. General **George Patton** pushed eastward toward Montgomery and helped to isolate the Germans at Tunis. The victory in North Africa (May 1943) gave the Allies access to the Mediterranean and a southern staging point for invading Europe. At the same time, the Soviets halted the Axis invasion of their homeland after a brutal six month siege of **Stalingrad**.

The Allies invaded Sicily July 1943 and the Italian mainland in September. The Italians surrendered on 8 September 1943, but the German forces in Italy continued fighting. It was not until June 1944 that the Allies inched their way into Rome.

On 6 June 1944, Eisenhower launched **Operation Overlord**, the largest amphibious invasion in history. Nearly 200,000 troops, 4,600 ships, and 11,000 planes attacked the Germans on the beaches of Normandy, France. Overlord opened a second front in Europe. The Germans fought back ferociously. By the end of the summer, the British had liberated the Netherlands and Belgium. A combined Free French, American, and Canadian army liberated Paris at about the same time.

Hitler was now caught between the Soviets driving from the east and the combined Allied forces moving rapidly from the west and south. In July, he tried to stem the tide by ordering the new **V-2 rockets** launched at Britain in massive incendiary raids. Nearly overcome by Allied air power, Hitler desperately threw ground forces against a weak section of the Allied line in Belgium. In the **Battle of the Bulge** (Dec. 1944 - Jan. 1945), the Allies were thrown back. However, a massive drive toward Germany from Poland by the Soviets, and another from Holland by the British forced the Germans to retreat. The Allies regained their momentum. With Berlin under attack, Hitler committed suicide on 30 April 1945. Field Marshal **Alfred Jodl** agreed to unconditional surrender on 8 May 1945.

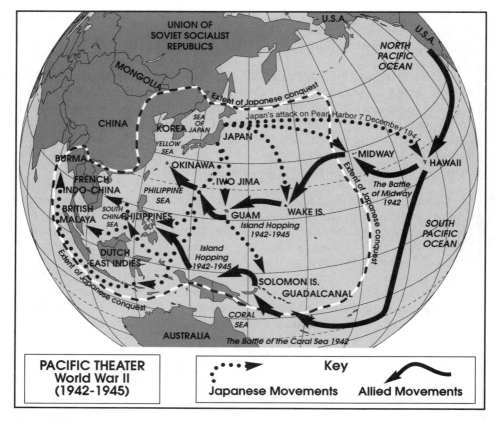

PACIFIC THEATER
World War II
(1942-1945)

Key

•••• ▶ Japanese Movements   ◥ Allied Movements

THE WAR IN THE PACIFIC

In 1943, Roosevelt finally allowed the military to turn some attention to the Pacific theater. By that time, Pacific Commander General **Douglas MacArthur** had already evacuated the Philippines, the British and Americans had retreated to Australia, and the Japanese had overrun most of Southeast Asia and Indonesia (Dutch East Indies). In mid-1942, U.S. Navy and Marine resistance had stopped the Japanese advance at the battles of the Coral Sea and Midway.

A successful Allied attack on Guadalcanal, just north of Australia, threw the Japanese into a defensive position. American commanders authorized a murderous "island-hopping" offensive through the Pacific. Intense cooperation between MacArthur and Admiral **Chester Nimitz** allowed the Americans to move simultaneously in the South and Central Pacific. Wake and Guam were recaptured by mid-1944. The Americans increased their devastating carrier air strikes on Japan itself. The drive toward the Japanese Islands grew more bloody and costly. In early 1945, it took 18,000 Allied casualties to capture Iwo Jima and 45,000 Allied casualties to take Okinawa.

Tragically, FDR died of a cerebral hemorrhage on 12 April 1945. Vice-President **Harry S Truman** became the nation's Commander-in-Chief. Shortly thereafter, the Germans surrendered. Truman focused his attention on the bloodbath in the Pacific. His advisors felt that the Japanese would not accept unconditional surrender, but would fight to the last. Truman increased air attacks on Japan, hoping for surrender. In mid-July, while at the **Potsdam Conference**, the President received word that an atomic weapon had been successfully developed by **J. Robert Oppenheimer** and a team of scientists working on the **Manhattan Project** in the New Mexico desert. Truman decided he could end the War quickly by authorizing the use of the bomb. On 6 August 1945, the first atomic bomb was dropped on **Hiroshima**, but there was no reply from the Japanese.

Iwo Jima Marine Memorial
Arlington Cemetery, Virginia
– PhotoDisc ©1994

On 9 August, a second bomb was dropped on the Japanese naval base of **Nagasaki**. The following day, Japanese Premier **Suzuki** offered to surrender if the Emperor **Hirohito** (1901-1989) was allowed to keep his throne. General MacArthur accepted the Japanese surrender for the Allies on 14 August 1945. America had over a million casualties in World War II (nearly 325,000 dead and 700,000 wounded).

World War II cost the American people more than 300 billion dollars. To finance it, Congress expanded the income tax system and required employers to withhold taxes from workers' paychecks. Major **war bond drives** were launched in workplaces and a movie-going public saw filmed appeals to buy bonds at every picture show. Famous entertainers of the era such as Kate Smith, Jane Froman, Eddie Cantor, Al Jolson, Frank Sinatra, Bob Hope, and Bing Crosby volunteered to tour the country staging **bond rallies** in major cities. The war bond purchases accounted for nearly two-thirds of government war revenues.

WARTIME DIPLOMACY

With the coming of the European war in 1939, Roosevelt changed his leadership role. As chief diplomat and commander-in-chief, FDR met personally with Allied leaders. Advisor Harry Hopkins laid the diplomatic groundwork for summit meetings in Casablanca (1943), Cairo (1943), Teheran (1943), and Yalta (1945). Overseas, FDR conferred with Britain's

☆ CAPSULE – THE HOME FRONT

World War II brought about monumental social and economic changes in Americans lives.

Industry Changed

- FDR got industries to patriotically donate the services of their top managers.
- The **War Production Board** forbade production of "nonessential items" (autos, kitchen appliances, toys).
- Manufacturing conversions were widespread. Silk stocking manufacturers switched to producing parachutes. Ford, Chrysler, and GM built tanks and planes. Kaiser Industries built prefabricated ship hulls and produced cargo transports in less than three months. Kaiser also developed the Army's General Purpose vehicle. The "GP" became known as the "Jeep."

Workers Changed

- The nation's GNP tripled by 1945.
- Federal spending jumped from $20 billion (1941) to almost $98.4 billion (1945).
- The **War Manpower Commission** coordinated the draft of nearly 14 million men into the armed forces while at the same time keeping a steady flow of trained workers moving into the nation's factories.
- Unemployment dropped to 1.9 percent by 1945.
- Average weekly earnings jumped from $25.25 in 1939 to $47.08 in 1945.
- The War Labor Board handled labor disputes and kept the country relatively strike-free.

NO TIME TO LET LOOSE!

It's a Fight to a Finish!

Women's Roles

- 17 million women entered the work force as men were drafted.
- Patriotic posters, film shorts, and a pop song glorified a new heroine, "Rosie the Riveter."
- Some industries set up day care and nursery schools near their defense plants.
- More than a quarter of a million women also joined newly created corps of the Army (WACs), Navy (Waves), Marines, and Coast Guard relieving men of non-combatant duties.

Rationing & Morale

- When consumer goods became scarce due to military production demands, the **Office of Price Administration** kept the inflation-prone economy working on a fair basis.
- The OPA imposed **price ceilings** and supervised the **rationing** program so that people would be able to get a fair share of goods in short supply (shoes, sugar, coffee, tires, gasoline).
- The people responded when "We Do Our Part" poster programs urged home front support for those doing the fighting.
- Even comic book characters were given wartime assignments; superhero *Captain America* started off as an Army recruit.

Cartoon drawing by O. Soglow. (OWI). National Archives.

- Hollywood studios produced such films as *Watch on the Rhine, Mrs. Miniver,* and *They Were Expendable* that deepened the support by focusing on the sacrifice of those struggling with the War.

Prime Minister Winston Churchill, the U.S.S.R.'s Premier Joseph Stalin, Free France's General Charles DeGaulle, and China's Generalissimo Jiang Jieshi (Chiang Kai-shek).

Two months before his death, FDR journeyed to the Soviet Union in February 1945. At the **Yalta Conference**, he met with Stalin and Churchill to plan for the final stage of the War. The Soviets had already conquered most of Eastern Europe and were ready to invade Germany. Roosevelt and Churchill persuaded a reluctant Stalin to hold free elections in Soviet-conquered territories. They laid the groundwork for the new **United Nations** peace organization. Stalin also promised to join the War against Japan as soon as he could.

British Prime Minister Winston Churchill, along with U.S. President Franklin Roosevelt and Soviet Premier Josef Stalin, attend the conference at Yalta.

(Library of Congress)

In July 1945, a final wartime summit took place at Potsdam, Germany. By then, Harry Truman had taken Roosevelt's place. He met with Churchill and Stalin to make agreements on the peacetime treatment of Germany and on the location of Polish borders. From World War II on, **summit meetings** and personal diplomacy became an important and burdensome responsibility for U.S. Presidents in the modern era.

U.S. MILITARY OCCUPATIONS

Unlike World War I, World War II ended without a general peace treaty. This failure paved the way for the tensions and suspicions that resulted in a Cold War between the Soviet Union and the western democracies.

Germany was placed under military occupation by the Allies (see map below). They split it into an eastern zone administered by the U.S.S.R. with Berlin as its capital, and a western zone jointly administered by Britain, France, and the United States with Bonn as its capital. Isolated inside the Soviet zone, Berlin later became the scene of much post-war tension.

Treatment of Japan was different. The U.S. tried about 4,000 Japanese officials for war crimes, executing only General Tojo and several other leaders. The Americans occupied and rapidly reconstructed the nation. Pacific commander General Douglas MacArthur was appointed military governor and oversaw the development of a democratic constitution adopted in 1947. In 1951, the former Allied nations, with the exception of the Soviet Union, signed a formal peace treaty with Japan.

Germany
Post
World War II

0   Miles   100

North Sea

Baltic Sea

BRITISH ZONE

NETHERLANDS

Berlin

POLAND

SOVIET ZONE

Bonn

BELGIUM

LUX

CZECHOSLOVAKIA

FRENCH ZONE

AMERICAN ZONE

FRANCE

AUSTRIA

SWITZERLAND

WORLD WAR II: IMPACT ON MINORITIES

The War created problems for minority groups at home and abroad. After Pearl Harbor, anti-Japanese feelings ran high. Fear of sabotage and espionage caused many unfounded charges to be leveled at Japanese aliens and American citizens of Japanese ancestry (**Nisei**).

Japanese-Americans were most densely settled in California. In the early spring of 1942, the War Relocation Authority had the Federal Bureau of Investigation round up 100,000 American citizens of Japanese ancestry. The WRA shipped them to ten relocation centers in Arizona, Utah, Arkansas, and several other western states. Most were detained there for the duration of the War. (Americans of Italian and German descent were not treated in similar fashion.)

This was apparently a racially-motivated denial of due process rights. It was challenged in the Supreme Court in 1944 in ***Korematsu v. U.S***. The Court upheld the government's actions on military urgency after Pearl Harbor and the "clear and present danger" rule based on the 1919 *Schenck* decision. The Nisei won appeals in the 1950s and 1960s

☆ CAPSULE – THE ASSEMBLY CENTERS

Japanese-Americans were most densely settled in California. In the early spring of 1942, the War Relocation Authority had the Federal Bureau of Investigation round up 100,000 American citizens of Japanese ancestry. The WRA shipped them to ten relocation centers in Arizona, Utah, Arkansas, and several other western states. Most were detained there for the duration of the War. (Americans of Italian and German descent were not treated in similar fashion.)

These young evacuees of Japanese ancestry are awaiting their turn for baggage inspection upon arrival at this Assembly Center. Turlock, CA, May 2, 1942. Dorothea Lange. (WRA). National Archives.

and partial compensation was made by the government for their suffering. In 1988, President Reagan signed a bill publicly apologizing to the Japanese American internees during the war and granted each of the 60,000 survivors a tax-free payment of $20,000.

The former leaders of Hitler's Third Reich on trial in Nuremberg, Germany. Shown in the photo above - Front Row from Left to Right: Hermann Göring, Rudolf Hess, Joachim von Ribbentrop, Wilhelm Keitel, Ernst Kaltenbrunner, Alfred Rosenberg, Hans Frank, Wilhelm Frick, Julius Streicher, Walther Funk, Hjalmar Schacht.
(Photo credit: U.S. National Archives)

The world was shocked by films of the Allied liberation of Hitler's concentration camps in Germany, Poland, and Eastern Europe. **The Holocaust** – the genocidal extermination of six million Jews – could not be brushed aside in dealing with the captured enemy leaders. More barbaric Nazi practices were revealed at the **Nuremberg Trials** conducted by the Allies in 1946. Twenty-two major Nazi leaders were placed on trial for violations of the basic rules of war and inhumane treatment of political prisoners. Half of the accused were sentenced to death, half received prison terms.

African Americans also suffered from racial policies during the War. African Americans servicemen were assigned to segregated units. Under the Fair Employment Practices Commission, the number of African Americans in industry tripled between 1940 and 1945 and wages quadru-

RESULTS OF WORLD WAR II	
Worldwide Costs	**Changes in World Order**
• 22 million military & civilian dead, 34 million wounded • over $110 billion in resources; over $230 billion in property damage • over 4 million displaced persons	• totalitarian systems overthrown (Germany, Italy, Japan) • Britain and France declined as world powers • U.S. and U.S.S.R. rise as dominant powers • U.S.S.R. set up satellite buffer nations in Eastern Europe • disruption of European overseas empires; rise of colonial independence movements • beginning of nuclear age • formation of the United Nations

pled. Government non-discrimination policies for defense plant workers drew civilians out of the South. Still, many trade unions in defense industries banned African Americans from membership. Some protested if African Americans received promotions. Mass migrations also caused race riots to break out in Los Angeles, Mobile, New York, and Detroit.

DEMOBILIZATION, INFLATION, AND STRIKES

Many people doubted whether President Truman could fill the shoes of Roosevelt. In the months following the War's end, President Truman showed strength. War-weary Americans clamored for a speedy demobilization. Concerned about Soviet behavior in Europe, President Truman wanted a very gradual dismantling of United States' power. Congress and the public criticized him for dragging the demobilization out.

As the economy converted to peacetime, consumer production gradually increased, and the administration ended rationing but fought with Congress to keep wartime price controls. Truman wanted to allow production (supply) to catch up with consumer demand to avoid the classic pattern of inflation and post-war recession. Inflation increased enormously as people who had sacrificed their desires and needs during the War now willingly paid high prices for scarce autos and appliances.

While pent-up money from wartime savings and bonds drove prices higher, everyday wages were not keeping up with inflation. Labor reacted to the inflation problem with a series of strikes for higher wages. In 1946, a United Mine Workers' strike so hurt the economy that Truman had to threaten to use the Army to keep coal production up. In the same year, he again threatened to use the Army to end a national railroad strike.

THE "G.I. BILL"

In 1944, as the fortunes of war began to change, Roosevelt had been farsighted enough to anticipate the domestic problems that would occur as the war moved toward its conclusion. To ease the economic dislocations of converting from wartime to peacetime, he had the War Production Board planning to let some industries increase their consumer production while cutting back on military output. As a gesture of gratitude to those who had done the fighting, he managed to have Congress pass the *Servicemen's Readjustment Act*, commonly called the *"G.I. Bill of Rights."* It provided for physical and vocational rehabilitation of wounded veterans, granted one year's unemployment compensation, and allowed for low cost business and housing loans. It also provided funds for veterans to continue their college and vocational educations – 7.8 million World War II veterans took advantage of the *G.I. Bill's* educational provisions. The Act helped to ease the impact on the economy of demobilizing thousands of servicemen by avoiding massive unemployment. In the long run, it created a better educated work force and stimulated construction on university campuses.

POST WAR INFLATION	
Too Much Demand	**Not enough Supply**
• consumers demanded goods denied during the War with savings and bonds built up during the war years • government ended OPA rationing restrictions • government demanded military goods for occupation troops • government demanded goods to rebuild Europe and Asia • government gave money for homes and education to veterans under the GI Bill	• manufacturers struggling to convert facilities to peacetime production • some companies trying to supply military needs and capital goods for rebuilding war-torn countries could not meet normal consumer demand

TRUMAN VS. CONGRESS

Congress resisted Truman's civil rights, housing, Social Security, and labor reforms. It did create an **Atomic Energy Commission** (AEC) to supervise military use of nuclear energy and research its future applications. However, growing inflation and the slow demobilization became issues in the 1946 Congressional elections. The Republicans regained control of Congress for the first time in sixteen years.

The new 80th Congress was more conservative than in the New Deal days. Truman's positions on civil rights pushed many Southern Democrats toward a **coalition** with the Republicans. Business-oriented Republicans overrode his veto of the anti-union *Taft-Hartley Act* in 1947. The *Act* outlawed closed-shops, permitted government intervention in strikes, and cancelled many of the collective bargaining gains made under the *National Labor Relations Act* of 1935.

The President did get Congress to enact the *Employment Act* (1946). It incorporated British economist John Maynard Keynes' ideas on government's role in keeping the economy stable. The *Act* created a **Council of Economic Advisors** to the president. It also equipped the government to use **demand management policy** (aggressive fiscal policy) to stimulate sluggish demand through tax reduction, job training for the structurally unemployed, and other spending policies.

Truman reorganized the military. Congress passed his *National Security Act* in 1947. The *Act* consolidated all military affairs under the Department of Defense, coordinated the military command under a **Joint Chiefs of Staff**, and formed the **Central Intelligence Agency** (CIA). Truman's energetic foreign policy of containment also earned him popularity. Stalin was breaking post war agreements in Eastern Europe and Iran, and Truman's tough diplomatic stance drew applause.

THE 1948 ELECTION

Perhaps Truman's scrappiness helped him to win the election of 1948. It is considered one of the greatest "come-from-behind victories" in the history of presidential elections. When the Democrats reluctantly nominated him, the Southern wing of the party walked out of the convention in opposition. They formed their own **States' Rights Party** (nickname: "Dixiecrats") and nominated Governor **Strom Thurmond** (SC). Another small, left-leaning group of Democrats also left the Party in protest to Truman's anti-Soviet policies. They formed a new Progressive Party and nominated former Vice President **Henry A. Wallace**.

With the Democrats split three ways, the Republicans could sense victory. They renominated their 1944 candidate, New York Governor **Thomas E. Dewey** (1902-1971). The overconfident Dewey ran a slow-paced, lackluster campaign. Truman threw himself into the campaign. Crisscrossing the country by train, he emphasized his down-to-earth style and the lack of cooperation from what he called a "Do-Nothing 80th Congress." No one expected him to win.

Truman edged Dewey by a mere 2 million popular votes on election day 1948. (Electoral results: Truman - 303, Dewey - 189, Thurmond - 39). Truman managed to attract a strong African American vote, the labor vote, moderate liberals, and those who agreed with his tough containment policies. Also, he had a strong enough **"coattail effect"** that voters selected Democratic candidates for U.S. Representatives and Senators, restoring the Democrats' control of Congress.

THE FAIR DEAL

With a slightly friendlier Congress, Truman was able to get more of his **Fair Deal** domestic program passed. A new *Federal Housing Act*, a revised *Fair Labor Standards Act* with an increased minimum wage, major expansion of Social Security, and federal assistance for city slum clearance programs were passed in his term. The Republican-Southern Democrat coalition still handed him defeats on programs to aid education and the small farmer, health insurance for the elderly, and enforcement of civil rights. As Chief Executive, Truman

Harry S Truman
Thirty-third President of the U.S.
– White House Historical Association

appointed a national **Civil Rights Commission** in 1947, issued executive orders to end segregation in the armed forces and in federal jobs, and had the Justice Department challenge segregation in federal housing projects. Despite opposition in Congress, Truman exerted effective leadership in domestic affairs.

PEACE WITH PROBLEMS (1945-1955)

FORMATION OF THE UNITED NATIONS

In the 1930s, Woodrow Wilson's dream of a League of Nations failed to preserve the peace. Nations refused to sacrifice their self interests and sovereignty to preserve world order. At the end of World War II, Franklin Roosevelt attempted to renew Wilson's dream. FDR devoted his last efforts to a new peace organization – the **United Nations**. President Roosevelt knew the organization would fail without the cooperation of the United States and the Soviet Union. At Teheran and Yalta, he bargained intensely with Stalin to make the United Nations a reality.

On 25 April 1945, President Truman opened a world conference at San Francisco to establish a charter for the United Nations organization. The U.N.'s most powerful unit, the **Security Council**, is dominated by the great powers. It negotiates peaceful settlements of international disputes or uses force to stop acts of aggression. Each of the five permanent members of the Security Council (Britain, China, France, U.S.A., and Russia) have a great power **veto**. Because they can block action, the organization has not lived up to initial expectations. However, the U.N. has achieved several goals in the years since its inception.

- World problems have been rapidly brought to public attention and openly debated.

- Significant humanitarian actions have been coordinated under its health and economic cultural aid programs in underdeveloped regions.

- Trusteeship programs have transformed former colonies into independent nations.

In 1948, the United Nations adopted the *Universal Declaration of Human Rights*. It sums up the aspirations of freedom-loving people: that all individuals should be able to live their lives in peace and dignity, free from the oppression of political forces and discrimination. This simple document has become a basis for justice and human dignity throughout the world.

DISPLACED PERSONS

World War II uprooted many in Europe. Large numbers could not return to their homes in Soviet-dominated nations. These "**displaced persons**" looked to the United States as a land traditionally open to the world's troubled peoples. The restrictive immigration acts of the 1920s barred large numbers of refugees especially from Eastern Europe. Plagued with problems of demobilization and economic readjustment, Congress moved slowly to aid such people. It took until 1948 for Congress to amend the immigration policy to permit the President to make emergency adjustments in the admission quotas. The government allowed an additional 200,000 carefully-screened persons to enter the country in the next two years.

ORIGINS OF THE COLD WAR

YALTA AND POTSDAM SUMMITS

Lack of agreement on a world peace structure left the post-war world in a chaotic state. The old world power structure had dissolved, and only two major industrial states emerged from the War stronger – the United States and the Soviet Union. These two **superpowers** dominated world politics for the next generation.

At Wartime summits, Stalin said the Soviet Union would maximize its security and protect its extensive borders by setting up friendly governments in the areas that its armies liberated. At Yalta, Churchill, and Roosevelt assumed Stalin would conduct free elections in these countries after a brief period of military occupation. Stalin, however, set up communist governments in the occupied nations.

At the Potsdam Conference (July, 1945), Churchill and Truman brought up the question of free elections in Poland, but Stalin brushed it aside. The Soviets wanted a buffer zone of small, communist satellite nations between themselves and the West.

American policy-makers began to see the world evolving into two armed camps polarized around the superpowers. Veteran State Department officials and diplomats experienced in dealing with the U.S.S.R., such as Dean Acheson, Averill Harriman, and George F. Kennan, were pessimistic. Former British Prime Minister Winston Churchill pronounced the European situation dismal when he claimed, "...an iron curtain has descended across the continent."

In February 1946, the Soviets refused to end their occupation of Iran. British oil interests appealed for help. The U.S.S.R. ignored the American and British complaints in the U.N. When the United States threatened military action, the Soviets withdrew.

FOUNDATIONS OF CONTAINMENT – THE TRUMAN DOCTRINE

In 1947, the Soviets again attempted to influence events on their southern border. The U.S.S.R. wanted concessions from the weak Turkish government on access to the Straits of the Dardenelles, leading to the Soviets' Black Sea ports. The United States and Britain sent stern notes and the Soviets backed off again. At the same time, the Soviets aided communist rebels trying to overthrow Turkey's neighbor, Greece. The British indicated to Truman that they were too weak to help the Greeks.

The memory of the disastrous Munich Conference, when the democracies appeased Hitler, was still fresh in most minds. The Soviets had to be stopped. Truman's advisors urged action. The President went before the Republican Congress and boldly stated that it was America's obligation to see that democratic nations would not be abandoned to communistic aggression. This idea gradually came to be known as the **Truman Doctrine**.

Congress responded positively to Truman's request, allocating the 400 million dollars to aid Greece and Turkey. The first foundation block of America's new **containment policy** was born: America would give military aid and training to nations resisting communist takeovers.

FOUNDATIONS OF CONTAINMENT – MARSHALL PLAN

Truman quickly followed up with a second foundation block of containment: economic aid to stabilize tottering regimes in western Europe. Truman tapped World War II Army Chief of Staff General George C. Marshall to serve as Secretary of State (1947-1949). On 5 June 1947, General Marshall proposed that the European economy could be stabilized by joint efforts of the European states and grants-in-aid from the U.S. Congress passed a $12 billion program called *The European Recovery Act*. Later it became known as the **Marshall Plan**. In the long run, the Plan offered $13.15 billion to stimulate the Western European economy. The extra production it stimulated in the U.S. undoubtedly helped to avoid the kind of 1930s style global depression that WW I had caused.

The Marshall Plan fostered cooperation that paved the way for a number of projects among Western European nations:

- **European Coal and Steel Community** (1952) was made up of France, West Germany, Belgium, and the Netherlands and organized to administer tariffs, prices, and supply vital industrial resources.

- **European Economic Community** (1957),a larger organization, was formed to break down tariff barriers and coordinate trade in Western Europe gradually became known as the "Common Market".

- **European Parliament** (1958) formed out of Common Market negotiations; this political assembly debated problems of mutual concern.

- **European Union** (1993) voters in the expanded Common Market countries approved to expand membership and create a unified trading bloc with its own currency (the euro or eurodollar).

☆ CAPSULE – THE BERLIN BLOCKADE AND AIRLIFT

As containment took shape, tension grew between the superpowers. The United States, Britain, and France agreed to merge the administration of their German occupation zones into a single Federal Republic of Germany (West Germany).

The U.S.S.R. wanted to keep Germany weak. The Soviets would not agree to reuniting the German nation. At the end of the War, the Allies agreed to divide the German capital into four zones. The eastern half of the city

became the Soviet Zone and the French, British, and Americans administered the western half. However, no provision was made for guaranteeing land and water access to the city through the surrounding Soviet Zone.

On 24 June 1948, the Soviets threw down the gauntlet. They blockaded all road, railroad, and canal routes to Berlin to get the other occupying nations to leave. Rather than use force on land, Truman chose to fly over the blockade. An elaborate **Berlin Airlift**, called "Operation Vittles," was devised. From June 1948 to September 1949, the U.S. and Royal Air Forces kept the western half of the city alive. Nearly a plane per minute landed with shipments of essential goods each day. Stalin, embarrassed by the show of moral strength, lifted the roadblocks in May of 1949.

FOUNDATIONS OF CONTAINMENT – THE NATO ALLIANCE

Four years of difficulties with the Soviets in Germany and Eastern Europe convinced Truman that he had to break with tradition. He knew economic aid and emergency military measures could not achieve containment of communism and Soviet aggression. Western Europe was too weak and unorganized to stop a move by Stalin's powerful Red Army. The U.N. could not move against aggression if the Soviets could exercise a Security Council veto. A standing military force was needed to deter aggression, and only America had the resources to form that force.

All this meant America had to enter into a permanent defense alliance for the first time since the French Alliance of 1778. It was a ponderous step. **Dean Acheson**, who served as Secretary of State from 1949 to 1953, carefully laid the groundwork with Congress and the European allies. The **North Atlantic Treaty Organization** (NATO) united ten nations of Western Europe with the

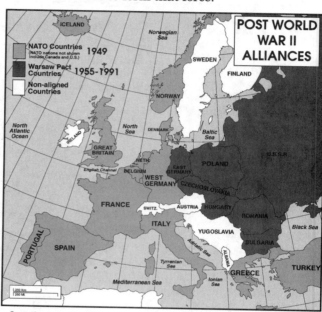

United States and Canada. Any attack on one member is considered an attack on all under the concept of **collective security**. This idea became the third foundation block of the containment policy.

FOUNDATIONS OF CONTAINMENT – THE POINT FOUR PROGRAM

President Truman also recognized that the U.S. role in containing communism would fail if it focused solely on Europe. The old European colonial empires were breaking up into new, underdeveloped nations then called the "Third World." Communist activities seemed to be sparking trouble in these new countries. In his State of the Union Address in January of 1949, Truman proposed the **Point Four Program** of tech-

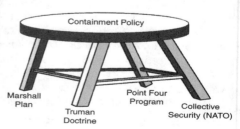

nological assistance to new, struggling nations. The intent of this foreign aid was to strengthen their economies to resist communist insurgent movements. The Point Four Program became the fourth foundation of the containment policy.

THE COLD WAR IN ASIA

THE UNITED STATES AND JAPAN

After the War, the Allies stripped Japan of its wartime territorial gains and its military power. General MacArthur helped Japan to create a democratic constitution that allowed only a small defensive military. The United States provided protection on a large scale. A defense agreement in 1949 eventually reduced U.S. occupation forces, but it allowed the United States to maintain bases.

As a result, Japan devoted its resources to peacetime production. The momentum of the communists in China caused Secretary of State Acheson to fear another large communist power in East Asia besides the U.S.S.R. The administration accelerated the rebuilding of Japan. The United States stepped up economic aid, paralleling the Marshall Plan in Europe. The U.S. government promoted American business investments in Japanese industrial growth.

As its economic recovery accelerated, Japan grew into a formidable capitalist democracy linked to the American market. An independent Japanese government took over the reins of power in 1949, just as China was taken over by the communists.

THE UNITED STATES AND CHINA

In China, the struggle between the Chinese Nationalist (or Guomindang) government under **Jiang Jieshi** (also called Chiang Kaishek) against **Mao Zedong**'s communist forces had been going on from the beginning of Japanese occupation in the 1930s. The United States supported the Nationalists during World War II.

Jiang Jieshi

After the War, the U.S. attempted to resolve the civil war through diplomatic mediation. Between 1945 and 1949, over $2 billion was sent to aid Jiang's Nationalist Chinese forces. However, corruption plagued the Nationalists. Some of the U.S. aid money and supplies for armies was traded to the communists by Jiang's own

Mao Zedong

officers. The Nationalists became associated with the powerful landed aristocratic class. The communists helped the peasants. In the end, the Nationalists defeated themselves.

On 1 October 1949, Mao Zedong proclaimed victory and established the new **Peoples' Republic of China**. Jiang and the Nationalist Chinese forces retreated to the island of Formosa (Taiwan) and set up a government in exile. The United States broke diplomatic relations with mainland China, and the two countries did not speak again for nearly a quarter of a century.

U.S.S.R. TESTS AN A-BOMB (1949)

Only a month before the loss of China to the communists, the U.S.S.R. announced a successful test of its first nuclear weapon. These two events,

coming in such rapid succession, were viewed as considerable setbacks for President Truman's containment policies. The Cold War power structure changed. The Republicans loudly criticized the Democrats for allowing such strategic blunders. Secretary of State Acheson came under assault for inept diplomacy. Some critics suggested that the State Department was riddled with communists who had "sold out" China.

☆ CAPSULE – THE COLD WAR TURNS HOT

After Japan's surrender in 1945, the Allies divided its Korean colony into two occupation zones. The U.S.S.R. occupied the north and the U.S. occupied the south. Post war tensions between them prevented reunification.

North Korea

South Korea

In the south, a U.N.-supervised election was held, the **Republic of Korea** emerged with a democratic constitution in 1948, and the U.S. withdrew its occupation forces. The U.S.S.R. quickly set up the **People's Republic of Korea** in the northern half of the peninsula. Skirmishes began between the two countries across the 38th Parallel border. Truman sent financial aid to help the South Koreans.

☆ CAPSULE – THE KOREAN CONFLICT

On the morning of 25 June 1950, North Korea attacked South Korea. The speed of North Korea's attack nearly pushed the U.N. and South Korean troops off the peninsula. The U.S. requested the U.N. Security Council to take action against the aggression. The Soviet Union was absent and unable to veto the Korean resolution. The U.N. voted to assist South Korea.

Truman acted quickly. Claiming a declaration of war was unnecessary, he ignored Congress, placed General MacArthur in command, and ordered U.S. troops into Korea where they were joined by small contingents of other U.N. members.

In September, MacArthur ordered a surprise attack behind the North Koreans. The brilliant amphibious landing at Inchon forced the North Koreans to retreat behind the 38th Parallel.

Truman then authorized MacArthur to enter North Korea, provided the Soviets or Chinese did not enter the War. MacArthur's U.N. forces pushed north almost to the Yalu River border of China. Nervous about United Nations' and United States' presence near its border, China invaded North Korea in November and pushed MacArthur's forces back to the 38th parallel.

Bloody fighting continued into 1951 until a cease-fire was declared. Peace negotiations lasted two years. The cost to the U.S. was 33,000 dead, 103,000 wounded, and $18 billion. An armistice was signed on 27 July 1953, restoring the border near the 38th parallel. The War ended in a stalemate that continues to this day.

MacArthur began criticizing Truman and the Joint Chiefs of Staff for restraining him from launching a massive counterattack against the Chinese. In one of the most controversial moves of his Presidency, Truman relieved MacArthur of command.

COLD WAR AT HOME

Domestically, the post war period was a stormy time. There was economic instability and Americans were not comfortable being the worldwide anti-communist defender of democracy. Soviet actions in Europe and Asia and President Truman's vigorous response caused many to grow fearful.

On top of all this, politicians claimed that communist subversion was widespread. The country began to show signs of paranoia.

- Truman responded to communist infiltration charges by forming a **Loyalty Review Board**. It investigated thousands of federal employees, some of whom were dismissed or resigned.

- Public and private employers required employees to file notarized loyalty oaths under pain of dismissal.

- In 1947, the House of Representatives' **Committee on Un-American Activities** launched an investigation of the American Communist Party. It issued contempt charges against leaders who refused to testify.

- In 1948, the Justice Department successfully prosecuted eleven American Communist Party leaders for violation of the *Smith Act* of 1940. The *Smith Act* made the teaching or advocating of the forceful overthrow of the U.S. government illegal. The communist leaders appealed, claiming the act violated their First Amendment right of free speech. In ***Dennis v. the United States*** (1951), the Supreme Court upheld the *Smith Act* and opened the door for many more prosecutions of Communist Party members in the early 1950s.

A full-blown anti-Red crusade began as the Committee on Un-American Activities held hearings all over the country. Refusal to answer questions that might incriminate oneself is a basic right protected by Fifth Amendment. Still, "taking the 5th" cast enough doubt on some witnesses – especially in Hollywood – to cause them to be "blacklisted" and lose their jobs.

In the late 1950s, the Supreme Court indicated that aspects of the *Smith Act* were unconstitutional. In ***Yates v. U.S.*** (1957), the Court ruled that speaking, studying, or teaching about theories of forcible overthrow of the government were not the same as participating in an actual conspiracy. In the same year, in ***Watkins v. U.S.***, the Court held that witnesses summoned before Congressional committees must be properly informed of the nature of the questions to be put to them and care must be taken to preserve their Constitutional rights.

THE ALGER HISS CASE

Amid the growing paranoia, California Congressman Richard Nixon achieved national attention as a member of the Committee on Un-American Activities. In mid-1948, sensational spy cases began to unfold. The Committee investigated a former State Department official, **Alger Hiss**. A former *Time* magazine editor by the name of **Whittaker Chambers** openly accused Hiss of espionage. Chambers was an admitted communist and Soviet agent.

In a sensational move, Chambers involved Representative Nixon in revealing microfilm of classified State Department documents. Chambers claimed Hiss passed these documents to Soviet officials in the 1930s. Hiss, then head of the prestigious Carnegie Endowment for Peace, vigorously denied the charges before televised Committee hearings. The Justice Department later charged Hiss with perjury. He was convicted in a series of sensational trials and served four years in prison. Nixon gained a U.S. Senate seat as a result of the Hiss episode.

The House Committee on Un-American Activities sponsored legislation to stop subversive activities in 1950. Congress passed the *McCarran Internal Security Act* which allowed the government to arrest and detain persons suspected of any affiliations with groups which might "...contribute to the establishment ...of totalitarian dictatorships in the United States." President Truman vetoed the McCarran bill. He claimed it would undermine the basic civil liberties of Americans. Congress easily overrode President Truman's veto.

The furor caused by the House Committee on Un-American Activities hearings led the FBI to broaden its espionage investigations. One investigation resulted in the famous **Rosenberg Case**. Ethel and Julius Rosenberg were arrested and accused of having arranged to pass U.S. atomic secrets to the Soviet Union during World War II. In 1951, a federal jury found them guilty of treason. Appeals continued for two years, but they were finally electrocuted in June 1953. As with the case of Sacco and Vanzetti in the Red Scare of the 1920s, there has been speculation that at least Ethel Rosenberg may have been a victim of a fear-ridden social environment.

McCARTHYISM

There was anti-communist activity in the U.S. Senate, also. Wisconsin Republican **Joseph R. McCarthy** began to make a series of shocking accusations about communist influence on high government officials. McCarthy never unearthed any conspiracy or any communists in government, but he came to symbolize the great anti-communist crusade of the early 1950s. As chairman of a Senate Committee on Government Operations investigations subcommittee, McCarthy led his own anti-communist investigations. He made brash charges and ignored the civil rights of those he subpoenaed to testify. He hinted at the disloyalty of General Marshall, Dean Acheson, and 1952 Democratic presidential candidate Adlai Stevenson.

The political pressure generated by McCarthyism touched many lives. Even Dr. J. Robert Oppenheimer, who had developed the first atomic bomb, was placed in the "security risk" category by the Eisenhower administration. Oppenheimer quit his government job in 1949 in opposition to the development of the more powerful hydrogen bomb. In 1954, he was working at Princeton, but was still

– Joseph R. McCarthy, U.S. Senate Speech, *Communists in Government Service*, February 1950
Photo: National Archives

a consultant to the U.S. Atomic Energy Commission. President Eisenhower directed that Oppenheimer's security clearance be suspended. Oppenheimer protested, but the AEC gave weak excuses. Years later, Oppenheimer was exonerated.

McCarthyism finally met its match when the Senator pledged to get the communists out of the U.S. Army. Millions of Americans watched the televised hearings. Senator McCarthy was shown to be reckless and irresponsible. His unpopularity became an embarrassment. The U.S. Senate officially censured him in 1954.

SUMMARY

The period from 1940 to 1950 was a mix of bewildering tragedy and triumph. World War II changed America's global position and transformed life at home. Government continued playing an active role after directing the War effort. The destruction of the War, the behavior of the Soviets, the competition of ideologies and of nuclear weaponry, were all powerful forces reshaping the country and the world. America took on a necessary but uncomfortable, and in some cases, unpopular role of world leadership.

LESSON ASSESSMENT

MULTI-CHOICE

1 Public support for Congressional neutrality legislation began to change after
   1 blitz attacks on Scandinavia, Holland, and Belgium
   2 Italy's conquest of Ethiopia
   3 Franco's victory in the Spanish Civil War
   4 the Munich Agreement

2 President Roosevelt rallied Americans to "become the great arsenal of democracy" to help
   1 South Korea against North Korea
   2 Jiang Jeshi against Mao Zedong
   3 the British and French appease Hitler
   4 Britain and the U.S.S.R. against the Axis

Base your answer to question 3 on the quotation below and your knowledge of U.S. history and government.

> "I suppose that history will remember my term of office as the years when the "cold war" began to overshadow our lives. I have hardly had a day in office that has not been dominated by this all-embracing struggle ... and always in the background there has been the atomic bomb."

3 The quotation best reflects the Presidential administration of
   1 Franklin D. Roosevelt   3 Herbert Hoover
   2 Harry S Truman   4 Adlai Stevenson

Base your answer to questions 4-7 on the statements below and your knowledge of U.S. history and government.

SPEAKER *A*: We must take action even if we are not sure it will work. To do nothing would be a repeat of the mistake made at Munich.
SPEAKER *B*: We must recognize the increasing interdependence of nations and join the United Nations.
SPEAKER *C*: Stopping the spread of communism can and must take several forms. We must be willing to do whatever is necessary.
SPEAKER *D*: Involvement in European affairs would be a mistake. We should not jeopardize our peace and prosperity over issues that control Europe's ambitions and rivalries.

4 Which Speaker best describes a basic attitude in foreign policy until the late 1800s?
   1 *A*   2 *B*   3 *C*   4 *D*

5   With which two speakers would Presidents Franklin Roosevelt and
    Harry Truman have been most in agreement?
    1   *A* and *B*   3   *B* and *D*
    2   *B* and *C*   4   *C* and *D*

6   Which speakers reflect the basic ideas behind the containment poli-
    cy?
    1   *A* and *C*   3   *C* and *D*
    2   *B* and *C*   4   *D* and *A*

7   The "Munich mistake" to which Speaker *A* refers is
    1   inflation   3   containment
    2   neutrality   4   appeasement

8   Which act effectively ended the Congressional policy of neutrality?
    1   The *Taft-Hartley Act*   3   The *Lend-Lease Act*
    2   The *Smith Act*   4   The *Reciprocity Act*

9   FDR and his advisors' initial strategy in fighting World War II was
    1   split Europe with an iron curtain
    2   focus on Europe and hold the line in the Pacific
    3   apprehend and detain all aliens in the United States
    4   steady bombing raids on the Philippines

**Base your answer to ques-
tion 10 on the poster and
quotation at the right and
your knowledge of U.S.
history and government.**

10 This poster was part of a
    program used in World
    War II to urge
    1   rationing vital com-
        modities
    2   buying of war bonds
        at home
    3   home front activities
        to conserve resources
    4   security while work-
        ing in defense plants

Remember child, Preserving
Food Helps Preserve Your
Democracy!

11 Reduction of the loss of American lives in the Pacific was a primary consideration in
   1 relocation of Japanese-Americans to internment camps
   2 Truman's decision to use the atomic bomb
   3 rationing food and critical materials on the home front
   4 forming the United Nations

12 Which of the following helped to convert the economy to peacetime by boosting demand?
   1 *Servicemen's Readjustment Act*
   2 *Universal Declaration of Human Rights*
   3 *National Security Act*
   4 *McCarran Internal Security Act*

13 The concept of collective security is best exemplified by the role of the United States in
   1 dropping the atomic bomb
   2 holding the Nuremberg Trials
   3 forming the North Atlantic Treaty Organization
   4 passing the G.I. Bill

14 The *Taft-Hartley Act* modified collective bargaining rights because it
   1 enhanced the power of labor unions
   2 allowed the government to interfere in strikes
   3 prohibited picketing places of employment
   4 increased pension benefits

Base your answer to question 15 on the chart at the right and your knowledge of U.S. history and government.

15 Which United States program is most likely reflected in the amounts of nonmilitary aid given from 1947-1950?
   1 Monroe Doctrine
   2 Marshall Plan
   3 The New Deal
   4 Arsenal of Democracy

U.S. Foreign Aid, 1946–1954
(Billions of Dollars)

NONMILITARY	YEAR	MILITARY
$ 4.0	1946	$ 0.7
$ 5.8	1947	
$ 5.0	1948	$ 0.1
$ 5.7	1949	$ 0.4
$ 4.3	1950	$ 0.2
$ 3.3	1951	$ 1.1
$ 2.8	1952	$ 1.8
$ 2.0	1953	$ 4.4
$ 1.7	1954	$ 3.5

16 After World War II, the United States was better able than its allies to adjust its economy from wartime to peacetime because the United States
   1 possessed nuclear weapons
   2 raised tariffs on imports
   3 had collected its war debt from the Allies
   4 had suffered no widespread wartime destruction

17 The response of a year-long airlift to the Soviet blockade of Berlin indicated
1 the effectiveness of United Nations' peacekeeping efforts
2 firm response to Soviet provocations
3 international disputes could be resolved through diplomatic channels
4 Congress would check presidential power in foreign affairs

18 Which element of the containment policy helped underdeveloped nations of the "Third World" resist communist insurgency by strengthening their economies?
1 Point Four Program   3 Berlin Airlift
2 Marshall Plan   4 NATO

19 After World War II, which action by President Truman helped stabilize the economy?
1 allowing displaced persons from Europe to enter the U.S.
2 slowing down demobilization of the armed forces
3 desegregating the armed forces
4 vetoing the *Taft-Hartley Act*

20 Truman's party splintered into three groups in the election of 1948 over
1 civil rights and containment
2 inflation and demobilization
3 veterans benefits and Social Security
4 refugees and nuclear arms

21 When Congress passed the *National Security Act* in 1947 creating the Department of Defense, the Joint Chiefs of Staff, and the Central Intelligence Agency it
1 demobilized the armed forces after World War II
2 restored the constitutional power over the military to the legislative branch
3 subjected all military decisions to judicial review
4 allowed the President to better manage the military

22 Which of the following occurred during the beginning of the Cold War in the late 1940s and early 1950s?
1 Congress prohibited all trade with nations associated with communist countries.
2 The United States refused to enter any military alliances with other countries.
3 Participation, or even past participation, in extremist movements was viewed as un-American.
4 A constitutional amendment required loyalty oaths be taken before voting in presidential elections.

23 Which is a valid conclusion about United States involvement in the Korean War?
1   The policy of containment was applied in Asia as well as in Europe.
2   United Nations economic sanctions are more effective than military action.
3   The American people will support United States participation in any war, whether declared or undeclared.
4   United States cooperation with wartime allies ends when the war ends.

24 President Harry Truman relieved General Douglas MacArthur of his command in the Korean conflict because
1   the U.N. forces were losing the War under MacArthur's command
2   MacArthur was planning to challenge Truman for the presidency
3   the U.N. wanted a non-American in command
4   MacArthur challenged the concept of civilian control of the military

25 In the 1950s, a number of individuals' constitutional rights were violated by
1   application of rationing rules
2   conversion from wartime to peacetime production
3   the activities of Senator Joseph McCarthy
4   reorganization of the armed forces

THEMATIC ESSAY QUESTION

Theme:

> **Government's Role in the Economy**
>
> Several actions taken by the U.S. government during and after World War II had significant effects on the national economy.

Task:

> Using your knowledge of United States history and government, write an essay in which you select *three* (3) actions taken by the U.S. government during or after World War II that altered economic life. For each one chosen,
> • describe the existing economic, social, or political conditions that prompted the action, and
> • discuss the impact of the change on the economic life of the nation.

Suggestions:
You may use any action from your study of United States history and government. You may wish to include actions such as the *Lend-Lease Act*, War Production Board activities, the G.I. Bill, rationing, the *Employment Act of 1946*, or the *Taft-Hartley Act*. **You are not limited to these suggestions.**

PRACTICE SKILLS FOR DBQ

Directions: The following task is based on the accompanying documents. The documents may have been edited for the purposes of this exercise. The task is designed to test your ability to work with historical documents. As you analyze the documents, take into account both the source of the documents and the author's point of view.

Historical Context:
After World War II, growing suspicion of Soviet actions led the United States government to make major alterations in its foreign policy.

Part A – Short Answer
The documents that follow present perceptions of U.S. foreign policy after World War II. Examine each document carefully, then answer the scaffold question that follows it.

Document 1

> "…it will be clearly seen that the Soviet pressure against the free institutions of the Western world is something that can be contained by the [skillful] and vigilant application of counter-force at a series of constantly shifting geographical and political points"
>
> – George F. Kennan, *Foreign Affairs*, July 1947

Questions for Document 1

1a What policy was Kennan recommending?

1b How was this policy different from traditional U.S. foreign policy?

Document 2

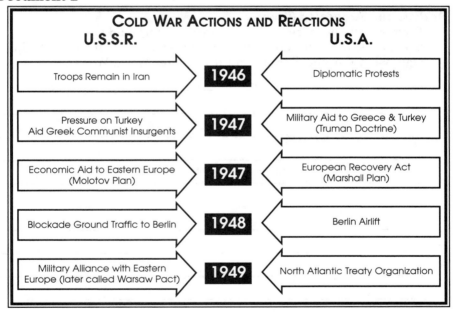

COLD WAR ACTIONS AND REACTIONS

U.S.S.R.		U.S.A.
Troops Remain in Iran	1946	Diplomatic Protests
Pressure on Turkey / Aid Greek Communist Insurgents	1947	Military Aid to Greece & Turkey (Truman Doctrine)
Economic Aid to Eastern Europe (Molotov Plan)	1947	European Recovery Act (Marshall Plan)
Blockade Ground Traffic to Berlin	1948	Berlin Airlift
Military Alliance with Eastern Europe (later called Warsaw Pact)	1949	North Atlantic Treaty Organization

Question for Document 2

What pattern of activity is portrayed in this chart?

Part B – Essay Response

Task: Using only the two documents, write one or two paragraphs discussing the change in U.S. foreign policy in the years after World War II.

State your thesis:

- use only the information in the documents to support your thesis position
- add your analysis of the documents
- incorporate your answers from the two Part *A* scaffold questions

_____

_____

_____

_____

Additional Suggested Task:

From your knowledge of United States history and government, make a list of other major alterations that the U.S. made in its foreign policy (beyond Europe) in the era after World War II.

_____

_____

_____

_____

_____

_____

_____

_____

_____

_____

_____

_____

_____

_____

_____

_____

★ **LESSON**

8

PAGE 273

THE WORLD IN UNCERTAIN TIMES

St. Patrick's Cathedral & Sculpture of Greek
Titan, Atlas, NYC, NY   – ©PhotoDisc 1993

THE WORLD IN UNCERTAIN TIMES
1950-1980

TOWARD A POST-INDUSTRIAL WORLD: LIVING IN A GLOBAL AGE

After World War II, the pace of global change accelerated. Interdependence among nations grew. Since the isolation of earlier times no longer worked, the United States tried to meet the challenges presented by the changes. America learned that seeking global cooperation was not easy. Conflicts arose frequently. The United States learned to consider the basic desire of all nations for sovereignty and control of their own destinies.

CHANGE WITHIN THE UNITED STATES

CHANGING ENERGY SOURCES

The United States is the largest consumer of energy in the world. Finding ways to meet this demand have resulted in some problems. Traditional fossil fuels (coal, oil) contribute to pollution. Dependence on petroleum imports have made Americans subject to the political and economic whims of other nations. Nearly 20% of America's electricity is generated by nuclear power plants, but the cost of building the nuclear plants is enormous. Many critics also question the safety of nuclear reactors. Although plant breakdowns and leakage of radiation are rare, a 1979 nuclear accident at Three Mile Island in Pennsylvania heightened awareness of the danger.

Cooling towers for nuclear reactors
(PhotoDisc ©1995)

Changing Materials

Stronger and lighter materials affect every aspect of modern life. Plastics are lighter and can retain strength for many years. Automobiles and airplanes use lighter metals and alloys to reduce weight and fuel consumption. The medical and communications industries use fiber optics, which sends light through minute fiber rods.

Changing Technology

Computers are a vital part of everyday life in America. Business and industry, government, the military, space agencies, and the medical field all depend on computer technology. The computer age has also created numerous social pressures and difficulties.

- fewer "**blue-collar**" jobs (industrial work) when automation and robotics replace human labor

- increased need for computer literacy to qualify for jobs in nearly all fields

- reduced individual privacy due to governments' and private data collecting organizations' greater capacity to access information on individuals

- enhanced information explosion as widespread access to the internet provides an almost limitless source of material

Changing Corporate Structures

Many corporations today are **multinational corporations**, especially in the manufacturing, mining, banking, petroleum, chemical, and high tech fields. They have the advantage of access to raw materials, cheap labor, and international markets. No single nation's laws can constrain them. Critics of multinationals fear corporations will interfere in the domestic affairs of nations. They also say **LDCs** (less developed countries) will be dominated by multinationals. American critics denounce multinationals for shifting operations overseas for cheaper labor.

Corporate mergers also changed the structure of American business. Firms that used to sell a single product merged with others into giant **conglomerates**, selling products in diverse fields. Some mergers combined two competing firms in the same product line, sometimes pushing the limits of antitrust laws.

CHANGING NATURE OF EMPLOYMENT

In 1800, most Americans were farmers. By 1900, the economy had shifted to industry, with factories providing many jobs. Since World War II, however, many older industries have closed or moved to other countries. Foreign competition and automation resulted in huge drops in the steel and textile industries, mining, and other blue collar jobs. Growth in today's economy is in service industries: information processing, health care, retailing, education, finance, food service, and recreation. America's post industrial age required a better educated work force.

CHANGE IN GLOBAL CONDITIONS

Changes in other parts of the world have had varying impact on the United States. There were a number of categories of significant global change.

- **World Population Growth** – Industrialized nations have seen population growth slow, but for most LDCs, population continues to grow at a fast pace. Recent efforts by India and China to limit child bearing have met with some success.

- **Agriculture** – Governments in many countries have taken advantage of the Green Revolution to increase food supply. However, other countries, especially Less Developed Countries, lack the money, knowledge, or climate to take advantage of this revolution.

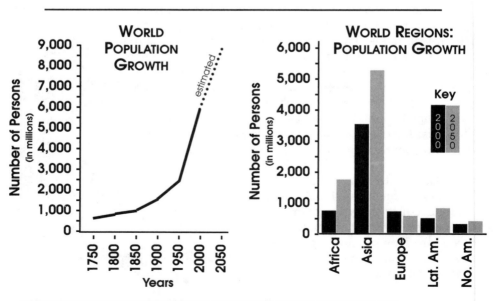

- **Manufacturing** – Many LDCs hoped that industrialization would bring a higher standard of living. This has often failed to occur, as rapid population growth, corrupt governments, lack of capital, and poor education hinder industrialization.

- **Environmental Concern** – Actions of one nation can affect many. Acid rain from factories falls in other countries. Nuclear testing over oceans can cause widespread fallout. Ozone depletion has occurred as a result of the release of the chemical compound CFC (chlorofluoro-carbon, used in refrigeration) into the upper atmosphere. Nations eager for industrialization have generally not placed high priorities on environmental protection.

- **Power Relationships** – For most of the second half of the 20th century, the United States and the Soviet Union were the two superpowers. Since the Soviet Union dissolved in 1991, no country has taken its place. America remains alone at the top. The **OPEC** cartel (Organization of Petroleum Exporting Countries) acts as an economic world power by controlling the supply and price of oil, but their effectiveness varies considerably from year to year.

CONTAINMENT AND CONSENSUS
1945-1960

EISENHOWER FOREIGN POLICIES

Under President **Dwight D. Eisenhower**'s administration (1953-1961), the United States attempted to maintain world peace while continuing the cold war campaign to check the spread of communism – especially in Asia. The increase of nuclear weapons and the introduction of long-range missiles gave international conflicts the potential for global destruction.

DOMESTIC POLITICS AND
CONSTITUTIONAL ISSUES UNDER EISENHOWER

As the Korean War ended in 1953, Eisenhower hoped to stimulate the economy by lifting government wage and price controls. Government defense and foreign aid spending renewed inflation during the rest of the 1950s, but it was offset by the steady growth of the economy. Demand for U.S. agricultural products lessened as European farmers recovered from World War II. To help American farmers, Eisenhower instituted a more flexible system of farm-price supports, hoping to reduce farmers' dependence on government subsidies and reduce overproduction. A federal **Soil Bank Plan** paid farmers to take land out of production and convert it to

☆ CAPSULE – EISENHOWER AND FOREIGN AFFAIRS

President Dwight Eisenhower with Secretary of State Dulles, assures President Ngo Dinh Diem the United States will to provide South Vietnam with military assistance.
(National Archive)

Achievements

- ended the Korean War, a stalemate with the country remaining divided near the 38th Parallel
- issued the **Eisenhower Doctrine**, which helped keep communists from gaining control of unstable Middle Eastern governments, such as Lebanon

Controversies

- supported the policies of Secretary of State John Foster Dulles of **brinkmanship** (to be constantly ready to use deterrent force) and **massive retaliation** (to destroy an attacking nation with nuclear weapons)
- expounded the **Domino Theory** and began long involvement in containing communism in Southeast Asia after French gave up their colonies
- CIA sent a U-2 spy plane over the U.S.S.R., then denied spying charges after the plane was shot down by the Soviets

pasture or forest. These plans did not solve the farm problem. Surpluses of supply mounted and many farmers lost money. Continued mechanization drove others out of agriculture altogether.

Labor unions won great gains at the bargaining table after World War II. Union members received cost of living raises, expanded pension benefits, and health insurance. In 1955, the nation's two giant, long-time rival labor organizations merged. The American Federation of Labor and the Congress of Industrial Organizations formed the new **AFL-CIO**. Corruption plagued some unions, however. Congress launched investigations against racketeering in the International Longshoremen's Association and the International Brotherhood of Teamsters. Out of these

THE WARREN COURT JUDICIAL ACTIVISM

DECISION	SIGNIFICANCE
Brown v. Board of Ed. of Topeka (1954)	Racial segregation of schools violated the Fourteenth Amendment.
Baker v. Carr (1962)	"One person, one vote" rule ordered states to set up Congressional Districts on equal basis.
Engel v. Vitale (1962)	State laws requiring prayers in schools violated the First Amendment.
Gideon v. Wainwright (1963)	State laws denying felony suspects legal counsel violated the Sixth Amendment.
Miranda v. Arizona (1966)	Authorities must inform accused persons of their "due process" rights under the Fifth and Sixth Amendment.

investigations came the ***Landrum-Griffin Labor Management Reporting and Disclosure Act*** (1957). The new law required unions to publish financial statements, hold regular elections, use secret ballots, end secondary boycotts, and forbade communists and convicted felons from holding union office.

In 1953, President Eisenhower appointed the governor of California, **Earl Warren**, as the 14th Chief Justice of the Supreme Court. For the next fifteen years, the Warren Court followed a policy of **judicial activism**. This meant that decisions of the Court not only provided interpretations of the Constitution, but initiated broad changes in American life. Critics claimed the Court was actually performing legislative tasks and taking power away from the individual and the legislative branch.

CIVIL RIGHTS

After the Civil War, the Thirteenth, Fourteenth, and Fifteenth Amendments freed former slaves, supposedly made them equal citizens, and nominally gave them suffrage. As Reconstruction ended, Southern state leaders found legal ways to circumvent these amendments and avoid equal treatment for African Americans. Jim Crow laws established de jure segregation throughout the South. The 1896 *Plessy* decision by the Supreme Court stated that racial separation was legal as long as facilities were equal. It quickly evolved that transportation, education, dining, and entertainment facilities were always separate, and rarely were they equal. Although many groups and individuals denounced social inequality, little change occurred until after World War II.

Rosa Parks breaks a Jim Crow Law in 1955 by sitting in the front of a bus.
UPI

☆ Capsule – Major Civil Rights Events: 1945-1960

- **1947** – Jackie Robinson became the first African American baseball player for the Brooklyn Dodgers
- **1954** – In *Brown v. Board of Education of Topeka, Kansas* (1954), the Supreme Court reversed the doctrine of "separate but equal" from the *Plessy* case. Segregation was declared unconstitutional because it violated the *Fourteenth Amendment's* "equal protection of the laws" provision.
- **1955** – Rosa Parks refused to give up her seat on a bus in Montgomery Alabama, and Martin Luther King Jr. organized a boycott of the buses, eventually forcing the city and bus company to desegregate facilities.
- **1957** – The schools in Little Rock, Arkansas refused to integrate their schools (a common event in the years immediately after the *Brown* decision). President Eisenhower refused to let such flagrant defiance of federal law go unanswered, and he sent in regular U.S. Army troops to escort African-American students into the school.
- **1957** – Congress passed the first *Civil Rights Act* since Reconstruction. The law created a Civil Rights Commission and sought to secure voting rights for African Americans in the South.
- **1960** – Freedom Riders rode buses to try to desegregate bus terminals in the South. Others engaged in sit-ins at restaurants. These tactics were called nonviolent, direct action, and civil disobedience. Protesters willingly went to jail to protest the unjust laws.

Sport Magazine

Jackie Robinson   Sports Magazine, 1947

PROSPERITY AND CONSERVATISM: 1950s

The 1950s was a time of prosperity. Postwar international stress, Korea, and McCarthyism left most Americans desirous of a more stable environment. The Eisenhower domestic policies were conservative by nature, and most people welcomed a lessening of government reform efforts after nearly three decades of upheaval.

EVIDENCE OF PROSPERITY: THE 1950s
• 50 million autos sold to Americans
• interstate Highway system begun and frequent travel is common
• television enters a majority of American homes
• G.I. Bill allows millions of veterans to go to college
• high birth rate results in the "baby boom"

MIGRATION AND IMMIGRATION

Prior to 1965, the National Origins Quota System from the 1920s gave preferential quotas to immigrants of "old" ethnic groups from Northern and Western Europe. Congress passed the **Immigration Act of 1965** to abolish the old National Origins System. The new regulations created a limit for the Eastern and Western Hemispheres and based admission on a first-come, first served-bases. Preference was given to relatives of American citizens and those with needed job skills. The result was new immigration from Asia and Latin America.

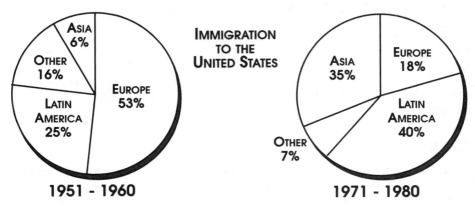

IMMIGRATION TO THE UNITED STATES

1951 - 1960: ASIA 6%, OTHER 16%, LATIN AMERICA 25%, EUROPE 53%

1971 - 1980: ASIA 35%, EUROPE 18%, LATIN AMERICA 40%, OTHER 7%

CITIES AND SUBURBS

During the 1950s, millions of new, affordable homes were built in suburbs for young families. Shortages of housing and crowded conditions in the cities made commuting from the suburban areas more reasonable. The G.I. Bill aided veterans in securing mortgages and gave even more incentive for construction. Thousands of single family houses were constructed, some using mass production techniques in the **Levittown** developments of New York and Pennsylvania. At the same time, many cities experienced a declining tax base as the middle class migrated to the suburbs or to other regions of the country. Businesses also left many cities, resulting in unemployment and urban decay. Many older cities of the Northeast and Mid-West (dubbed the "**Rust Belt**" by the mass media) were on the brink of bankruptcy by the 1960s.

CITY POPULATION CHANGE 1950-1990 (SOURCE: U.S. BUREAU OF CENSUS)		
CITY	POPULATION IN 1990	CHANGE 1950-1990
New York	7,322,564	-569,393
Los Angeles	3,485,398	+1,515,040
Chicago	2,783,726	-837,236
Houston	1,630,553	+1,034,390
Philadelphia	1,585,577	-486,028
San Diego	1,110,549	+776,162
Detroit	1,027,974	-821,594
Dallas	1,006,877	+572,415
Phoenix	983,403	+876,585
San Antonio	935,933	+421,170

As the table (above right) shows, some cities did prosper. Retirees, immigrants, and white urban dwellers of the Northeast moved to the South and West. The "**Sun Belt**" cities offered warmer climates, expanding job markets, and a lower cost of living.

DECADE OF CHANGE – 1960s

The general peace and prosperity of the Eisenhower years disintegrated as the 1960s progressed. Television brought the Vietnam War and urban riots into living rooms and divided public opinion as it had not been since the Civil War. By the end of the decade, the nation soured on social reform programs that had held great promise when the 1960s had dawned.

THE KENNEDY YEARS

In the election of 1960, Massachusetts Senator **John F. Kennedy** became the first Catholic elected as President of the United States. The Democrats "balanced the ticket" by selecting Senator **Lyndon B. Johnson** of Texas to appeal to Southern Protestant voters.

THE "NEW FRONTIER" PROGRAM

The youth-oriented Kennedy promised to lead a new generation of Americans to a "New Frontier" with energetic proposals for the space program, civil rights, urban renewal, social welfare, and a new image in foreign policy. Congress approved some of President Kennedy's proposals, but rejected others.

Rejected by Congress
- federal aid to education
- medical care for the poor and elderly
- tax cuts
- civil rights protections

Passed by Congress
- lower tariffs
- increased minimum wage
- increased Social Security benefits
- aid to depressed cities
- expansion of the space program

White House Historical Association
Washington, D.C.

President Kennedy used his executive powers in an effort to reduce civil rights violence in the South. After the *Brown* decision, few Southern school integrated. In 1962, **James Meredith** attempted to become the first African American student to register at the University of Mississippi. Mississippi's governor barred Meredith's entry. The President sent in federal troops to stop riots and see that Meredith enrolled in the school, but not before two people were killed.

KENNEDY'S ACTIONS IN FOREIGN AFFAIRS

- **Cuban Problems** – In 1958, rebels led by Fidel Castro overthrew Cuban dictator Fulgencio Batista. Unexpectedly, Castro immediately denounced the United States and announced that Cuba would be a communist state, allied with the Soviet Union. After breaking relations with Cuba, Eisenhower approved a Central Intelligence Agency plot to train and assist Cuban refugees in launching a counterrevolution. When Kennedy came into office, he went ahead with the plan. In April 1961, two thousand Cuban rebels landed at the Bay of Pigs with U.S. assistance. An air strike from Guatemala by CIA trained Cuban fighter pilots never materialized. A planned revolt inside Cuba never took place. The invaders were captured, and both Castro and the Soviets denounced the United States.

NO PERMISSION HAS BEEN GRANTED BY N&N PUBLISHING COMPANY, INC TO REPRODUCE ANY PART OF THIS BOOK

- **Cuban Missile Crisis** – Additional difficulties with Cuba developed in 1962, when American U-2 planes provided pictures of Soviet built missile bases with nuclear capacity being constructed in Cuba. Kennedy invoked the Monroe Doctrine and publicly condemned the Soviet intrusion as a threat to the entire Western Hemisphere. The President ordered a naval blockade of Cuba. Soviet leader Khrushchev finally backed down and agreed to remove the missiles. In an attempt to ease tensions, the United States, Soviet Union, and over 100 nations signed the **Nuclear Test Ban Treaty** in 1963. This prohibited testing of nuclear weapons in the atmosphere, underwater, or in outer space.

- **Latin American Aid** – Kennedy offered an aid program called the Alliance for Progress. This ten year program poured over 20 billion dollars into Latin American republics for housing, school, hospitals, and factories. In return, the governments were to have initiated political reforms to achieve greater economic opportunity for the masses, but few were truly effective.

- **The Peace Corps** – Kennedy created a people-to-people program to get Americans personally involved in helping people in underdeveloped nations. Participants used they skills to help other nations develop agricultural, educational, and medical facilities.

- **The Berlin Wall** – Berlin remained a divided city from World War II, and thousands of people escaped annually from communism in the East to freedom in the West. Khrushchev ordered the East German government to seal off the flow of refugees by building a 25 mile wall between the two sectors. The Kennedy Administration condemned the East Germans for cutting off thousands of Germans from relatives and jobs.

ASSASSINATION IN DALLAS

On 22 November 1963, Lee Harvey Oswald shot and killed President Kennedy in a motorcade in Dallas. Vice President Lyndon Baines Johnson was immediately sworn in as the nation's leader. Two days later, Jack Ruby, a Dallas bar owner, shot and killed Oswald. After much investigation, the **Warren Commission**, led by the Chief Justice, concluded that the assassination was not part of a larger conspiracy. Both Oswald and Ruby acted alone, though skeptics remained un-convinced.

LYNDON JOHNSON – GREAT SOCIETY

Lyndon Baines Johnson had over 20 years of experience in Congress before becoming President. In 1964, Johnson was elected in his own right by polling more than 60% of the popular vote against Republican Senator Barry Goldwater of Arizona. President Johnson undertook a sweeping reform program called the **Great Society**. He envisioned a society in which poverty, illiteracy, hunger, and racial injustice would be eliminated. All Americans would enjoy freedom, equality, and

Lyndon Johnson
36th U.S. President
(White House)

A VARIETY OF GREAT SOCIETY ACTIONS

Action	Results
Twenty-fourth Amendment (1964)	banned the use of poll taxes (voting fees) in federal elections
Civil Rights Acts (1964, 1968)	the 1964 Act outlawed discrimination in employment and in public accommodations connected with interstate commerce; the 1968 Act banned discrimination in housing and real estate
Project Head Start (1965)	gave funds for developmental assistance to disabled children and children from low-income families
Medicare (1965)	extended Social Security benefits to provide health insurance for the elderly
Elementary & Secondary Education Act (1965)	funded libraries, textbooks, and supplementary education centers to help Native Americans, migrants, and low income families
Voting Rights Act (1965)	federal examiners registered African American voters; also suspended all literacy tests; (by the end of 1965 a quarter of a million new African American voters had been registered)
VISTA (1966)	this "domestic Peace Corps" used volunteers to run programs to help teach job skills in poverty areas
Job Corps (1966)	provides vocational training, health care, and personal counseling to disadvantaged youth in order to help them find work
Medicaid (1966)	provides medical payments for low income, blind, and disabled (funded jointly by U.S. federal and state agencies)
Department of Housing and Urban Development (1965)	administers programs for mortgage insurance for home-buyers, low-income rental assistance, and programs for urban revitalization
Department of Transportation (1966)	administers environmental safety and an efficient national transportation system

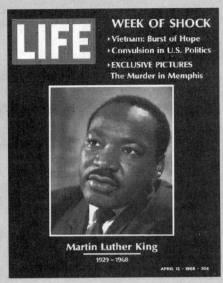

WEEK OF SHOCK
› Vietnam: Burst of Hope
› Convulsion in U.S. Politics

› EXCLUSIVE PICTURES
The Murder in Memphis

Martin Luther King
1929 – 1968

APRIL 12 · 1968 · 35¢

LETTER FROM A BIRMINGHAM JAIL

"We will match your capacity to inflict suffering with our capacity to endure suffering. We will meet your physical force with our soul force. We will not hate you, but we cannot obey your unjust laws. Do to us what you will and we will still love you. Bomb our homes and threaten our children; send your hooded perpetrators of violence into our communities and drag us out on some wayside road, beating us and leaving us half dead, and we will still love you. But we will soon wear you down by our capacity to suffer. And in winning our freedom, we will so appeal to your heart and conscience that we will win you in the process."

– Martin Luther King, Jr., *Letter from a Birmingham Jail*, April 16, 1963

prosperity. It would involve substantially expanding the role of the federal government in everyday life.

The Great Society programs helped millions, but the problems they addressed failed to go away. Great Society's scope was enormous, and so was its cost. The unpopularity of Johnson's foreign policies gradually undercut support for his domestic reforms.

CONTINUED DEMANDS FOR EQUALITY: THE CIVIL RIGHTS MOVEMENT

The movement for racial equality, begun in earnest after the Supreme Court's landmark decision in *Brown v. Board of Education of Topeka* (1954), continued in the Johnson years. The Civil Rights Movement encompassed a growing variety of organizations, advocating different means of achieving equality.

- **NAACP** – The National Association for the Advancement of Colored People was founded by W.E.B. DuBois and others in 1909. The NAACP used legislative pressures and legal challenges (the *Brown* decision is an example) to actively protest racial injustice.

- **National Urban League** – Founded in 1910, it has worked mainly to assist African Americans migrating to Northern cities from the rural South. It fought constantly against **de facto segregation** to improve urban living conditions and took a leading role in seeking fair treatment for minorities in industry.

- **SCLC** – The Southern Christian Leadership Conference was formed by Dr. Martin Luther King, Jr. and other ministers after the Montgomery bus boycott (1956-1957). Its leaders used nonviolent, direct action techniques to confront injustice through marches and public demonstrations of civil disobedience. While under arrest for leading nonviolent marches, Dr. King wrote his famous *Letter from a Birmingham Jail*. In it, Dr. King equated the nonviolent struggle of African Americans with the struggle of early Christians and the Indian independence movement of Mohandas Gandhi.

- **SNCC** – The Student Non-violent Coordinating Committee was formed in 1960 by college students arranging sit-in demonstrations at segregated restaurants in the South. As the 60s progressed, SNCC became increasingly militant as white resistance to integration grew. SNCC leader Stokley Carmichael questioned the nonviolent tactics of Dr. King. Carmichael's calls for militant "Black Power" alienated some political figures as well as some general popular support of the movement among liberals.

- **CORE** – The Congress of Racial Equality was organized in 1942 to promote peaceful means of calling attention to racial discrimination. CORE organized the Freedom Riders of 1961, which staged demonstrations in segregated buses, terminals, and waiting rooms in the South.

- **Black Muslims**– In the 1960s, the Black Muslims held that true equality was nearly impossible under the U.S. political system. They began a movement for a separate American state within the United States. Malcolm X became the foremost spokesman for the group. Malcolm X was beginning to advocate more active accommodation with U.S. society rather than separatism, when he was assassinated by a rival Muslim faction. This more inclusive approach continued in later decades.

- **Black Panthers** –- This most radical group of the Sixties encouraged violent revolution by the African American population and armed take-over of the country. Few supported their fierce tactics, and many were arrested or forced to go underground.

1960s CIVIL RIGHTS LEGISLATION	
LAW	**DESCRIPTION**
Civil Right Acts of 1964	attaches stiff criminal penalties for discrimination in voting and employment; ends segregation in most public facilities; withholds federal funds from school districts and communities practicing discrimination
Civil Rights Act of 1968	bans discrimination in rental units and real estate transactions and gives broader federal protection to civil rights workers; prohibits the hiring and classification of employees; makes it illegal for unions to discriminate on the basis of race, color, religion, sex, and national origin in their membership practices
Voting Rights Act of 1965	suspends literacy tests in counties where more than half the population cannot vote; provides federal help to register new voters; began action to end state use of poll taxes
Voting Rights Act of 1970	ends all literacy tests and establishes 30-day residency requirements

CIVIL RIGHTS ADVANCES: LEGISLATIVE AND JUDICIAL

The persistent effort of the Civil Rights Movement gradually influenced the legislative and executive branches of the federal government to take actions for justice and equality in America. Congress in 1964 proposed, and the states ratified, the *Twenty-fourth Amendment*, which prohibited the poll tax in federal elections. In addition, the judicial branch continued to move and shape public policy which it had begun with the *Brown* decision.

DEMANDS FOR EQUALITY: WOMEN

In 1900, women made up 17% of the work force; by 1997, the figure had grown to 46%. Women continue to dominate clerical positions, domestic work and patient care in hospitals. At the same time, the number of women in professional, managerial, and supervisory positions has increased. Many important women's issues have come into focus since 1970.

- **Equal Rights Amendment** – Proposed by Congress in 1972, but failed to gain the required ratification by 3/4 of the states. Opponents feared laws which protect women would be nullified, and that the general terminology of the amendment would be too susceptible to court interpretations.

THE SUPREME COURT
WASHINGTON

⭐ CAPSULE – SUPREME COURT DECISIONS FURTHERING EQUALITY

Court Case	Decision
Baker v. Carr (1962)	The Court applied the *Fourteenth Amendment* to bring about equally-sized election districts. The Court ruled that inequality in representation violated the equal protection clause. As a result, state and local governments now reapportion (redraw) their election districts following each census to guarantee the concept of "one person, one vote."
Heart of Atlanta Motel Inc. v. United States (1964)	The motel refused to serve African Americans, but the Court ruled that Congress had the constitutional authority to apply the *Civil Rights Act* of 1964 to the business in question, since the public accommodation engaged in interstate commerce.
Swann v. the Charlotte Mecklenburg Board of Education (1971)	The Court approved busing of students to schools in different parts of communities to achieve racial balance.
Bakke v. the Regents of the University of California (1978)	The Court ruled that affirmative action programs, which set aside a certain percentage of positions for African Americans and other minorities were constitutional. However, the Court went on to stress that such programs must be administered in such a way that the rights of others are not violated.

- **Abortion** – In *Roe v. Wade* (1973), the Supreme Court invalidated all state laws which prohibited abortion. Many women's groups saw it as a victory for women's rights (freedom of choice). Others saw abortion as murder and formed Right to Life Movements, with the goal of getting the Court to reverse *Roe*, or prohibit abortion with a Constitutional amendment. Neither has occurred, and abortion, though restricted in some states, remains legal.

- **Equal Pay for Equal Work** – Statistics indicate that women earn considerably less than men. Some states passed "equal-pay-for-equal-work" laws, which mandate the same pay scale for jobs requiring similar skills.

RISING CONSCIOUSNESS OF HISPANIC AMERICANS

The Hispanic (or Latino) population of the United States doubled from 1970 to 1990, and some projections indicate that nearly 25% of the population will be of Hispanic ancestry by the year 2050. Hispanics account for much of the immigration to the United States. About 60% of Hispanics are of Mexican origin, 12% are from Puerto Rico, and 5% from Cuba. Significant numbers also come from the Dominican Republic, Central America, and other islands of the Caribbean. In recent years, Hispanic political influence has increased. A number of Congressional delegations have Hispanic representation, and non-Hispanic politicians are paying increased attention to issues that are important to the Hispanic community. In recent years several key issues for Hispanics have been the focus of national attention.

- **Availability of Bilingual Opportunities** – To provide equal opportunity, Federal legislation requires bilingual ballots in certain communities, and many school districts provide bilingual education.

- **Protection for Farm Laborers** – Many Hispanics found work as migrant farm workers, living in deplorable conditions. **Cesar Chavez** organized the United Farm Workers and led boycotts of produce to bring attention to harsh conditions. Over the years, conditions slowly improved as federal, state, and local governments became more involved in the regulation of migrant farm operations.

- **Immigration Policies** – Hispanics seek fairness in immigration policies, and protection from discrimination for recent arrivals. Other Americans at times voiced complaints that Cubans fleeing the Castro dictatorship were welcome with open arms, while other refugees from political oppression in the Caribbean, such as Haitians, received far less consideration.

DEMANDS FOR EQUALITY: NATIVE AMERICAN MOVEMENT

Long one of the most impoverished groups in America, the Native Americans organized the **American Indian Movement** (AIM) in 1968. They demanded equal rights and greater government concern for the problems of Native Americans. AIM developed into a militant organization, using direct and often violent action to gain publicity and achieve their goals. In recent years several key issues for Native American have been the focus of national attention.

- **Less Paternalistic Attitude** – For decades, the federal Bureau of Indian Affairs treated Native Americans with a paternalistic attitude. Slowly, Native Americans were given more control over their affairs.

☆ CAPSULE –
PROTECTION OF THE RIGHTS OF THE ACCUSED

Through a series of Supreme Court decisions, those accused of crimes gained important constitutional protections in the 1960s. These decisions resulted in widespread change in the way authorities treated criminal suspects.

- ***Mapp v. Ohio*** (1961) – A suspect was handcuffed by police in her apartment, who then conducted a search without a warrant. The Court ruled that this was an illegal search because of the *Fourth Amendment* guarantee against unreasonable search and seizure.

- ***Gideon v. Wainwright*** (1963) – The suspect, Clarence Gideon, could not afford a lawyer, and was found guilty. The Court ruled that the *Sixth Amendment* guarantee of a lawyer means a state must provide the accused with a lawyer if the accused can not afford one.

- ***Miranda v. Arizona*** (1966) – Suspect Ernesto Miranda was questioned by police about a rape and kidnapping case, and then arrested. Miranda appealed to the Court, arguing that the police should have told him of his constitutional right against self incrimination. The Court agreed, and to be sure that suspects know their *Fifth* and *Sixth Amendment* rights, those who are detained must be told before any questioning of their right to remain silent and their right to a lawyer.

- **Honoring Past Treaties** – Agreements which gave land to Native American tribes centuries ago were broken as the government needed to build highways, reservoirs, and other public facilities. Before 1970, such land seizures were common, but recently, Native Americans have increasingly gone to court over treaty violations and have won most of the time.

YEARS OF TURMOIL:
THE VIETNAM WAR (1965-1972)

The Vietnam War was the longest and (except for the Civil War) the most divisive conflict in the nation's history. A former French colony, Vietnam was divided at 17° N. Latitude (the 17th Parallel) when the French left in 1954. A communist rebel group headed by Ho Chi Minh took control in the North, while anti-communists controlled the South. The United States was to supervise elections to unite the country in 1956, but the elections were never held. Meanwhile, Ho Chi Minh gave increasing support to a communist insurgent movement in the South – the **Viet Cong**. By the early 1960s, the Viet Cong grew into a major threat, and President Kennedy increased U.S. commitment by sending 15,000 military personnel as advisors.

ESCALATION OF THE WAR

As part of the containment policy, the **Domino Theory** continued to influence American foreign policy-makers during the Kennedy and Johnson years. The Theory's premise was that if one weak nation fell to communism, others around it would similarly topple. Policy-makers felt that a stand had to be made in Vietnam if the surrounding nations were to survive the communist threat. In 1964, U.S. ships were reportedly fired upon by North Vietnamese gunboats in the Gulf of Tonkin. Congress subsequently passed the *Tonkin Gulf Resolution*, which authorized the President to "take all necessary action to protect American interests" in the region. Essentially the Johnson Administration took the Resolution as carte blanche (unrestricted power) to conduct a full-scale war without a declaration from Congress.

Over the next four years, Johnson sent 500,000 U.S. troops to Vietnam. Yet, American military intervention failed to stop the communist penetration into the South. Guerrillas attacked towns and villages, then retreated into

U.S. Troop Escalation During The Vietnam War

JFK   LBJ   Nixon

(y-axis: Thousands Of Troops — 100, 200, 300, 400, 500, 600)
(x-axis: 1960, '63, '66, '69, '72, '74)

the rain forests. During the 1968 Vietnamese New Year holiday, the Viet Cong and North Vietnamese launched the Tet Offensive. It showed that the enemy had been little weakened by over three years of American effort. Fighting continued until 1973.

PROTESTS AT HOME

As the Vietnam War escalated, an increasing number of Americans, nicknamed "doves," demanded immediate withdrawal from what they viewed as an unjust war. Anti-war protests in major cities drew hundreds of thousands of people. The draft itself became a hated symbol of the War, and some protesters burned their draft cards or fled to Canada to avoid the draft. Civil rights leaders protested that a disproportionate number of African Amer-

Memorial Stone for the four students who died during an anti-war demonstration at Kent State University on 4 May 1970.
Photo - Kent State History Archives

icans were being drafted. Radical groups, such as the **Students for a Democratic Society** lead marches and protests on the nation's campuses. On the Kent State campus of the University of Ohio, National Guardsmen killed four students during a protest. A more radical group, the **Weathermen**, engaged in terrorist tactics, burning buildings and planting bombs. A small number of young people rejected American traditional value altogether, adopting outlandish clothes and experimenting with drugs. Some of these "hippies" and "flower children" rejected society altogether, living in "back-to-nature" communes and enclaves in San Francisco's Haight-Ashbury and New York's Greenwich Village.

IMPACT OF THE WAR ON SOCIETY

The Vietnam conflict had a critical impact on America. The Great Society programs suffered as billions of tax dollars were diverted to the military. War spending caused inflation which made everything more costly. In addition, the American military command was widely criticized for its conduct of the War. Top generals assured President Johnson and the public that the Vietnam War was being won while asking for more and more money and troops. As the War became increasingly unpopular, demands grew for legal limits on the President's power to involve the country in military conflict. Whereas Johnson received all the criticism for escalating the Vietnam War, all the blame for the catastrophic misadventure should not rest on his shoulders. It should be remembered that Congress passed the *Tonkin Gulf Resolution* in 1964 and continued to fund the war effort.

A TREND TOWARD CONSERVATISM: 1972-1980

The period of upheaval and change during the 1960s was followed by a more conservative period in the 1970s and 1980s. The protests and civil disorders convinced many Americans that law and order had broken down. The failure in Vietnam led to increased caution in the area of foreign policy. The momentum of the Civil Rights Movement also evaporated in the domestic turbulence of the late 1960s.

All of this was reflected in the 1968 presidential election. Johnson, sensing his unpopularity, declared he would not run. For the Democrats, Vice President Hubert Humphrey carried the Johnson Administration's big spending, pro-war legacy, while for the Republicans, former Vice President Richard Nixon called for toning down government excesses and "peace with honor." Staunchly conservative George Wallace of Alabama polled 13.5% of the vote as a third party candidate. Nixon received 301 electoral votes to Humphrey's 191, but Nixon only received 43.4% of the popular vote.

Richard Nixon
37th President of U.S.
White House Historical Association

THE NIXON PRESIDENCY 1969-1974

DOMESTIC POLICIES AND EVENTS

ENVIRONMENTAL AND CONSUMER LEGISLATION

Congress created the Environmental Protection Agency to enforce regulations flowing from the *Clean Air*, *Resource Recovery Act*, and *Water Pollution Control Act*. Business complained that compliance was complicated and costly. To protect consumers, the Consumer Products Safety Commission was created in 1972, and the *Truth in Lending Act* required consistent disclosure of finance charges and annual percentage rates in consumer credit arrangements. **Ralph Nader** became a strong and intense spokesman for consumer rights. His book, *Unsafe at Any Speed* (1965) was highly critical of the lax production methods and unsafe vehicles of the U.S. auto industry.

SELF-DETERMINATION FOR NATIVE AMERICANS

In 1970, President Nixon sent a message to Congress proposing a policy of self-determination for Native Americans. The new policy would turn over the administration of most of the federal programs to the tribes. A final version of the measure did this to some extent, but Native Americans continued to complain of government interference. In a similar action, the administration began to name Native Americans to management positions in the Bureau of Indian Affairs.

PENTAGON PAPERS

In 1971, the *New York Times* was given a confidential study made by the Defense Department on the Vietnam War. Named the *"Pentagon Papers,"* the documents revealed the misleading and dishonest statements made by the military and the government during the War. The Nixon Administration went to the Supreme Court to halt publication of the documents, but lost the case. ***New York Times Company v. United States*** (1971) was considered a major victory for the First Amendment protection of freedom of the press.

FOREIGN POLICY ACCOMPLISHMENTS

On taking office, President Nixon appointed Harvard professor Dr. Henry Kissinger as special White House advisor on national security. Later appointed Secretary of State, Kissinger played a pivotal role in the shaping of foreign policy during the Nixon and Ford years. He made frequent trips to the U.S.S.R., China, and the Middle East.

NIXON'S FOREIGN POLICY	
COUNTRY	U.S. INTERESTS
Vietnam	withdraw troops, place burden on South Vietnam
China	economic benefits, eventual diplomatic ties
U.S.S.R.	slowing the arms race through SALT

VIETNAM WITHDRAWAL

In the 1968 campaign, Nixon had promised "peace with honor" in Vietnam. He pledged to end the War, but with the "mission accomplished." Through a process he called "Vietnamization," Nixon shifted more responsibility to the South Vietnamese to conduct the War. After several years of intense bombing by the United States, the North Vietnamese finally agreed to a cease fire. In 1973, as the U.S. withdrew from Vietnam, Congress moved to limit presidential war-making power. Under the ***War Powers Act***, the President must report the movement of troops to Congress within 48 hours. Congress must then vote within 60 days to continue military action. Periodic Congressional approval has to be secured to continue military actions.

American troops came home, but North Vietnamese troops remained in the South Vietnamese countryside. Vietnamization failed. Within two years of American evacuation, South Vietnam and Cambodia were overrun by the communists. Americans came away disillusioned as to their power and role in the world. Out of the Southeast Asian quagmire came the **Nixon Doctrine**. It said that the United States should continue to honor its treaty obligations in Asia, but actual combat troops would have to be provided by the nation directly involved in the conflict.

OPENING TO CHINA

For over twenty years, the United States officially backed the exiled Nationalist Chinese government of Jiang Jieshi (Chiang Kai-shek) on Taiwan. Nixon and Kissinger decided to investigate the possibility of establishing contact with Mao's communist government on the mainland. They hoped a new, more cordial relationship with communist China might indirectly force the Soviet leaders (who were not on good terms with Mao) to be more accommodating to America. Nixon's trip to China in 1972 resulted in no significant agreements, but did pave the way for trade and cultural exchanges. In 1979, President Carter opened full diplomatic relations with communist China, while still maintaining trade relations with Taiwan.

DETENTE

Nixon also became the first President to visit the Soviet Union. He hoped to relax Cold War tensions and limit the nuclear arms race with the communist superpower through a policy of **détenté**. From this new initiative came the *Strategic Arms Limitation Treaty* (SALT, 1972), which slowed but did not halt the proliferation of nuclear weapons. Questions about types of weapons and verification by each side prevented further progress. Nixon also reached an agreement to allow the U.S.S.R. to buy American grain, which benefitted farmers but drove up the price in America.

WATERGATE

In the 1972 presidential election, President Nixon received better than 60% of the popular vote, defeating Democratic challenger Senator George McGovern (SD) by 520-17 electoral vote margin. Despite the overwhelming victory, Nixon was in serious difficulty a year later. His Vice President, Spiro Agnew, was forced to resign over evidence of bribe-taking while Governor of Maryland. Meanwhile, investigations of a botched burglary at the Democratic Party headquarters in the Watergate apartment complex in Washington D.C. revealed a pattern of illegal activities by members of the Republican Committee to Reelect the President.

Nixon claimed to have no knowledge of the **Watergate Scandal**, but he had routinely made tape recording of all his conferences and phone conversations in the White House. Nixon refused to turn over the tapes to Senate investigators, claiming "executive privilege." In *United States v. Nixon* (1974), the Supreme

Court disagreed and forced Nixon to turn over the tapes. On the tapes the President discussed ways to "cover up" the illegal activities. The House Judiciary Committee recommended impeachment, but Nixon resigned in August 1974 before any vote was taken in the full House. Vice President Gerald Ford (appointed 9 months earlier to replace Agnew) was elevated to the presidency.

THE FORD AND CARTER PRESIDENCIES

Gerald Ford
38th U.S. President
(White House)

After Watergate, both Presidents **Gerald Ford** (1974-1977) and **Jimmy Carter** (1977-1981) experienced difficult times in the White House. Economic woes and foreign problems plagued both men. Each year, the government spent more than it collected, and annual deficits of 100 billion dollars became common by the end of the 1970s.

President Ford was the first person to occupy the White House by virtue of appointment. A month after taking office, Ford used his Constitutional power to grant a general pardon to former President Nixon. While Ford's intentions appeared honorable, the controversial move cost him votes in the 1976 presidential election which he barely lost to Carter (51%-49% popular / 297-240 electoral).

Jimmy Carter
39th U.S. President
(White House)

DOMESTIC CONCERNS:

* **Oil Crisis** – As the largest energy consumers in the world, Americans had been importing oil in ever increasing quantities in the post World War II period. But in 1973, OPEC (Organization of Petroleum Exporting Countries) embargoed oil shipments to nations which supported Israel. In 1979, a revolution in Iran resulted in a another oil shortage. The price increased from $2.50 a barrel at the start of the 1970s, to $35.00 by the end. Federal, state, and local authorities tried to ease the energy crisis by rationing gasoline, imposing a 55 miles-an-hour speed limit, and temporarily closing schools. Both Ford and Carter tried to implement comprehensive national energy plans, but were rejected by Congress. Efforts to fund wind and solar power research and develop synthetic fuels found little support. Higher fuel prices helped to increase spiraling upward inflation. Dependency on

foreign oil was reduced somewhat with the completion of the Alaskan North Slope Pipeline and consumers turning to smaller, more fuel-efficient cars. Increased oil supplies and stable prices during the 1980s and 1990s caused many Americans to lose interest in energy conservation.

- **Space Program** – After the triumph of reaching the Moon in 1969, government deficits and a decline in interest led to a more modest space program in the 1970s. The *Skylab* space station was in orbit for several years, permitting astronauts to do research. Through the 1980s and 1990s, NASA launched reusable space shuttles. Unmanned space probes (*Explorer*, *Galileo*, *Magellan*, and *Voyager*) reached other planets, sending back important data and pictures.

- **Bilingual and Handicapped Legislation** – The 1975 *Voting Rights Act* required bilingual ballots in districts with large populations of non-English speaking voters. The *Bilingual Education Act* mandated public schools to teach students in their native languages while they were learning English. Congress came to the aid of the handicapped and dis-

KEY PROVISIONS OF THE AMERICANS WITH DISABILITIES ACT (1990)

- Properties open to the public must be made accessible to disabled people.

- Employers may not discriminate against disabled people in hiring, advancement, compensation, or training, and must adapt the workplace if necessary.

- Public transportation must be accessible to those in wheelchairs.

abled by passing the *Rehabilitation Act* of 1973 which forbade discrimination in jobs, education, and housing. In 1975, Congress required free public education for all physically and mentally disabled students. The *Americans with Disabilities Act* (1990) required that most public places be accessible to the disabled.

- **Environmental Concerns** – The Environmental Protection Agency was created in the Nixon Administration and made significant progress in cleaning up the nation's water and air. New concerns arose over the disposal of hazardous chemical wastes. In 1977, homes built near a chemical dump called **Love Canal** near Niagara Falls (NY) had to be abandoned when residents were stricken with illnesses and birth defects. Congress created a "super fund" of several billion dollars to clean up dangerous sites. A 1979 accident at the **Three-Mile Island** nuclear facility in Pennsylvania increased public awareness of the risks of nuclear generators. The Nuclear Regulatory Commission tightened safety procedures, and denied one completed power plant at **Shoreham** on Long Island (NY) from opening.

FOREIGN POLICIES

During the 1970s, it sometimes appeared as though the once mighty United States was at the mercy of international forces beyond its control. Less Developed Countries blocked U.S. desires in the United Nations, and Arab oil countries seemed to be manipulating the economy. The United States signed the **Helsinki Accords** in 1975 to halt violations of human rights in nations such as Cuba, South Africa, Uganda, and the U.S.S.R. However, American ability to secure lasting change in these nations was limited.

☆ CAPSULE – MIDDLE EAST AFFAIRS

SUCCESS: THE CAMP DAVID AGREEMENTS

In 1978, President Carter brought together Egyptian President Anwar Sadat and Israeli Premier Menachem Begin at the presidential retreat at Camp David, Maryland. The three leaders worked out a peace agreement that was signed at the White House the following year. The Camp David Agreements ended thirty years of hostility between Egypt and Israel, and gave Israel official recognition as well as access the Suez Canal. Israel evacuated the Sinai Peninsula, and negotiations dealing with the issue of self-determination for Palestinian refugees began. The peace agreement became President Carter's major achievement in foreign policy. Tragically, Sadat was assassinated by Egyptian opponents of the agreement. After many years, Palestinians were granted self rule in some of their lands, but an independent Palestinian state remained stalled.

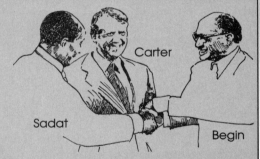

Carter

Sadat

Begin

FAILURE:
THE IRANIAN HOSTAGE CRISIS

In 1979, the dictatorial rule of the Shah of Iran led to a revolution. The Shah fled, eventually ending up in the United States for medical treatment. The revolution resulted in the creation of an Islamic Republic presided over by Ayatollah Rullah Khomeini. When the United States refused Iranian demands for the Shah's return, militant students in Iran attacked the U.S. embassy and took 50 U.S. employees hostage. President Carter's attempts to negotiate for the hostages' release proved futile. Iran was in revolutionary chaos. A secret rescue attempt failed, and Secretary of State Cyrus Vance resigned over the problem. The hostage crisis, combined with the Soviet invasion of Afghanistan, inflation, and the energy crisis, cast doubts on Carter's leadership ability. The Republicans sensed victory in the polls, and Ronald Reagan won a sweeping victory in 1980. The Iranians needed money, and in return for releasing frozen Iranian bank assets in the U.S., the hostages were released after Ronald Reagan took his oath of office on 20 January 1981.

In late 1979, Soviet forces invaded Afghanistan in support of a Marxist regime. President Carter stopped grain shipments and organized a boycott of the 1980 Moscow Olympics, but to little effect. (The Soviets left Afghanistan in 1989 after ten unsuccessful years of fighting). Carter signed an agreement that gave the Panama Canal back to Panama over a period of time, but many in America criticized the action as compromising the security of the United States. The Carter Administration's foreign policy is most remembered for two events: The successful Camp David Agreements and the disastrous Iranian Hostage Crisis (see chart on page 299).

SUMMARY

As the 1970s came to a close, Americans had witnessed three decades of enormous change. An abundance of consumer goods helped place a majority of Americans in the comfortable middle class, yet poverty still existed. A lost war in Vietnam and a disgraced President Nixon led many citizens to question the actions of government. The nation's dominance in world affairs became less certain. However, opportunities for those who in the past faced discrimination, especially women and African Americans, increased. By the end of the 1970s, equality and justice for all, though still not fully reached, was becoming a much more realistic goal.

LESSON ASSESSMENT

MULTI-CHOICE

1 An increasing amount of personal information about American citizens has been placed on computers. This raises concerns for many about
   1 arrests without warrants
   2 the right of privacy
   3 freedom of speech
   4 separation of Church and state

2 The United States sells manufactured products to Less Developed Countries and purchases raw materials from these nations. This fact illustrates
   1 finance capitalism
   2 pooling of resources
   3 global interdependence
   4 economic protectionism

3 The terms "brinkmanship" and "massive retaliation" were used in discussions about
   1 integration of public schools
   2 the role of the Federal Reserve Board
   3 the Cold War with the Soviet Union
   4 the activist role of the Supreme Court

4 The armistice that ended the Korean War in 1953 resulted in
   1 a democratic government for all of Korea
   2 a communist government for all Korea
   3 withdrawal of all communist forces from North Korea
   4 the continuation of a divided Korea

5 "Separate educational facilities are inherently unequal"
   – Brown v. Board of Education (1954)
   The effect of this Supreme Court ruling was to
   1 establish affirmative action programs in schools
   2 require the integration of public schools
   3 force states to spend an equal amount on each public school student
   4 ban religious schools

6 The use of federal marshals in 1957 to protect African American students in Little Rock, Arkansas was significant because it
   1 was the first time martial law had been declared in the United States
   2 led to federal takeover of many Southern public schools
   3 strengthened control of education by state governments
   4 showed that the federal government would enforce court decisions on integration

7   "… there are two types of laws: There are just laws and there are unjust laws. I would be the first to advocate obeying just laws. One has not only a legal but a moral responsibility to obey just laws. Conversely, one has a moral responsibility to disobey unjust laws."
                                                                    – Martin Luther King Jr.

This statement is a justification of the concept of
1   reverse discrimination   3   civil disobedience
2   ethnic assimilation   4   cultural pluralism

8   Which development was a result of the other three?
1   The *Civil Rights* and *Voting Rights Acts* of the 1960s were passed.
2   African Americans were barred from voting in several states.
3   State laws supported racial segregation.
4   Several civil rights movements were formed.

9   From the end of World War II until the 1980s, the United States carried out its foreign policy mainly by
1   giving in to foreign demands
2   avoiding any situation that might involve the nation in a conflict
3   acting forcefully to obtain and control colonies
4   taking a variety of actions to prevent the spread of communism

10 President Lyndon Johnson's Great Society program was aimed at reducing social pressures caused by
1   poverty and urban deterioration
2   the war in Vietnam
3   environmental pollution
4   political corruption

11 Protests against United States involvement in Vietnam grew in the late 1960s and early 1970s mainly because many Americans
1   believed that the war was unjust
2   objected to the drafting of college students
3   feared nuclear war with the Soviet Union
4   opposed participation in conflicts involving the United Nations

12 The intent of the *War Powers Act* of 1973 was to limit the President's power to
1   send troops to rescue Americans held captive by terrorists in foreign nations
2   use troops to defend against an armed attack on the United States
3   send troops to stop a riot in an American city
4   commit troops to major military operations in a foreign nation

13 The main reason the *Voting Rights Act* of 1965 removed the literacy test as a voting qualification was that
  1 different standards of literacy had been applied to different groups of voters
  2 a majority of voters were unable to read election ballots
  3 technology had made voter literacy unnecessary
  4 the cost of achieving literacy was too high

14 One criticism of affirmative action programs is that these programs
  1 ignore the needs of women in business and education
  2 lead to discrimination against more qualified people
  3 have a negative effect on immigration
  4 have not eliminated segregated housing patterns

15 Which issue continues to be a major goal of the women's rights movement in the United States?
  1 having women serve as officers in the military
  2 guaranteeing women equal pay for equal work
  3 enabling women to serve in the President's Cabinet
  4 admitting women to medical schools

16 The Supreme Court of the United States has influenced representative government by ruling that
  1 each state should have two Senators in Congress
  2 the President should be elected directly by the people
  3 congressional districts should be approximately equal in population
  4 each state should have the same number of members in the House of Representatives

17 During the administration of President Richard Nixon, U.S. policy toward communist China was characterized by
  1 repeated attempts to introduce democratic principles in Chinese elections
  2 increasing hostility and isolation
  3 the signing of a mutual defense pact
  4 a relaxation of strained relations

18 In *United States v. Nixon* (1974), the Supreme Court ruled against excessive use of
  1 the line item veto   3 executive privilege
  2 presidential pardons   4 the electoral college

19 The Camp David Agreements negotiated during the Carter Administration were significant because the Agreements
  1 brought peace between two longstanding enemies
  2 resulted in cheaper oil for the United States
  3 led to increased human rights in communist nations of Eastern Europe
  4 reduced the number of nuclear weapons aimed at the U.S.

Base your answer to question 20 on the graph at the right and on your knowledge of U.S. history and government.

20 Which conclusion can be drawn from the information in the graph?
1   In 1983, America imported most of its oil from OPEC members.
2   Between 1978-1983, the United States reduced its dependence on OPEC.
3   The United States paid more for oil in 1983 than it did in 1978.
4   The United States used less oil in 1983 than it did in 1978.

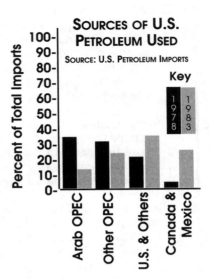

SOURCES OF U.S. PETROLEUM USED

SOURCE: U.S. PETROLEUM IMPORTS

THEMATIC ESSAY

Directions: Write a well-organized essay that includes an introduction, several paragraphs explaining your position, and a conclusion.

Theme:

> The federal government acted in a variety of ways in the period 1950-1990 to promote equality and protect the rights of minority and oppressed groups in American society.

Task:

> Describe *three* (3) actions taken by the federal government from 1950-1990 that furthered equality and protected the rights of minority or oppressed groups in the United States. For *each* action described:
>
> • identify the action undertaken by federal authorities
> • describe what the federal action did
> • show how the action helped a particular minority or oppressed group

Suggestions:
You may use any federal action in the time period indicated. Some suggestions you might wish to consider are: *Brown v. Board of*

Education (1954), *Miranda v. Arizona* (1966), *Civil Rights Act* of 1964, *Voting Rights Acts, Bilingual Education Act, Americans with Disabilities Act,* self determination for Native Americans. **You are *not* limited to these suggestions.**

Practice Skills for DBQ

Directions: The following task is based on the accompanying documents. The documents may have been edited for the purposes of this exercise. The task is designed to test your ability to work with historical documents. As you analyze the documents, take into account both the source of the documents and the author's point of view.

Historical Context:
Between 1950-1980, the United States acted in a variety of ways to protect its national interests in foreign nations.

Part A – Short Answer
Analyze the documents and answer the questions that follow each document

Document 1

Question for Document 1
According to the author of the cartoon, what would happen if Vietnam fell?

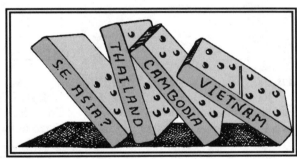

Document 2

"The meeting between the leaders of China and the United States is to seek the normalization of relations between the two countries and also to exchange views on questions of concern to the two sides. In anticipation of the inevitable speculation which will follow this announcement, I want to put our policy in the clearest possible context. Our action in seeking a new relationship with the People's Republic of China will not be at the expense of our old friends."

– President Richard Nixon, July 15, 1971

Question for Document 2 (on page 306)

2 *a* Why did President Nixon wish to begin a new relationship with the People's Republic of China?

2 *b* Why did President Nixon think that some might be concerned about the new relationship?

Part B – Essay Response

Task: Using only the information in the documents, write a one or two paragraph discussion of the motives behind U.S. foreign policy in the Post World War II era.

State your thesis:
- use only the information in the documents to support your thesis position
- add your analysis of the documents
- incorporate your answers from the two Part *A* scaffold questions

_____

_____

_____

_____

Additional Suggested Task:
From your knowledge of United States history and government, make a list of additional examples of how the United States acted to protect its national interests in foreign affairs between 1950-1980.

_____

_____

_____

_____

_____

_____

_____

_____

_____

_____

1980-

REAGANOMICS (1981-1989)
SUPPLY SIDE ECONOMICS (1981)
SANDRA O'CONNOR TO SUPREME COURT (1981)
NEW FEDERALISM (1982)

INVASION OF GRENADA (1983)

1985-

IMMIGRATION REFORM (1986)
CHALLENGER DISASTER (1986)

AMERICA
ASTRIDE
THE MILLENNIUM

1990-

SAVINGS & LOAN CRISIS (1989-1992)

U.S.S.R. COLLAPSES (1991)

PERSIAN GULF WAR (1991)

NAFTA AGREEMENT (1994)

1995-

CLINTON IMPEACHMENT (1998)

U.S. INTO KOSOVO (1999)

2000-

ELECTORAL VOTE CONTROVERSY (2000)

TERRORIST ATTACKS (2001)

2ND WAR IRAQ (2003)

Members of the crew of the 10th flight of the U.S. Space Shuttle Challenger: commander Francis R. "Dick" Scobee; pilot Michael J. Smith; mission specialists Judith A. Resnik, Ellison S. Onizuka, and Ronald E. McNair; and payload specialists Gregory Jarvis and Christa McAuliffe, a schoolteacher. Seventy-three seconds into the flight on Jan. 28, 1986, with no warning from real-time sensors on board or on the ground, and in full view of those watching there at the Kennedy Space Center and on television, the external tank exploded and with it the Challenger. The crew perished. (NASA Photo)

AMERICA ASTRIDE THE MILLENNIUM

Ronald Reagan
Presidential Library

THE NEW FEDERALISM

President Reagan's victory in the 1980 Presidential election brought many Republican candidates into office on his coattails. This resulted in Republican control of the U.S. Senate for the first time in thirty years. In the 1984 election, Reagan easily defeated Democrat Walter Mondale (MN). President Reagan called his domestic agenda the **New Federalism**. His goal was to shift federal programs in education, health, welfare, and transportation to state and local authorities. State officials welcomed control over such programs, but they voiced concern about paying for them. In the end, the federal government cut or reduced only a few programs. The states were unable to finance most of the programs themselves, and the federal government continued massive funding while trying to cut taxes.

DOMESTIC POLICIES DURING THE REAGAN ADMINISTRATION

SUPPLY-SIDE ECONOMICS

Reagan tried to boost the economy through **supply-side economic policy**. This approach was based on the belief that by reducing various taxes and government spending, more money would be freed up for new investment capital. As the economy expanded, it would increase supplies of goods and services. Eventually, in this "trickle down" approach, industrial growth was expected to trigger new employment and expand national wealth. As the entire economy grew, there would be more incomes to be

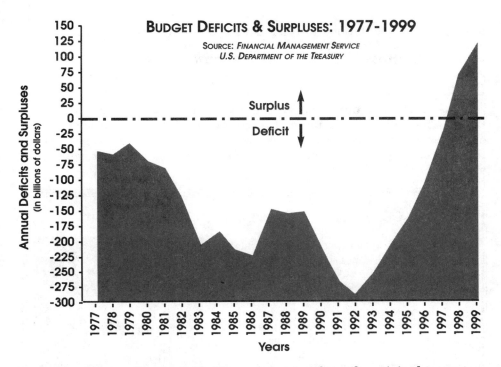

BUDGET DEFICITS & SURPLUSES: 1977-1999

SOURCE: FINANCIAL MANAGEMENT SERVICE
U.S. DEPARTMENT OF THE TREASURY

Surplus ↑

Deficit ↓

Annual Deficits and Surpluses (in billions of dollars)

Years

taxed to make up for the initial loss of revenue from the original tax cuts. The plan excited the public as tax cuts always do, pressuring Congress to support the basic plan. Critics, however, claimed that the federal budget cuts harmed millions of poor, and the rich would prosper at the expense of the middle and lower classes.

BUDGET DEFICITS

Congress passed Reagan's proposal to cut taxes by 25%. At the same time, Reagan wanted more military spending and Congress increased domestic social-welfare programs. Eventually, the "Reaganomics" tax cut did increase revenue, but government spending increased at a faster rate. This caused **budget deficits** (annual imbalances when federal spending exceeds revenue). Deficits soared, borrowing increased, and interest payments became a major government expense in themselves. Government demand for money kept inflation high, and the deficit problem plagued the government for another two decades.

ENVIRONMENTAL POLICIES

The campaign for environmental protection that began in the 1970s slowed in the Reagan years. Secretary of the Interior James G. Watt weakened or cut regulations that provided protection to the environment, wildlife, and national parks. The Reagan Administration also increased the number of permits for offshore oil drilling and strip-mining, both potentially dangerous to the environment. Administration officials said the numerous regulations interfered with free enterprise and economic growth, and that their actions stimulated the economy.

CIVIL RIGHTS

The Reagan Administration reduced federal involvement in civil rights. The individual states had to enforce busing, affirmative action, and prosecution of civil rights violations. Civil rights leaders condemned this approach, saying it negated the progress made since the *Brown* decision.

☆ CAPSULE – SUPREME COURT SHIFTS TO RIGHT

Reagan's conservative approach reignited support for overturning liberal Supreme Court decisions of the Warren Court. President Reagan supported unsuccessful attempts to pass constitutional amendments to allow school prayer and ban abortions. Reagan did manage to reinforce the Supreme Court's judicial restraint by appointing conservative judges to the Court (William Rehnquist as Chief Justice, **Sandra O'Connor**, the first woman, Antonin Scalia, and Anthony Kennedy).

Photo: Supreme Court

COURT RETURNS AUTHORITY TO THE SCHOOLS
Tinker v. Des Moines School District, 1969
(First Amendment – free speech)
Two students were suspended from school for wearing black armbands in protest of the Vietnam War. The students said the Constitutional guarantee of free speech protected this form of protest. Agreeing with the students, the Court ruled that this symbolic type of speech is protected by the 1st Amendment. However, speech that is disruptive of the educational process can be restricted.

New Jersey v. TLO, 1985
(Fourth Amendment – search and seizure)
School officials found a student smoking in school, and conducted a search of the student's purse, in which not just cigarettes, but drugs and and drug related items were found. The student claimed this was an unreasonable search. The Court ruled in favor of the school authorities, saying that in a school, only "reasonable suspicion" (instead of probable cause) is necessary for a search. It posited that schools have a duty to promote a safe environment for learning.

OTHER DOMESTIC CONCERNS
DURING THE 1980s

POVERTY IN AN AFFLUENT SOCIETY

Despite economic growth, poverty remained a problem, especially in inner cites and for those on fixed incomes. Some blamed the New Federalism and supply-side economics. The job market provided few opportunities for those with limited education and skills. Poorly administered state programs and inadequate educational systems in many areas also shared the blame. Communities struggled to deal with the issue of homelessness among people with emotional problems, and those addicted to alcohol or drugs.

THE FARMERS' DILEMMA

Inflation drove farm prices to record levels during the 1970s, but overproduction and reduced demand during the 1980s resulted in falling prices. Foreclosures and bank failures grew in agricultural regions of the country.

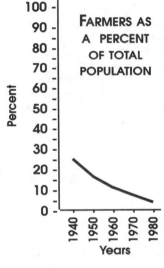

FARMING IN THE UNITED STATES
1940-1980

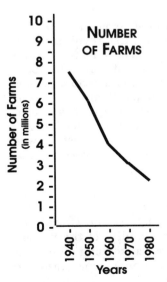

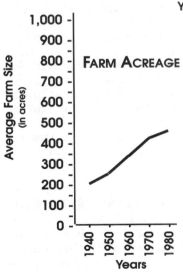

SOURCES OF IMMIGRATION

Despite restrictions imposed in 1965, millions of illegal aliens continued to enter the nation. To reduce the number of illegal immigrants, Congress passed the ***Immigration Reform and Control Act*** of 1986. The law granted legal status to "illegals" who had entered the U.S. before 1982. However, it also provided strict punishment for employers who continued to hire illegals. Critics claimed the law was unfair and discriminated against poorer Hispanic groups, especially Mexican workers. The untimely legislation was ineffective in solving the problem of illegal immigration.

ELDERLY POPULATION GROWTH

According to government projections, by 2020 larger numbers of elderly will pressure the Social Security System to pay more benefits than it collects in taxes. Such a situation could bankrupt the system by the middle of the 21st century. Society will also have to find ways to deal with the problems of affordable medical care and housing for the elderly.

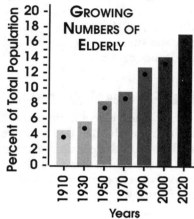

GROWING NUMBERS OF ELDERLY

Years

REAGAN'S FOREIGN POLICY

President Reagan promised to restore America's strength and pride on the international front. He hoped to reverse some of the foreign policy humiliations of the previous decade. Many of the policies were controversial.

CENTRAL AMERICA AND CARIBBEAN

President Reagan vigorously opposed communist expansion. During the 1970s and 1980s, Cuba secretly supported Marxist revolutions in Nicaragua and Grenada. President Reagan denounced Nicaragua and Grenada as centers of Cuban and Soviet communist influence. In 1983, U.S. troops joined those of other Latin American nations to stop a Soviet-Cuban communist coup in the island nation of Grenada. Reagan also sent aid to the Nicaraguan contras (anti-communist guerrilla group based in Honduras), though battles with Congress limited some funding. Nicaragua's communist Sandinista government led by Daniel Ortega was voted out of office when international pressure forced the government to hold elections.

MIDDLE EAST: TERRORISM AND HOSTAGES

In the 1980s, Lebanon's civil war between Muslims and Christians continued. Seeing the conflict as a threat to the stability of the region, President Reagan sent Marine units to aid U.N. peace-keeping efforts. In October, 1983, Muslim extremists crashed a bomb-laden truck into the

Marine headquarters, killing 241 U.S. servicemen. The United States could do little to stop Muslim factions from taking numerous hostages in Lebanon through the 1980s. A decade-long war between Iran and Iraq threatened oil supplies from the Persian Gulf. American naval forces escorted tankers of friendly Kuwait through danger zones, and kept the Persian Gulf open to shipping.

Muslim extremists, backed by the PLO, Libya, and /or Iran, committed terrorist acts throughout Western Europe. Terrorists bombed a nightclub in Berlin, hijacked airplanes, took over the *Achille Lauro* cruise ship, and planted a bomb that caused the crash of a Pan Am jet in Scotland, killing 270 (mostly Americans) in 1988. The U.S. sometimes managed to punish those responsible (the *Achille Lauro* terrorists and those responsible for the Pan Am bombing). In 1986, Reagan ordered U.S. jets to bomb the headquarters of Libya's Muammar Qaddafi, a supporter of terrorism. However, many other terrorists evaded capture, some with the help of friendly governments in the Middle East.

TRADE POLICY

U.S. foreign trade experienced a mounting deficit in the 1980s. Attempts to place quota restrictions on the flood of cars and electronic equipment from Japan, and manufactured goods, clothes and toys from other markets failed. U.S. consumers benefitted from the greater choice of goods at lower prices. However, American workers faced unemployment as domestic producers cut back or ceased production. Reagan, and his successor, President **George Bush** (1989-1993), resisted pressure from business and unions for stronger retaliation against foreign governments.

SOUTH AFRICAN LINKS

South Africa's domestic policy of **apartheid** (racial separation by law) posed a problem for U.S. policymakers. Over 70% of South Africa's population was black, yet they were second class citizens. Nearly all nations condemned apartheid, but there was disagreement over what actions the United States should take. Some wanted the U.S. government to sever all trade relations with South Africa. Others urged stockholders of corporations doing business in South Africa to **divest** (sell off their stock). Supporters of American corporations pointed out that these companies were more likely to treat black Africans as equals and provide greater opportunity.

The Reagan Administration imposed limited economic sanctions, but resisted demands to end all ties. In 1990, The South African government released African National Congress leader **Nelson Mandela** after 28 years in prison. In 1994, in the first election open to all citizens of South Africa, Nelson Mandela was elected President, and a new constitution based on racial equality was implemented.

Soviet Relations

President Reagan opposed the 1970s policy of détente. As a professional cold war warrior, he took a strong position against Soviet expansion, and he promoted rebuilding U.S. military strength as a deterrent. Reagan spent billions on researching the **Strategic Defense**

President Reagan & General Secretary Gorbachev signing the INF Treaty in the East Room of the White House, 8 December 1987.
(National Archives and Record Administration)

Initiative (nicknamed "Star Wars"). He condemned the Soviet invasion of Afghanistan, and Soviet imposition of martial law in Poland.

By the late 1980s, relations with the Soviets improved under their new leader, **Mikhail Gorbachev**. The Soviet leader started economic reform (*perestroika*) and political openness (*glasnost*), and he trimmed the Soviet military presence in Eastern Europe. Reagan and Gorbachev held frequent summits, and moved vigorously toward arms reduction.

Iran-Contra Affair

In 1986, congressional investigators revealed that members of the Reagan Administration illegally sold weapons to Iran. The officials then diverted the funds to the contra rebels in Nicaragua. Federal courts convicted several White House staff members of violating federal laws which prohibited such clandestine aid. Congress criticized President Reagan for his inattention to these illegal activities, and his lax administrative procedures. Reagan broke no laws, but many critics questioned his lack of control over staff and foreign policy makers.

President George Bush and First Lady Barbara National Archives

THE 1990s: BUSH AND CLINTON

Under the 22nd Amendment, the popular Reagan could not run for a third term. In the 1988 presidential race, Reagan's Vice President, **George Bush**, defeated the Democratic nominee, Massachusetts Governor Michael Dukakis (426-111 electoral votes). Bush was the first sitting vice president to win the presidency since Martin Van Buren in 1836. Domestic problems plagued Bush's administration, however.

A serious economic recession hit the country during his second year in office. Overuse of credit led to declines in purchasing and production. The Federal Deposit Insurance Corporation had to pay billions to depositors of many failed saving and loans institutions. Downsizing by corporations led to increased unemployment, especially among middle class white collar (managerial level) workers. Federal deficits grew, and the Federal Reserve's efforts to loosen the money supply worked slowly. In 1992, Bush lost his bid for reelection to Democratic Governor **William J.** ("**Bill**") **Clinton** of Arkansas (370-168 electoral votes). Clinton won a second term in 1996, but faced a hostile Republican majority in the House and the Senate for most of his tenure.

DOMESTIC ISSUES

THE AIDS CRISIS

AIDS (Acquired Immuno-Deficiency Syndrome) became a major health concern. Up to 100,000 new U.S. cases appeared each year. Over 40 million worldwide contracted AIDS. Conflicts arose over methods to slow the spread of AIDS, payment for medicine, and the rights of confidentiality of individuals with AIDS. Safe sex practices or abstinence and the avoidance of contaminated blood are currently the best defense against the disease.

HEALTH CARE PROBLEMS

Affordable health care became a major issue in the 1990s. A significant number of individuals had no health insurance. A growing number of workers were losing protection because of the high cost of medical care, making insurance premiums too expensive for individuals and employees. Some Americans preferred expansion of current programs to cover the uninsured. Others called for a complete overhaul of the insurance system. They believed government should provide universal health coverage.

SOCIAL CONCERNS - LIFE AND DEATH

The abortion debate continued with additional rulings by the Supreme Court. In *Planned Parenthood v. Casey* (1992), the Supreme Court allowed the states to impose certain restrictions on abortions (waiting periods, parental consent for minors).

A new issue before the Court involved the withdrawal of life support systems for terminally ill and the right to die. In *Cruzan v. Director, Missouri Department of Health* (1990), the Court said that states were free to develop their own polices regarding terminally ill people. In some instances, life support could be removed (though not in this particular case). Also controversial during the 1990s were the activities of a Michigan doctor, Jack Kervorkian, who helped terminally ill patients commit suicide. In 1999, Kervorkian was found guilty of murder for his role in a suicide.

CAMPAIGN FINANCE REFORM

During the 1990s, there was a large increase in the amount of money flowing into the two major parties. Some came from **PACs** – Political Action Committees which are formed to influence the decisions of government officials. Individuals and businesses face many restrictions when giving to candidates, but PACs do not. Another controversial source of money was from "soft money"; virtually unlimited amounts given to political parties (instead of directly to candidates). Courts have ruled that most mandatory spending limits are unconstitutional, because such limitations restrict the free speech rights of citizens. In 2002, Congress finally banned "soft money" and some political advertising, with the courts upholding the reform.

THE ECONOMY

By the end of the 1990s, American economic indicators were the best they had been in decades. Unemployment and inflation were down, interest rates remained stable, and the stock market reached record

U.S. TRADING PARTNERS			
(ranked by value of exports, 1997; In billions of dollars)			
Nation	Imported from U.S.	Exported to U.S.	Deficit for U.S.
Canada	151	168	- 17
Mexico	71	85	- 14
Japan	65	121	- 56

highs. Federal, state, and local governments collected billions in added revenue, and budget surpluses were common. The federal government saw yearly deficits become surpluses of over $100 billion annually. Yet, trade deficits remained high, as the American people's appetite for imports greatly exceeded the value of American exports.

TRIALS OF PRESIDENT CLINTON

In 1998, President Clinton admitted he had not told the entire truth to Special Prosecutor Kenneth Starr about an improper relationship with a White House intern. By the end of the year, the House of Representatives voted for two articles of impeachment against the President: lying under oath and obstructing justice. In early 1999, Chief Justice Rehnquist presided over a trial in the Senate. (It was the second such trial in history; Andrew Johnson's 1868 trial was the first). The Senate failed to muster the necessary $2/3$ majority to remove the President, and Clinton remained in office.

FOREIGN ISSUES

THE PERSIAN GULF CONFLICT

In August 1990, Iraqi dictator Saddam Hussein annexed oil rich Kuwait. With congressional approval, President Bush sent 500,000 U.S. troops to the region to block any further

Iraqi aggression. A coalition of 23 nations was formed to support American actions. When economic pressure failed to persuade Hussein, the U.S. began five weeks of intense bombing of Iraq in January 1991, followed by a 100 hour ground invasion of Kuwait and Iraq. The Iraqi troops quickly surrendered and Kuwait was liberated by February 27th. However, Saddam Hussein remained in power in Baghdad.

PANAMA

U.S. officials indicted Panamanian military leader Manuel Noriega for drug trafficking in 1988. After further conflicts between American military personnel and Noriega, President Bush ordered U.S. troops to invade Panama, capture Noriega, and transport him to stand trial in the United States. He was convicted on drug-related charges and sentenced to 40 years in prison.

INTERVENTION IN THE BALKANS

A bloody civil war erupted in the Balkans as the "original" Yugoslavia disintegrated. Timeless ethnic and religious conflicts fueled the breakup of the former communist nation. Serbian nationalists fought Croats and Muslims for power in the west central state of Bosnia. As the deaths, destruction, and dislocation of people mounted, the European Community, NATO, and the U.N. all sought to end the fighting.

In 1993, the United States reluctantly agreed to military participation in a peacekeeping mission. American forces went to the region again in 1997 when a Yugoslav-Serbian "ethnic cleansing" campaign began against ethnic Albanians living in Kosovo province. Thousands of Kosovar refugees fled into Albania and Macedonia. A U.S. and NATO bombing campaign forced the aggressors to agree to a truce in 1999.

COLLAPSE OF COMMUNISM AND THE SOVIET UNION

Soviet President Mikhail Gobachev's political and economic reforms spread to the U.S.S.R.'s Eastern European satellites. Poland, Hungary, Czechoslovakia, Rumania, Bulgaria, and Albania all ousted communist leaders. Democratic government and market reforms blossomed. The Berlin Wall was torn down, and the two Germany's reunited in 1991.

Inside the Soviet Union, Gorbachev's economic reforms floundered. The Soviet Republics began to break away from Russia. After less than 70 years of existence, the once powerful U.S.S.R., created by Lenin after his Boshevik Revolution, passed into history. Gorbachev resigned from the Communist Party and was soon forced from power. Boris Yeltsin took over as President of Russia. The newly independent republics disagreed on many issues regarding trade, currency, and military matters. New governments in Ukraine, Belarus, and Kazakhstan were unstable, and civil wars plagued some regions.

American response to all the change was to support the Russian reforms with economic aid and private investment. In the hope of ending the cold war, negotiations continued with Russia over the deployment of weapons and defense systems. Emigration to the United States increased dramatically, as Russians freely left their country. The former communist nations of Poland, Hungary, and the Czech Republic became members of NATO.

NAFTA

With Congressional support, President Clinton signed the **North American Free Trade Agreement** (NAFTA) in 1994. This economic alliance with Canada and Mexico reduced tariff and trade restrictions between these two nations and the United States. The U.S. also joined the World Trade Organization, which attempts to settle disputes over trade, the environment, labor standards, and questions arising from foreign investment. On other trade issues, Congress approved a trade bill with China in 2000, despite the dismal human rights record of the Chinese. Within a few years, America's growing demand for inexpensive chinese goodsled to record trade deficits.

THE 2000 PRESIDENTIAL ELECTION

In the summer of 2000, the Democratic convention nominated Vice President **Albert Gore** (TN) as its candidate. The Republicans nominated the conservative son of former President George Bush, Texas Governor **George W. Bush**. Neither the issues (use of projected budget surpluses, the future of Social Security, tax cuts) nor the candidates stirred the public. This impassive attitude translated into the closest election since 1876. In congressional races, the Republicans maintained their narrow advantage in the House, while they held the Senate by the barest majority. (Several months later, Vermont Republican Senator Jeffords left the party to become an independent, and the Democrats took control of the Senate; they lost it again in the 2002 election.)

Although Vice President Gore won the total popular vote, he did not obtain a majority of electors. It was unclear if Bush had an electoral majority. A tight and muddled contest for Florida's 25 electoral votes would tip the balance. Bush appeared the victor in Florida, but recounts were ordered by state authorities. Both sides claimed voting irregularities and flawed ballots. Courts ordered several recounts which narrowed Bush's leads, but then other courts halted further recounts.

President George W. Bush speaks to a Joint Session of Congress February 27, 2001. Behind: Vice President Richard Cheney (left) and Speaker of the House J. Dennis Hastert (right)
WHITE HOUSE PHOTO BY PAUL MORSE

After a month of such confusion, the United States Supreme Court ruled (**Bush v. Gore**) that the Florida state courts had acted questionably in reexamining only certain ballots, and it ordered the recounts stopped. Gore conceded and Florida officials certified Bush as the winner just before the Electors met to vote in the 50 state capitals. A repeat of the electoral fiasco was avoided in 2004, as Bush was the clear winner over Senator John Kerry, MA.

George W. Bush became the second son of a President to serve (John Quincy Adams was the first in 1825). At his inauguration, Bush called on the nation to unite after the bitter election struggle, and live out the nation's promise of justice and opportunity "through civility, courage, compassion, and character." In his first year, President Bush was able to exceed expectations, but no leader could have been prepared for what was about to happen to the country.

TERRORIST ATTACKS ON SEPTEMBER 11

On September 11, 2001, nineteen extremists belonging to the terrorist group **Al Qaeda** (Arabic for "the base") hijacked four American commercial airliners. One plane went down in western Pennsylvania, and a second slammed into the Pentagon near Washington, D.C. The greatest damage occurred when the hijackers flew the other two planes directly into the twin towers of the World Trade Center in New York City. The mammoth buildings collapsed from the enormous fires resulting from the impact. Over 3,000 people died in these attacks. Over 2,000 of the deaths occurred at the World Trade Center and included 343 New York City firefighters, rescue workers, and law enforcement officials that rushed to the disaster scene to assist.

Many Americans compared the Sept. 11 terrorist assault to the surprise attack at Pearl Harbor in 1941. While all of the actual hijackers died, President Bush vowed to punish those who had ties to Al Qaeda, both at home and abroad. With worldwide cells, and funded and led by Saudi millionaire **Osama bin Laden**, Al Qaeda's main bases were in Afghanistan. It had previously been suspected of bombing U.S. embassies in Kenya and Tanzania and tragically attacking the *USS Cole* at anchor in Yemen.

Osama bin Laden
Al Qaeda Terrorist Leader

FOR ADDITIONAL INFORMATION: WWW.PBS.ORG/FRONTLINE/

The **Taliban**, a radical Islamic group that ruled Afghanistan, provided vital support for Al Qaeda's training bases. In 2002, President Bush ordered U.S. forces to the area and engaged terrorist strongholds. Afghan opponents of the Taliban and NATO troops joined to drive the radical Islamists from power and capture suspected Al Qaeda operatives. By 2004, Afghans adopted a new constitution and Hamid Karzi was elected president. Taliban resurgencies and increases in illegal opium production engendered instability and required continued U.S. and NATO presence.

By the end of 2002, the Taliban and Al Qaeda were in disarray abroad, but the September 11 attacks greatly affected domestic affairs. The government increased security at airports and public events and tightened immigration under the 2001 **Patriot Act** (reauthorized in 2006). The Act raised civil rights issues of due process, search, and seizure as often occurs in times of insecurity. Economic effects of the attacks included recession and increased unemployment. The travel and transportation industries suffered serious declines. Federal, state, and local governments struggled with mounting security costs in the face of declining tax revenues. As a result, stock prices fell and even suffered greater declines due to corporate financial manipulation scandals.

President Bush pushed Congress for tax cuts to stimulate the sagging economy, helping employment and housing starts, and stimulating the stock market. Public confidence inched upward as 2004 progressed.

In the election in 2004, Ohio's 20 electoral votes gave President Bush the needed margin of victory over Senator John Kerry (D, MA), and the Republicans retained control of Congress. In 2005, Senate approval of Bush's appointments of Associate Justice Samuel Alioto and Chief Justice **John Roberts** nudged the U.S. Supreme Court toward more conservative decisions.

In the 2006 midterm elections, the Democrats regained control of Congress and elected **Nancy Pelosi** (D-CA) as the first woman Speaker of the House, and relations with the White House became strained. Congress became more openly critical of the administration's foreign policy and military involvement in Iraq. They held many hearings, including investigations into the firing of U.S. Attorneys by the Justice Department, all of which characterized the power struggle. Unable to gain public support for immigration reform, the government failed to pass the Secure Borders, Economic Opportunity, and Immigration Reform Act of 2007. Public concern over rising gas prices and a fizzling real estate boom contributed to record low approval rates for the President and Congress.

THE SECOND WAR IN IRAQ

In 2001, the Bush Administration charged Iraq with violations of the post-Gulf War (1991) U.N. resolutions prohibiting dictator Saddam Hussein's power group from amassing nuclear, chemical, and biological weapons. Saddam methodically thwarted U.N. inspections and U.S. proposals for military action against his illicit manoeuvres. President Bush and Britain's Prime Minister Blair eventually formed a 68-nation coalition that invaded Iraq in 2003. Saddam's totalitarian regime disintegrated in less than two months with the dictator and his key Baath Party henchmen being captured, tried, and (many) executed in the ensuing years.

Subsequently, Iraqi sectarian opposition and suicide bombings hindered the coalition's reconstruction efforts. Iraqis adopted a new constitution in 2004, held parliamentary elections in 2005, and established a new government in 2006, but discord between the majority Shi'a and Sunni Muslim sects continued to to threaten stability. U.S. and coalition forces and newly trained Iraqi forces struggled against opponents of the new government (Saddam loyalists, insurgents, Al Qaeda, and foreign religious and political infiltrators'). As casualties mounted and Coalition members withdrew, support for the Bush policies declined at home.

SUMMARY
As the Cold War faded into history, the United States became the world's leading power. As part of the global community, numerous conflicts in foreign countries drew America's interest. As part of a global economy, interdependence broadened U.S. interests in the world marketplace. Prosperity grew, but not without problems. Poverty was reduced, but still affected more than 12% of the population. With people living longer, the aging required a greater share of the nation's resources. Moving into a new millennium precipitated unprecedented issues at home and abroad.

LESSON ASSESSMENT

MULTI-CHOICE

President Nixon Plans Trip to China to Meet with Chairman Mao
President Carter Signs New Panama Canal Treaty
President Clinton Concludes Trade Agreement with Japan

1   Each of the headlines above illustrates an action of a President fulfilling his role as
   1   head of his political party   3   chief diplomat
   2   commander in chief   4   chief legislator

Base your answer to question 2 on the graph at the right and on your knowledge of U.S. history and government.

2   The trend indicated in the graph has been largely the result of
   1   technological and scientific advances in agriculture
   2   a reduction in immigration to the United States
   3   repeated natural disasters in agricultural regions
   4   the refusal of banks to make any loans to farmers

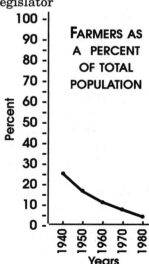

FARMERS AS A PERCENT OF TOTAL POPULATION

3   The "trickle down" economic theory of President Herbert Hoover and the "supply side" economic policies under President Ronald Reagan were based on the idea that
    1   balanced budgets are essential to economic success
    2   local governments do not have the capacity to solve economic problems
    3   economic growth depends on making increased amounts of capital available to businesses
    4   economic stability is the responsibility of federal monetary agencies

4   A major difference between United States immigration policy in the mid 19th century and in the 1980s was that the most recent policy
    1   excludes certain races   3   is more restrictive
    2   excludes political refugees   4   favors skilled workers

5   Raising import duties and placing quotas on foreign manufactured goods during the 1980s was an example of
    1   technological competition   3   lowering inflation
    2   supporting free trade   4   economic protectionism

6   President Reagan's desire to rid countries of communist influence was shown by his
    1   sending troops to Lebanon in 1983
    2   providing aid to the Nicaraguan contras
    3   protection of Kuwait in the Iran - Iraq conflict
    4   bombing of the headquarters of Muammar Qaddafi

7   Critics of President Reagan's environmental record said that
    1   foreign nations were being given control of the national lands
    2   the Reagan proposals favored business interests
    3   the federal lands were producing too little in revenue
    4   pollution controls were too strict

8   In *New Jersey v. TLO* (1985), the Supreme Court ruled that
    1   all searches of student possessions on school grounds are unconstitutional
    2   authorities must obtain a warrant to search student possessions
    3   students can be searched only after a crime has been committed
    4   in schools, the necessary proof to conduct a search is less than in other instances

9   President Clinton's impeachment and Senate trial was an example of the operation of
    1   federalism   3   eminent domain
    2   checks and balances   4   concurrent powers

10 NAFTA led to increased trade between the United States and
   1 Japan and China   3 Great Britain and France
   2 Canada and Mexico   4 Brazil and Argentina

11 The United States made cuts in defense spending during the 1990s
   in part because
   1 the Constitution limited spending during peacetime
   2 the United Nations agreed to share the cost of defense with the
      United States
   3 the Cold War ended
   4 there were no armed conflicts in the world during the 1990s of
      concern to the United States

12 What is a moral problem that developed during the latter part of the
   20th century as a result of scientific and technological advances?
   1 The ability of the medical profession to prolong life artificially
      has raised the issue of the desirability of such actions.
   2 The development of the computer has permitted business and
      industry to produce more information at a faster rate.
   3 New sources of energy are needed to satisfy energy requirements.
   4 A knowledge explosion has resulted as people have engaged in
      more research programs.

13 The main reason President Clinton sent U.S. military forces into
   Haiti and Bosnia was to
   1 establish permanent military bases in these nations
   2 help secure peace in these nations
   3 stop illegal immigration to the United States from these nations
   4 obtain needed mineral resources

14 Those who support the public financing of election campaigns would
   hope to
   1 prevent incumbents from winning reelection
   2 create a third party
   3 reduce the influence of big contributors
   4 reduce the cost of voting for individual voters

15 Many Americans were reluctant to grant trading privileges to communist China because of their disappointing record on
   1 repayment of loans
   2 human rights for its citizens
   3 producing quality goods
   4 shipping goods on time from foreign ports

THEMATIC ESSAY

Directions: Write a well-organized essay that includes an introduction, several paragraphs explaining your position, and a conclusion.

Theme:

> The federal government tried a variety of ways to meet the economic needs of the people between 1975-2000.

Task:

> Describe *three* (3) federal actions that helped satisfy an economic need or problem between 1975-2000. For *each* action selected:
> - state and describe the specific federal action
> - explain the purpose of the action
> - discuss why some opposed the action

Suggestions:
You may use any federal action that answers the question within the time period. Suggestions include construction of the Alaskan Oil Pipeline, President Reagan's "Supply side" economic plan, federal farm subsidies, Federal Reserve Board interest rate increases, increases in the Social Security payroll tax, or NAFTA (North American Free Trade Agreement). **You are *not* limited to these suggestions.**

PRACTICE SKILLS FOR DBQ

Directions: The following task is based on the accompanying documents. The documents may have been edited for the purposes of this exercise. The task is designed to test your ability to work with historical documents. As you analyze the documents, take into account both the source of the documents and the author's point of view.

Directions:
Read the documents in Part *A* and answer the question(s) after each document. Then read the directions for Part *B* and write your essay.

Historical Context:
The population of the United States has historically undergone change, and continues to do so in a variety of ways.

Part A – Short Answer
Analyze the documents and answer the questions that follow each document

Document 1

Question for Document 1

Describe the trend that took place between 1970-2000.

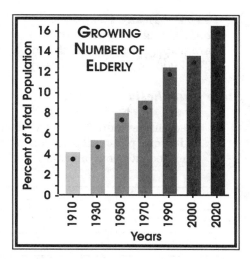

Document 2

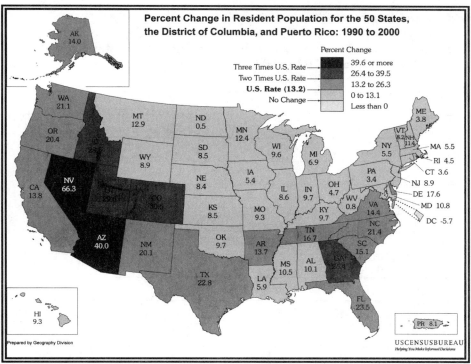

Questions for Document 2

2a In what regions of the country did the states see the greatest increases?

2b In what regions of the country did the states see the smallest increases?

Part B – Essay Response

Task: Using the information from the documents, write a one or two paragraph discussion of the impact of population changes between 1970-2000 on American society.

State your thesis:

- use only evidence from the documents to support your response
- add your personal analysis of the documents
- incorporate your answers to the two Part A scaffold questions

_____

_____

_____

_____

Additional Suggested Task:

From your knowledge of United States history and government, make a list of additional examples of how the United States population changed from 1970 to 2000.

_____

_____

_____

_____

_____

_____

_____

_____

_____

_____

_____

_____

_____

_____

_____

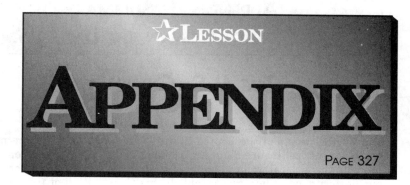

☆ LESSON

APPENDIX

APPENDIX 1: SUMMARY OF THE CONSTITUTION OF THE UNITED STATES

THE U.S. CONSTITUTION

PREAMBLE

We the people of the United States, in order to form a more perfect union, establish justice, insure domestic tranquility, provide for the common defense, promote the general welfare, and secure the blessings of liberty for ourselves and our posterity, do ordain and establish this Constitution of the United States of America.

ORIGINAL CONSTITUTION

Article I   Establishes Congress as a bicameral legislative branch (House of Rep. & Senate); how members are chosen and terms; lists 17 specific powers plus the "elastic clause;" presidential veto and override; actions prohibited

Article II   Establishes executive branch with President and Vice President; duties of office; how elected; appointment power; checks on power, including impeachment procedure

Article III   Establishes judicial branch, with Supreme Court and its jurisdiction; how Congress sets up lower federal courts; defines treason

Article IV   Declares equality among the states, extradition, admission of new states, Congress' authority over territories; requires republican form of government in all states

Article V   Establishes procedure for amending the Constitution

Article VI   Declares Constitution the supreme law of the land

Article VII   Establishes procedure for the 13 states to ratify the new Constitution

CONSTITUTIONAL AMENDMENTS

BILL OF RIGHTS (1791)

1st Amendment   freedom of speech, press, assembly, free exercise of religion

2nd Amendment   right to bear arms

3rd Amendment   forbids government from quartering of troops in peacetime

4th Amendment	protects against unwarranted search
5th Amendment	protects rights of accused to due process; eminent domain
6th Amendment	protects rights to fair trial & counsel
7th Amendment	right of jury trial in civil cases
8th Amendment	protects against cruel punishment & excessive bail
9th Amendment	rights not specifically mentioned still exist
10th Amendment	powers not specified in Constitution left to states and people

SUBSEQUENT AMENDMENTS

11th Amendment	(1795) suits by citizens of one state against a particular state must be heard in the latter's courts not in Federal ones
12th Amendment	(1804) electors must use separate ballots for President and Vice President
13th Amendment	(1865) abolishes slavery
14th Amendment	(1868) defines citizenship, application of due process, and equal protection
15th Amendment	(1870) defines citizens' right to vote
16th Amendment	(1913) allows federal income tax
17th Amendment	(1913) direct popular election of United States Senators
18th Amendment	(1919) manufacture, sale, importation, & transportation of alcoholic beverages forbidden in U.S. (repealed by 21st Amend.)
19th Amendment	(1920) right of women to vote
20th Amendment	(1933) redefines term of President & sessions of Congress
21st Amendment	(1933) repeal of prohibition amendment (18th)
22nd Amendment	(1951) limits Presidential terms
23rd Amendment	(1961) provides presidential electors for District of Columbia
24th Amendment	(1964) abolishes poll taxes: federal elections
25th Amendment	(1967) defines succession to presidency & disability of president
26th Amendment	(1971) eighteen year-old citizens may vote in federal elections
27th Amendment	(1992) sitting Congress may not raise own salary

Appendix 2:
Landmark Decisions of the Supreme Court

| Case & Date | Key Word | Supreme Court |
Issues		Landmark Decision
Marbury v. Madison (1803)	Judicial Review	The Court decided part of a 1789 Congressional law contradicted the Constitution and declared it void. (First time the Court checked the power of Congress.)
separation of power; checks and balances the power to interpret the constitutionality of laws passed by Congress		
McCulloch v. Maryland (1819)	Federalism	The Court decided that federal agencies could not be taxed by state government since "the power to tax is the power to destroy."
state v. national power; implied power		
Gibbons v. Ogden (1824)	Federalism	The Court decided that only Congress could make rules on commerce between states.
state v. national power; Interstate commerce		
Worcester v. Georgia (1832)	Native Americans	The Court decided that only the federal government had jurisdiction to deal with Indian nations.
state v. national power; judicial supremacy		
Dred Scott v. Sanford (1857)	citizenship; slavery; property	The Court decided that slaves were personal property of their owners protected by the 5th Amendment and that Congress could not make laws prohibiting slavery.
property rights; citizen rights		
Civil Rights Cases (1883)	Citizenship	In a group of five related cases, the Court decided that Congress could make laws to control discriminatory actions by states but not by private individuals.
Congressional power; 14th Amendment; discrimination		

Case & Date / Issues	Key Word	Supreme Court Landmark Decision
Wabash, St. Louis & Pacific RR v. Illinois (1886) interstate commerce	state regulatory power limits	The Court decided that Congress must set the general rules on interstate commerce and that states were very limited in actions to control interstate transportation.
United States v. E.C. Knight Co. (1895) state regulation of commerce; Congressional power	anti-trust; interstate commerce	The Court reasserted that Congress has the power to make rules on activities directly linked to interstate commerce, but that under the 10th Amendment, states could regulate activities of interstate corporations that take place within the state.
In Re Debs (1895) freedom of speech; support for general welfare	commerce clause	The Court ruled that the federal government has the power to halt a strike that affects the nation's general welfare (in this case mail delivery).
Plessy v. Ferguson (1896) 14th Amendement's equal protection of the law	separate but equal	The Court ruled that state laws providing "separate but equal" accommodations for the races did not violate the Constitution's equal protection of the law clause, and that these laws did not conflict with federal regulation of interstate commerce.
Northern Securities Co. v. United States (1904) commerce; restraint of trade	antitrust	The Court ruled that it was constitutional to apply Congress' antitrust laws to a holding company set up to eliminate interstate railroad competition.
Lochner v. New York (1905) employer/employee contracts; property rights; substantive due process; public welfare	use of personal property; contracts	The Court ruled that a New York law went beyond its "police power" to protect the public welfare and violated the employer's economic rights ("liberty to contract with employees").
Muller v. Oregon (1908) contracts; state's interest in worker protection; equal protection of law	working conditions for women	The Court ruled that an Oregon law to protect women from overwork was within the state's "police power" to protect the public welfare and did not violate the equal protection for employer's economic rights to make contracts with employees.

Case & Date / Issues	Key Word	Supreme Court Landmark Decision
Schenck v. United States (1919) freedom of speech; Congressional war power	clear and present danger; war powers	The Court ruled that the 1st Amendment did not protect a citizen's freedom of speech if a public statement posed a "clear and present danger" to the nation's security during a world war.
Schechter Poultry Corporation v. United States (1935) executive and legislative power	New Deal economic legislation	The Court ruled that a congressional act unconstitutionally gave the President power (to regulate interstate commerce) that belonged only to Congress.
Korematsu v. United States (1944) executive power; war power; 14th Amendment equal protection; 5th Amendment right to "life, liberty, and property"	forced relocation	The Court ruled that a military situation permitted Congress and the President to deprive an entire race of basic 5th and 14th Amendment rights in the interest of national security.
Brown v. Board of Education of Topeka (1954) equal protection; state's rights to educate	racial segregation of schools	The Court ruled that the mere act of legally segregating schools by race violated the concept of equal treatment (14th Amendment) no matter how equal a state made the physical facilities in the schools.
Watkins v. United States (1957) self-incrimination; due process; congressional power	UnAmerican activities	The Court ruled that citizens testifying before congressional investigating committees must be granted the same civil rights under the Bill of Rights they would have in any legal proceeding.
Mapp v. Ohio (1961) right to privacy; unwarranted search and seizure	unwarranted search; privacy	The Court ruled that the use of evidence seized in an unwarranted search of an individual's home violated the 4th and 14th Amendments.
Baker v. Carr (1962) equal voting rights; equal protection	reapportionment; representation	The Court ruled that , under the 14th Amendment, seats in a state legislature must be apportioned on a population basis.

Case & Date / Issues	Key Word	Supreme Court Landmark Decision
Engel v. Vitale (1962) 1st Amendment: establishment of religion	school prayer; state religious requirement	The Court ruled that requiring students to recite a non denominational New York State Board of Regents prayer violated the 1st Amendment's prohibition on the establishment of religion.
Gideon v. Wainwright (1963) right to attorney; state v. individual rights; due process	rights of accused, due process	The Court ruled that the Sixth Amendment's due process guarantee of the right to counsel applied to all felony cases (not just in federal courts) and that the state government must provide a defense attorney for indigent accused persons.
Heart of Atlanta Motel v. United States (1964) property rights; commerce clause	discrimination	The Court ruled that the commerce clause of the Constitution justified the Civil Rights Act of 1964 prohibition of racial discrimination in "any place of public accommodation" whose operations affect interstate commerce.
Miranda v. Arizona (1966) self-incrimination (5th amendment), due process (6th amendment), equal protection (14th amendment)	rights of accused	The Court ruled that unless a criminal suspect is informed of the right to counsel and the right against self-incrimination during police interrogation, evidence so obtained may not be used to prosecute the suspect.
Tinker v. Des Moines (1969) freedom of speech; state's right to educate	symbolic silent speech	The Court ruled that the wearing of arm bands to make a political statement was protected by the 1st Amendment as "symbolic speech." As long as there was no substantial or material interference with the educational process, it could not be interfered with by school officials.
New York Times v. United States (1971) executive power v. free press	free press, prior restraint, Pentagon Papers	The Court ruled that "prior restraint" (prohibiting information from being published) inhibits freedom of the press (1st Amendment) and that the government bore a "heavy burden" of justifying such restraint
Roe v. Wade (1973) privacy; abortion rights; personal choice reserve power of the state	abortion rights; personal liberty, right-to-life	The Court ruled with some qualification that state laws prohibiting abortions were unconstitutional. (first 3 mos. = no state interference; second 3 mos. = state could interfere based on mother's health; third 3 mos. = state could interfere to protect unborn child)

Case & Date / Issues	Key Word	Supreme Court Landmark Decision
United States v. Nixon (1974) impeachment; executive privilege, separation of power	separation of power	In the issue of the president withholding information from a Congressional investigation, the Court ruled that the president's executive privilege cannot "prevail over the fundamental demands of due process of law in the fair administration of criminal justice."
New Jersey v. TLO (1985) unwarranted search (4th amendment)	student rights; right to privacy; unwarranted search	The Court ruled that because of a school's educational mission, school officials need only "reasonable suspicion" of a student's unlawful behavior to conduct a reasonable search (as opposed to the police needing more specific "probable cause").
Cruzan v. Director, Missouri Dept. of Health (1990) right to die; police power; due process, equal protection (14th amendment)	right to die; police power	The Court ruled that due process under the 14th Amendment entitled a "clearly competent' person to refuse life-prolonging medical treatment (artificial life support).
Planned Parenthood of Southeastern Pennsylvania v. Casey (1992) privacy; abortion; due process, *Roe* decision	privacy; abortion	The Court ruled that states could seek to control abortion through reasonable waiting periods and parental consent for minors as long as the controls were not unduly burdensome and did not present substantial obstacles to procedures protected by the Roe decision of 1973.
Veronia School District v. Acton (1995) student search and seizure	school search and seizure, student drug testing	The Court ruled that, to maintain student safety and to fulfill the educational mission of the school, drug testing of student athletes was constitutional.

INDEX AND GLOSSARY

Abolitionism, Abolition Movement (anti-slavery movement), 106, 165

Abortion (see *Roe v. Wade*, 289)

Acculturation (modification of the culture of a group or an individual as a result of contact with a different culture; immigrants adapting to their new culture), 143

Acheson, Dean (1893-1971; Sec'y. State for Truman), 255, 258, 259, 260, 264

Achille Lauro (1988 Mid-East terrorist attack on cruise ship in Mediterranean), 313

Adams, John (1735-1826; revolutionary leader; 2nd President), 58, 60, 72, 94, 95

Adams, John Quincy (1767-1848; 6th President of the United States, 1825-1829), 320

Adams, Samuel (1722-1803; Revolutionary leader; member of both Cont. Congresses; signed *Dec. of Independence*; governor of MA, 1794-1797), 54, 55

Addams, Jane (1860-1935; Progressive social reformer - settlement houses), 168, 180

AEF (see American Expeditionary Force)

AFL or A.F.L.-C.I.O. (national alliance of labor unions founded in the 1880s), 138, 278

Affirmative action programs (special hiring quotas for minorities), 289

Afghanistan (1979; U.S.S.R. invasion), 300

African National Congress (ruling party in S. Africa; prior to 1990, an outlawed revolutionary group that opposed the apartheid government rule), 314

Age of Reason (see Enlightenment)

Agnew, Spiro (1918- 1996); resigned as vice president under Nixon, 1969-1973; Gov. MD, 1966-1968), 296

Agrarian protest (see Grange, Populist Party)

Agricultural Adjustment Act (1933; AAA- New Deal farm relief), 218, 220

Aguinaldo, Emilio (1869-1964; Philippine leader of a rebellion against Spanish rule, 1896-1898, and rebel against American authority, 1899-1901), 180

AIDS (Acquired Immuno-Deficiency Syndrome; immunological disorder caused by the retrovirus HIV, causes increased susceptibility to infections and rare cancers; transmitted primarily by venereal routes or exposure to contaminated blood), 315

Alaskan North Slope pipeline, 298

Albany Plan of Union (1754; Franklin's proposal that the colonies form a self-governing federation under the British crown), 49, 53

Alger, Horatio (1832-1899; writer of inspirational books of industrial era heroes), 133

Alliance for Progress (JFK's aid program for Latin America), 284

Allied Powers (in WW I: Britain, France, Russia, later Italy and the U.S.; in WW II: Britain, U.S., U.S.S.R., China, Canada, and Free French), 185, 186, 187, 240, 241, 242, 243, 244, 245, 248, 250, 257

Al Qaeda (Arabic for "the base""; Islamic terrorist group emerged in the 1990s nder leadership of a radical Saudi businessman Osama bin Laden; responsible for 9/11/2001 attacks on U.S.), 319, 320

Amendments, amendment process (formal revision of, addition to, or change, as in a bill or a constitution), 78, Appendix 1

American Dream (ideal of a happy and successful life to which all may aspire), 204

American Expeditionary Force (AEF - U.S. military in WW I), 186

American Federation of Labor (AFL; organization composed primarily of craft unions founded in 1886), 138

American Indian Movement (AIM - Native American civil rights group formed in 1968), 291

American Party - "Know-Nothings" (1840s-1850s; anti-immigrant nativist group), 145

American Protective Association (1890s; anti-immigrant nativist group), 145

American Railway Union (founded in 1893 by Eugene Debs; see Pullman Boycott), 139

American Revolution (1775-1783 rebellion of Britain's North American colonies), 55-61, 165

Americans with Disabilities Act (1990; extended comprehensive civil rights protections to the disabled), 298

Americanization Process (see acculturation), 143

Amnesty Act (1872 - general pardon for Confederate officials by Congress), 124

Anarchists (advocating the abolition of all government), 188, 204, 209

Anasazi (Native American people inhabiting southern CO and UT and northern NM and AZ from about A.D. 100; whose descendants are Pueblo peoples), 39

Anthony, Susan B. (1820-1906; feminist suffragist leader; instrumental in the passage of legislation that gave married women legal rights over their children, property, and wages; co-founded the American Woman Suffrage Association), 165, 168

Anti-Federalists (opponents of U.S. Constitution's ratification c. 1788-89), 75

Anti-Imperialist League (prominent Americans opposed the acquisition of colonies by the U.S.), 180

Anti-Klan Law (see Ku Klux Klan), 124

Anti-Saloon League (prohibitionist group reached national scale in 1895), 169, 210

Anti-trust suits (stopping monopolies), 137, 171, 172, 173, 207

Antiquities Act (1906; federal land preservation), 172

Apartheid (19th - 20th c. South African policy of total separation of races), 313-314

Appalachian Mountains, 28, 29, 30, 31, 33, 54

Appeasement (Europeans' conceded to Hitler's aggressive acts, c. 1938-40), 237-238

Arbitration (third party dictates settlement in labor-management or international disputes), 140

Arkies (Great Plains farmers - esp. Arkansas - displaced by 1930s Dust Bowl disaster; focus of Steinbeck's *Grapes of Wrath*), 222

Armstrong, Louis (1900-1971; musician; influenced the development of jazz), 212

Articles of Confederation (first U.S. government, 1778-1789), 70-73

Arsenal of Democracy (FDR's pre-WW II preparation speech), 241

Assimilation (process whereby a minority group gradually adopts the customs and attitudes of the prevailing culture), 143

Astair, Fred (1899-1987; Hollywood entertainer; 1930s musicals), 222

Atlantic Charter (WW II aims for U.S. and Britain), 241

Autocracy (Government by a single person having unlimited power; despotism), 185

Atomic Energy Commission (1946-1975; independent government agency licenses and regulates civilian uses of nuclear materials; succeeded the Manhattan Project; became Nuclear Regulatory Commission, 1975), 252

Austin, Stephen (1793-1836; colonizer and political leader; worked to make Texas a state of Mexico but later helped TX settlers gain independence, 1836), 104

Axis Alliance (1936 informal cooperation between Italy and Germany, formalized in 1939, Japan joined in 1940), 236, 238, 239

Aztec (people of central Mexico whose civilization was at its height at the time of the Spanish conquest in the early 16th century), 39

Baker v. Carr (1962; equity in Congressional district apportionment), 279, 289, Appendix 2

Bakke v. the Regents of the University of California, (1978; court ordered care in the use of racial quotas in affirmative action programs to avoid reverse discrimination), 289

Baltimore, Lord (Calvert, Cecil,1605-1675; Second Baron of Baltimore; recipient of the Maryland proprietorship, 1634), 47

Bank of the United States (1791 independent financial control agency created by Hamilton's controversial stretching of the powers of Congress; Jackson's controversial 1832 veto), 102-104

Baruch, Bernard (1870-1965; stock broker, public official, and political adviser for every President from Wilson to Kennedy; key manager of WW I economy), 203

Batista, Fulgencio (Cuban dictator overthrown by Castro), 283

Battle of Bunker Hill (low elevation in the Charlestown section of Boston, MA; first major Revolutionary War battle took place on nearby Breed's Hill on June 17, 1775), 58

Battle of the Bulge (12/1944-01/1945; Hitler's last offensive in France to stop Allied movement toward Germany), 243

Bay (body of water partially enclosed by land but with a wide mouth, affording access to the sea), 29

Bay of Pigs Invasion (04/1961; CIA-backed botched attempt overthrow Castro), 283

Begin, Menachem (1913-1992; Israeli prime minister, 1977-1983; shared the 1978 Nobel Peace Prize with Anwar el-Sadat of Egypt), 299

Bell, Alexander Graham (1847-1922; inventor of the telephone in 1876), 133

Bellamy, Edward (early socialist reform work: Looking Backward, 1888), 154

Berlin Blockade and Airlift (1948-1949; Soviet blockade of city relieved by Allies air supplies), 257

Berlin Wall (1961-1989; Soviets ordered blocking off of E. Berlin; divided communist and free sections of Berlin), 284, 318

Bessemer Process (see Kelly-Bessemer)

Bethune, Mary McLeod (1875-1955; educator who sought improved racial relations and educational opportunities for African Americans; advisor to FDR; delegate to first UN meeting, 1945), 221

BIA (see Bureau of Indian Affairs)

Bicameral legislature (lawmaking body divided into 2-houses), 72, 79

bin Laden, Osama (Saudi businessman sponsor of Al Qaeda terrorist activities), 320

Big Stick, The (Theodore Roosevelt's aggressive Lat. Am. foreign policy), 182

Bilingual Education Act (1975 mandate that children be taught in their native language while learning English), 298

Bill (draft of a proposed law presented for approval to a legislative body), 81

Bills of attainder (laws declaring persons guilty without right of trial), 81

Bill of Rights (1791 - U.S. Constitutional amendments 1-10 stating fundamental personal rights of citizens), 77-78, Appendix 1

Black Codes (post civil war legal & economic restrictions on former slaves.), 122

Black Muslims (Nation of Islam; founded in 1930s; anti-integrationist in the 1960s; main group dissolved in 1970s to blend with worldwide orthodox Islam; 1970s Detroit-based Farrakhan group emerged as advocates of black male solidarity and intensive work with youth in inner-city black communities), 287

Black Panthers (1960s militant civil rights group), 287

Black Power (post 1966 militant civil rights activities), 287

Blacklist (lists of undesirable employees circulated in an industry), 140, 262

Blitzkrieg (swift, sudden military offensive, usually by combined air and mobile land forces; Nazis - WW II attack on Poland), 238, 239

Blue-collar jobs (industrial workers), 275, 276

B'nai B'rith ("sons of the covenant"; oldest and largest American Jewish service organization; founded in 1843 in NYC by Jewish immigrants), 169

Bolsheviks (communist group led late 1917 revolution in Russia), 139, 188, 203

Bond rallies (raising money on WW II home front), 245

Bonus Army (veterans' march on Washington 1932, lobby for military pensions; broken up by force), 216

Border states (slave states that did not rebel against the Union), 108

Boss / Bossism (see political boss), 125, 170

Boston Massacre (1770; squad of British troops fired into an unruly crowd killing three men outright and mortally wounding two others), 56

Boxer Rebellion, The (anti-imperialist movement in China, 1900), 178

Boycott (organized abstaining from doing business with someone to force them to accept a condition), 57, 139, 140, 279, 280, 290

Brandeis, Louis (1856-1941; activist Supreme Court assoc. justice, 1916-1939), 170

Brinkmanship (confrontational Cold War diplomacy; see Dulles), 278

Brooklyn Bridge (1869-83; first great suspension bridge in the U.S. that had cables formed from parallel steel wires that were spun in place), 141

Browder, Earl (U.S. communist leader), 223

Brown, John (1800-1859; abolitionist; raided the U.S. arsenal at Harper's Ferry (VA) in an aborted effort to liberate Southern slaves), 107

Brown v. Board of Ed. of Topeka (1954 - school desegregation), 127, 279. 280, 283, 286, Appendix 2

Bryan, William Jennings (1860-1925; Populist/Democratic leader; unsuccessful bids for the presidency in 1896, 1900, 1908; "Cross of Gold" speech advocating free silver, 1896; defense of fundamentalism in the Scopes trial, 1925), 154, 209

Buchanan, James (1791-1868; 15th President, 1857-1861; could not prevent the South from seceding from the Union), 107

Budget deficit (amount by which gov't. revenue falls short of meeting expenses), 309

Budget surplus (amount by which government revenue exceeds meeting expenses; an overabundance of income), 319

Bull Market (wild speculation before 1929 stock market crash), 214

Bunche, Ralph (1904-1971; civil rights leader; Nobel Peace Prize, 1950), 221

Bureau of Indian Affairs (BIA; an agency of the U.S. Department of the Interior set up to handle Indian affairs), 291, 295

Bureaucracy / Bureaucrat (power concentrated in an immense hierarchy of governmental agencies), 85-86, 220

Burns, George & Gracie Allen (radio/TV entertainers), 223

Bush, George H.W. (1924- ; 41st President; ambassador to the U.N.and China; director of the CIA; Vice President (1981-1989), 313, 315, 317

Bush, George W. (1946- ; 43rd President; Governor of Texas, 1995-2001; son of Pres. George H.W. Bush), 83, 319-320

Business cycle (see cycle of demand)

Cabinet (heads of executive agencies function as advisory group to president), 94

Cabot, John (1450-1498; Italian-born explorer [Giovanni Caboto] who commanded the English expedition that discovered the North American mainland in
1497), 41

Calhoun, John C. (1782-1850; Senator, Vice President, states rights spokesman),
101

Calvert, Cecil (see Lord Baltimore)

Camp David Agreements (1979 Egyptian-Israeli accords), 299, 300

Capitalism (system in which the means of economic production and distribution
are privately owned; development balanced by reinvestment of profits), 131

Carmichael, Stokley (1941-1998; militant "black power" civil rights leader of
SNCC), 287

Carnegie, Andrew (1835-1919; industrialist and philanthropist who amassed a
fortune in the steel industry), 134, 135, 139, 142, 180

Cartel (international trade organization with monopolistic power), 277

Carter, Jimmy (1924- ; 39th President, 1977-1981; negotiated the Camp David
accords between Egypt and Israel, 1979; Gov. GA 1971-1975), 297, 298, 299

Cartier, Jacques (1491-1557; French explorer who navigated the St. Lawrence
River in 1535 and laid claim to the region for France), 41

Castro, Fidel (1936- ; Cuban rebel leader; created communist state, 1959), 283,
284

Catt, Carrie Chapman (1859-1947; major role in the ratification of the *19th
Amendment* giving women the vote; founded the League of Women Voters),
168

Caucus (gathering of political leaders often to choose candidates), 102

Central Intelligence Agency (CIA; U.S. espionage agency created in 1947; coordi-
nates other agencies in the intelligence community), 252, 278, 283

Central Powers (Austria, Germany, Turkey WW I alliance), 185, 189

Chamberlain, Neville (British Prime Minister, 1937-1940; advocated a policy of
appeasement toward the fascist regimes of Europe), 237

Chambers, Whittaker (1901-1961; member of the Communist Party; testified
before the House Un-American Activities Committee; implicated Alger Hiss),
263

Charter (document issued by a sovereign, legislature, or other authority, creating
a public or private corporation), 44, 45, 46, 47

Chavez, Cesar (1927-1993; organized the United Farm Workers [UFW]), 290

Checks and Balances (gov't. structure that grants power to various branches to
keep the other branches within specific bounds), 75, 78

Cherokee Nation (Native American people formerly inhabiting the western
Carolinas, eastern Tennessee, and northern Georgia; present-day populations in northeast Oklahoma and western North Carolina; U.S. government
removed them to OK Indian Territory in the 1830s), 39, 150

Chicago, Milwaukee & St. Paul Railway Co. v. Minn. (reinforced the federal commerce power over the states, 1889), 153

Chief Diplomat (presidential role of carrying out foreign policy), 82

Chief Executive (presidential role of implementing laws of Congress), 82

Chief Legislator (unofficial presidential role of suggesting laws to Congress), 82

Chief of State (presidential role - ceremonial head of government), 82

Chinese Exclusion Act (1882; immigration restriction), 146

Chinese Nationalists (also Guomindang; Party of Jiang Jieshi; ruling power
group in China 1924-1947), 259-260

Chiang Kai-shek (see Jiang Jieshi)

Churchill, Winston (1874-1965; British prime minister, 1940-1945 and 1951-
1955; led Great Britain through WW II), 241, 247-248, 255

CIA (see Central Intelligence Agency)

Civil disobedience (intentional public breaking of laws deemed unjust), 280, 287

Civil liberties (basic personal rights and protections in U.S. Constitution, Bill of Rights, and other amendments), 77

Civil Rights Acts (1957, 1964, 1968), 280, 288, 289

Civil Rights Cases (Court held that the *13th* and *14th Amendments* did not allow Congress to legislate on private or social actions of citizens), 126, Appendix 2

Civil Rights Commission (1947), 254, 280

Civil Rights Movement, 280, 286-288

Civil service (distribution of government jobs through fair competitive examinations; see *Pendleton Act*), 165

Civil War (war between factions or regions of the same country; in U.S., 1861-1865 conflict between the Union and the Confederacy), 108-111

Civil Works Administration (1933; federally financed building projects to make work for the unemployed), 218, 219

Civilian Conservation Corps (CCC; 1933-1942; unemployed, unmarried young men enlisted to work on conservation and resource-development projects such as soil conservation, flood control, and protection of forests and wildlife), 218, 219, 221

Clay, Henry (1777-1852; U.S Representative, Senator, Sec'y of State; Missouri Compromise, 1820, Compromise of 1850), 101, 105, 106

Clayton Anti-Trust Act (l914; made up deficiencies in the *Sherman Anti-Trust Act* of 1890 in combatting monopolistic practices), 174

Clean Air Act (1970; curbed auto emissions), 294

Clear and present danger rule (gov't. suspends rights in national stress), 187, 249

Clemenceau, Georges (French WW I leader), 187

Cleveland, (Stephen) Grover (1837-1908; 22nd and 24th President, 1885-1889 and 1893-1897)

Clinton, Bill (William J., 1946- ; 42nd President, 1993-2001; Gov. AR, 1978-80, 1983-93), 315, 317, 319

Coalition (an alliance of small groups to achieve majority control of a government or organization), 243, 252, 253, 317

Coalition Provisional Authority (U.S.-led group of countries that provided troops and support for the Iraqi liberation and supervised the occupation after defeat of Saddam Hussien regime in 2003-2004), 320

Coattail effect (in an election, the success of a strong, popular candidate may pull votes for other candidates in the same party), 253, 308

Cold war (political tension and military rivalry between nations that stops short of full-scale war), 255, 259, 260, 262, 277, 296, 314, 319

Collective bargaining (labor-management negotiation on wages and working conditions), 138, 140, 219

Columbian Exchange (early Native American - European contacts), 41, 42

Columbus, Christopher (1451-1506; Italian explorer in the service of Spain; convinced that Earth was round, he attempted to reach Asia by sailing west from Europe, thereby encountering America in 1492; made three subsequent voyages to the Caribbean), 38, 40-41

Commander in chief (role of the President as head of the U.S. military forces), 82

Command economy (functional arrangement for exchange of goods and services following decisions by government agencies), 202, 203

Commerce clause (Constitutional power to Congress to regulate trade), 137, 167

Commerce Department (cabinet dept. created in l903 to aid business development), 94, 133, 172

Committee on Un-American Activities (1938-1975; House of Representatives investigations on communism and subversive activities; renamed Internal Security committee, 1969-1975), 263 common law (system of laws originated and developed in England based on court decisions, on the doctrines implied in those decisions, and on customs and usages rather than on codified written laws), 45

Common Market (see European Union)

Communism (government in which the state plans and controls the economy; a single, often authoritarian party holds power to make progress toward a social order in which all goods are equally shared by the people; Marxist-Leninist version advocates the overthrow of capitalism by the revolution of the proletariat), 223, 234, 255, 256, 258, 259, 260, 262, 263, 264, 277, 278, 279, 283, 284, 292, 295, 296, 312, 318-319

Compromise of 1850 (five laws enacted by Congress aimed at ending sectional disputes that threatened the Union), 106

Computers, 275

Concurrent power (power shared by several divisions of gov't.), 80

Confederate States of America (name adopted by the states that seceded from the U.S. in 1860-61 to form an independent nation), 107, 108, 110, 111, 120-124

Confederation (union of sovereign states retaining power locally), 71

Conglomerates (large, highly diversified corporations), 275

Congress, The (federal legislative body of U.S.), 71, 72, 73, 74, 77, 79-81, 82, 84, 85, 94, 96, 97, 98, 99, 102, 104, 105, 109, 120-123, 124, 125, 126, 171, 173, 174, 178, 179, 185, 186, 202, 203, 205, 207, 208, 209, 210, 214, 218, 219, 220, 233, 234, 235, 237, 239, 241, 251, 252, 253, 254, 255, 256, 258, 262, 263, 278, 280, 281282, 283, 285, 288, 292, 293, 294, 295, 297, 298, 309, 312, 314, 316, 317, 319

Congress of Industrial Organizations (CIO; 1930s-1950s, major national labor union; rival of AFL, merged with AFL in 1955), 278

Congress of Racial Equality (CORE - 1940s civil rights organization became active in the 1960s), 287

Conscription (see draft)

Conservation (attempts to preserve the natural environment), 172

Conspicuous consumption (lavish indulgence by the very rich, c. industrial era), 142

Constitution (fundamental law of U.S.), 59, 70-86, 95, 96, 97, 100, 102, 105, 109, 124, 126, 220, Appendix 1

Containment policy (post WW II foreign policy to restrain growth of communism on global scale), 256-261, 278, 292

Continent (one of the principal land masses of the earth), 29, 38

Continental Congress (delegates from the 13 original American colonies /states; U.S. government, 1774-1789; declared independence, fought the Revolution, managed country under the *Articles of Confederation*), 56-58, 71

Continental Divide (in the Rockies; line that divides those rivers that run east from those that flow west), 30

Conversion (also reconversion; economic dislocations - recessions and depressions - experienced as nations readjust from war production [demobilize] and government imposed restrictions to normal market economic activity), 204, 251

Coolidge, (John) Calvin (1872-1933; 30th President, 1923-29), 191, 207, 214, 215, 233

Cooper, James Fenimore (1789-1851; novelist remembered for his novels of frontier life – *The Last of the Mohicans*), 103

Cooperatives (farmers organization to combat high railroad shipping charges), 152

Copperheads (Lincoln's critics; Northerners who sympathized with the South during the Civil War), 109

Cornwallis, Charles (1738-1805; British military leader; commanded forces in NC during the American Revolution; surrendered at Yorktown in 1781), 60

Corporations (business organization drawing capital from large group of share holding owners), 132, 133, 136, 275, 315

Coughlin, Charles E. (1891-1979; "radio priest" of the 1930s-40s; national broadcasts were critical of New Deal; isolationist, antisemitic, and pro-fascist), 223

Council of National Defense (WWI war effort management organization), 202-203

County (territorial division of a state or colony exercising administrative, judicial, and political functions), 48

Court Packing Plan (FDR's 1937 attempt to influence Supreme Court decisions), 220

Coureurs de bois (15th-16th C. fur trappers of New France / Canada), 43

Craft unions (labor organizations for skilled trades), 138

Credit Mobilier Scandal (Grant era railroad scandal), 125

Crime of '73 (refusal of gov't. to increase silver coinage issue), 153

Critical Period (1781 to 1789 - troubled time under *Articles of Confederation*), 71-72

Crosby, Bing (singer-actor, radio, cinema, TV), 223, 245

Cross of Gold (Bryan's 1896 campaign speech in favor of free silver), 154

Cruzan v. Director, Missouri Dept. of Health (1990 life support issue), 316, Appendix 2

Cuba (U.S. protect. after Sp. Am. War; 1962 missile crisis), 179, 180, 283, 284, 299

customs duties (tax charged by a government on imports; see tariffs), 54

Cullen, Countee (1903-1946; Harlem Renaissance poet; *Colors, Copper Sun*), 212

Cultural pluralism (society made up of a blend of numerous cultures), 143

Cumberland Road (also National Road; first federal highway in the U.S.; authorized by Congress in 1806; chief road to the West), 99

Cycle of demand (ebb and flow of demand which causes the economy to expand and contract at intervals; also business cycle), 213

Darrow, Clarence (1857-1938; lawyer known for highly publicized defense of lost causes; Scopes evolution trial, 1925), 209

Dartmouth College v. Woodward (1819, legal sanctity of contracts), 96

Dawes General Allotment Act (1887 - attempt to distribute tribal lands and resettle Native Americans), 150

Debs, Eugene V. (1855-1926; industrial era labor union and Socialist Party leader), 140, 186

Declaration of Independence (summary of the reasons the colonies revolted against Britain in 1776; authored primarily by Thomas Jefferson; employs the natural-rights theories of John Locke), 57, 58-59, 320

Declaration of Sentiments (Elizabeth Stanton's proclamation at the 1848 Seneca Falls women's rights convention), 165

De facto segregation (racial separation by informal means - as in neighborhood settlement patterns), 287

Deficit spending (spending of public funds in excess of revenues), 219

De jure segregation (racial separation by legal statutes), 124, 127, 279

Delegated power (specifically assigned in Constitution), 78, 80

Demand (amount of a commodity or service that people are ready to buy for a given price), 131, 202, 213, 217

Demobilize (disband military structures), 204, 251

Democratic Party (evolved in early 19th C. from Democratic Republicans; modern party tends to be the more liberal of the two major parties; support comes from the lower and middle class, urban dwellers, ethnic minorities, and unions; generally favors welfare, and government economic intervention), 216, 217, 315, 319

Democratic republic (broad-based franchise allows most citizens to select representatives who do the decision-making in a government), 78

Democratic-Republicans (early U.S. political party organized by Jefferson & Madison), 94, 95

Dennis v. U.S. (1951; upheld the 1940 *Smith Act* on modified freedom of speech rights for communists), 262

Department of Transportation (DOT, est. 1966), 94, 285

Depression (severe and prolonged economic slow down characterized by low production and high unemployment), 204, 213

Destroyers-for-Bases Deal (1940; FDR's pre-WW II entry executive order for indirect aid to Britain), 239

Détenté (a relaxation of tense diplomatic relations between adversaries), 296

Developing nations of Asia, Latin America, and Africa (see LDCs)

Dewey, Thomas E. (1902-1971; NY Governor 1943-1955; Republican nominee for President, 1944,1948), 253

Diaz, Porfiro (1830-1915; Mexican general and dictator; dominated Mexico from 1876 to 1911; catered to the rich and foreign investors), 182

Dickinson, John (1732-1808; PA Revolutionary political leader and pamphleteer; work: *Letters from a Farmer in Pennsylvania*, 1767-1768), 55, 71

Displaced persons (WW II refugees), 255

Dissenters (those who disagrees in opinion or belief; dissidents), 44, 46

Divest (to sell off or otherwise dispose of), 314

Dix, Dorothea (1802-1887; pioneer in movement for treatment of the mentally ill), 103

Dixiecrats (see States' Rights Party)

Doctrine of Nullification (see nullification)

Dollar Diplomacy (Taft administration approach to using business investment to further U.S. foreign policy interests), 182

Domino Theory (1950s-1960s foreign policy underpinning that if one small country in a region succumbs to communist insurgency, others will quickly fall, prompting large outlays of preemptive aid from the U.S.), 278, 292

Douglass, Frederick (1817-1895; abolitionist and journalist who escaped from slavery; became an influential lecturer in the North and abroad), 106

Downsizing (reduction of large corporations in the early 1990s), 315

Dred Scott v. Sanford (1857;Court ruling, Negroes–slave or free–were not included and were not intended to be included in the category of citizen as the word was used in the U.S. Constitution; the Missouri Compromise was unconstitutional), 107, 330

DuBois, W. E. B. (19th -20th century civil rights leader; founded NAACP), 127, 169, 286

Due process (proper and fair admin. of legal procedures), 77, 124, 126, 170, 249, 279

Dukakis, Michael (Gov. MA, unsuccessful Democratic Pres. candidate, 1988), 315

Dulles, John Foster (1888-1959; Sec'y. of State for Eisenhower; containment), 278

Dust Bowl, The (protracted drought disaster on Great Plains in 1930s), 222

Duties (a tax charged by a government, especially on imports; see tariffs), 54

Economic contraction (decline - see depression and recession), 204

Economics (social science that deals with the production, distribution, and consumption of goods and services and with the theory and management)

Edison, Thomas Alva (1847-1931; inventor who patented more than a thousand inventions: microphone , phonograph, incandescent lamp; world's first central electric power plant, 1882), 133

Eisenhower Doctrine (containment actions in Middle East), 278

Eisenhower, Dwight D. (1890-1969; 34th President, 1953-1961; supreme commander of the Allied Expeditionary Force, 1943-1945), 243, 264, 277-282

El Alamein in Egypt (WW II Allied victory), 243

Elastic clause (Article I sec. 8, clause18 gives Congress power to stretch meaning of its 17 assigned powers to meet new situations), 80-81, 97

Elastic currency (gov't. ability to manage money supply to stabilize the economy), 174

Elderly (problems of growing population segment), 312

Electoral College (traditional name for the group of officials that elects the presidents and Vice Presidents of the U.S.), 74, 83-84

Electors of the President (after the popular vote, officials selected in each state cast the official electoral votes for president and vice president in December), 83

Elementary and Secondary Education Act (1965; 1st major U.S. program of direct financial assistance to schools; part of President Johnson's War on Poverty), 285

Eliot, T.S. (1888-1965; American-born British critic and writer), 212

Elkins Act (1903 - expanded power of Interstate Commerce Commission), 172

Ellington, Duke (1899-1974; jazz composer, pianist, and bandleader; *Mood Indigo, Sophisticated Lady*), 212

Emancipation Proclamation (1863; declared slaves free in rebelling states), 110

Embargo (prohibition by a gov't. on certain or all trade with a foreign nation), 98 239

Embargo Act (attempt to keep U.S. from being drawn into Napoleonic wars), 98

Emergency Quota Act (1921 - discriminatory immigration quotas begun), 146

Emerson, Ralph Waldo (1803-1882; writer, philosopher; essays regarded as landmarks of American thought and literary expression), 103

Eminent domain (under the 5th Amendment personal property can only be taken by the government if fair compensation is made to the owner), 329

Employment Act of 1946 (gov't. adopted Keynsian discretionary actions stabilize economy), 252

Encomienda (New World colonial Spanish plantation, usually employed slaves), 42

Engel v. Vitale (1962 - school prayer decision), 279, Appendix 2

English Bill of Rights (1689; limited the power of English monarchs and invested increased power in Parliament), 45, 59

Enlightenment (philosophical movement of the 18th century that emphasized the use of reason to scrutinize previously accepted doctrines and traditions and that brought about many humanitarian reforms; influenced *Declaration of Independence* and gov't. forms of the Constitution), 47, 59, 73

Enumerated Power (see delegated power; usually Congress' 17 powers in Art. I, 8)

Environmental concern (Relating to ecological altering of the environment), 294

Environmental Protection Agency (EPA; established in 1970, as an independent agency in the executive branch of the U.S. government to permit coordinated and effective government action on behalf of the environment), 294

Equal protection of law (see *14th Amendment*)

Equal Rights Amendment (intended to outlaw discrimination based on sex; originally introduced in 1923, it received support in the 1970s and 1980s, but failed to be ratified by 38 states), 288

Era of Good Feeling (1820s - a time of political cooperation), 101

Erie Canal (1817 - 1825; artificial waterway extending about 360 miles across central NY from Albany to Buffalo), 99

Espionage Act (1917; limited WW I dissent), 187

European Economic Community (see European Union)

European Parliament (legislative body for the European Union), 257

European Recovery Act (see Marshall Plan)

European Union (1993; formerly the Eur. Community and the Common Market), 257

Evans, Walker (1903-1975; photographer noted for images of the rural South), 222

Excise Tax (internal tax imposed on the production, sale, or consumption of a commodity or the use of a service within a country: excises on tobacco, liquor, and long-distance telephone calls), 96, 97

Ex parte Milligan (1866- limits of Presidential power in wartime), 109

Ex post facto laws (retroactive legislation- making something a crime after the act has been committed - forbidden in Constitution), 81

Executive branch (branch of government charged with putting into effect a country's laws and the administering of its functions), 82-84, 94

Executive privilege (claim by presidents refusing to share information with Congress or the courts that disclosure would compromise either national security or the principle of separation of powers; see *United States v. Nixon*), 96, 296

*F*air Deal (domestic program of Truman), 253

Fair Labor Standards Act (1937- federal minimum wage, other labor rights), 219

Fall, Albert (Sec'y. of Interior for Harding; Teapot Dome scandal), 205

Farewell Address (see Washington's *Farewell Address*)

Fascist (system of government marked by centralization of authority under a dictator, stringent socioeconomic controls, suppression of opposition through terror and censorship, and belligerent nationalism and racism), 232, 233, 235, 237, 238

Fazenda (New World colonial Portuguese plantation, usually employed slaves), 40

FDIC (see Federal Deposit Insurance Corporation)

"Fed" (see Federal Reserve System)

Federal Deposit Insurance Corporation (1933; FDIC- New Deal agency protects depositors by insuring their bank accounts; absorbed FSLIC in 1989), 219, 315

Federal Emergency Relief Administration (FERA- New Deal relief measures), 218

Federal Reserve System (1913; "The Fed"; central bank of the U.S.; holds deposits of the commercial banks and operates a nationwide check-clearing system; serves as the basic controller of credit in the economy), 174

Federal System (see federalism)

Federal Theater Project (New Deal aid for arts), 222

Federal Trade Commission (maintains free and fair competition in business; takes action against monopoly, and unfair trade practices), 133, 174, 207

Federal union (see federalism)

Federalism (political union with a strong central government with some power shared among smaller components), 75, 80

Federalist Papers, The (essays in defense of new U.S. Constitution by Hamilton, Jay, and Madison, 1788), 77

Federalists (supporters of the Constitution in ratification struggle, also early U.S. political party founded by Hamilton and John Adams), 75-76, 94, 95

Fifteenth Amendment (1870; states could not deny citizens suffrage because of race or previous slavery), 124

Finney, Charles Grandison (1792-1875; religious revivalist leader in 1840s; president of Oberlin College in Ohio, 1851-1866), 103

Gandhi, Mohandus (1869-1948; sought independence in India through non-violent, direct actions), 287

Garfield, James A. (1831-1881; 20th President, 1881; assassinated), 165

Garland, Hamlin (1860-1940; agrarian writer, work: *Son of the Middle Border*), 94

Garland, Judy (1930s-60s film actress and singer; *The Wizard of Oz*), 222

Garrison, William Lloyd (1805-1879; abolitionist leader; published the antislavery journal *The Liberator*, 1831-1865), 106

Garvey, Marcus (1887-1940; civil rights-separatist leader in 1920s), 169

GATT (see General Agreement of Trade and Tariffs)

GDP (see Gross Domestic Product)

General Agreement on Tariffs and Trade (GATT; U.N.-sponsored overseer of world trade 1948-1995; see World Trade Organization, 319)

General Assembly (U.N.'s main deliberating body), 254

Gentlemen's Agreement (1907- restrictions on Japanese immigration), 146

George, David Lloyd (British WW I leader), 187

George, Henry (industrial era philosopher / author), 154

George III (English monarch during American Revolution), 56, 59

Georgia, 47

Geographic terms, 26, 29

G.I. Bill of Rights (*Servicemen's Readjustment Act*, 1944; aid for returning veterans and post WW II economic recovery), 251, 252, 281

Gibbons v. Ogden (1824 - upheld Congressional power to regulate interstate commerce), 96, Appendix 2

Gideon v. Wainwright (1963- Sup. Ct. ruled on rights of poor to legal defense), 279, 291, Appendix 2

Gilded Age (term used by Mark Twain to describe the post-Civil War period– an era characterized by the ruthless pursuit of profit, government corruption, conspicuous consumption, and vulgarity in taste), 142, 164

Glass-Steagall Banking Act (sets up federal bank examinations, FDIC), 219

Glasnost (U.S.S.R. internal political and economic reform program initiated by Gorbachev), 314

GNP (see Gross National Product)

Goldman, Emma (WW I radical dissenter), 187

Goldwater, Barry (1909-1998; U.S. Sen., AZ, 1953-1987; pres. candidate, 1964), 285

Gompers, Samuel (1850-1924; labor leader; president of the American Federation of Labor, 1886-1924; won higher wages, shorter hours, and greater freedom for union members), 138, 180, 203

Good Neighbor Policy (1930s; FDR's efforts to improve U.S.-Latin Am. relations), 234

Gorbachev, Mikail (1931- ; Soviet leader 1985-1990; dissolved U.S.S.R.), 314, 318

Gore, Albert (1948- ; U.S. representative, 1977–85 and senator, 1985–92 [TN]; vice president, 1993-2001), 83, 319-320

GOP ("Grand Old Party"; nickname for Republican Party)

Gospel of Wealth, The (Andrew Carnegie's social philosophy), 142

Gould, Jay (1836-1892; American financier and speculator of industrial era), 125

Graduated income tax (individual taxes scaled to income; see Sixteenth Amendment)

Grandfather clauses (South's voting restrictions on former slaves), 124

Grange laws (see Grange Movement)

Grange Movement (agrarian reform group), 152

Grant, Ulysses S. (1822-1885; 18th President; Union Civil War commander), 110, 125

Great Awakening (1720-1750; widespread revival of interest in Calvinist religion; also Second Great Awakening: 1840s revival challenged Calvinist dogma), 52, 103

Great Compromise (1787; settled issue of representation in Congress), 75

Great Depression (1929-1941; global economic collapse of the 1930s), 212-223, 232

Great Plains (large, grassland grain-producing region in central North America, stretching from Canada to Texas), 31

Great Society (Lyndon Johnson's social welfare reform program), 285-286

Greeks (classical influence on American constitutional government), 73

Green Revolution (popular term coined in the 1960s to describe the recent transfer and diffusion of agricultural technology from the technologically developed countries to less technologically advanced agricultural areas), 276

Grenville, George (British prime minister, 1763-1765; instigated *Stamp Act*, 1765, which provoked rebellious activities in the American colonies), 54

Gross Domestic Product (GDP; post-1980s basic statistical indicator of economic activity; measures the total value of all nation's production of goods and services [excluding national firms' overseas installations] in a given year)

Gross National Product (GNP; pre-1980s basic statistical indicator of economic activity: measures the total value of all nation's production of goods and services [including national firms' overseas installations] in a given year), 213, 214, 216

Guadalcanal (1942-43 WW II battle; S.W. Pacific island), 244

Guerrilla warfare (small band, hit-and-run fighting tactics), 180, 292

Gulf (large area of a sea or ocean partially enclosed by land, especially a long landlocked portion of sea opening through a strait), 28-29

Habeas corpus (constitutional protection writ guaranteeing that an accused person be informed [given a writ] of charges against them or released), 81

Hamilton, Alexander (1755-1804; soldier / politician; 1st U.S. Secretary of the Treasury, 1789-1795), 76-77, 94, 95, 97, 136

Hancock, John (1737-1793; Revolutionary leader; pres. of Continental Congress; 1st to sign the *Declaration of Independence*; served 9 terms as governor of MA), 55

Handicapped Americans (see *Rehabilitation Act of 1973*)

Harding, Warren G. (29th President ,1921-1923; corrupt administration), 187, 190, 191, 204, 205, 206, 207, 215, 233

Harlem Renaissance (artisticworks of the 1920s and early 1930s that renewed of racial pride through an emphasis on African cultural heritage), 212

Harriman, W. Averill (1891-1986; diplomat of WW II and Cold War era, ambassador to U.S.S.R., Governor of NY), 255

Harris, Joel Chandler (1848-1908; post Civil War southern author, work: *Uncle Remus: His Songs and His Sayings*), 143

Haudenosaunee Union (see Iroquois Confederacy)

Hawaii, 178

Hawley-Smoot Act (1930; kept protective tariffs high), 207, 214

Hawthorne, Nathaniel (1804-1864; writer; moralistic novels and short stories), 103

Hay, John, (1838-1905; Secretary of State, 1898-1905), 178

Haymarket Riot (1886; violent labor confrontation related to strike at Chicago's McCormack Reaper Co.), 138

Hayes, Rutherford B. (1822-1893; 19th President ,1877-1881), 126

Haywood, William "Big Bill" (1869-1928; socialist who helped found the Industrial Workers of the World, 1905), 139, 187

Hearst, William Randolph (1863-1951; newspaper and magazine publisher; beginning with the *San Francisco Examiner* in 1887, built the world's largest publishing empire, comprising 28 major newspapers), 143

Heart of Atlanta Motel Inc. v. United States (1964; Court upheld *Civil Rights Act* of 1964's prohibition of racial discrimination in places of public accommodation if operations affect interstate commerce), 289, Appendix 2

Helsinki Accords (human rights and defense perimeters of Europe, 1975), 299

Hemingway, Ernest (1899-1961; post WW I author; work: *The Sun Also Rises*), 212

Hemisphere (northern or southern half of the Earth as divided by the equator or eastern or western half as divided by a meridian), 29

Henry, Patrick (1736-1799; Revolutionary leader and orator; member of the VA House of Burgesses and the Continental Congress; governor of Virginia, 1776-1790), 55

Hepburn Act (1906 - continued Federal control over interstate commerce), 172

Hirohito, Japanese Emperor (1901-1989; Emperor of Japan, 1926-1989; advocated unconditional surrender that ended WW II; renounced his divine status), 245

Hiroshima (city of southwest Honshu, Japan; US nuclear bombing, 1945), 245

Hiss, Alger (1904 -1996; public official; accused of espionage at the height of the 1950s Communist scare; convicted of perjury in controversial case), 263

Hitler, Adolf (1889-1945; German Nazi leader), 232, 233, 235, 237, 238, 241, 242, 243

Ho Chi Minh (1890-1969: communist rebel leader; N. Vietnamese leader), 292

Holding companies (stock pool designed to indirectly monopolize an industry), 133

Holocaust, The (WWII genocide of Jews and others by the Nazis), 250

Home front (civilian activities of a country at war), 246-247

Homestead Act (1862; free land to induce settlement of the American West), 147, 151

Homestead Strike (1892; Bloody strike against Carnegie Steel Co. in PA), 139

Homesteaders (western pioneer settlers), 147, 150

Hoover, Herbert (1874-1964; 31st President, 1929-1933), 203, 214, 215-217, 233

Hopkins, Harry L. (1890-1946; key New Deal administrator and FDR advisor), 245

Horizontal integration (near monopolistic control over one basic aspect of an industry; cf. vertical integration), 134

House of Burgesses (colonial VA legislature, c. 1619), 48

House of Representatives (lower chamber of U.S. nat'l. legislature), 74, 79, 122, 317

Housing and Urban Development, Department of (HUD; 1965; federal programs relating to housing and city improvement), 285

Houston, Sam (1793-1863; led the Texan struggle for independence; president of the Republic of Texas, 1836-1844; served as U.S. senator and governor), 104

How the Other Half Lives (1890- analysis of urban poverty, Jacob Riis), 167

Hudson, Henry (b? - d. 1611; English navigator and explorer who discovered Hudson River on expedition for the East India Company, 1609), 41

Hughes, Charles Evans (1862-1948; gov. of NY, 1906-1910; associate justice of the U.S. Supreme Court, 1910-1916; sec'y of state, 1921-25; chief justice, 1930-1941), 190

Hughes, Langston (1902-1967; writer made important contributions to the Harlem Renaissance; works include *Weary Blues*, *The Ways of White Folks*), 212

Hull, Cordell (1871-1955; sec'y of state, 1933-1944; laid groundwork for UN), 234, 241

Hull House (1889- Jane Addams Chicago settlement house), 168

Human rights (fundamental entitlements all persons enjoy as protection against state conduct prohibited by international law or custom; mistreatments condemned include extrajudicial or summary execution, disappearance (in which people are taken into custody and never heard of again); torture; arbitrary detention or exile; slavery or involuntary servitude; discrimination on racial, ethnic, religious, or sexual grounds; violation of free expression, free association), 254, 299

Hussein, Saddam (Iraq's dictator; see Persian Gulf Conflict), 317-318, 320

Hypothesis (see thesis)

Immigration (to enter and settle in a country or region to which one is not native), 143-146, 281, 290, 312

Immigration Act of 1965 (abolished 1920s National Origins system), 281

Immigration Reform and Control Act (1986), 312

Impeach (to charge (a public official) with improper conduct in office before a proper tribunal), 79, 82, 122, 297, 317

Imperialism (policy of extending a nation's authority by territorial acquisition or by the establishment of economic and political hegemony over other nations), 180

Implied power (not specifically enumerated power, but broadly hinted at in Constitution; see elastic clause), 80-81, 97

Impressment (act of seizing people or property for public service or use), 98

In Re Debs (1895; Court ruled fed. gov't. could use *Sherman Antitrust Act* to end a strike that threatened the national welfare), Appendix 2

Inca civilization (Quechuan peoples of highland Peru who established an empire from northern Ecuador to central Chile before the Spanish conquest), 39

Indentured servants (colonial era laborers bound by contract for a specified term), 51

Indian Removal Act (1830; see Cherokee nation), 149

Indian Reorganization Act (1934, *Wheeler-Howard Act*, authorized the purchase of additional lands for Indians, created a revolving-credit fund to be used for tribal enterprises, invoked strict conservation practices on Indian lands), 221

Indian Service scandal (1876; Grant Era scandal), 125

Indirect democracy (citizens select representatives to do the decision-making in gov't.)

Industrial revolution (historical transformation of traditional society by dramatic increase in per capita production through the mechanization of manufacturing and other processes carried out in factories), 128-130, 132-137, 141-143

Industrial Workers of the World (IWW or "Wobblies"; revolutionary socialist union, formed in 1905 by the Western Federation of Miners), 139

Inflation (significantly rising prices not balanced by rising productivity), 251, 252, 293, 297, 309

Initiative (Progressive reform in some states which requires action by legislature on demand of certain percentage of electorate), 169

Injunction (court order forbidding an action - employers use injunctions to avoid strikes by unions), 140

Installment plan (paying for an item in small payments over extended period), 206

Interlocking Directorates (same group serve on different boards of directors to coordinate business in an industry and form an indirect monopoly), 133

Intolerable Acts (1774 - colonists' label for the laws enacted by the British Parliament in response to the Boston Tea Party), 56

International Ladies Garment Workers Union (ILGWU; industrial labor union representing workers in the women's garment industry established in 1900), 138

Interstate (activities taking place in several states), 80

Interstate Commerce Act (1887; regulates power of railroads), 137, 153

Interstate Commerce Commission (1887-1996; ICC; policing agency for oversight of surface transportation; now done by Commerce Dept.), 137, 153, 172

Interventionism (policy of interfering with the internal affairs of another sovereign nation), 181-183

Intrastate (activities taking place solely within a state), 80

Investment capital (resources used to expand business operation), 131, 277

Iran (country of southwest Asia), 299, 313, 314, 317-318

Iran-Contra Affair (activities in Reagan administration), 314

Iran-Iraq War (1980-1989), 313

Iranian hostage crisis (1979-81; militant students took 66 U.S. embassy employees as hostages and demanded return of Muhammad Reza Shah Pahlavi for trial), 299

Iron Curtain (Churchill's phrase for post-WW II separation of Eastern and Western Europe into communist and free nations), 255

Iroquois Confederation (loose union of Native American groups inhabiting NY; originally the Mohawk, Oneida, Onondaga, Cayuga, and Seneca peoples composed the Five Nations; after 1722 the Tuscaroras joined to form the Six Nations), 39, 73

Irving, Washington (1783-1859; writer remembered for *Rip Van Winkle* and *The Legend of Sleepy Hollow*), 103

Isolationism (foreign policy that seeks to keep a nation in neutral and unaligned status), 232, 233-237

Iwo Jima (island 750 mi. S. of Tokyo; bloody WW II battle in Pacific, 2/'45), 244

Jackson, Andrew (1767-1845; 7th President, 1829-1837; defeated the British at New Orleans in 1815), 99, 101-102, 104

Jackson, Helen Hunt (1830-1885; writer known for her works concerning the injustices suffered by Native Americans), 150

Jackson, Thomas J. "Stonewall" (1824-1863; Confederate general who commanded troops at both battles of Bull Run - 1861 and 1862), 110

Jamestown (1607 – first permanent English settlement in America.; named for the reigning monarch, James I), 44, 47

Jay, John (1745-1829; revolutionary leader, diplomat and jurist; served in Continental Congress; negotiated peace with Great Britain, 1782-1783; first chief justice of the U.S. Supreme Court, 1789-1795; NY governor, 1795-1801), 60, 76

Jay's Treaty (1794- kept infant U.S. out of war), 98

Jazz music (style of music, native to America, characterized by a strong but flexible rhythmic understructure with solo and ensemble improvisations on basic tunes and chord patterns), 211

Jefferson, Thomas (1743-1826; political philosopher, diplomat, educator, and
architect; 3rd President ,1801-1809; drafted the *Declaration of Independence*,
1776), 57, 58-59, 72, 94, 95, 98, 99-100
Jiang Jieshi (1887-1975; also Chiang Kai-shek, Nationalist China's generalissi-
mo; opponent of Mao), 247, 259-260
Jim Crow laws (see de jure segregation), 124, 126, 212, 279, 280
Job Corps (1960s Great Society employment retraining & youth assist.), 285
Jodl, Alfred (German WW II Field Marshal), 243
Johnson, Andrew (1808-1875; 17th President, 1865-1869; Vice President, 1864-
65; impeached and acquitted, 1868), 120, 122, 123
Johnson, Lyndon B. (1908-1973; 36th President, 1963-1969, U.S. Rep & Sen.,
TX), 284, 285, 286, 292-294
Joint Chiefs of Staff (1947; combined U.S. military command), 252
Joint Defense Board (1940; Canadian-U.S. WWII military cooperation), 239
Joint stock company (16th-19th C. private investment groups used by English to
finance exploration routes and colonies), 42, 43, 44, 45
Jones Act (1917- U.S. citizenship for Puerto Ricans), 180
Judicial activism (initiating public policy through court decisions with broad
interpretations of constitutional law), 279
Judicial Branch, The (Federal court structure), 72, 75, 85
Judicial restraint (curtailing the courts' practice of broadening public policy
through liberal interpretation of basic law), 310
Judicial review (Supreme Court power to determine the constitutionality of acts
of Congress, the president, federal agencies, or state laws and actions), 85,
96
Judiciary Act of 1789 (see *Marbury v. Madison*), 85, 96
Justice Department (federal government's legal office; headed by the cabinet-
rank attorney general responsible for the enforcement of federal laws, repre-
sents the government in all legal matters, and gives advice and opinions to
the president and the heads of the executive departments; includes the
Federal Bureau of Investigation), 94, 133
Jungle, The (1906; muckraking Sinclair novel led to *Meat Inspect. Act*), 167

Kansas-Nebraska Act (1854; established the territories of Kansas and Nebraska
with slave status determined by popular sovereignty and repealed the
Missouri Compromise of 1820), 107
Kellogg-Briand Pact (1928, attempt to outlaw aggression among nations), 191
Kelly, William (1811-1888; Pittsburgh iron manufacturer; patented a pneumatic
process for making steel in 1857), 129, 133
Kelly-Bessemer Process (pneumatic process for making steel from iron), 129, 133
Kennan, George F. (1904 – ; State Dept. official in Truman Administration,
worked out containment policy), 255
Kennedy, Anthony (1936- ; associate justice of the U.S. Supreme Court, 1988),
310
Kennedy, John F. (1913-1963; 35th President, 1961-63; U.S. Sen., MA), 282-284
Kent State (1970 anti-Vietnam protest, 4 students killed), 293
Kervorkian, Jack (controversial MI doctor; advocates physician-assisted suicide),
316
Keynes, John Maynard (1883-1946; British economist; advocated deficit spending
by gov't. for demand stimulation), 217, 252
King George's War (1744-1748; extension of Anglo-French imperial rivalry in the
early 18th C.), 52
King, Jr., Martin Luther (1950s-'60s non-violent civil rights leader), 280, 286, 287

Kissinger, Dr. Henry (American diplomat; national security adviser,1969-1975 and Secretary of State, 1973-1977 under Presidents Nixon and Ford negotiated Vietnam cease-fire), 295, 296

Knights of Labor (early national labor union), 138

Know-Nothings (19th c. anti-immigrant party), 145

Korean Conflict (After World War II the Soviet- and U.S.-occupied territories formed separate republics on the East Asian peninsula; a Soviet-backed invasion of the south led to U.N. intervention between 1950-1953), 260-261, 278

Korematsu v. U.S. (1944, suit against internment of Am. citizens of Japanese ancestry during WW II, see clear & present danger rule), 249, Appendix 2

Khomeini, Ayatollah Rullah (1900-1989; Shi'ite leader and head of state, 1979-1989; leader of Iranian Revolution), 299

Khrushchev, Nikita S. (1894-1971; Soviet leader, 1956-64), 284

Kosovo (province of Yugoslavia; scene of ethnic rebellion, 1999; NATO force deployed to end ethnic cleansing), 318

Ku Klux Klan (secret society organized in the South after the Civil War; reasserted white supremacy through terrorism; reorganized in GA in 1915), 124, 145, 209

Kuwait (U.S. protection of oil tankers in Persian Gulf), 317-318

Kwakiutl (Native American people inhabiting parts of coastal British Columbia and northern Vancouver Island), 39

LaFayette, Marquis Marie-Joseph Paul de (1757-1834; French soldier / politician; served on Washington's staff in the Am. Rev.), 59

LaFollette, Robert (1855-1925; politician and reformer, served as a U.S. Senator, WI, 1906-1925), 170

Laissez-faire (economic philosophy which seeks to minimize governmental interference with the economy), 131, 136, 202, 206, 207

Lake (large inland body of fresh water or salt water), 29

Lame duck (elected official serving during the period between failure to win an election and the inauguration of a successor; an ineffective person; a weakling), 107

Landon, Alf (1887-1987; KS Gov.; 1936 Republican presidential candidate), 220

Landrum-Griffin Labor Management Reporting and Disclosure Act (1957 - control of corruption in labor unions), 279

Landslide vote (an overwhelming victory in an election), 220

Lange, Dorothea (1895-1965; photographer; 1930s portraits of rural workers), 222

LDCs (see Less Developed Countries)

League of Nations (post-WW I international peace organization conceived by Pres. Wilson - U.S. never joined), 187, 189, 190, 191, 233, 235, 236, 237, 254

Lee, Ann (1736-1784; "Mother Ann"; founder of the Shakers in U.S, 1776), 103

Lee, Robert E. (1807-1870; Confederate commander; victories included: Bull Run, Fredericksburg, and Chancellorsville; surrendered at Appomattox, 1865), 110

Leigh, Vivian (1930s-1950s film actress; *Gone with the Wind*), 223

Lend-Lease Act (1941; U.S. aid to all WWII Allies), 241, 242

Less Developed Countries (LDCs; low level of industrial development, high poverty level, vulnerability to international economic conditions, and poor quality of life), 275, 276

Letter From a Birmingham Jail (1963 statement of philosophy of social justice by Dr. Martin Luther King), 286, 287

Levittown (examples of suburban growth after WW II), 281

Lewis, Meriwether and Clark, William (led the 1803-1806 Louisiana Territory expedition from St. Louis to the mouth of the Columbia River), 99

Lewis, Sinclair (1885-1951; novelist satirized middle-class America; works: *Main Street, Babbitt, Elmer Gantry*), 212

Liberator, The (19th c. militant anti-slavery newspaper of Wm. Lloyd Garrison), 106

Liliuokalani (1838-1917; last Hawaiian sovereign ruler, 1891-1893), 178

Limited government (political principle of restricting gov't. power), 75

Lincoln, Abraham (1809-1865; 16th President, 1861-65; led the Union during the Civil War; emancipated slaves in the South), 106-111, 120-122

Literacy tests (citizens must pass exam to vote - used to keep poor blacks from voting in the South), 146

Literacy Test Act (1917 - immigration restricted to those literate in native language), 146

Little Rock Crisis (1957; desegregating Southern schools), 280

Livingston, Robert (1746-1813; NY Revolutionary leader and diplomat; helped draft *Declaration of Independence*; negotiated the Louisiana Purchase, 1803), 58

Lloyd, Henry Demerest (Progressive Era social philosopher), 154

Lobby (group organized to influence legislation), 97

Lochner v. New York (1905; questioned labor legislation), 170, Appendix 2

Locke, John (1632-1704; English Enlightenment political philosopher), 47, 59, 73

Lockout (withholding of work from employees and closing down of a workplace by an employer during a labor dispute), 140

Lodge, Henry Cabot (1850-1924; Senate majority leader, 1918-1924; opposed U.S. membership in the League of Nations), 189

Long, Huey (1893-1935; LA Gov., 1928-1932 / U.S. Sen., 1930-1935; FDR opponent), 223

Longfellow, Henry Wadsworth (1807-1882; 19th-century poet), 103

Loose constructionists (broad, flexible interpretations of the Constitution), 80, 95, 100

Lord Baltimore (see Baltimore)

Louisiana Purchase (1803; 1st major addition of territory; constitutionality questioned), 99-100

Love Canal, (1971-1977 Niagara Falls, NY toxic waste controversy), 298

Lowell, Francis Cabot (1775-1817; MA merchant; launched U.S. textile industry), 129

Loyalists (individuals maintaining loyalty to an established government, or sovereign during war or revolutionary change), 60

Loyalty oaths (citizens being required to pledge allegiance to their country as a condition of employment), 262

Lusitania (British ship torpedoed by Germans; moved U.S. toward entering WW I), 184

Lyon, Mary (1797-1849; founded the 1st institution of higher learning for women), 103

MacArthur, Douglas (1880-1964; WW II Pacific commander, military governor of occupied Japan, Korean War commander; fired by Truman), 244, 245, 248, 259, 261

Madison, James (1751-1836; fourth President, 1809-1817; member of the Continental Congress and Constitutional Convention, 1787), 72, 76, 77, 94, 95, 98

Magna Carta (charter of English political and civil liberties granted by King John at Runnymede in June 1215), 45, 59

Mahan, Alfred T. (1840-1914; naval officer and historian; prompted a worldwide buildup of naval strength prior to World War I), 176

Mail order houses (mass retailing - through the U.S. Postal Service), 152

Maize (yellow corn), 39

Malcolm X (1925-1965; Black Muslim minister, civil rights activist, assassinated by rival group after converting to orthodox Islam), 287

Manager of economic prosperity (unofficial role of the president taking actions which keep the economy on an even keel), 82

Manchuria (Northeast China; site of Japanese aggression in 1930s), 236

Mandela, Nelson (1918 - ; President of South Africa, 1994-1999; leader of African National Congress; imprisoned for 28 years in South Africa), 319

Manhattan Project (1942-1945; developed atomic bomb), 245

Manifest Destiny (emotional drive for territorial expansion), 104, 177

Mann, Horace (1796-1859; reforms influenced public education), 103

Mao Zedong (communist Chinese revolutionary leader), 259-260, 296

Mapp v. Ohio (1961; Supreme Court ruled illegal search and seizure evidence inadmissible in state court), 291, Appendix 2

Marbury v. Madison (1803 decision established Supreme Court's power of judicial review), 85, 96, Appendix 2

Margin (buying stocks on some sort of credit arrangement; difference between the cost and the selling price of securities or commodities), 207, 214

Market economy (functional arrangement for exchange of goods and services following decisions made through the interaction of buyers and sellers), 131, 202, 213

Marshall Plan (1948 - 1952; 16 participating countries received $13.15 billion in U.S. aid; post WW II economic recovery), 256, 258

Marshall, George C. (1880-1959; WW II military chief; Sec'y. of State and Defense under Truman), 243, 256

Marshall, John (Chief Justice, U.S. Supreme Court, 1801-1835), 76, 85, 96, 102

Massachusetts Bay Colony (the Puritan-dominated Massachusetts Bay Company unified several earlier commercial settlements at Plymouth, Gloucester, and Salem and governed by charter from 1629 – 1684),44, 46

Massive retaliation (Dulles' diplomatic tool to deter aggression by major military buildup in 1950s), 278

Maximillian Affair (failed French attempt take over Mexico, setting up an Austrian Archduke as emperor in 1860s), 181

Maya (Mesoamerican Indian people inhabiting southeast Mexico, Guatemala, and Belize, whose civilization reached its height between A.D. 300-900), 39

Mayflower Compact (Plymouth settlers agreed to establish and to be bound by a "Civil Body Politic"– a temporary government modeled after a Separatist church covenant), 48

McCarthy, Joseph R. (1908-1957; U.S. Senator, WI, led controversial anti-communist crusade in early 1950s), 263-264

McCarthyism (Joe McCarthy's practice of publicizing accusations of political disloyalty or subversion with insufficient regard to evidence), 263-264

McCarran Internal Security Act (1950s anti-subversive legislation; communistfront and communist action organizations must register with Attorney General), 263

McCulloch v. Maryland (1819, denied state power to tax federal gov't.), 96, Appendix 2

McKay, Claude (1890-1948; poet of Harlem Renaissance), 212

McKinley, William (1843-1901; 25th President, 1897-1901), 154, 178, 179

Meade, George G. (1815-1872; Union commander at Gettysburg, 1863), 110

Meat Inspection Act (1906- first major consumer legislation), 171, 172

Medicaid (1960s Lyndon Johnson's Great Society public welfare system providing medical treatment of poor), 285

Medicare (1960s Lyndon Johnson's Great Society public welfare system providing medical treatment of elderly), 285

Mediation (settlement of disputes by neutral third party), 140

Mellon, Andrew (1855-1937; Secretary of the Treasury, 1921-1932), 207

Melting Pot (a theory of immigrant assimilation), 143

Melville, Herman (1819-1891; writer of allegorical masterpiece *Moby Dick,* 1851), 103

Mercantilism (also mercantile system; closed trading system involving immense profit for mother country, while using colonies as market for goods), 45, 49, 53

Meredith, James (civil rights advocate, 1st African American to enter U. of Mississippi), 283

Mergers (strongest firm(s) absorb competitors to form a monopoly), 133

Meridian (imaginary great circle on Earth's surface passing through the North and South geographic poles), 29

Mesabi (MN iron ore deposit), 29, 129

Mexican Cession (1848; large land area [AZ, CA, CO, NM, NV, UT] ceded to U.S. by the treaty ending Mexican War), 104, 105

Mexican War (1846-1848 conflict fomented by U.S. annexation of Texas), 105

Midway (Pacific battle- WW II turning point), 244

Middle-class (usually the average level of economic or social status), 142, 206, 208

Middle Passage (trip from Africa in slave ships), 51

Military Reconstruction Plan (1867; Radical Republican Congress set up post-war reconstruction), 123

Minutemen (men ready to fight on a minute's notice just before & during the Revolutionary War), 58

Miranda v. Arizona (1966; Supreme Court clarified rights of criminally accused persons), 279, 291, Appendix 2

Mississippi River (chief river of the U.S., rising in the lake region of northern Minnesota and flowing about 3,781 km (2,350 mi) generally southward to enter the Gulf of Mexico through a huge delta in southeast Louisiana), 28, 29, 31, 32, 43, 61, 99, 110

Missouri Compromise (1820; an attempt to solve the sectional disputes between free and slave states), 105

Mixed economy (functional arrangement for exchange of goods and services combining market and command structures)

Model T (mass production; popular middle class Ford auto), 135, 206

Mohawk (Native American people formerly inhabiting northeast NY along the Mohawk and upper Hudson valleys north to the St. Lawrence River, with present-day populations chiefly in southern Ontario and extreme northern NY), 39

Mondale, Walter (1928- ; Vice President, 1977-1981; U.S. senator, MN, 1964-1977; unsuccessful Democratic presidential candidate, 1984), 308

Monopoly (company or group having exclusive control over a commercial activity), 133, 136, 137, 171, 173

Monroe Doctrine, The (1823; declared U.S. opposition to European interference in the Americas), 100, 181-182, 233

Monroe, James (1758-1831; 5th President, 1817-1825;acquisition of Florida, 1819; Missouri Compromise, 1820; Monroe Doctrine, 1823), 100, 181

Montesquieu, Baron de la Brede et de (1689-1755; philosopher and jurist of the early French Enlightenment; wrote *The Spirit of the Laws*, 1748), 73

Montevideo Conference, (1933; pledged to end intervention in Latin America), 234

Montgomery, Bernard L. (1891-1976; British WW II supreme commander), 243

Montgomery Movement (1955-1956; city bus desegregation led by Dr. King), 280, 287

Montgomery Ward (early mail-order business, 19th C.), 133, 152

Morgan, J.P. (John Pierpont Morgan, 1837-1913; Wall St. financier - philanthropist noted for his reorganization and control of major railroads, consolidation of the U.S. Steel Corporation in 190), 135, 171

Mormonism (a way of life practiced by members of the Church of Jesus Christ of Latter-day Saints founded by Joseph Smith in 1830), 103

Morrill Land Grant Act (1862; agricultural colleges created), 151

Mott, Lucretia (1793-1880; social reformer active in the antislavery movement), 168

Mountain (natural elevation of the Earth's surface having considerable mass, generally steep sides, and a height greater than that of a hill), 29

Muckrakers (journalists who expose corruption and scandal), 154, 167, 168

Muir, John (1838-1914; naturalist who promoted the creation of national parks and reservations), 172

Muller v. Oregon (1908, limits on women's working hours upheld), 170, Appendix 2

Multinational corporations (owning enterprises in more than one country), 275

Munich Conference (1938 - Hitler appeased; Britain and France gave in to Hitler's demand for occupation of Sudetenland in western Czechoslovakia), 237-238

Munn v. Illinois (1877; states could regulate railroads), 137, 153

Mussolini, Benito (1883-1945; fascist dictator of Italy), 233

NAACP (see National Association for the Advancement of Colored People)

Nader, Ralph (1934 - ; late 20th early 21st cent. consumer rights spokesman; pres. candidate in 2000), 294

NAFTA (see North American Free Trade Agreement)

Nagasaki (city of western Kyushu, Japan; nuclear bombing by U.S., 1945), 245

Napoleon (1769-1821; Emperor of the French (1804-1814), 99-100

Napoleonic Wars (1803-1815 wars with France; U.S. tried to remain neutral), 98

Nast, Thomas (1840-1902; political cartoonist; anti-corruption crusader), 125

National Association for the Advancement of Colored People (NAACP; major civil rights group; c. 1909, Niagara Falls, NY), 127, 286

National nominating convention (formal meeting of members, representatives, or delegates of a political party as method of selecting presidential candidates; began c. 1830), 102

National debt (cumulative money owed by a government to investors [individuals, businesses, nonprofit organizations, and other governments] incurred to finance annual budget deficits whenever government spending exceeds tax revenues, fees, and other income)

National Industrial Recovery Administration (1933, NIRA - New Deal regulation/stimulation of industry; permitted businesses to draft "codes of fair competition," subject to presidential approval, that regulated prices, wages, working conditions, plant construction, and credit terms), 218

National Labor Relations Act (1935 - Wagner Act: assured right of organization and collective bargaining for unions), 219

National Recovery Administration (NRA; see *National Industrial Recovery Act*)

National Road (see Cumberland Road)

National Origins Act (1924-1965; immigration system based on preference quotas for certain groups), 146, 209

National Security Act (1947; reorganized military after WWII), 252

National Urban League (civil rights group founded in 1910; sought industrial jobs for African Americans; aided southern migrants moving to northern cities), 287

Native Americans (member of any of the aboriginal peoples of the Western Hemisphere), 38-45, 71, 149-150, 291-292, 294-295

Nativist (organized opposition to immigrants), 145

NATO (see North Atlantic Treaty Organization)

Navigation Acts (17th C. series of statutes by the English Parliament, formed the basis of the mercantilist trading system in the early British Empire), 49, 54

Neutrality Acts of 1935, '36, '37 (pre-WW II isolationist sentiment; see chart for differences), 235, 236, 237,239

New Deal (FDR's reform programs to help in Great Depression), 216-223

New England Town Meeting (assembly of the qualified voters of a community for the purpose of attending to public business; originated with the first settlers of Massachusetts Bay; church membership was the major qualification), 48

New Freedom (Wilson's domestic Progressive reform program), 173

New Federalism (Reagan's shift of more welfare responsibilities to local gov't.), 308

New Frontier (JFK's legislative program), 282-283

New Immigrants Pattern (Southern and Eastern European groups coming in large numbers after 1890), 144, 281, 312

New Jersey v. TLO (1985; school search & seizure powers), 310, Appendix 2

New Nationalism (T. Roosevelt's general legislative program; also Square Deal), 173

New South (industrial development after the Civil War), 130-131

New York Times v. United States (1971; freedom of the press in the *Pentagon Papers* dispute), Appendix 2

Newlands Act (1902 - national parks), 172

Ngo Dinh Diem (1901-1963; South Vietnamese leader 1954-63, assassinated), 278

Niagara Movement (founding of NAACP), 127

Nicaragua (anticommunism activities of the Reagan administration), 312-313

Nimitz, Admiral Chester (1885-1966; WW II Pacific naval commander), 244

Nineteenth Amendment (1920; provides men and women with equal voting rights), 168, 174, 209, Appendix 1

Nisei (person born in America of parents who emigrated from Japan), 249

Nixon Doctrine (curtailing American use of power against communist insurgency after the Vietnam withdrawal), 296

Nixon, Richard M. (1913-1994; U.S. rep. & senator [CA]; vice president, 1953-61; 37th President, 1969-74; Watergate scandal; resignation, pardon), 263, 294-297

Non-violent, direct action (protest tactics of the civil rights movement), 280, 287

Noriega, Manuel (1934- ; Panamanian dictator, 1983-89; indicted and imprisoned by U.S. for drug trafficking, 1992), 318

Normalcy (normality – state or fact of being typical; Warren Harding's 1920 campaign misnomer for wanting the country to return to normal, pre-Progressive and pre-war conditions), 204

Norris, Frank (muckraking writer; works include: *The Octopus, The Pit*), 167

Norse (also Viking; relating to medieval Scandinavia or its peoples), 40

North American Free Trade Agreement (1994 NAFTA – U.S., Can., Mex. phased out trade barriers over 15 yr. period), 319

North Atlantic Treaty Organization (1949; NATO - multi-nation defense alliance; first permanent peacetime military alliance for the U.S), 258

North Korea (Soviet ally attacked S. Korea, 1950 to begin the Korean War), 260, 261

Northern Securities Co. v. U.S. (1904, first Federal prosecution and breakup of a monopoly), 171, Appendix 2

Northwest Ordinance (1787; procedures for admission of states), 72, 149

Nuclear power, 274, 298

Nuclear Test-Ban Treaty (1963, U.S.-U.S.S.R., plus 100 other nations pledged no more atmospheric testing), 284

Nullification (individual states deciding that a federal law is invalid and refusing to enforce it), 101

Nuremberg Trials (Allied trials of Axis war criminals, 1945-1946), 250

Nye Committee (1935 report led to new neutrality laws), 233

Oakies (Great Plains farmers displaced by 1930s Dust Bowl disaster; focus of Steinbeck's *Grapes of Wrath*), 222

Ocean (any principal division of the body of salt water that covers 70% of the earth, including the Atlantic, Pacific, and Indian Oceans), 29

O'Connor, Sandra Day (1930 – 1st woman associate justice of Supreme Court), 310

Office of Economic Opportunity (OEO - major Great Society job retraining and anti-discrimination agency)

Office of Price Administration (administered WW II rationing), 247

Oglethorpe, James (1696-1785; English soldier, philanthropist; secured a charter for the colony of Georgia in 1732), 47

Oil Crisis (1973, 1979, Arab and OPEC nations used economic embargo and supply manipulations against Western nations, 1973), 297

Okinawa (4-6/1945; WW II Pacific battle, 650 mi. S.E. of Japan), 244

Old Folks' Crusade (New Deal Era campaign by Dr. Francis Townsend), 223

Old Immigrants Pattern (predominance of WASP-related groups before 1890), 144

Olney, Richard (Sec'y of State and Attorney Gen. for Cleveland), 181

Olympics (U.S. boycott of the1980 Summer Games in Moscow), 300

O'Neill, Eugene (1888-1953; 20th C. plays: *Mourning Becomes Electra*), 212

OPA (see Office of Price Administration)

OPEC (see Organization of Petroleum Exporting Countries)

Open Door Policy (1900; U.S. advocated equal trading rights in China should be guaranteed to all foreign nationals), 178

Operation Overlord (code name for WW II - Allied invasion of Europe, 1944), 243

Oppenheimer, J. Robert (1902-1967; physicist directed development of the first atomic bomb, 1942-1945), 245, 264

Organization of Petroleum Exporting Countries; OPEC cartel created by 5 oil producing countries in 1960 to counter oil price cuts of American and European oil companies; oil boycotts of the mid-1970s; now 12 members), 277, 297

Orlando, Vittorio (Italian Premier at Versailles, 1918-19), 187

Oswald, Lee Harvey (1963 JFK assassin), 284

Owen, Robert (British manufacturer and social reformer who attempted to establish a cooperative community at New Harmony in Indiana, 1825-1828), 103

PAC (see Political action committee)

Paine, Thomas (1737-1809; Anglo-American writer and revolutionary; wrote the pamphlets *Common Sense* and *The Crisis* in 1776; published *The Rights of Man* in 1792 defending the French Revolution), 58

Palestine Liberation Organization (PLO; umbrella organization founded in 1964 for several groups of Palestinians engaged in a struggle to liberate their homeland; recognized in 1974 by U.N. as sole legitimate representative of Palestinian people), 313

Palmer, A. Mitchell (1872-1936; U.S. attorney general,1919-21; initiated the 1919-20 Palmer Raids against alleged radicals and subversives during the Red Scare period following WW I), 188, 204

Palmer Raids (see Palmer)

Pan-American Union (early 20th C. inter-American peace organization, predecessor of Organization of American States), 234, 239

Panama Canal Zone (1903-1999; 648 sq.mi. U.S. corridor that ran through the middle of the Republic of Panama from the Atlantic to the Pacific Ocean), 183, 318

Panama Invasion (December 1989, U.S. armed forces remove dictator Manuel Noriega and restore elected government), 318

Parallel (imaginary lines representing degrees of latitude that encircle the earth parallel to the plane of the equator), 29

Parish (administrative unit in southern states that corresponds to a county), 48

Parks, Rosa (triggered Montgomery Movement, 1955-56), 280

Partnership (limited business contract arrangement entered into by two or more persons in which each agrees to furnish a part of the capital and labor, and by which each shares a fixed proportion of profits and losses), 132

Party caucuses (small leadership group picks candidates), 102

Patriot Act (2001, reauthorized in 2006- ; Passed after September 11, 2001 attacks; expanded law enforcement authority to fight domestic and foreign terrorism; eased restrictions on foreign intelligence gathering inside the U.S.), 320

Patroon (landholder in New Netherland who, under Dutch colonial rule, was granted proprietary and manorial rights to a large tract of land), 42

Patton, Gen. George S. (1885-1945; U.S. WW II 3rd Army cdr. in Europe), 243

Paul, Alice (1885-1977; founded separatist National Woman's Party in 1916; wrote first equal rights amendment to be considered by Congress, 1923), 168

Peace Corps (JFK international program of volunteers to personally aid people in underdeveloped nations), 284

Pearl Harbor (1941 Japanese attack on U.S naval base in Hawaii drew U.S. into WW II), 240, 241

Pelosi, Nancy P. (1940- ; U.S. Representative, D-CA, 1987 - ; 1st woman selected as Speaker of the U.S. House Representatives, 2007), 320

Pendleton Act (civil service examination system initiated, 1883), 165

Peninsula (piece of land that projects into a body of water and is connected with the mainland by an isthmus), 29

Penn, William (1644-1718; English Quaker colonizer in America; received proprietary rights to the colony of Pennsylvania in 1681), 46

Pentagon Papers, The (secret study by Dept. of Defense stated gov't. falsified Vietnam War reports to public; intensified anti-Vietnam War demonstrations), 295

Peoples' Republic of China (name adopted by Mao's communists after defeating the Nationalist forces in 1949), 260

Perestroika (Gorbachev's internal political & economic reforms in U.S.S.R.), 314

Perry, Matthew C. (1794-1858; naval cdr. opened trade with Japan 1854), 177

Pershing, John (1860-1948; U.S. general; WW I commander), 184, 186

Persian Gulf Conflict (U.S. involvement in protecting oil shipping), 317-318

Pétain, Field Marshal Henri (surrendered France to Nazis, 1940), 238

Phillips, Wendell (1811-1884; leading abolitionist spokesman), 106

Philanthropy (effort to increase the well-being of humankind, as by charitable aid or donations), 134, 136

Philippines (U.S. colony 1898-1946), 179, 180, 241, 244

Picketing (group of persons stationed outside a place of employment, usually during a strike, to express grievance or protest and discourage entry by non-striking employees or customers), 140

Pilgrims (English Separatists from the Anglican Church who founded the colony of Plymouth in 1620), 46, 48

Pinchot, Gifford (1865-1946; conservationist and politician; served as chief of the U.S. Forest Service, 1898-1910), 171

Pinckney's Treaty (1795- Spain gave right of deposit in New Orleans for western farmers), 98

Pit, The (1903- muckraking novel by Norris), 167

Plain (extensive, level, usually treeless area of land), 29, 149

Planned Parenthood v. Casey (1992 decision upheld *Roe*), 316, Appendix 2

Plateau (elevated, comparatively level expanse of land; a tableland), 29

Platt Amendment (1901 - U.S. grants Cuban independence), 180

Plessy v. Ferguson (1896 - allowed de jure segregation, sets "separate but equal" rule), 126, 279, 280, Appendix 2

PLO (see Palestine Liberation Organization)

Pluralistic society (see cultural pluralism)

Poe, Edgar Allan (1809-1849; writer known for macabre poems and short stories), 103

Point Four Program (1949 technical-assistance program designed to improve living standards by helping people in underdeveloped countries; containment policy to strengthen LDCs against communist insurgency), 258-259

Poland (borders and freedom in question in WWII summit meetings), 248, 250, 255

Political Action Committees (PACs; organizations established by private, special interest groups to support candidates for public office – labor unions, corporations, trade associations; e.g., 4500 PACs distributed $201.4 million to congressional candidates in the 1995-96 election), 316

Political boss (professional politician who controls a party or a political machine), 170

Political parties (organizations of common political interest), 102

Polk, James Knox (1795-1849; 11th President, 1845-1849; established the 49ºN parallel as the U.S. northern border, Mexican War), 105

Poll taxes (fees charged in order to vote, see *24th Amendment*), 124, 285, 288

Pools (combination of firms for monopolistic ends), 132

Popular Sovereignty (territorial slavery decided by each state), 106, 107

Populism (see Populist Party)

Populist (People's) Party (1892 - western reform group primarily agrarian), 153-154

Potsdam (1945, WW II summit; Stalin-Truman-Churchill/Attlee), 248, 255

Powderly, Terence V. (1849-1924; reform leader of Knights of Labor), 138

Powhatan (Native American union of E. Virginia in the 16th and 17th C.), 39

Prairie (extensive area of flat or rolling, predominantly treeless grassland, especially the large tract or plain of central North America), 29

Prayer, school (see *Engel v. Vitale*), 279, 310

Preamble (preface to the *U.S. Constitution*), 75, Appendix 1

Radical Republicans (extreme wing of Republican Party bent on punishment of the South; led Reconstruction Era), 122-126

Randolph, A. Philip (1889-1979; labor and civil rights leader, 1920s-1960s; organized FDR's Fair Employment Practices Committee), 221

Rankin, Jeannette (1880-1973; leader in the women's suffrage movement; first woman U.S. representative, 1917-1919 and 1941-1943; pacifist), 168, 187

Ratification (1787-88 battle to accept the U.S. Constitution), 75-77

Rationing program (WW II government controlled consumer supplies of critical goods), 247

Reagan, Ronald (1911- 2004; 40th President, 1981-1989; brought about end of Cold War and improved relations with the Soviet Union), 308-310, 312-313

Real wages (actual purchasing power of dollars earned), 130

Recall (a public election to remove an official from office; reform sought by Populists & Progressives), 169

Recession (economic slowdown characterized by ꞈeclining production and rising unemployment for more than 9 straight months of falling GDP), 213, 315

Reciprocate (make a return for something given or done; other countries retaliate against high tariffs with increased tariffs of their own), 101, 207, 208, 234

Reciprocity Act (1934, New Deal action to reduce international trade barriers), 234

Reconstruction (1865-1877; programs for reform of South after Civil War), 120-126

Reconstruction Finance Corporation (RFC - Hoover's attempt to stimulate economy in Great Depression through business loans), 215

Recovery (period of economic improvement and growth after a contraction; short-term government actions to stimulate slow economic activity), 213, 217

Red Scare (1918-1919; paranoiac response to fear of socialist and anarchist activities after WW I; see Palmer), 188, 204, 263

Redeemer governments (Southern white-supremacists regain control after Reconstruction), 126

Redemptioners (colonial emigrant from Europe who paid for the voyage by serving for a specified period as a bondservant; cf., indentured servant), 144

Referendum (to decide a public issue in a general election; democratic reform sought by Populists and Progressives), 169

Reform (actions to abolish abuse or malpractice; improve by alteration, correction of error, or removal of defects; put into a better condition), 164-175, 216-223

Reform in America (survey of major movements), 164, 165

Region (large, indefinite portion of the Earth's surface), 29

Rehabilitation Act (1973; federal law providing improved public access and facilities for the handicapped and forbidding discrimination against them), 298

Rehnquist, William H. (1924- ; associate justice of the U.S. Supreme Court 1972-1986; chief justice, 1986 -), 310, 317

Relief (government actions to relieve economic misfortune), 217

Renaissance (humanistic revival of classical art, architecture, literature, and learning that originated in Italy in the 14th C. and later spread throughout Europe), 40

Reparations (compensation or remuneration required from a defeated nation as indemnity for damage or injury during a war; especially as a cause of economic difficulties in Europe after WW I), 187, 232

Representative government (see republic; republican forms), 75

Representatives, House of, (lower chamber of U.S. national legislature), 74, 79, 83

Republic (political order in which the supreme power lies in a body of citizens who are entitled to vote for officers and representatives responsible to them), 75, 78

Republic of Korea (democratic southern half of Korea, created in 1948; attacked by North Korea in 1950), 260-261

Reserved powers (by virtue of the 10th Amendment powers not specifically assigned or delegated to the national government are left to the states), 80, 81

Resource Recovery Act (1971; environmental action under Nixon), 294

Revenue (income of a government from all sources appropriated for the payment of the public expenses; e.g., taxes, tariffs), 97, 125, 309

Right of deposit (privilege granted by Pinckney's Treaty with Spain allowing U.S. farmers to transfer goods shipped down the Mississippi through Spanish New Orleans to export ships), 98, 99

Right to Life and "freedom of choice" (opposing sides in abortion question), 289

Right to petition (privilege of citizens to formally request government action, see 1st Amendment), 77, 97

Riis, Jacob (investigative journalist of the industrial-Progressive Era), 167, 168

River (large natural stream of water emptying into an ocean, a lake, or another body of water and usually fed along its course by converging tributaries), 29

Robber barons (derogatory name for ruthless industrialists), 136

Roberts, John G. (1955- ; became 17th Chief Justice of U.S. Supreme Court, 2005), 320

Robinson, Jackie (1947; first African American player in Major League Baseball), 280

Rockefeller, John Davison (1839-1937; oil industry monopolist), 134, 171

Roe v. Wade (1973 - controversial abortion decision), 289, Appendix 2

Rogers, Ginger (1930s-'40s Hollywood actress-dancer), 222

Romans (classical influences on American government), 73

Rommel, Gen. Erwin (1891-1944; WW II German tank commander, "Desert Fox"), 243

Roosevelt Corollary to the Monroe Doctrine (1903; U.S. to act as protector of the Western Hemisphere, adopts interventionist approach), 182

Roosevelt, Eleanor (1884-1962; diplomat, writer, and 1st Lady of the U.S., 1933-1945; delegate to the U.N., 1945-1952 / 1961-1962), 221

Roosevelt, Franklin D. (1882-1945; 32nd President, 1933-1945; Governor of NY, 1929-1932), 216-221, 233-239, 241, 242-247, 251

Roosevelt, Theodore (1858-1919; 26th President, 1901-1909; Spanish-American War hero; NY Governor, 1899-1900; vice president, 1901), 167, 170-173, 179, 182, 183

Rosenberg case (atomic secrets spy case of early 1950s; the first U.S. civilians executed for espionage), 263

"Rosie the Riveter" (fictional heroine - symbolic of home front role in WW II), 246

Rousseau, Jean-Jacques (1712-1778; French philosopher / writer held humanity is essentially good but corrupted by society; work: *The Social Contract*), 47, 73

Royal colony (a large tract of land owned and operated by a sovereign, with revenues going to the monarch or national government), 44, 45, 46-47

Ruby, Jack 1963; (murdered JFK assassin Lee Harvey Oswald), 284

"Rust Belt, The" (decaying industrial centers of N.E and Mid-west, 1960s-80s), 282

Sacajawea (1787-1812; Native American guide and interpreter on Lewis and Clark Expedition, 1805-1806), 99

Sacco-Vanzetti trial (1920s; due process questions in case of 2 anarchists' accused of murder), 209, 263

Sadat, Anwar (1918-1981; President of Egypt, 1970-1981; shared the 1978 Nobel Peace Prize with Israeli Prime Minister Menachem Begin; assassinated by Islamic fundamentalists), 299

Saddam Hussein (Iraqi dictator, 1980- ; defeated in Persian Gulf Conflict), 317-318

St. Lawrence River (major river of southeastern Canada/ northeastern U.S., flowing northeast from Lake Ontario to the Atlantic Ocean), 31

Salary Grab (1873 - Grant Era scandal), 125

SALT Treaty (see *Strategic Arms Limitation Treaty*)

Salutary neglect (general ignoring of mercantilist regulations during the colonial period by British officials until after the French and Indian War), 53

Sanger, Margaret (1883-1966; nurse campaigned widely for birth control; founded organization that became the Planned Parenthood Federation in 1942), 168

S & L Crisis (see Savings & Loan failure)

Savings & Loan Failures (bank deregulation crisis - 1985-1995), 315

Sault Sainte Marie Canals (canals of upper MI opened Great Lakes raw materials for industrial trade), 129

Scabs (worker who refuses membership in a labor union; employee who works while others are on strike; a strikebreaker), 140

Scalia, Antonin (1936- ; appointed an associate justice of the U.S. Supreme Court in 1986), 310

Schechter Poultry Corp. v. United States (1935 - Court struck down New Deal's NIRA), 220, Appendix 2

Schenck v. United States (1919- civil rights in wartime; see clear and present danger rule), 187, 249, Appendix 2

Scopes Monkey Trial (1925 - controversy over teaching evolution), 209

Scott, Winfield (1786-1866; military officer in War of 1812; commander in Black Hawk War, Second Seminole War, and Mexican War; Lincoln's 1st chief-of-staff in Civil War), 105

Sea (tract of water within an ocean; relatively large body of salt water completely or partially enclosed by land), 29

Sears, Roebuck & Co. (early mail-order business, 19th c.), 152

Secret ballot (reform sought by Populists & Progressives; also Australian Ballot), 169

Secretary of State (cabinet officer in charge of foreign affairs), 94, 178, 181, 278, 299

Sectionalism (loyalty to one's state or region surpassing one's nation), 100, 101

Securities and Exchange Commission (1934; SEC -protects investors against malpractice in the securities and financial markets), 218, 219

Security Council (major power arm of U.N.), 254, 261

Segregation (racial separation, either by law [de jure] or by practice [de facto]), 212, 221, 279, 280, 283, 288

Selective Service Acts (military conscription, draft laws), 186, 203

Senate (upper chamber of U.S. national legislature), 74, 79, 189, 191, 233, 263-264

Senators, direct election of U.S. (see 17th Amendment)

Seneca Falls Convention (1848, first national U.S. women's rights meeting), 165

Separation of Power (3 branches of U.S. government to avoid tyranny), 73, 75, 78, 96

Service industries (industries involved in transportation, communications, and public utilities; wholesale and retail trade, finance, insurance, real estate, and government; and professional and personal services such as health care, accounting, entertainment, education, and food services), 276

Servicemen's Readjustment Act (see *"GI Bill"*)

Settlement houses (19th and early 20th C. aid for immigrants, industrial poor), 168

Seven Years' War (18th c. Anglo-French imperial struggles world wide), 52

Seventeenth Amendment (Progressive era change to avoid entrenched power and decrease influence of special interests, allowed popular election of U.S. senators instead of state legislative selection), 175

Shakers (Quaker reform sect originating in England in 1747, practicing communal living and observing celibacy), 103

Sharecropping (payment of land rent with agricultural produce), 130

Shays, Daniel (1747-1825; insurrectionist who raided a government arsenal in Springfield, MA, to protest the state legislature's indifference to the economic plight of farmers, 1787), 71

Shays' Rebellion (see Daniel Shays)

Sherman, William T. (1820-1891; Union general; commander of all Union troops in the West, 1864; captured Atlanta in 1864 and led a destructive March to the Sea), 110

Sherman Anti-trust Act (1890; 1st gov't. attempt to regulate monopolies), 137, 174

Significance of the Frontier in American History, The (F.J. Turner's historical theory positing westward expansion as key force on American experience), 148

Sinclair, Upton (1878-1968; muckraking writer and reformer; novels include *The Jungle*, 1906), 167

Sioux (Native American peoples, also known as the Dakota, inhabiting the northern Great Plains from Minnesota to eastern Montana and from southern Saskatchewan to Nebraska), 39

Sit-ins (non-violent civil rights protest tactic), 280, 287

Sixteenth Amendment (gives Congress the power to "lay and collect taxes on incomes, from whatever source derived"), 174

Skyscrapers (tall, industrial era urban architecture), 141

Slater, Samuel (1768-1835; textile manufacturing pioneer in 1790s New England), 129

Slavery (social institution based on ownership, dominance, and exploitation of one human being by another), 38, 44, 51, 74, 105-111, 121, 122, 123, 124

Smith Act (1940 *Alien Registration Act* required registering of all aliens residing in the U.S.; made it a crime to advocate or teach the violent overthrow of the government or to belong to a group advocating or teaching it), 239, 262

Smith, Adam (see *Wealth of Nations*)

Smith, Bessie (1894-1937; leading jazz and blues singer in the 1920s), 212

Smith, Joseph (1805-1844; founder of the Mormons or Latter-day Saints), 103

SNCC (see Student Non-violent Coordinating Committee)

Social Darwinism (application of "survival of fittest" to human behavior, justification for ruthless business practices of industrial era), 142

Social Gospel movement (1870 to 1918; attempt by liberal Protestant clergy to bring the power of faith to bear on the social problems of the industrial era day; active group Christian Labor Union), 166

Social Security System (1935; government program provides economic assistance to persons faced with unemployment, disability, or agedness, financed by assessment of employers and employees), 218, 219, 253, 312

Socialist (follower of a social system in which the means of producing and distributing goods are owned collectively and political power is exercised by the whole community), 172, 186-187, 188, 223

Socialist Party (1900s coalition of worker interests weakened after WWI; regained some strength during the Depression of the 1930s; abandoned presidential campaigns after 1948; Socialist Workers Party, more militantly allied with international communism, was founded in 1937), 223

Soil Bank Plan (Eisenhower era farm conservation), 277

Solid South (primacy of Democratic Party from Civil War to late 20th C.), 128
Sons of Liberty (intercolonial organization to oppose the *Stamp Act*), 55
South Africa (problem of apartheid), 313-314
South Carolina, 47
South Carolina Exposition and Protest (Calhoun's 1830 statement on states rights protested the Tariff of Abominations), 101
Southern Christian Leadership Conference (SCLC, 1957 - Dr. King's group broadened the civil-rights effort through peaceful but potent demonstrations), 287
Sovereignty (complete independence and self-government)
Soviet Union (U.S.S.R. - Union of Soviet Socialist Republics; lands of the old Russian Empire governed by the Communist Party of the Soviet Union, 1917-1991), 234, 236, 238, 241, 243, 247, 248, 250, 254, 255-258, 260, 261, 262, 263, 264, 277, 278, 283, 284, 295, 296, 299, 300, 314, 318-319
Spanish-American War (1898; marked the emergence of the U.S. as a great power and the advent of U.S. overseas imperialism), 179, 180, 181
Speaker of the House (presiding officer of the U.S. House of Representatives), 79
Square Deal (Theodore Roosevelt's Progressive philosophy), 171
Stalemate (situation in which further action is blocked; a deadlock), 185
Stalin, Josef (1879-1953; successor of Lenin, dictator/premier of the U.S.S.R., 1926-1953), 234, 238, 241, 247-248, 255, 258
Stalingrad (1941, turning point of Nazi invasion of U.S.S.R.), 243
Stamp Act (1765-66; first direct tax imposed by Britain on its American colonies; levied on legal and commercial documents as well as printed material, such as newspapers and pamphlets; Americans opposed the tax because it violated the newly enunciated principle of "No taxation without representation"), 54
Stamp Act Congress (general intercolonial conference; met in 1765 in NYC; issued a declaration of American rights and grievances), 54
Stanton, Elizabeth Cady (1815-1902; feminist and social reformer), 165, 168
Stanton, Edwin (Secretary of War under Lincoln and Johnson), 121, 122
Star Wars (see Strategic Defense Initiative)
States' rights (opposition to power of Federal government), 106
States' Rights Party (nicknamed the Dixiecrats; 1948 Southern opposition to Truman's civil rights program), 253
Steffens, Lincoln (1866-1936; journalist. As managing editor of *McClure's Magazine*, 1902-1906), 167
Steinbeck, John (1902-1968; novelist, novel of Dust Bowl, *The Grapes of Wrath*), 222
Stephens, Uriah (early U.S. labor leader - Knights of Labor), 138
Stereotyping (form of prejudice; giving a fixed characterization to a group), 145
Stevens, Thaddeus (1792-1868 [PA]; Radical Republican congressional leader, 1859-1868; led the impeachment proceedings against President Andrew Johnson), 123
Steuben, Baron Friedrich Wilhelm von (1730-1794; Prussian-born American Revolutionary military leader troops under Washington), 59
Stone, Lucy (1818-1893; social reformer; founder of the American Woman Suffrage Association, 1869), 168
Strategic Arms Limitation Treaty (SALT; 1972; US/USSR nuclear arms reduction agreement; antiballistic missile [ABM] treaty by which the two countries agreed to limit the number of ABM sites; *SALT II* attempted to extend and refine original, but failed to achieve Senate ratification 1972 *SALT*), 296
Strategic Defense Initiative (Reagan's "Star Wars;" proposed space missile defense system), 314
Streetcars (industrial era mass transit), 141

Strict constructionists (believe in precise interpretations of Constitutional), 80, 95

Strike (to cease working, in support of demands made upon an employer), 138-140

Strong, Rev. Josiah (1847-1916; social justice advocate & pro-imperialist of 1880s), 176

Student Non-violent Coordinating Committee (SNCC; founded 1960 to coordinate sit-ins and voter registration campaigns in the South; became more radical after 1966; disintegrated in 1970s), 287

Students for a Democratic Society (SDS- radical anti-Vietnam group), 293

Submarine warfare (as a cause of U.S. entry into WW I), 184, 185

Suburbia, suburbs (residential region around a major city; growth after WW II), 206, 281-282

Subway systems (industrial era urban mass transit), 141

Sudetenland (region of Czechoslovakia taken by Hitler in 1939), 237

Suffrage (the right to vote), 102, 168, 174

Suffragist (crusades for women's right to vote; note: the term "suffragette" was used in Britain, not in the American movement), 168

Summit meetings (personal diplomacy among world leaders), 245-247, 255-256, 314

Sun Belt (South and West developing in the 1970s), 282

Superpower (powerful and influential nation, especially a nuclear power that dominates its allies or client states in an international power bloc), 255

Supply (Economics: amount of a commodity available for meeting a demand or for purchase at a given price), 202, 251

Supply side economics (gov't. stimulus through tax incentives to industry and richer classes; similar to "trickle down" concept), 308-309

Supreme Court (highest federal court in the U.S., consisting of nine justices and having jurisdiction over all other courts in the nation), 85, 96, 107, 109, 122, 126, 127, 134, 135, 137, 150, 153, 170, 171-172, 174, 187, 207, 220, 249, 262, 279, 286, 289, 291, 295, 296, 310, 316, 320

Sussex Pledge (1916; Germans agreed to stop sub. attacks on merchant vessels), 185

Suzuki (Japanese premier, surrendered in WW II), 245

Swan v. the Board of Education of Charlotte-Mecklenburg (1971- upheld busing as desegregation technique), 289

Sweatshops (factory with poor working conditions), 137

Taft, William Howard (1857-1930; 27th President, 1909-1913; chief justice of the U.S. Supreme Court, 1921-1930), 170, 171-172, 173, 182

Taft-Hartley Labor Management Relations Act (1947; cut power of labor unions), 252

Taliban (radical militant Islamic fundamentalist group controlled Afghanistan in the 1980's-2002 period, sheltered Al Qaeda terrorists), 320

Talkies (talking motion pictures introduced in the late 1920s), 211

Tarbell, Ida (1857-1944; muckraker: *History of the Standard Oil Co.*, 1904), 167

Tariff of Abominations (1828 - exceptionally high duties became subject of Southern protests), 101

Tariffs (duties, taxes on imports), 74, 101, 173, 176, 207

Taylor, Zachery (1784-1850; 12th President, 1849-1850; commander in Black Hawk War, Second Seminole War, and Mexican War), 105

Tax revenue (see revenue)

Tea Act (1773 - Parliament tried to force Americans to buy East India Co. tea; triggered the Boston Tea Party), 56

Teapot Dome Affair (1920s Harding era scandal), 205

Teller Resolution (1898 - promise of Cuban independence), 180

Temperance (restraint in the use of or abstinence from alcoholic liquors; see prohibition movement), 210

Tenement (rundown, low-rental apartment building whose facilities and maintenance barely meet minimum standards), 141

Tenure of Office Act (Radical Republican law used as ploy to impeach Andrew Johnson), 122

Terrorism (use of acts of violence for political purposes), 313

Tet Offensive (massive Viet Cong attack 1968 leads to questions about U.S. role), 293

Textiles (first major U.S. industry), 129

Thesis ([hypothesis is a more precise term, but thesis is more commonly used]; a theory to be proven; proposition that is maintained by argument), 15, 17, 18, 23, 24, 148

Third World Countries (underdeveloped nations of Asia & Africa; see LDCs), 258

Thirteenth Amendment (1865 addition to the Constitution abolished slavery), 122, 124, Appendix 1

Thomas, Norman (1884-1968; 1920s-1940s socialist leader and founder of the American Civil Liberties Union), 223

Thoreau, Henry David (1817-1862; writer; *Walden, On Civil Disobedience*), 103

Three-Fifths Compromise (slavery question in Constitutional Convention), 74

Three R's (Relief, Recovery, Reform [in New Deal]), 217

Three Mile Island (PA nuclear plant accident, 1979), 274, 298

Thurmond, Strom (1902 – ; SC Governor, oldest U.S. Senator; led opposition wing of Democrats - Dixiecrats - against Truman in 1948), 253

Tilden, Samuel (Gov. of NY, Democratic Presidential candidate, 1876), 126

Tinker v. DesMoines (1969 - symbolic speech protected by First Amendment), 310, Appendix 2

Tojo, General (Japanese WW II commander), 248

Toomer, Jean (Jean Toomer, 1894-1967; writer best known for experimental novel, *Cane*, 1923, on lives of Southern rural blacks and their Northern urban movement; Harlem Renaissance), 212

Tonkin Gulf Resolution (Congressional permission for Johnson to escalate troops in Vietnam), 292, 293

Tory (American who favored the British side during the period of the American Revolution; see Loyalist), 60

Townsend, Francis (1867-1960; physician and social reformer; plan for government-sponsored old-age pension was a precursor of *Social Security Act* of 1935), 223

Townshend Acts (1767- Parliament levied repressive mercantile duties on many items imported to the American colonies; cause of American Revolution), 54

Trade deficit (imports exceeding exports), 313

Trail of tears (forced government relocation of Native Americans under President Jackson), 150

Transcendentalism (mid-19th C. literary and philosophical movement; asserts the existence of an ideal spiritual reality that transcends observed scientific knowledge); 103

Transportation, Dept. of, (DOT; 1966; responsible for policies aimed at environmental safety and an efficient national transportation system that can also facilitate national defense), 285

Treaty of Alliance (1778 - France recognized the government of the U.S. during the Revolution and committed financial and military aid), 60

Treaty of Ghent (1814; settled War of 1812), 99

Treaty of Guadelupe-Hidalgo (1848: ended U.S.-Mexican War and provided considerable western territory), 105

Treaty of Paris, 1783 (ended American Revolution), 61

Treaty of Paris, 1898 (ended Spanish American War), 179

Treaty of Tordesillas (1494 - Spain & Portugal divided Western Hemisphere colonial rights), 41

Treaty of Versailles (or *Pact of Paris, 1919*; ended WW I, punished Germany with financial reparations and created League of Nations; rejected by U.S. Senate), 187, 188, 191, 232

Triangle Shirtwaist Co. fire (1911 NYC disaster spurred factory safety reforms), 138

Trickle-down theory (government stimulation of economy through business assistance and tax cuts for the rich to spur investment; also supply-side economics), 217, 308

Triple Alliance (pre-WW I alliance of the Central Powers: Germany, Austria-Hungary, and Italy), 184

Triple Entente (pre-WW I alliance: France, Great Britain, Russia), 184

Truman Doctrine (aid for containment of communist expansion in Europe), 256, 257

Truman, Harry S (1884-1972; 33rd President, 1945-1953; authorized the use of the atomic bomb against Japan; implemented the Marshall Plan, NATO; U.S. involvement in Korean War, 1950-1953), 245, 248, 251, 252-256, 258, 260, 261, 262, 263

Trust (combination of firms or corporations for the purpose of reducing competition and controlling prices throughout a business or an industry), 133, 134, 135, 137, 171, 172, 173

Truth, Sojourner (1797?-1883; abolitionist and feminist; became a leading preacher against slavery and for the rights of women), 106

Truth-in-Lending Act (1969 - consumer protection: banking, installment buying), 294

Tubman, Harriet (1820?-1913; abolitionist. escaped MD slave who became the most renowned conductor on the Underground Railroad), 106

Turner, Frederick Jackson (1861-1932; historian; emphasized the importance of the frontier in American history), 148

Tuskegee Institute (Booker T. Washington's technical training school for blacks), 127

Twain, Mark (1835-1910; pen name of industrial era author, humorist Samuel L. Clemens; works: *Tom Sawyer, Huckleberry Finn, Gilded Age*), 142, 143, 180

Tweed Ring (NYC political corruption in Grant Era), 125

Tweed, William Marcy (1823-1878; Democratic boss of NYC in the 1860s; defrauded the city of millions of dollars before being exposed and convicted in 1873), 125

Twenty-fourth Amendment (outlawed poll taxes in federal elections, 1964), 285, 288

Two Treatises on Government (1662; 17th c. British enlightenment philosopher John Locke's work - influenced framers of the Constitution), 73

Tydings-McDuffie Act (1946; U.S. granted Philippines independence), 180

U-2 incident (1960; U.S. spy plane shot down in U.S.S.R., pilot Francis Gary Powers captured and found guilty of espionage; released in 1962), 278

Uncle Remus' Stories (post Civil War Southern literature - Joel Chandler Harris), 143

Uncle Tom's Cabin (Harriet Beecher Stowe's abolitionist novel, 1852), 106

Underground Railroad (secret, organized efforts by northerners to help escaped slaves find safe shelter in the free states or Canada), 106

Underwood Tariff (1913; Progressive Era attempt to lower tariffs), 173

Unicameral legislature (having only one House in government), 72, 74

United Nations (post-WW II international peace organization), 241, 254, 261, 318

United States Constitution (1789- present; system of fundamental laws and principles that outlines the functions and limits of the U.S. government), 73-86, 94, 95, 96, 100, 101, 102, 107, Appendix 1

United States v. Butler (1935; Supreme Court struck down New Deal's agricultural program), 220

United States v. E.C. Knight (1895; Court narrowed its interpretation of the Constitution's commerce clause in interpreting the *Sherman Antitrust Act*), Appendix 2

United States v. Nixon (1974; Supreme Court ruled against "executive privilege"), 296, Appendix 2

Universal Declaration of Human Rights (1947; backing for basic rights; see Eleanor Roosevelt), 254

Universal Negro Improvement Association (Marcus Garvey's separatist back-to-Africa movement in 1920s), 169

U.S.S.R. (see Soviet Union)

Unrestricted submarine warfare (as a cause of U.S. entry into WW I), 184, 185

Unsafe at Any Speed (1965; Ralph Nader book on U.S. auto industry), 294

Unwritten constitution (executive precedents, judicial decisions, expansions of legal power and procedure not officially in the Constitution), 94-97

Urban League (see National Urban League)

Urbanization (process of the society's central activities taking place in cities), 141

V-2 rockets (Germany's Vengeance Weapon 2; liquid-propellant rocket; more than 4,300 were launched against England and Holland, 1944-1945), 243

Van Buren, Martin (1782-1862; eighth President, 1837-1841; U.S. Senator, NY, 1821-1828; Secretary of State, 1829-1831; Vice President, 1833-1837), 315

Veronia School District v. Acton (1995; upheld school authorities power to require drug testing of athletes), Appendix 2

Vertical integration (near monopolistic control over all the basic aspects of an industry; cf horizontal integration), 134

Veto power (executive power to nullify legislation), 81, 104, 120, 121, 122, 254, 252, 254, 261

Victorian ideal (idealized vision of women as delicate, weaker members of the society c. 1890s), 143, 211

Viet Cong (communist insurgent forces in Vietnam War), 292-293

Vietnam War (1954-1973 conflict in Southeast Asia involving the U.S. in resisting communist insurgency), 292-293

Vietnamization (Nixon's idea of putting more and more responsibility on the South Vietnamese themselves to win the war), 295

Vigilante groups (sought unofficial law and order in old west), 151

Viking (see Norse)

Villa, Pancho (Mexican revolutionary leader c. 1913), 184

VISTA (see Volunteers in Service to America)

Voice of the People (presidential role as spokesperson on national concerns), 82
Voltaire (pen name of François Marie Arouet; 1694-1778; Enlightenment French
  philosopher and writer; *Candide*, 1759, *Philosophical Dictionary*, 1764), 73
Volunteers in Service to America (VISTA; 1960s program to aid underprivileged),
  285
Voting Rights Acts (1965, 1970, 1975 insured proper procedures against racial
  discrimination), 285, 288

Wabash, St. Louis, and Pacific Railway v. Illinois (1886 - states could regulate
  railroads), 137, 153, Appendix 2
Wade Davis Bill (1864 attempt of Congress to run Reconstruction), 120, 121
Wallace, George (Gov. of AL: 1963-1967, 1971-1979, and 1983-1987; ran for
  President in 1968 and 1972), 294
Wallace, Henry A. (FDR's 2nd Vice President; ran for President against Truman
  in 1948), 253
War of 1812 (fought between the U.S. and Great Britain from June 1812 to the
  spring of 1815), 98-99
War bond drives (WW II patriotic pressures to finance war effort), 245
War Hawks (land-hungry pro-war Congressmen in 1812 era), 98
War Labor Board (WW I and WW II management of labor force), 203, 246
War on Poverty (see Great Society)
War Manpower Commission (WW II management of labor), 246
War Powers Act (1973; post Vietnam Congressional move to limit Pres. power),
  295
War Production Board (WW II economic command structure for industry), 246
Warren Commission (1963-64; investigated JFK assassination), 284
Warren Court (followed a policy of judicial activism), 279
Warren, Earl (Chief Justice of the Supreme Court, 1953-1969), 279, 284
Washington Conference (1921-1922; attempt to stop post-WWI naval arms race),
  190
Washington, Booker T. (post Civil War civil rights leader), 127, 169
Washington, George (1732-1799; commander of American forces in the
  Revolutionary War, 1775-1783; presided over Constitutional Convention,
  1787; first President of the U.S., 1789-1797), 58, 59, 60, 72, 76, 77, 94, 96-98,
  233
Washington's *Farewell Address* (1796; recommended neutrality for future genera-
  tions), 98, 233
Watt, James (1938 - ; Sec'y of Interior under Reagan, 1981-83), 309
Water Pollution Control Act (1970s environmental reform under Nixon along with
  the *Water Quality Control Act*), 294
Watergate Affair (1973-1974 election scandal - Nixon resignation), 296-297
Watkins v. U.S. (1957; federal witness protection stipulations in Congressional
  hearings; further clarified right of free speech position on the *Smith Act* after
  Dennis decision), 262, Appendix 2
Wealth of Nations (1776, Scots philosopher Adam Smith's attack against mercan-
  tilism and outline of the market economic system), 136-137
Weathermen (a radical extremist offshoot of SDS in Vietnam era), 293
Weaver, Robert (1907-1997; first African American to hold a cabinet post in the
  U.S. government; service during the New Deal), 221
Webster, Daniel (1782-1852;U.S. Representative NH, 1813-1817 and MA, 1823-
  1827; U.S. Senator for MA, 1827-1841 / 1845-1850; advocated preservation of
  the Union; served twice as Secretary of State), 101

Westinghouse, George (1846-1914; engineer and manufacturer; 400 patents, including the air brake -1869), 133

Whiskey Rebellion, The (PA farmers protest Hamilton's excise tax, 1794), 96

Whiskey Ring (scandal in Grant era), 125

White House (official residence of the President since 1800; also journalistic phrase denoting executive branch of the U.S. government), 82, 215

Whitman, Walt (1819-1892; poet who used unconventional meter and rhyme), 103

Willard, Emma (1787-1870; educator who was an early proponent of higher education for women), 103

Williams, Roger (1603-1686; Puritan cleric expelled from Massachusetts; founded Providence in 1636 as a community based on religious freedom and democratic ideals; obtained a royal charter for Rhode Island in 1663), 46

Wilson, Woodrow (1856-1924; 28th President, 1913-1921; WW I; prohibition; Treaty of Versailles; established the League of Nations won 1919 Nobel Peace Prize; governor of NJ), 170, 173,-174, 184, 187-189, 202-203, 205

Wobblies (see Industrial Workers of the World)

Women's Christian Temperance Union (1876 - prohibitionists), 169, 210

Women's International League for Peace and Freedom (WW I pacifists), 187

Women's Movement (Suffrage, 1960s), 165, 168, 288-290

Woodhull, Victoria (1838-1927; WY advocate of woman suffrage; first woman to run for the U.S. presidency, 1872), 165

Worcester v. Georgia (1832 challenge by Cherokee nation for protection against land confiscation by a state), 150, Appendix 2

Works Progress Administration (WPA; 1935-1943; relief programs to preserve persons' skills and self-respect by providing useful work during a period of massive unemployment), 220, 221

World Court (1920s and 1930s; U.S. isolationists kept U.S. from joining international peace organization in 1920), 191

World Leader (unofficial presidential role of representing the most powerful nation on earth and its close allies), 82

World Trade Organization (1995; WTO; a U.N.-affiliated multilateral commission moderates trade disputes among its 116 member states), 319

World War I (1914-1918; U.S. entry in 1917), 184-191, 202-205, 208, 209, 210, 234, 238, 239, 233, 238, 239, 248

World War II (1939-1945; U.S. entry in 1941), 236, 238-252, 254, 255, 256

Wounded Knee (1973, 3 month AIM civil rights demonstrations vs. federal authorities at site of 1890s massacre in SD), 150

Writs of Assistance (blanket search warrant under which British customs agents could investigate and ransack any house in their search for smuggled goods), 54, 78

Writs of habeas corpus (constitutional protection that accused be informed of charges against them or released), 81

Xenophobia (exaggerated fear of foreigners; emotional underpinning of nativism), 145, 209

Yalta Conference (1945 WW II leaders summit), 245-248, 255

Yates v. U.S. (1957- Court modified its 1951 Dennis position on the Smith Act; ruled that teaching communism or other revolutionary theories did not in itself constitute grounds for conviction; only proof that direct action had been urged to topple the government could result in conviction), 262

Yellow-dog contract (agreement—usually signed as a condition of employment—between employees and an employer that prohibits the workers from becoming involved in union activities), 140

Yellow journalism (exploiting, distorting, or exaggerating the news to create sensations and attract readers), 143, 179

Yeltsin Boris (1931 - ; Russian reform president, 1991-2000), 318

Yeoman (farmer who cultivates his own land), 51, 72

Young, Brigham (1801-1877; Mormon religious leader after the 1844 assassination of founder Joseph Smith; established Salt Lake City as center for the church), 103

Zenger, John Peter (1697-1746; colonial printer whose acquittal [1735] of libel charges in NYC established a legal precedent for freedom of the press), 48

Zimmerman Note (Jan. 1917 proposal for a German Mexican alliance inflamed U.S. anti-German sentiment before WW I entry), 185

Part I
Answer all questions in this part.

Directions (1-50): For each statement or question, select the word or expression that, of those given, best completes the statement or answers the question.

Base your answers to questions 1 and 2 on the map below and on your knowledge of social studies.

North America, 1803

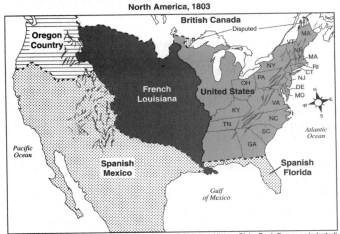

Source: *Exploring American History*, Globe Book Company (adapted)

1   Which geographic feature was the boundary line between the United States and French Louisiana in 1803?
    (1) Appalachian Mountains   (3) Mississippi River
    (2) Great Lakes   (4) Rocky Mountains

2   If the Great Plains were shown in this map, they would be located mostly in
    (1) French Louisiana   (3) the Oregon Country
    (2) Spanish Mexico   (4) the original thirteen states

3   Which document included John Locke's idea that people have the right to overthrow an oppressive government?
    (1) Mayflower Compact   (3) Declaration of Independence
    (2) Northwest Ordinance   (4) Bill of Rights

4   Many colonies objected to the Albany Plan of Union (1754) mainly because
    (1) the colonies had just been given representation in Parliament
    (2) the plan gave too much power to Native American Indians
    (3) threats to colonial safety had ended
    (4) colonial assemblies did not want to give up their individual power

5   Thomas Paine's publication Common Sense was most influential in persuading American colonists to support
(1) additional British taxes on the colonies
(2) colonial independence
(3) the Whiskey Rebellion
(4) continued ties with Great Britain

6   A major weakness of government under the Articles of Confederation was that
(1) the large states received more votes in Congress than small states did
(2) the national government could not enforce its laws
(3) too much power was given to the president
(4) state governments could not coin money

7   To address the concerns of many Antifederalists during the debate over ratification of the Constitution, the Federalists agreed that
(1) political parties would be formed
(2) states would retain control of interstate commerce
(3) slavery would be eliminated by an amendment
(4) a bill of rights would be added

8   During the Constitutional Convention of 1787, the Great Compromise resolved a conflict over
(1) presidential power   (3) representation in Congress
(2) the issue of nullification (4) taxes on imports

9   The United States Constitution requires that a national census be taken every ten years to
(1) provide the government with information about voter registration
(2) establish a standard for setting income tax rates
(3) determine the number of members each state has in the House of Representatives
(4) decide who can vote in presidential elections

10 According to the United States Constitution, the president has the power to
(1) nominate federal judges   (3) grant titles of nobility
(2) declare war   (4) reverse Supreme Court decisions

11 In the 2000 presidential election, which aspect of the electoral college system caused the most controversy?
(1) A state can divide its electoral votes among different candidates.
(2) States with few electoral votes have no influence on election outcomes.
(3) The selection of electors varies among states.
(4) The winner of the popular vote might not get the majority of the electoral vote.

12 In his Farewell Address, President George Washington advised the nation to avoid permanent alliances because he believed that the United States
(1) would risk its security by involvement in European affairs
(2) had no need for the products or markets of Europe
(3) possessed military power superior to any European nation
(4) needed to limit European immigration

13 The decision in *Marbury v. Madison* (1803) expanded the power of the Supreme Court by
   (1) restricting the use of the elastic clause
   (2) establishing the power of judicial review
   (3) upholding the constitutionality of the National Bank
   (4) interpreting the interstate commerce clause

14 Prior to 1850, what was a main reason the North developed an economy increasingly based on manufacturing while the South continued to rely on an economy based on agriculture?
   (1) Protective tariffs applied only to northern seaports.
   (2) Geographic conditions supported different types of economic activity.
   (3) Slavery in the North promoted rapid economic growth.
   (4) Manufacturers failed to make a profit in the South.

15 The *Declaration of Sentiments*, adopted during the Seneca Falls Convention in 1848, is most closely associated with the rights of
   (1) immigrants
   (2) enslaved persons
   (3) Native American Indians
   (4) women

16

I. Actions Taken by President Abraham Lincoln During the Civil War
A. Increased the size of the army without congressional authorization
B. Arrested and jailed anti-Unionists without giving a reason
C. Censored some anti-Union newspapers and had some editors and publishers arrested

Which statement is most clearly supported by these actions of President Lincoln?
   (1) Wartime emergencies led President Lincoln to expand his presidential powers.
   (2) President Lincoln was impeached for violating the Constitution.
   (3) Checks and balances effectively limited President Lincoln's actions.
   (4) President Lincoln wanted to abolish the Bill of Rights.

17 In the late 1800s, the creation of the Standard Oil Trust by John D. Rockefeller was intended to
   (1) protect small, independent oil firms
   (2) control prices and practices in the oil refining business
   (3) increase competition among oil refining companies
   (4) distribute donations to charitable causes

18 Passage of the Dawes Act of 1887 affected Native American Indians by
   (1) supporting their cultural traditions
   (2) attempting to assimilate them into mainstream American culture
   (3) forcing their removal from areas east of the Mississippi River
   (4) starting a series of Indian wars on the Great Plains

19 The changes in American agriculture during the late 1800s led farmers to
    (1) grow fewer cash crops for export
    (2) request an end to agricultural tariffs
    (3) demand a reduced role for government in agriculture
    (4) become more dependent on banks and railroads

20 The Supreme Court cases of *Wabash, St. Louis & Pacific R.R. v. Illinois*
    (1886) and *United States v. E. C. Knight Co.* (1895) were based on laws that
    were intended to
    (1) limit the power of big business
    (2) support farmers' efforts to increase the money supply
    (3) maintain a laissez-faire approach to the economy
    (4) improve working conditions for immigrants

21 The Spanish-American War (1898) marked a turning point in United States
    foreign policy because the United States
    (1) developed a plan for peaceful coexistence
    (2) emerged as a major world power
    (3) pledged neutrality in future European conflicts
    (4) refused to become a colonial power

**Base your answers to questions 22 and 23 on the cartoon below and on your
knowledge of social studies.**

Woman's Holy War
Grand Charge on the Enemy's Works

Source: Currier and Ives,
Library of Congress (adapted)

22 The "Holy War" illustrated in the cartoon was an effort to
    (1) recruit women soldiers   (3) ban the sale of alcoholic beverages
    (2) promote world peace   (4) spread Christian religious beliefs

23 Women gained a victory in the "war" shown in the cartoon through the
    (1) ratification of a constitutional amendment
    (2) legalization of birth control
    (3) expansion of missionary activities overseas
    (4) repeal of national Prohibition

24 A primary reason for the establishment of the Open Door policy (1899) was to
  (1) protect United States trade in the Far East
  (2) gain control of the Panama Canal Zone
  (3) encourage Chinese immigration to the United States
  (4) improve relations with Russia

Base your answers to questions 25 and 26 on the statements below that discuss immigration laws in the early 20th century, and on your knowledge of social studies.

Speaker A: A literacy test as a requirement for immigration to the United States is reasonable. Great numbers of uneducated workers take jobs and good wages from our workers.

Speaker B: Requiring literacy of immigrants is unfair. It will keep people out because they lacked the opportunity to gain an education.

Speaker C: A literacy test will allow more people from northern and western Europe to enter. They are similar to the majority of the United States population.

Speaker D: Literacy is not an issue. The real purpose of this law is to discriminate against immigrants from certain parts of the world.

25 Supporters of literacy tests to restrict immigration would most likely favor the views of Speakers
  (1) A and C   (3) B and D   (2) B and C   (4) A and B

26 The immigrants referred to by Speaker D were mainly from
  (1) Canada and Mexico   (3) western Europe
  (2) South America   (4) southern and eastern Europe

Base your answer to question 27 (next page) on the map below and on your knowledge of social studies.

Suffrage Legislation, 1890–1919

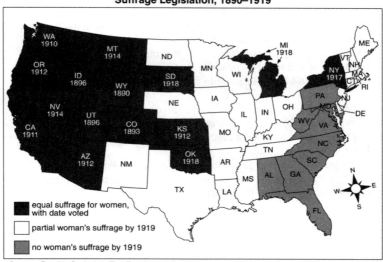

Source: Sandra Opdycke, *The Routledge Historical Atlas of Women in America*, Routledge (adapted)

27 What does the map show about woman's suffrage legislation before ratification of the federal woman's suffrage amendment in 1920?
(1) Opposition to woman's suffrage was strongest in the New England states.
(2) New York was the first state to grant women the right to vote in state elections.
(3) State legislatures never gave women the right to vote.
(4) Many western states granted women suffrage before passage of the 19th amendment.

28 During the Progressive Era, public demands for direct consumer protection resulted in passage of the
(1) Pure Food and Drug Act
(2) Fair Labor Standards Act
(3) Underwood Tariff
(4) income tax amendment

29 The Federal Reserve System helps to regulate
(1) the annual federal budget
(2) state sales tax rates
(3) Social Security payments
(4) the nation's money supply

30 Which issue was the focus of the Supreme Court decision in *Schenck v. United States* (1919)?
(1) freedom of speech for war protesters
(2) relocation of ethnic minority groups
(3) use of detention camps for enemy aliens
(4) integration of military forces

31 During the Harlem Renaissance of the 1920s, African American authors and artists used literature and art to
(1) end segregation of public facilities
(2) promote affirmative action programs
(3) celebrate the richness of their heritage
(4) urge voters to elect more African Americans to political office

32 Which economic condition was a major cause of the Great Depression?
(1) high wages of industrial workers
(2) deficit spending by the federal government
(3) inability of industry to produce enough consumer goods
(4) uneven distribution of income between the rich and the poor

33 The march of the "Bonus Army" and referring to shantytowns as "Hoovervilles" in the early 1930s illustrate
(1) growing discontent with Republican efforts to deal with the Great Depression
(2) state projects that created jobs for the unemployed
(3) federal attempts to restore confidence in the American economy
(4) the president's success in solving social problems

Base your answer to question 34 on the cartoon below and on your knowledge of social studies.

The Galloping Snail

Source: Burt Thomas, *Detroit News* (adapted)

34 The cartoonist is commenting on President Franklin D. Roosevelt's efforts to
   (1) veto several bills sent him by Congress
   (2) end New Deal programs
   (3) gain quick passage of his legislation
   (4) slow down the legislative process

35 Critics of the New Deal claimed that the Tennessee Valley Authority (TVA) and the Social Security System threatened the United States economy by
   (1) applying socialist principles   (3) decreasing government spending
   (2) imposing unfair working hours (4) eroding antitrust laws

Base your answer to question 36 on the ration card shown below and on your knowledge of social studies.

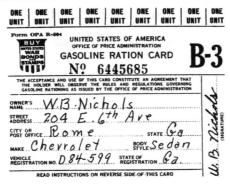

36 The use of this card, issued by the federal government, was intended to
   (1) help the automobile industry   (3) increase the use of gasoline
   (2) support the troops in wartime   (4) decrease the cost of automobiles

A goal of the Marshall Plan (1948) was to
(1) rebuild Japan after World War II
(2) provide military aid to the Warsaw Pact
(3) establish a Pan-American military alliance system
(4) provide economic aid to European nations threatened by communism

38 Which heading is most appropriate for the partial outline below?

```
I._____
   A.  The House Un-American Activities Committee
   B.  Loyalty review boards
   C.  Bomb shelters
   D.  Watkins v. United States (1957)
```

(1) Results of World War I   (3) Problems of Urbanization
(2) The Cold War at Home   (4) Reactions to Immigration

Base your answer to question 39 on the statement below and on your knowledge of social studies.

. . . Whenever normal agencies prove inadequate to the task and it becomes necessary for the Executive Branch of the Federal Government to use its powers and authority to uphold Federal Courts, the President's responsibility is inescapable.

In accordance with that responsibility, I have today issued an Executive Order directing the use of troops under Federal authority to aid in the execution of Federal law at Little Rock, Arkansas. This became necessary when my Proclamation of yesterday was not observed, and the obstruction of justice still continues. . . .
                    — President Dwight D. Eisenhower, September 24, 1957

39 The situation described in this statement grew out of efforts to
   (1) uphold the Voting Rights Act
   (2) pass a constitutional amendment ending poll taxes
   (3) enforce the decision in *Brown v. Board of Education of Topeka*
   (4) extend the Montgomery bus boycott to Little Rock

Base your answers to questions 40 and 41 on the cartoon below and on your knowledge of social studies.

Source: Herblock, *Washington Post*, 1974 (adapted)

40 The conflict that was the focus of the cartoon involved President Richard Nixon's attempt to
(1) increase the number of troops in Vietnam
(2) withhold evidence in the Watergate scandal
(3) impose mandatory wage and price controls
(4) improve relations with the People's Republic of China

41 The cartoon illustrates the constitutional principle of
(1) federalism
(3) representative government
(2) checks and balances
(4) civilian control of the military

42 Population increases that resulted from the baby boom of the 1950s and 1960s contributed to a
(1) housing surplus
(3) reduction in government services
(2) drop in immigration
(4) rise in demand for consumer goods

43 The 1961 Bay of Pigs invasion and the 1962 missile crisis are conflicts directly related to United States relations with which two nations?
(1) the Dominican Republic and Haiti
(2) Cuba and the Soviet Union
(3) China and Japan
(4) North Korea and South Korea

44 What was a central issue in the Supreme Court cases of *Gideon v. Wainwright* (1963) and *Miranda v. Arizona* (1966)?
(1) freedom of religion
(3) rights of the accused
(2) voting rights
(4) property rights

45 The economic policies of President Ronald Reagan (1981–1989) and
President George W. Bush (2001–present) are similar in that both
(1) balanced the federal budget
(2) expanded welfare programs to end poverty
(3) used tax cuts to encourage economic growth
(4) decreased military spending

46 Since the 1990s, the primary issue concerning the health care system in the
United States has been the
(1) increasing cost of medical care (3) safety of medical procedures
(2) shortage of prescription drugs (4) reorganization of hospitals

47 Books such as *Uncle Tom's Cabin, How the Other Half Lives*, and *The
Feminine Mystique* all show that literature can sometimes
(1) expose government corruption
(2) cause violent revolution
(3) begin military conflict
(4) encourage social reform

48 The Progressive movement (1900–1920) was primarily a response to
problems created by
(1) abolitionists   (3) industrialization
(2) nativists   (4) segregation

49 The term Dust Bowl is most closely associated with which historical
circumstance?
(1) a major drought that occurred during the 1930s
(2) logging practices in the Pacific Northwest in the 1950s
(3) an increase in pollution during the 1960s
(4) the migration to the Sun Belt in the 1970s

50 The Camp David Accords and the Persian Gulf War both show the desire of
the United States to
(1) create stability in the Middle East
(2) expand trade with Asian nations
(3) maintain friendly relations with Europe
(4) provide economic stability in Latin America

Answers to the essay questions are to be written in the separate essay booklet.
In developing your answer to Part II, be sure to keep these general definitions in mind:
(a) describe means "to illustrate something in words or tell about it"
(b) discuss means "to make observations about something using facts, reasoning, and argument; to present in some detail"

Part II
THEMATIC ESSAY QUESTION
Directions: Write a well-organized essay that includes an introduction, several paragraphs addressing the task below, and a conclusion.

Theme: Influence of Geographic Factors on Governmental Actions

> Actions taken by the United States government have often been influenced by geographic factors. Some of these factors include location, climate, natural resources, and physical features.

Task:

> Identify two actions taken by the United States government that have been influenced by geographic factors and for each
> * State one reason the United States took the action
> * Describe how a geographic factor influenced the action
> * Discuss the impact of the action on the United States

You may use any action taken by the United States government that was influenced by a geographic factor. Some suggestions you might wish to consider include the Lewis and Clark expedition (1804–1806), issuance of the Monroe Doctrine (1823), Mexican War (1846–1848), Commodore Perry's opening of Japan (1853), passage of the Homestead Act (1862), purchase of Alaska (1867), construction of the Panama Canal (1904–1914), entry into World War II (1941), passage of the Interstate Highway Act (1956), and involvement in the Persian Gulf War (1991).

You are not limited to these suggestions.

Guidelines:
In your essay, be sure to:
* Develop all aspects of the task
* Support the theme with relevant facts, examples, and details
* Use a logical and clear plan of organization, including an introduction and a conclusion that are beyond a restatement of the theme

In developing your answer to Part III, be sure to keep these general definitions in mind:
(a) explain means "to make plain or understandable; to give reasons for or causes of; to show the logical development or relationships of "
(b) discuss means "to make observations about something using facts, reasoning, and argument; to present in some detail"

Part III
DOCUMENT-BASED QUESTION

This question is based on the accompanying documents. It is designed to test your ability to work with historical documents. Some of the documents have been edited for the purposes of the question. As you analyze the documents, take into account the source of each document and any point of view that may be presented in the document.

Historical Context:

Since World War II, conflicts in Asia have played a major role in the Cold War. One of these conflicts arose in Vietnam. United States involvement in this conflict was sometimes controversial. The decision to send troops to Vietnam had a major impact on American society and on United States foreign policy.

Task:

Using information from the documents and your knowledge of United States history, answer the questions that follow each document in Part A. Your answers to the questions will help you write the Part B essay, in which you will be asked to

- Explain the reasons for United States involvement in Vietnam
- Discuss the impact of the Vietnam War on American society
- Discuss the impact of the Vietnam War on United States foreign policy

Part A
Short-Answer Questions
Directions: Analyze the documents and answer the short-answer questions that follow each document in the space provided.

Document 1

... At the present moment in world history nearly every nation must choose between alternative ways of life. The choice is too often not a free one.

One way of life is based upon the will of the majority, and is distinguished by free institutions, representative government, free elections, guarantees of individual liberty, freedom of speech and religion, and freedom from political oppression.

The second way of life is based upon the will of a minority forcibly imposed upon the majority. It relies upon terror and oppression, a controlled press and radio, fixed elections, and the suppression of personal freedoms.

I believe that it must be the policy of the United States to support free peoples who are resisting attempted subjugation [control] by armed minorities or by outside pressures.

I believe that we must assist free peoples to work out their own destinies in their own way. ...

Source: President Harry Truman, Address to Congress (Truman Doctrine), March 12, 1947

1a According to President Harry Truman, what is *one* problem when governments are controlled by the will of a minority? [1]

_____

_____

b According to President Truman, what policy must the United States support? [1]

_____

_____

Document 2a

... Communist aggression in Korea is a part of the worldwide strategy of the Kremlin to destroy freedom. It has shown men all over the world that Communist imperialism may strike anywhere, anytime.

The defense of Korea is part of the worldwide effort of all the free nations to maintain freedom.

It has shown free men that if they stand together, and pool their strength, Communist aggression cannot succeed. ...

Source: President Harry Truman, Address at a dinner of the Civil Defense Conference, May 7, 1951

2a According to President Harry Truman, why was it important for the United States to help defend Korea? [1]

_____

_____

Document 2b

Another Hole in the Dike

Source: Fred O. Seibel, *Richmond Times-Dispatch,*
May 5, 1953 (adapted)

2b Based on this cartoon, what problem did the United States face in Asia by 1953? [1]

_____

_____

Document 3

> ### THE NATURE OF THE CONFLICT
> . . . The world as it is in Asia is not a serene or peaceful place.
> The first reality is that North Viet-Nam has attacked the independent nation of South Viet-Nam. Its object is total conquest.
> Of course, some of the people of South Viet-Nam are participating in attack on their own government. But trained men and supplies, orders and arms, flow in a constant stream from north to south.
> This support is the heartbeat of the war. . . .
>
> ### WHY ARE WE IN VIET-NAM?
> Why are these realities our concern? Why are we in South Viet-Nam?
> We are there because we have a promise to keep. Since 1954 every American President has offered support to the people of South Viet-Nam. We have helped to build, and we have helped to defend. Thus, over many years, we have made a national pledge to help South Viet-Nam defend its independence.
> And I intend to keep that promise. . . .

Source: President Lyndon B. Johnson, Speech at Johns Hopkins University, April 7, 1965

3   According to President Lyndon B. Johnson, why was the United States
    involved in Vietnam? [1]

    _____

    _____

Document 4a

> ... When the country looks to Lyndon Johnson these days, it gains the
> inescapable impression that Vietnam is America's top priority. Mr.
> Johnson uses the bully pulpit [power] of the Presidency (not to mention
> the Rose Garden) time and again to tell a painfully divided nation why
> it is fighting and must continue to fight in Southeast Asia. No amount
> of resistance—and it is growing—can blunt [lessen] his resolve. Few
> question his personal resolve on the Negro [African American] problem
> (he is, after all, the President who proclaimed "We Shall Overcome!" in a
> speech three years ago). But his public posture [position] here projects
> none of the sense of urgency that marks his Vietnam crusading. ...

Source: "The Negro in America: What Must Be Done," *Newsweek*, November 20, 1967

Document 4b

"First things first!"

Source: Charles Brooks,
Birmingham News (adapted)

4   According to these documents, what were *two* effects of the Vietnam War on
    American society? [2]

    (1) _____

    _____

    (2) _____

    _____

Document 5a

Anti-Vietnam War protesters march down Fifth Avenue in New York City on April 27, 1968. The demonstration attracted 87,000 people and led to 60 arrests. Also on the 27th, some 200,000 New York City students boycotted classes.

Source: *The Sixties Chronicle*, Legacy Publishing

Document 5b

This article appeared in the *New York Times* three days after the Kent State shootings.

> ### Illinois Deploys Guard
> More than 80 colleges across the country closed their doors yesterday for periods ranging from a day to the remainder of the academic year as thousands of students joined the growing nationwide campus protest against the war in Southeast Asia.
>
> In California, Gov. Ronald Reagan, citing "emotional turmoil," closed down the entire state university and college system from midnight last night until next Monday. More than 280,000 students at 19 colleges and nine university campuses are involved.
>
> Pennsylvania State University, with 18 campuses, was closed for an indeterminate [indefinite] period.
>
> In the New York metropolitan area about 15 colleges closed, some for a day, some for the week, and some for the rest of the term.
>
> A spokesman for the National Student Association said that students had bee staying away from classes at almost 300 campuses in the country. . . .

Source: Frank J. Prial, *New York Times,* May 7, 1970

5 Based on these documents, state *two* ways the Vietnam War affected American society. [2]

(1) _____

_____

(2) _____

_____

Document 6

After the Vietnam War ended in 1975, large numbers of Vietnamese refugees settled in Westminster, California.

"Little Saigon" in Westminster, California

Source: Bailey and Kennedy, *The American Pageant*, D. C. Heath and Co., 1991

6   According to this photograph, how have Vietnamese immigrants contributed to American society? [1]

_____

_____

Document 7

> . . . Within sixty calendar days after a report is submitted or is required to be submitted pursuant to section 1543(a)(1) of this title, whichever is earlier, the President shall terminate any use of United States Armed Forces with respect to which such report was submitted (or required to be submitted), unless the Congress (1) has declared war or has enacted a specific authorization for such use of United States Armed Forces, (2) has extended by law such sixtyday period, or (3) is physically unable to meet as a result of an armed attack upon the United States. Such sixty-day period shall be extended for not more than an additional thirty days if the President determines and certifies to the Congress in writing that unavoidable military necessity respecting the safety of United States Armed Forces requires the continued use of such armed forces in the course of bringing about a prompt removal of such forces. . . .

Source: War Powers Act, 1973

7   Based on this document, state *one* way in which the War Powers Act could limit United States involvement in foreign conflicts. [1]

_____

_____

Document 8

> ... Fourteen years after the last United States combat units left Vietnam, at least 15 men who were there have made their way into Congress.
>
> ### Each Draws His Own Lesson
> Some are Republicans, like Representative David O'B. Martin of upstate New York; some are Democrats, like Representatives H. Martin Lancaster of North Carolina and John P. Murtha of Pennsylvania; some are conservatives, and some are liberals. Each has drawn his own lesson from having participated in the war, and each applies the experience in his own way to the issues of foreign policy he confronts as a legislator.
>
> Some support military aid to the Nicaraguan rebels, some oppose it. A few favored sending the Marine contingent to Beirut in 1982, though most say they had grave reservations. Some see the Soviet threat in larger terms than others.
>
> But the Vietnam experience has given almost all of them a sense of seasoned caution about using American military power without having the broad support of the American people. And this translates into some sober views on the limitations of force, especially in impoverished countries torn by internal strife. ...

Source: David K. Shipler, "The Vietnam Experience and the Congressman of the 1980's,"
New York Times, May 28, 1987

8 According to this article, how has the experience of many Congressmen who served in Vietnam affected their views on when to use American military force? [1]

_____

_____

Document 9

Comments on United States participation in Operation Desert Storm and Persian Gulf War, 1991

> "By God, we've kicked the Vietnam syndrome once and for all!" So said President George Bush in a euphoric [joyful] victory statement at the end of the Gulf War, suggesting the extent to which Vietnam continued to prey on the American psyche more than fifteen years after the fall of Saigon. Indeed the Vietnam War was by far the most convulsive and traumatic of America's three wars in Asia in the 50 years since Pearl Harbor. It set the U.S. economy on a downward spiral. It left America's foreign policy at least temporarily in disarray, discrediting the postwar policy of containment and undermining the consensus that supported it. It divided the American people as no other event since their own Civil War a century earlier. It battered their collective soul.
>
> Such was the lingering impact of the Vietnam War that the Persian Gulf conflict appeared at times as much a struggle with its ghosts as with Saddam Hussein's Iraq. President Bush's eulogy for the Vietnam syndrome may therefore be premature. Success in the Gulf War no doubt raised the nation's confidence in its foreign policy leadership and its military institutions and weakened long-standing inhibitions against intervention abroad. Still it seems doubtful that military victory over a nation with a population less than one-third of Vietnam in a conflict fought under the most favorable circumstances could expunge [erase] deeply encrusted and still painful memories of an earlier and very different kind of war. . . .

Source: George C. Herring, "America and Vietnam: The Unending War," *Foreign Affairs*, Winter 1991/92

9   According to this document, what was *one* impact of the Vietnam War on United States foreign policy? [1]

_____

_____

Part B

Essay

Directions: Write a well-organized essay that includes an introduction, several
paragraphs, and a conclusion. Use evidence from at least five
documents in the body of the essay. Support your response with
relevant facts, examples, and details. Include additional outside
information.

Historical Context:
Since World War II, conflicts in Asia have played a major role in the Cold
War. One of these conflicts arose in Vietnam. United States involvement in
this conflict was sometimes controversial. The decision to send troops to
Vietnam had a major impact on American society and on United States
foreign policy.

Task: Using information from the documents and your knowledge of United
States history, write an essay in which you

- Explain the reasons for United States involvement in Vietnam
- Discuss the impact of the Vietnam War on American society
- Discuss the impact of the Vietnam War on United States foreign
  policy

Guidelines:
In your essay, be sure to:
- Develop all aspects of the task
- Incorporate information from at least five documents
- Incorporate relevant outside information
- Support the theme with relevant facts, examples, and details
- Use a logical and clear plan of organization, including an introduction
  and conclusion that are beyond a restatement of the theme

Part I
Answer all questions in this part.

Directions (1-50): For each statement or question, select the word or expression that, of those given, best completes the statement or answers the question.

1   In the pamphlet *Common Sense*, Thomas Paine urged the American colonists to
   (1) oppose the French colonization of North America
   (2) compromise with the British
   (3) reaffirm their loyalty to King George III
   (4) declare their independence from Great Britain

2   What was the primary reason for holding the Constitutional Convention of 1787?
   (1) outlaw slavery in both the North and the South
   (2) place taxes on imports and exports
   (3) revise the Articles of Confederation
   (4) reduce the power of the federal government

3   Which idea did the Founding Fathers include in the Constitution that allows Congress to meet the needs of a changing society?
   (1) federalism   (3) the elastic clause
   (2) separation of powers   (4) States rights

4   The major reason Antifederalists opposed ratification of the Constitution was because they believed
   (1) amending the Constitution was too easy
   (2) too much power was given to the states
   (3) a federal court system would be too weak
   (4) individual rights were not adequately protected

5   Which power was delegated to the federal government in the United States Constitution?
   (1) establishing an official religion
   (2) controlling interstate commerce
   (3) regulating marriage and divorce
   (4) granting titles of nobility

Base your answers to questions 6 and 7 on the quotation below and on your knowledge of social studies.

   . . . The Privilege of the Writ of Habeas Corpus shall not be suspended, unless when in Cases of Rebellion or Invasion the public Safety may require it. . . .

   — Article I, Section 9, Clause 2, United States Constitution

6   This clause of the Constitution expresses the idea that
    (1) civil liberties are not absolute
    (2) revolution is essential to democracy
    (3) national defense is less important than individual rights
    (4) freedom of the press is guaranteed

7   During which war was the writ of habeas corpus suspended by the president?
    (1) Revolutionary War   (3) Mexican War
    (2) War of 1812   (4) Civil War

8   Which heading best completes the partial outline below?

    ```
    I. _____
        A.  Political parties
        B.  Committee system in
        C.  Judicial review
        D.  President's cabinet
    ```

    (1) Unwritten Constitution   (3) Electoral Process
    (2) Constitutional Amendments   (4) Checks and Balances

9   •   The United States government taxes gasoline.
    •   New York State law requires a sales tax on many goods.

    These two statements best illustrate the principle of

    (1) concurrent powers   (3) reserved powers
    (2) property rights   (4) popular sovereignty

10 Which statement about the United States House of Representatives is accurate?
    (1) Representatives are chosen by the legislatures of their states.
    (2) The Constitution allows each state two representatives.
    (3) The number of representatives from each state is based on its population.
    (4) The political party of the president always holds a majority of House seats.

11 Lobbying groups like the National Rifle Association (NRA) and the National Education Association (NEA) can influence government decisions because they
    (1) directly choose the leaders of Congress
    (2) work to elect legislators who support their views
    (3) pay the salaries of elected officials
    (4) become members of third political parties

12 The Mississippi River system was an important economic resource during the first half of the 1800s because it was used to
    (1) irrigate desert lands
    (2) transport farm goods to market
    (3) move immigrants to the Northeast
    (4) produce hydroelectric power

13 Washington's Proclamation of Neutrality (1793), Jefferson's Embargo Act (1807), and the Monroe Doctrine (1823) were all efforts to
(1) avoid political conflicts with European nations
(2) directly support European revolutions
(3) aid Great Britain in its war against France
(4) promote military alliances

14 Under the leadership of Chief Justice John Marshall (1801–1835), the United States Supreme Court issued decisions that
(1) declared racial segregation laws unconstitutional
(2) gave states the power to tax the Bank of the United States
(3) increased the ability of Congress to limit the powers of the president
(4) established the supremacy of federal laws over state laws

15 What was a major reason that slavery expanded in the South in the first half of the 1800s?
(1) Federal government regulations favored Southern exports.
(2) New inventions led to an increase in cotton production.
(3) Most early textile mills were built in the South.
(4) The federal government encouraged the importation of enslaved persons.

16 President Andrew Jackson used the spoils system to
(1) veto bills he disliked
(2) enforce Supreme Court decisions
(3) move Native American Indians off their traditional lands
(4) provide jobs to political party supporters

17 The slogan "Fifty-four forty or fight!," the annexation of Texas, and the Mexican War all relate to the
(1) theory of nullification
(2) practice of secession
(3) belief in Manifest Destiny
(4) idea of due process

18 The Homestead Act (1862) attempted to promote development of western lands by
(1) creating a system of dams for crop irrigation
(2) providing free land to settlers
(3) removing all restrictions on immigration
(4) placing Native American Indians on reservations

19 Which two geographic features most influenced United States foreign policy throughout the 19th century?
(1) Atlantic Ocean and Pacific Ocean
(2) Gulf of Mexico and Missouri River
(3) Great Lakes and Hudson River
(4) Appalachian Mountains and Rocky Mountains

20 In the second half of the 1800s, the federal government encouraged the building of transcontinental railroads by
(1) giving land to the railroad companies
(2) purchasing large amounts of railroad stock
(3) forcing convicts to work as laborers
(4) taking control of the railroad trust

21 Which action marked the end of Reconstruction in the United States?
   (1) ratification of the 14th amendment
   (2) withdrawal of federal troops from the South
   (3) creation of the Freedmen's Bureau
   (4) impeachment of President Andrew Johnson

22 During the late 1800s, which group strongly supported an open immigration policy?
   (1) conservationists   (3) factory owners
   (2) nativists   (4) southern farmers

23 What was a major goal of the Dawes Act (1887)?
   (1) to provide a tribal legislature to govern all reservations
   (2) to remove the Cherokees from the southeastern United States
   (3) to strengthen Native American Indian tribal unity
   (4) to encourage assimilation of Native American Indians

24 The theory of Social Darwinism was often used to justify the
   (1) creation of the Ku Klux Klan
   (2) formation of business monopolies
   (3) use of strikes by labor unions
   (4) passage of antitrust laws

25 The national income tax, free and unlimited coinage of silver, and the direct election of senators were proposals that were included in the
   (1) Declaration of Sentiments
   (2) Republican plan for Reconstruction
   (3) Populist Party platform
   (4) Federal Reserve System

26 Prior to entering World War I, the United States protested Germany's use of submarine warfare primarily because it
   (1) violated the Monroe Doctrine
   (2) discouraged immigration to the United States
   (3) posed a direct threat to American cities
   (4) violated the principle of freedom of the seas

27 What was a primary reason for the great migration of African Americans to northern cities during World War I?
   (1) Job opportunities were available in northern factories.
   (2) Jim Crow laws in the South had been repealed.
   (3) Voting rights laws had been passed in northern states.
   (4) The federal government had guaranteed an end to discrimination.

28 Which characteristic of the 1920s is illustrated by the trial of Sacco and Vanzetti?
   (1) hostility toward woman's suffrage
   (2) support for segregation
   (3) opposition to separation of church and state
   (4) intolerance toward immigrants

Base your answers to questions 29 and 30 on the map below and on your knowledge of social studies.

United States Territory and Leases, 1857–1903

Source: Maps.com (adapted)

29 The main purpose of this map is to illustrate the
  (1) sources of important natural resources
  (2) development of United States imperialism
  (3) growth of the Atlantic slave trade
  (4) results of the Spanish-American War

30 The conclusion that can best be supported by the information on this map is that construction of the Panama Canal was motivated by the desire of the United States to
  (1) raise the living standards of Latin American people
  (2) increase naval mobility and expand overseas markets
  (3) improve relations with Latin American and Asian nations
  (4) maintain a policy of collective security

31 The national policy of Prohibition ended when the states
  (1) strengthened food and drug laws
  (2) legalized alcohol for medical purposes
  (3) ratified the 21st amendment
  (4) banned interstate shipment of alcoholic beverages

Base your answer to question 32 on the cartoon below and on your knowledge of social studies.

The Trojan Horse at Our Gate

Source: Carey Orr, *The Chicago Tribune*,
September 17, 1935 (adapted)

32 The main idea of the cartoon is that the New Deal
   (1) threatens the Constitution and the American people
   (2) threatens the two-party political system
   (3) provides American citizens with greater political freedom
   (4) provides protection from foreign tyranny

33 President Franklin D. Roosevelt's Good Neighbor policy was designed mainly to
   (1) reduce border conflicts with Canada
   (2) increase acceptance of minorities within the United States
   (3) encourage Germany and the Soviet Union to resolve their differences
   (4) improve relations with Latin America

34 One result of President Franklin D. Roosevelt's New Deal was that it
   (1) raised the national debt   (3) deregulated the stock market
   (2) weakened labor unions   (4) repealed federal antitrust laws

Base your answer to question 35 (next page) on the illustration below and on your knowledge of social studies.

Source: Library of Congress (adapted)

35 The main purpose of the World War II coupons shown in this illustration was to
   (1) choose men for the draft
   (2) conserve essential goods for military use
   (3) encourage increased production of consumer goods
   (4) pay defense contractors for military hardware

36 In which pair of events is the second event a response to the first?
   (1) Truman Doctrine → D-Day Invasion
   (2) Manhattan Project → Lend-Lease Act
   (3) Holocaust → Nuremberg War Crimes trials
   (4) Germany's invasion of Poland → Munich Conference

37 United States foreign policy changed following World War II as the United
   States
   (1) became more involved in world affairs
   (2) returned to a policy of isolationism
   (3) rejected membership in the United Nations
   (4) pursued a policy of appeasement toward the Soviet Union

38 President Harry Truman's order requiring loyalty checks and the Senate
   hearings led by Joseph McCarthy were both responses to
   (1) excessive spending by the armed forces after World War II
   (2) racial discrimination against African Americans
   (3) fear of communist influence in government
   (4) control of labor unions by known criminals

39 As a result of the Interstate Highway Act of 1956, the United States experienced
   (1) increased suburban growth
   (2) the elimination of urban renewal programs
   (3) less air pollution from motor vehicles
   (4) a reduction in United States dependence on foreign oil

40 The Supreme Court decisions in *Gideon v. Wainwright* (1963) and *Miranda v.
   Arizona* (1966) resulted in
   (1) an increase in the power of the police to obtain evidence
   (2) a clarification of rules pertaining to cruel and unusual punishment
   (3) a limitation of a citizen's right to an attorney
   (4) an expansion of rights for persons accused of crimes

41 A major effect of the Watergate scandal of the 1970s was that it
   (1) led to the Arab oil embargo
   (2) reduced people's trust in government
   (3) resulted in term limits for elected officials
   (4) increased presidential power

42 In the Camp David Accords (1978), President Jimmy Carter succeeded in
   (1) returning the Panama Canal Zone to Panama
   (2) suspending grain sales to the Soviet Union and China
   (3) providing a foundation for a peace treaty between Egypt and Israel
   (4) freeing hostages being held in Iran

43 Which event is most closely associated with the end of the Cold War?
    (1) passage of the North American Free Trade Agreement (NAFTA)
    (2) establishment of a policy of détente with the Soviet Union
    (3) invasion of Afghanistan by the Soviet Union
    (4) fall of the Berlin Wall

44 Which event led to the other three?
    (1) United States overthrow of the Taliban in Afghanistan
    (2) passage of the Patriot Act
    (3) September 11, 2001, terrorist attacks against the United States
    (4) creation of the Department of Homeland Security

45 Which person's action was most closely associated with the abolitionist movement?
    (1) William Lloyd Garrison's publication of *The Liberator*
    (2) Booker T. Washington's commitment to African American education
    (3) Thurgood Marshall's legal argument in *Brown v. Board of Education of Topeka*
    (4) Martin Luther King, Jr.'s leadership of the Birmingham march

46 "Neither slavery nor involuntary servitude, except as a punishment for crime whereof the party shall have been duly convicted, shall exist within the United States, or any place subject to their jurisdiction."

    This statement is part of the
    (1) Missouri Compromise
    (2) Kansas-Nebraska Act
    (3) Dred Scott decision
    (4) 13th amendment to the Constitution

Base your answer to question 47 on the song lyrics below and on your knowledge of social studies.

Brother, Can You Spare a Dime?

. . . Once I built a tower, up to the sun, brick and rivet and lime.
Once I built a tower, now it's done-- Brother, can you spare a dime? . . .
— E. Y. Harburg and J. Gorney

47 These song lyrics are most closely related to
    (1) the writers of the Harlem Renaissance
    (2) unemployment during the Great Depression
    (3) the "Lost Generation" following World War I
    (4) business expansion during the 1950s

48 Which pair of events shows a correct cause-andeffect relationship?
    (1) secession of South Carolina → election of Abraham Lincoln
    (2) United States enters the Spanish-American War → sinking of the USS *Maine*
    (3) passage of the Meat Inspection Act → publication of *The Jungle*
    (4) Soviets launch *Sputnik* → United States lands astronauts on the Moon

49 The Marshall Plan (1948) and the Cuban missile crisis (1962) are most closely associated with
(1) the establishment of the Peace Corps
(2) the creation of the Alliance for Progress
(3) United States–Soviet relations during the Cold War
(4) an increase in trade between the United States and Cuba

50 Which federal government program has been most affected by the longer life expectancy of people in the United States?
(1) Medicare   (3) War on Poverty
(2) Americans with Disabilities Act   (4) No Child Left Behind Act

---

Answers to the essay questions are to be written in the separate essay booklet. In developing your answer, be sure to keep these general definitions in mind:

(a) <u>explain</u> means "to make plain or understandable; to give reasons for or causes of; to show the logical development or relationships of "
(b) <u>discuss</u> means "to make observations about something using fact, reasoning, and argument; to present in some detail"

Part II
THEMATIC ESSAY QUESTION

Directions: Write a well-organized essay that includes an introduction, several paragraphs addressing the task below, and a conclusion.

Theme: Change — Industrialization

> During the 19th century, the United States experienced tremendous industrial growth. This industrial growth resulted in many changes in American life.

Task:

> Identify *two* changes in American life that resulted from industrial growth in the United States and for each change
> - Explain how industrialization contributed to this change
> - Discuss one positive or one negative effect of this change on American life

You may use any appropriate change in American life that resulted from industrial growth. Some suggestions you might wish to consider include increased immigration, new inventions or technologies, growth of labor unions, growth of monopolies, growth of reform movements, and increased urbanization.

You are *not* limited to these suggestions.

Guidelines:
In your essay, be sure to
- Develop all aspects of the task
- Support the theme with relevant facts, examples, and details
- Use a logical and clear plan of organization, including an introduction and a conclusion that are beyond a restatement of the theme

In developing your answer to Part III, be sure to keep this general definition in mind: discuss means "to make observations about something using facts, reasoning, and argument; to present in some detail"

Part III
DOCUMENT-BASED QUESTION

This question is based on the accompanying documents. The question is designed to test your ability to work with historical documents. Some of the documents have been edited for the purposes of the question. As you analyze the documents, take into account the source of each document and any point of view that may be presented in the document.

Historical Context:

The woman's suffrage movement of the 1800s and early 1900s and the civil rights movement of the 1950s and 1960s had many similar goals and used similar methods to achieve these goals. Yet these movements also had many different goals and used different methods to achieve them.

Task:

Using information from the documents and your knowledge of United States history, answer the questions that follow each document in Part A. Your answers to the questions will help you write the Part B essay, in which you will be asked to

- Discuss the similarities *and/or* the differences between the woman's suffrage movement of the 1800s and early 1900s and the civil rights movement of the 1950s and 1960s in terms of
  — the goals of the movements *and*
  — the methods used by the movements to achieve these goals

Part A
Short-Answer Questions

Directions: Analyze the documents and answer the questions that follow each document in the space provided.

Document 1A

On November 5, 1872, Susan B. Anthony, along with sixteen other women, went to the local polling booth in Rochester to vote in the general election. She was arrested and made this statement during her trial. In the trial, she was convicted and fined.

> . . . Miss Anthony.[speaking] — May it please your honor, I will never pay a dollar of your unjust penalty. All the stock in trade I possess is a debt of $10,000, incurred by publishing my paper— The Revolution— the sole object of which was to educate all women to do precisely as I have done, rebel against your man-made, unjust, unconstitutional forms of law, which tax, fine, imprison and hang women, while denying them the right of representation in the government; and I will work on with might and main to pay every dollar of that honest debt, but not a penny shall go to this unjust claim. And I shall earnestly and persistently continue to urge all women to the practical recognition of the old Revolutionary maxim, "Resistance to tyranny is obedience to God.". . .

Source: Ida Husted Harper, *The Life and Work of Susan B. Anthony*, Vol. I, The Hollenbeck Press, 1898

1 According to Susan B. Anthony, why did she refuse to pay a fine? [1]

_____

_____

Document 2

Suffragists' Machine
Perfected in All States
Under Mrs. Catt's Rule

Votes for Women Campaign Is
Now Run with All the Method
of Experienced Men Politicians

. . . A suffrage publishing company, whose first President was Mrs. Cyrus W. Field, and whose present President is Miss Esther Ogden, is one of the important auxiliaries of the National American Suffrage Association's work. It has proved so successful as a business proposition that in January of this year, after two years of work, it declared a dividend of 3 per cent. This publishing company issues fliers, leaflets, books, posters, and suffrage maps. Incidentally, it produces, as an adjunct of the propaganda work, playing cards, stationery with "Votes for Women" printed on it, calendars, dinner cards, and postcards; also parasols, &c. [etc.], for use in parades. Last year this company issued 5,000,000 fliers. . . .

Source: *New York Times*, April 29, 1917

---

2 According to this *New York Times* article, what was *one* way that the National American Suffrage Association drew attention to its cause? [1]

_____

_____

Document 3

Suffragists' Parade, c. 1913

Source: Library of Congress

| Wisconsin Women Have Had School Suffrage Since 1900 | Connecticut Women Have Had School Suffrage Since 1893 | In All But 4 States Women Have Some Suffrage |

White House Picketer, 1917

Document 3b

Source: Miles Harvey, *Women's Voting Rights*, Children's Press

3a What was a goal of the women shown in these photographs? [1]

_____

_____

b As shown in these photographs, what was *one* method being used by women to achieve their goal? [1]

_____

_____

Document 4

Twelve Reasons
Why Women Should Vote

1. BECAUSE those who obey the laws should help to choose those who make the laws.
2. BECAUSE laws affect women as much as men.
3. BECAUSE laws which affect WOMEN are now passed without consulting them.
4. BECAUSE laws affecting CHILDREN should include the woman's point of view as well as the man's.
5. BECAUSE laws affecting the HOME are voted on in every session of the Legislature.
6. BECAUSE women have experience which would be helpful to legislation.
7. BECAUSE to deprive women of the vote is to lower their position in common estimation.
8. BECAUSE having the vote would increase the sense of responsibility among women toward questions of public importance.
10. BECAUSE hundreds of thousands of intelligent, thoughtful, hard-working women want the vote.
11. BECAUSE the objections against their having the vote are based on prejudice, not on reason.
12. BECAUSE to sum up all reasons in one—IT IS FOR THE COMMON GOOD OF ALL.

VOTE FOR WOMAN SUFFRAGE
GIVE THIS TO A FRIEND AND ASK HIM TO VOTE FOR IT

MASSACHUSETTS WOMAN SUFFRAGE ASSOCIATION
Headquarters: 585 Boylston St., Boston

Source: Massachusetts Woman Suffrage Association

(Note: The original version of this flier
did not include a Reason 9.)

4   According to this document, what were *two* arguments suffragists used in this 1915 flier in support of their goal? [2]

(1) _____

_____

(2) _____

_____

Document 5

> . . . At these meetings [about the treatment of African Americans on buses], we discussed not only the two women who had been arrested, but also a number of additional bus incidents that never found their way into court, no doubt because the victims were black passengers. Several of the white drivers were determined to harass our people at every opportunity. For example, when the bus was even slightly crowded, they would make blacks pay their fare, then get off, and go to the back door to enter. Sometimes they would even take off with a squeal as a passenger trudged toward the rear after paying. At least once a driver closed the back door on a black woman's arm and then dragged her to the next stop before allowing her to climb aboard. Clearly this kind of gratuitous [unnecessary] cruelty was contributing to an increasing tension on Montgomery buses. We tried to reason with local authorities and with bus company officials. They were polite, listened to our complaints with serious expressions on their faces, and did nothing.
>
> On December 1, 1955, Mrs. Parks took her now-famous bus ride and set events in motion that would lead to a social revolution of monumental proportions. . . .

Source: Ralph David Abernathy, *And the Walls Came Tumbling Down*, Harper & Row

5*a* According to Ralph David Abernathy, what was a goal of African Americans in Montgomery, Alabama? [1]

_____

_____

b According to Ralph David Abernathy, what was *one* method used by African Americans to address their concerns? [1]

_____

_____

Document 6a   **Document 6b**

College students face a hostile crowd at a southern "Whites Only" lunch counter in 1963.

African American college students wait for service or forcible removal from a "Whites Only" lunch counter..

Source: Juan Williams, *Eyes on the Prize*, Viking

Source: Gary Nash et al., ed., *The American People*, Pearson Longman

6a Based on these photographs, identify *one* method used by these civil rights activists to achieve their goals. [1]

_____

_____

b What was *one* specific goal of the civil rights activists shown in these photographs? [1]

_____

_____

Document 7

April 16, 1963
Birmingham, Alabama

. . . You may well ask: "Why direct action? Why sit-ins, marches and so forth? Isn't negotiation a better path?" You are quite right in calling, for negotiation. Indeed, this is the very purpose of direct action. Nonviolent direct action seeks to create such a crisis and foster such a tension that a community which has constantly refused to negotiate is forced to confront the issue. It seeks so to dramatize the issue that it can no longer be ignored. My citing the creation of tension as part of the work of the non-violent-resister may sound rather shocking. But I must confess that I am not afraid of the word "tension." I have earnestly opposed violent tension, but there is a type of constructive, nonviolent tension which is necessary for growth. Just as Socrates felt that it was necessary to create a tension in the mind so that individuals could rise from the bondage of myths and half-truths to the unfettered [free] realm of creative analysis and objective appraisal, we must see the need for nonviolent gadflies [activists] to create the kind of tension in society that will help men rise from the dark depths of prejudice and racism to the majestic heights of understanding and brotherhood. . . .

Source: Martin Luther King, Jr., "Letter from Birmingham Jail," 1963

7a   According to Martin Luther King, Jr., what was *one* method of achieving the goals of the civil rights movement? [1]

_____

_____

b   According to Martin Luther King, Jr., what was a method of achieving the goals of the civil rights movement? [1]

_____

_____

Document 8

200,000 MARCH FOR CIVIL RIGHTS IN ORDERLY WASHINGTON RALLY

WASHINGTON, Aug. 28 — More than 200,000 Americans, most of them black but many of them white, demonstrated here today for a full and speedy program of civil rights and equal job opportunities.

It was the greatest assembly for a redress of grievances that this capital has ever seen.

One hundred years and 240 days after Abraham Lincoln enjoined the emancipated slaves to "abstain from all violence" and "labor faithfully for reasonable wages," this vast throng [crowd] proclaimed in march and song and through the speeches of their leaders that they were still waiting for the freedom and the jobs. . . .

Source: *New York Times*, August 29, 1963

8a According to this *New York Times* article, what method was used by these activists to achieve their goals? [1]

_____

_____

b According to this *New York Times* article, what was a specific goal of these activists? [1]

_____

_____

Document 9

JERICHO, U.S.A.

Source: Herblock, *Washington Post,* March 21, 1965 (adapted)

9   As shown in this Herblock cartoon, what was a specific goal of these marchers in their effort to gain equal rights? [1]

_____

_____

Part B

Essay

Directions: Write a well-organized essay that includes an introduction, several paragraphs, and a conclusion. Use evidence from *at least* **five** documents in the body of the essay. Support your response with relevant facts, examples, and details. Include additional outside information.

Historical Context:
The woman's suffrage movement of the 1800s and early 1900s and the civil rights movement of the 1950s and 1960s had many similar goals and used similar methods to achieve these goals. Yet these movements also had many different goals and used different methods to achieve them.

Task: Using information from the documents and your knowledge of United States history, write an essay in which you

> • Discuss the similarities and/or the differences between the woman's suffrage movement of the 1800s and early 1900s and the civil rights movement of the 1950s and 1960s in terms of
> — the goals of the movements and
> — the methods used by the movements to achieve these goals.

Guidelines:
In your essay, be sure to
- Develop all aspects of the task
- Incorporate information from *at least* **five** documents
- Incorporate relevant outside information
- Support the theme with relevant facts, examples, and details
- Use a logical and clear plan of organization, including an introduction and a conclusion that are beyond a restatement of the theme